A Celebration of Poets

CALIFORNIA
GRADES 4-6
SPRING 2009

A Celebration of Poets
California
Grades 4-6
Spring 2009

An anthology compiled by Creative Communication, Inc.

Published by:

1488 NORTH 200 WEST • LOGAN, UTAH 84341
TEL. 435-713-4411 • WWW.POETICPOWER.COM

All rights reserved. No part of this book may be reproduced or transmitted in any form or by any means, electronic or mechanical without written permission of the author and publisher.

Copyright © 2009 by Creative Communication, Inc.
Printed in the United States of America

ISBN: 978-1-60050-293-4

FOREWORD

Earlier this year I received a phone call from an individual who was sending in a poem written by a friend's son. Through the conversation it was revealed that the person I was talking to was the author, poet and playwright, John Tobias. His poem, "Reflections on a Gift of Watermelon Pickle Received from a Friend Called Felicity" is one of my favorite poems. Starting with the line "During that summer, when unicorns were still possible…" his poem takes me back to all the magical summers that I had where anything could happen. I was given a treat in that Mr. Tobias recited his poem and related the story that inspired it. What I gained most from the conversation was that the inspiration for any writing may seem to come from an event, but it is really written from a lifetime of experiences.

I also received a letter this spring from a young lady who was published in one of our anthologies in 1999. Now a published author working on her second novel, she took the time to write and thank Creative Communication for giving her the start for her writing career. The poets in this anthology are beginning writers. Yet, as they continue in their writing, the experience of being a published author will hopefully be an inspiration to them. As they gain a lifetime of experiences, I hope they will continue to write and share themselves through poetry.

As you read each student's poem, realize that every famous author started somewhere. I hope that I will continue to receive letters from authors who relate that we were the first place they were published. Will one of these authors become famous? Anything is possible.

I hope you enjoy this anthology and the poets who share their lives through words.

Thomas Worthen, Ph.D.
Editor
Creative Communication

WRITING CONTESTS!

Enter our next POETRY contest!
Enter our next ESSAY contest!

Why should I enter?
Win prizes and get published! Each year thousands of dollars in prizes are awarded throughout North America. The top writers in each division receive a monetary award and a free book that includes their published poem or essay. Entries of merit are also selected to be published in our anthology.

Who may enter?
There are four divisions in the poetry contest. The poetry divisions are grades K-3, 4-6, 7-9, and 10-12. There are three divisions in the essay contest. The essay divisions are grades 3-6, 7-9, and 10-12.

What is needed to enter the contest?
To enter the poetry contest send in one original poem, 21 lines or less. To enter the essay contest send in one original non-fiction essay, 250 words or less, on any topic. Each entry must include the student's name, grade, address, city, state, and zip code, and the student's school name and school address. Students who include their teacher's name may help their teacher qualify for a free copy of the anthology. Contest changes and updates are listed at www.poeticpower.com.

How do I enter?

Enter a poem online at:
www.poeticpower.com
or
Mail your poem to:
   Poetry Contest
   1488 North 200 West
   Logan, UT 84341

Enter an essay online at:
www.studentessaycontest.com
or
Mail your essay to:
   Essay Contest
   1488 North 200 West
   Logan, UT 84341

When is the deadline?
Poetry contest deadlines are August 18th, December 3rd, and April 13th. Essay contest deadlines are October 15th, February 17th, and July 15th. Students can enter one poem and one essay for each spring, summer, and fall contest deadline.

Are there benefits for my school?
Yes. We award $15,000 each year in grants to help with Language Arts programs. Schools qualify to apply for a grant by having 15 or more accepted entries.

Are there benefits for my teacher?
Yes. Teachers with five or more students published receive a free anthology that includes their students' writing.

For more information please go to our website at **www.poeticpower.com**, email us at editor@poeticpower.com or call 435-713-4411.

TABLE OF CONTENTS

POETIC ACHIEVEMENT HONOR SCHOOLS	1
LANGUAGE ARTS GRANT RECIPIENTS	7
GRADES 4-5-6	11
TOP POEMS	12
HIGH MERIT POEMS	22
INDEX	223

Spring 2009 Poetic Achievement Honor Schools

* Teachers who had fifteen or more poets accepted to be published

The following schools are recognized as receiving a "Poetic Achievement Award." This award is given to schools who have a large number of entries of which over fifty percent are accepted for publication. With hundreds of schools entering our contest, only a small percent of these schools are honored with this award. The purpose of this award is to recognize schools with excellent Language Arts programs. This award qualifies these schools to receive a complimentary copy of this anthology. In addition, these schools are eligible to apply for a Creative Communication Language Arts Grant. Grants of two hundred and fifty dollars each are awarded to further develop writing in our schools.

Aliso Elementary School
    Lake Forest
        Linda Brown*
        Lynne Weber

Andasol Avenue Elementary School
    Northridge
        Laura McGovern*

Aviara Oaks Elementary School
    Carlsbad
        Syndi Lyon*

Barstow Intermediate School
    Barstow
        Janna Swierczek*

Bernice Ayer Middle School
    San Clemente
        Susan Borowicz*

Bethany Lutheran School
    Vacaville
        Cathy Hays*

Big Springs Elementary School
    Simi Valley
        Robin Boswell-Thomas*
        Tracy Bowden*
        Matt Guzzo*

Blessed Sacrament School
    Los Angeles
        Bunnee Blum
        Salvador Callela
        Joy Gillett

Canyon View Elementary School
    San Diego
        Renie Martin*

Carlthorp School
    Santa Monica
        Laura Bickel
        Dr. Leslie Johnson*

Century Community Charter School
    Inglewood
        Mrs. McLaughlin*

A Celebration of Poets – California Grades 4-6 Spring 2009

Challenger School – Ardenwood
Newark
  Rebecca Arnold*

Charles Armstrong School
Belmont
  Kate Agoglia
  Julie Brady
  Maggie Dale
  Daniel DeLuca
  Melissa Fedoronko
  Penne Tognetti

Cimarron Education Center
Palmdale
  Laura Mitobe*

Clayton B Wire Elementary School
Sacramento
  Paul Bowling
  Mr. Tateishi*

Clover Avenue Elementary School
Los Angeles
  Nancy Vinicor*

Coeur d'Alene Avenue Elementary School
Venice
  Joyce Koff*

Corpus Christi School
San Francisco
  Theodore R. Langlais*

Daves Avenue Elementary School
Los Gatos
  Cathy Fisher*
  Mrs. Setziol*

Dingeman Elementary School
San Diego
  Leigh Morioka*

Dorris-Eaton School
Walnut Creek
  Brad Breilein
  Maggi Brown
  Mary Dickens*
  Claudia Fredriksson*
  Deeni Schoenfeld

Duveneck Elementary School
Palo Alto
  Mangla R. Oza*

Eastwood Elementary School
Westminster
  Kym Slingerland*

El Monte Elementary School
Concord
  Kurt Adkins*

Francis Parker School
San Diego
  Cindy Garetson*

Garden Grove Elementary School
Reseda
  Anne Morrison*

George Washington Charter Elementary School
Palm Desert
  Kym Blackburn*

Grant Elementary School
Petaluma
  Mary Reynolds*

Heather Elementary School
San Carlos
  Jennifer Lenci
  Michelle Marino*
  Sheila Sevilla*

Highland Oaks Elementary School
Arcadia
  Rose Gant*

Poetic Achievement Honor Schools

Horace Mann School
    Beverly Hills
        Ms. Rogers*

Islamic School of San Diego
    San Diego
        Aisha Boulil*

Jackson Elementary School
    Sanger
        Debbie Galloway
        Carol Gingrich
        Joseph Kutka
        Chris Mimura
        Debbi Santos

James B Davidson Middle School
    San Rafael
        Laura Edelen*

John Muir Elementary School
    Stockton
        Teri Dix
        Beth Largen*
        Mrs. Winterhalder

Joseph M Simas Elementary School
    Hanford
        Claudia Davis*
        Mr. Mwangi

Kadima Heschel West Middle School
    West Hills
        Barbara Hudock*

Kentwood Elementary School
    Los Angeles
        Roberta Guarnieri*
        K. Mc Broom*

La Costa Heights Elementary School
    Carlsbad
        Jan Patterson*

Ladd Lane Elementary School
    Hollister
        Lynn Parsons*

Lake Forest Elementary School
    Lake Forest
        Myrna Erickson*

Lockeford Elementary School
    Lockeford
        Lark Lieb*

Lydiksen Elementary School
    Pleasanton
        Linda Boveda*

Mayfield Jr School of the Holy Child Jesus
    Pasadena
        Madelyn DeVanon*
        Debbie St. John*

Montessori Family School
    El Cerrito
        Sarah McKinney*

Notre Dame School
    Chico
        Stephanie Beyers*

Ocean Air School
    San Diego
        Yvonne Sansom*

Packinghouse Christian Academy
    Redlands
        Theresa J. Moore*

Santa Fe Springs Christian School
    Santa Fe Springs
        Kathy Winger*

Santa Rosa Technology Magnet School
    Camarillo
        Michelle Bennett*

Sonoma Charter School
    Sonoma
        Bob Edmondson*

St Alphonsus School
    Los Angeles
        Margaret Kirby*

St Andrew's Episcopal School
    Saratoga
        Kristy Sumwalt*

St Anne School
    Laguna Niguel
        Donna D. Vandenberg*

St Charles Catholic School
    San Diego
        Mrs. Gorlitz*

St John's Parish Day School
    Chula Vista
        Connie Walker*

St Louis De Montfort School
    Santa Maria
        Cindy Hubbard*

St Pancratius Elementary School
    Lakewood
        Norman Ashbrooke*

St Raphael School
    Santa Barbara
        Christine Epley
        Barbara Malvinni*

St Timothy School
    Los Angeles
        Sally David*

Stone Ranch Elementary School
    San Diego
        Mrs. Seckington
        Jeremy Vincent*

The Mirman School
    Los Angeles
        Dr. Julia Candace Corliss*
        Bonnie Muler*
        Wendy Samson*
        Mrs. Walker*

Theodore Roosevelt Elementary School
    Burbank
        Tiffany Kaloustian*

Upper Lake Elementary School
    Upper Lake
        Janice Klier*

Wagon Wheel Elementary School
    Trabuco Canyon
        Jill LeFevre*
        Mr. Tobenkin

Language Arts Grant Recipients 2008-2009

After receiving a "Poetic Achievement Award" schools are encouraged to apply for a Creative Communication Language Arts Grant. The following is a list of schools who received a two hundred and fifty dollar grant for the 2008-2009 school year.

Acushnet Elementary School, Acushnet, MA
Benton Central Jr/Sr High School, Oxford, IN
Bridgeway Christian Academy, Alpharetta, GA
Central Middle School, Grafton, ND
Challenger Middle School, Cape Coral, FL
City Hill Middle School, Naugatuck, CT
Clintonville High School, Clintonville, WI
Coral Springs Middle School, Coral Springs, FL
Covenant Classical School, Concord, NC
Coyote Valley Elementary School, Middletown, CA
Diamond Ranch Academy, Hurricane, UT
E O Young Jr Elementary School, Middleburg, NC
El Monte Elementary School, Concord, CA
Emmanuel-St Michael Lutheran School, Fort Wayne, IN
Ethel M Burke Elementary School, Bellmawr, NJ
Fort Recovery Middle School, Fort Recovery, OH
Gardnertown Fundamental Magnet School, Newburgh, NY
Hancock County High School, Sneedville, TN
Haubstadt Community School, Haubstadt, IN
Headwaters Academy, Bozeman, MT
Holden Elementary School, Chicago, IL
Holliday Middle School, Holliday, TX
Holy Cross High School, Delran, NJ
Homestead Elementary School, Centennial, CO
Joseph M Simas Elementary School, Hanford, CA
Labrae Middle School, Leavittsburg, OH
Lakewood High School, Lakewood, CO
Lee A Tolbert Community Academy, Kansas City, MO
Mary Lynch Elementary School, Kimball, NE
Merritt Secondary School, Merritt, BC
North Star Academy, Redwood City, CA

Language Arts Grant Winners cont.

Old Redford Academy, Detroit, MI
Prairie Lakes School, Willmar, MN
Public School 124Q, South Ozone Park, NY
Rutledge Hall Elementary School, Lincolnwood, IL
Shelley Sr High School, Shelley, ID
Sonoran Science Academy, Tucson, AZ
Spruce Ridge School, Estevan, SK
St Columbkille School, Dubuque, IA
St Francis Middle School, Saint Francis, MN
St Luke the Evangelist School, Glenside, PA
St Matthias/Transfiguration School, Chicago, IL
St Robert Bellarmine School, Chicago, IL
St Sebastian Elementary School, Pittsburgh, PA
The Hillel Academy, Milwaukee, WI
Thomas Edison Charter School - North, North Logan, UT
Trinity Christian Academy, Oxford, AL
United Hebrew Institute, Kingston, PA
Velasquez Elementary School, Richmond, TX
West Frederick Middle School, Frederick, MD

Grades 4-5-6

Note: The Top Ten poems were finalized through an online voting system. Creative Communication's judges first picked out the top poems. These poems were then posted online. The final step involved thousands of students and teachers who registered as online judges and voted for the Top Ten poems. We hope you enjoy these selections.

Top Poem Grades 4-5-6

The Ocean

Wind whistles in the vacant meadow
Birds fly on the ocean shore
As the wind gets harder and faster
Fish try to swim as the air chills the ocean's salty stay
The ocean waves get to a very high tide
People walk away from the ancient old crusty pier
Children play with daily visited souvenirs
Hear dolphins near
Surfers in the blasted waves surf a wave
Then say "hey"
The ocean floor is very cold
Fish and creatures dive below
People think how cool it is to see the ocean and its habitat
The sun's sunset sinks in to the earth
Like getting pulled away by a giant tow truck
It's great to live near water and it's great to be alive

Matt Caniglia, Grade 4
Sierra Oaks K-8 School

Top Poem Grades 4-5-6

Greeting

The land is held in a damp embrace
A lonely calm moves in the air
Cloud and earth lie, face to face
Parched fields call to the mist for care
Fog curls down with its fingers wet
And gently strokes the arid soil

The sun beats upon the broken ground
A faint breeze rustles the brittle grass
A cackle of birds, the only sound
Golden hills bend as heat waves rise
I listen and wait, yet I can't say why
Birds are specks in a blue vault of sky

Chloe Carothers-Liske, Grade 5
Montessori Family School

Top Poem Grades 4-5-6

Remaking America

Put aside your riches,
Fame,
and greed,
And be helpful to America.
Get ready for a challenge unlike any other.
We need memories and hope,
Peace and trust will slowly grow,
Our courage will sprout,
If we nurture it.
Hope,
Peace,
Trust,
Life,
Love,
Mixed together by Lady Liberty,
Will make the bricks,
To remake America.

Sophie Cobarrubia, Grade 4
Canyon View Elementary School

Top Poem Grades 4-5-6

Jewels of Poetry

The Jewels of Poetry hide themselves
in a sparkling chest of letters.
The Jewels of Poetry
hang on necklaces of paragraphs
and bracelets of letters.
The Jewels of Poetry dance like flames
with the ocean current.

The Jewels of Poetry then hide
as someone swims down into the ocean blue.
The Jewels of Poetry breathe in the scent
of newly made paper.

The Jewels of Poetry are then passed around
to children, like candy.
The Jewels of Poetry are also passed out often
to adults, like apples.
But the Jewels of Poetry are really one thing
everyone knows:
words.

Isabella Gordon, Grade 4
The Mirman School

Top Poem Grades 4-5-6

The Monster Under Your Bed

Dad told me the truth a while ago,
I believe what he said; I have my doubts though.
He said there's a monster, that's under my bed,
It's downright scary, enough to be said.

It has 26 eyes, a cheek on its nose,
15 arms, 20 legs, they look like they froze!
18 halves of his body, 1 red, one blue,
I shouldn't even start on the color of its poo.

It loves to eat birds, medium rare.
And it doesn't really care,
Whether it's a sparrow, a woodchuck, a penguin on ice,
Or a parrot with 3,000 types of wood lice!

If one sees you, then a boom and a bam!
It'll gobble you up and say, "tastes like ham!"
So avoid it if you don't want to be like Shawn,
Who got digested and expelled and is fertilizing his lawn!

So when this monster thinks you're sleeping at night,
Sleep with on eye open; all right?
I told you; remember what I said
'Bout the monster that lives under your bed.

Edward Im, Grade 5
Lydiksen Elementary School

Top Poem Grades 4-5-6

Pull Me Back to Last Summer

Missing the moment, wishing I could go back,
Wanting it to happen all over again.
I want to jump into you,
Photo, to be in the moment.
I have seen you on my shelf for too long
Waiting for me to jump in.

Reach out your long, colorful arm.
Pull me into the bright, happy sun.
Let me run with my cousins and eat watermelon
With the juice running down my chin.

Would it be the same, or
Would it ruin my memories
So that they turn less fond?
Would I get bored or be too old to
Enjoy what you have to offer?
No, I would smile brightly,
Let the sun reflect
Off my shining teeth.

I would laugh and run and roll
On the grass, never losing the smile
Plastered on my face.

Erica Jaffe, Grade 6
Carlthorp School

Top Poem Grades 4-5-6

A Piece of Me

A piece of me desires,
To turn the hours back,
To right my wrong decisions,
To gain anything I lack.

A piece of me is longing,
To zoom forward into time,
To find the undiscovered,
To see money in its prime.

But the dominant piece of me,
Will only leave time ticking by,
Though the present is all that I have now,
I'll live on without a sigh.

Natalie Martinez, Grade 6
Cimarron Education Center

Top Poem Grades 4-5-6

The 3 R's

The 3 R's help the world you see,
It makes a global difference for you and me.
The first R says to reduce and save energy.
If you don't take long when you water your lawn
You'll be saving all the animals from human harm.

The second R says to reuse your old clothes from before.
Then if you donate your clothes to the poor
They'll have a little more to be thankful for.

The last R says that we have to recycle to save our power too.
We help our world to conserve every year through and through.
We take care of our environment
And make our world's R's our commitment.

Alisaundre Morallos, Grade 4
St Pancratius Elementary School

Top Poem Grades 4-5-6

Storm

Streaking from the sky, like silvery lances,
Shattering upon impact
Falling wasted into glassy puddles,
Sending gray rings racing across the surface.
Dripping from the gutters,
Thrumming angrily on the windows,
Leaving trails as they slip down the glass.
Wetting the ground and shaking the flowers,
The raindrops rage a hopeless war against the earth.

Sophia Pelosi, Grade 5
Duveneck Elementary School

Top Poem Grades 4-5-6

The Things We No Longer Know

We live on this Earth aware of almost nothing
Of the things we can do
And the things that could change.
The dust we kick up with our dirty feet
Are the things we regret.
The sand in between our toes
Are the memories we choose not to notice.
And the grass that sways against our faces
Is our forgetfulness.
The Earth is filled with what-ifs.
When do the actions come in?
When one person stands up
The rest of the crowd sits down in their seats.
When will the mossy rocks
That sit on mountains for thousands of years be our happiness?
When will the piney evergreen trees be our pride?
And when will the vast wide ocean be our calmness?
The things we no longer know nor care about
Are hidden beneath our lies
In something that has been true
Ever since mankind sprung from Mother Nature.

Devan Udall, Grade 4
North Oakland Community Charter School

Yellow Fever

I am as sly as an assailant
I will kill without warning
I will sabotage lives
I immerse you with death
I will kill with out grief
I am as frightening as death itself
I long to find you
My attacks are groundless
You dread finding me
Do not expect to live
You will die
You cannot stop me
You will not stop me
Give up it is inept
You will have to endure me
I last all summer and autumn
My only enemy is your friend
My enemy is frost
I am
Yellow Fever

Zak Hovey, Grade 6
St Andrew's Episcopal School

My Heart

My dad is my heart
Because without him I will die
He is supportive
So I support him
He is nice
But not with mice
He is lovable and playful
I think he is funny and silly
He is cool
But does not act like a fool
He is skinny
But does not wear a bikini
When my mom is mad
I don't get sad
Because my dad is there for me
He is a Dodger fan
So he likes to play baseball
But he is playful and careful
He is awesome…
He is my dad

Maria Valdez, Grade 6
Century Community Charter School

Dragon

D ark crazy creatures
R aging flaming fire
A ttacks you when it's mad
G oing on a lot of adventures
O ut in the freedom
N ever turns away from its prey

Nicholas Molina, Grade 5
Joseph M Simas Elementary School

The Truth About the World

Strife and Envy rule the world.
The world may be full of Joy, Love, Happiness.
But…it doesn't make a meaning.
Because the world is as it always was, full of Hate and Destruction.
My name is Power. My father is Control, my mother? Wealth.
My best friend is Destruction, my enemy is Hope.
I love the world. Because the truth is a lie.
The truth is what I had said.
The truth of the world.
The truth about the world.
Is full of lies.

Freddy Lisitsa, Grade 6
Horace Mann School

Horsefly

Though it's not very large, your eyes will pop,
Mesmerized, you hear it's hooves, clip clop.
With it's clear, glistening wings,
You hear it's playful rings.
Nah! It shouts when full of joy, wanting to play a game,
It's brown coat shakes along with its long, thick mane.
When it's head drops, and you hear a buzz it doesn't wish to be bothered,
The creature is very smart, so it doesn't need to be mothered.
Its eyes so large, you can even hear it blink,
And yet so gray because when people spot it all they can say…
Oooooo!
Aaaaaa!

Sara Dunnet, Grade 6
Big Springs Elementary School

Music

Music from rock to pop
It makes you wiggle, jump and hop.

Music from jazz to classical
So beautiful, joyful, and magical.

Some people don't like music
They don't know how to use it.

Music is to dance, to enjoy, to be happy or sad
Music can be slow, fast, loud, or not that bad.

Music can make you leap
But it can also make you sleep.

Music can come in many ways
Some music comes in opera, concert, people even sing on highways.

Artist, band, orchestra
Teacher, professor, maestra.

Oh music! Oh music you are a part of my life
I will like music even with a wife.

Sebastian Torres, Grade 6
St Charles Catholic School

Teach Me to Walk So I May Not Fall
Teach me to walk brother so I may not fall
Teach me to see so I may not be blind
Teach me to read so I may thrive
Teach me to love so I do not sob
Though I will learn these things I will never forget you
I will always need you to get back up
So teach me to walk brother so I may not fall

I'll teach you to walk but first learn to fall
I'll teach you to see if you teach me
I'll teach you to read to see you thrive
I'd teach you to love but clearly you already know how
Charlie Bennett, Grade 5
Mayfield Jr School of the Holy Child Jesus

Mrs. K
Mrs. K is always there
Helping me whenever I need it
She's caring and loving
Her aloha spirit spreads through everyone
Strong through thick and thin
Compassion throughout the room
She will always have a place in my heart
Zoe Baer, Grade 5
Theodore Roosevelt Elementary School

Softball
Softball is a great sport
you can play many different positions
and if you make a great play, fans and family
members cheer you on.
In softball you also have a lot of teammates, who
consider you as friends, but they're really there to
play some ball.
Sara Stephenson, Grade 5
George Washington Charter Elementary School

Rainbow
I wish I were a vivid rainbow,
Brilliant and bright,
Gleaming like fireworks,
Arching like a bridge,
Reflecting sunlight off sparkling raindrops.
Gwen Maly, Grade 5
Lake Forest Elementary School

Friends for Life
When I'm with my friends I'm so glad they're there.
My friends make me laugh and have fun.
We're always there for each other.
I love them as if they were my sisters.
Nothing and nobody can make us stop being friends.
To me God put us together for a reason
And that reason is to stay friends forever and ever.
Gabriela Seda, Grade 5
St Louis De Montfort School

Hurricane
I wish I were a dreadful hurricane,
Disastrous and destructive,
Spinning and twirling like a horrible nightmare,
Dangerous and terrifying like a wicked monster,
Finally flooding the sandy shore.
Adam Knerr, Grade 5
Lake Forest Elementary School

7 Little Pit-Bulls
7 little pit-bulls playing with sticks,
one broke its leg and then there were 6.

6 little pit-bulls learned the jive,
one liked it and then there were 5.

5 little pit-bulls knocked on the door,
one got smushed and then there were 4.

4 little pit-bulls had some tea,
one had too much and then there were 3.

3 little pit-bulls found a clue,
one solved it and then there were 2.

2 little pit-bulls looked for fun,
one wandered off and now there is 1.

1 little pit-bull had a son,
they moved away and now there are none.
Justin Brown, Grade 5
Kentwood Elementary School

I Know…
I know…
I know the feeling of
The pages slipping on my fingers
The first words rolling through my mind
I know jumping into the pages
Becoming a character alongside the main one
Doing crazy things, fun adventures
I know hearing the last words
Closing my dreams until new ones come
I reach for another
I know reading
I know the pencil flying across the paper
Straight squiggly lines cover the white sheet
Circles squares and other shapes too
Make up something wonderful
No person has ever seen
Suddenly I flip the pencil over
And rub vigorously
My work disappears
I start over
I know drawing
Kira Oson, Grade 6
Francis Parker School

Rose
People call me beautiful,
I guess I am
My pinks are cheerful
My red, bright
My white is soothing
My petals give off a strong fragrance
I see my friends get cut
And taken away
It hurts my insides
To see them leave
So I try to look sad
My color fades
I droop and turn brown
Then he comes to cut me.
Jessica Blough, Grade 4
Daves Avenue Elementary School

Dylan
You are my personal tree
that gives me shade
with the softest leaves.
Keep me warm.
I come so close to you
reach up
and climb.
Together
we have the warmest heart of all.
Monique Sheps, Grade 6
St Timothy School

Friends
Joey is funny
Steven is an A student
Dominic is too
Cole Astamendi, Grade 5
Theodore Roosevelt Elementary School

The Night
The night is cold
The night is dark
The night is scary
The night has noises
The night is weird
The night is quiet
The night is wet
The night has bugs
The night is crowded
The night is bright
The night is not crowded
The night has stars
The night is beautiful
The night is big
The night is ugly
The night can be anything you want.
Nathan Cho, Grade 4
Stone Ranch Elementary School

Anthony Rivera
Fast as speed of light
Lightning comes to play at night
Sun comes lightning goes.
Anthony Rivera, Grade 5
Andasol Avenue Elementary School

Monkeys
Eating bananas
Shrieking at passing monkeys
Swinging through the trees
Ethan Koler, Grade 4
Sonoma Charter School

Rose
One beautiful rose,
Starts to lose its petals,
How gently they fall.
Carley Gomez, Grade 5
Packinghouse Christian Academy

The Meadow
I love the meadow,
so colorful and sweet.
It makes me smile,
when the grass tickles my feet.
There are blooms all around,
and I laugh as I run.
When I visit the meadow,
I have so much fun.
Jocelyn Jackson, Grade 6
Fort Washington Elementary School

Poetry
Poetry is smooth,
A wind of rhythm,
Light, color, a twinkle
From a star.

Poetry is the
Way you feel,
See and hear.

Poetry is what
You and I imagine
Everyday and night,

Poetry is growing with
Excitement inside your mind!

Poetry is everything around you,
Poetry is the way nature gently
Calls for you,
Like a ladybug on a rose blossom,
Poetry inside your head.
Savannah Alfaro, Grade 4
Oak Grove Elementary School

Boring
Boring
is
doing
nothing
you want something
anything
to happen
something fun
or exciting
but
still
nothing
happens
Alexander D'Souza, Grade 4
Daves Avenue Elementary School

DC Comics
Heroes
Heroic, cool
Fitting, flying, working
Strong, costumes, bad, ugly
Masking, kidnapping, lying
Weak, machines
Villains
Luis Angel Angulo, Grade 5
St Louis De Montfort School

Moonlight Tonight
I looked out
my window and
saw a bright light.
I thought to myself,
what can that be
on this clear,
starless night?
Shiny, shimmery,
mysterious and
bright — oh look,
it's the moon!
What a beautiful
sight! It shines
down upon me
I feel blessed in
its might. What
an awesome joy
to be under the
moonlight tonight!
Briana Quinteros, Grade 6
Corpus Christi School

Blue Dolphins
Hot sun glistens on
the blue dolphin's fins while it
swims in the ocean.
Erik Nelson, Grade 5
Joseph M Simas Elementary School

I Am From

I am from a home
Where Papa's old snooker table is played
Where you wake up to the smell of French toast
And where we make our famous family raviolis

I am from a yard
Where smelly old lamb pens lay deserted
Where the dogs roam in search of a bone
And where the big redwood trees sway

I am from a family
Where my brother goes pheasant hunting
Where people go horse back riding
And where we rush in a hurry to get my lamb to fair

Jillian Gabski, Grade 5
Notre Dame School

Sorrow

Sorrow is like gray
And is also like dark clouds before a storm
It is like having a bad day
It reminds me of the time when there was a huge thunderstorm
It makes me feel sad inside but fun when walking in the rain
It makes me want to run in the rain

Olivia Djahanchahi, Grade 6
St Anne School

Green

Green is a frog that jumps so high.
Green is a cute turtle that walks so slow.
Green is a leaf that drops from a tree.
Green is a soldier who fights to be free.
Green is the grass in my front yard.
Green is a gummy worm that tastes so great.
Green is mold that I have to scrape.
Green is a grasshopper that jumps far.
Green is slime that feels like tar.

Michael Rayala, Grade 4
Stanton Elementary School

Jackson Hole, Wyoming

I sit in my chair
The window open and I feel the breeze of fresh air
The mountains are turning purple
And the day is turning into night
This is something I don't want to fight
I look to my right and see the Sleeping Indian made of rock
I look up in the dark sky and see a hawk
I look down to my pond below
And see my dad catch a fish while he bellows
I see a fox scamper into the tall grass
It disappeared so fast
I see a moose in the trees
Oh how I feel so free

Faith Doney, Grade 5
Mayfield Jr School of the Holy Child Jesus

Insane Brother

My brother is insane!
I try to make him stop,
But he doesn't listen
When I yell "DO NOT!"
I get mad and angry,
So I scream, "STOP"
Every time I yell it
He gives a karate chop.
He broke my mom's special vase,
Also the TV.
I thought he was nice,
But maybe that's just me.
He's funny and hilarious,
But not nice at all.
He bothers me and laughs
Mostly when I fall.
I hope I can carry on with it,
And someday it will stop,
But I just heard something breaking,
"Brother you need to STOP!"

Rebekah Garcia, Grade 4
Oak Grove Elementary School

Lightning Bolt

I wish I were a destructive lightning bolt,
Fast and furious,
Flaming high in the sky like a monstrous dragon,
Lighting up the world with a single flash,
Striking angrily with hot fire.

Saam Kashani, Grade 5
Lake Forest Elementary School

I Am From

I am from a home
With a neighborhood filled with laughter
With friends that have an everlasting friendship
And a home that lets me share my dreams

I am from food
With spices that are put into fresh Longanisa
And baked lumpia with vegetables
With juicy, ripe, guavas growing from my mama's tree

I am from relatives
Who passed down my family name
Deep memories in an old house and babies on the walls
Many memories and photos kept in booklets

I am from love
That regenerated from grandmas and grandpas
That passed down the emotion
And built up the family's love and care

That is where I am from

Drew Ferrer, Grade 4
Stone Ranch Elementary School

Ryan, He's My Bro
Ryan is his name
Playing baseball is his game
He wears dark shades
But he's the Sun Man
He waddles like a penguin
And farts like a dog
He jams to rock
And he rocks to hip-hop
He's funny like a monkey
And as strong as an ox
He rides his bike
And runs through Ikea
He's a car loving dude
On the beach he can be rude
He's very smart
And likes to drive a go-cart
He is my brother
I love him so
Today, tomorrow, and always you know
His nickname is Yi-Yi
And he's my bro
Bryan Williams, Grade 6
Century Community Charter School

Fog
I wish I were a wispy fog,
Swift and stealthy
Poising like a nonchalant ghost,
Moving like a slow monster,
Drifting away when my time is over.
Jordan Mann, Grade 5
Lake Forest Elementary School

Mom
My mommy loves me so much
She is careful and helpful
And she keeps me healthy
She checks if I need help
Even though she is very busy
I love her delicious foods
That she cooks
I like it when she's funny
She makes me happy and calm
She tries to keep the house clean
I know she can be a great fan
Because she's Mexican
She is honest and friendly
Just like me
She keeps me clean
She's with me day and night
To protect me
She is sweet and soft
As a spongy marshmallow
She loves me and I love her
Itaide Galvan, Grade 6
Century Community Charter School

If I Were in Charge
If I were in charge of my home,
I would have sleepovers every night, no chores,
Tons of allowance to spend on whatever I want,
And candy whenever I want without getting cavities.

If I were in charge of my school,
It would start at ten o'clock and only on certain days.
There wouldn't be any homework or tests,
Your friends would be in your class.
You could eat in class, you could choose what you learn,
And have a longer recess.

If I were in charge of the world,
There would be no bullies or criminals,
Everyone had a mansion, no wars, unlimited money, and robot helpers.
There would never be Global Warming,
No animal could be endangered, and everybody would always be happy.
Isabelle Chun, Grade 5
Duveneck Elementary School

Me…
I haven't yet discovered,
Who I'm supposed to be,
I have so many options,
But I still can't figure out me!

When I look in the mirror,
I see a young girl staring back,
I'm still trying to figure out,
What it is that this girl seems to lack.
She is still in her adolescent stages,
And everything is still changing, just like a book with turning pages.
She knows what she's supposed to do, during her time on Earth,
She's full of different ideas and knowledge, things have been in her mind since birth.
When she finally figures out, who and where she's supposed to be,
She'll always follow God because she knows He is more important than she.
Quinn Quesenberry, Grade 6
Round Valley Elementary School

The Touch of Hope
Sitting at my bedside, would be my selfless mother
Her purpose for this deed, would be her sick daughter
Coughing, sniffling, writhing in pain
Never will the immoral virus cut you a break
Gazing into hope's eyes like the sun rupturing through the clouds
A great effort, from both my mother and me
The voices in my head chant,
"Get better, get better!"
Gagging down that medicine
That tastes like acid rain!
As I sit up she smoothes my hair
A rat's nest it is, sticking out in all directions
As her wintry hand rests on my cheek
All my worries float away

Chelsea Cantos, Grade 5
Clover Avenue Elementary School

Special

I am just a boy.
Every morning I wake up just like other kids.
I wake up during dawn and the night I rest.
People say I am nothing but to me I am very special.
I live and I learn and I live.
I am just a boy.

Aaron Zalmai, Grade 4
Garden Grove Elementary School

Great Basketball

Great basketball, great basketball
Such a wonderful sport!

If you want your team to win,
You have to show support

Great basketball, great basketball
I hope your team wins

If your team doesn't win,
Then I'll just play with little pins

Great basketball, great basketball
You dribble the ball down the court

The whole crowd cheers for you, so you have to show effort

Great basketball, great basketball
That's all you need to know
But I'll see you at your next game show.

Nicolas Vargas, Grade 5
St Pancratius Elementary School

Preschool

I sat there in the car
with my mom and dad
a large building towering over me
Was this a prison
What did I do wrong
I didn't deserve this
Whatever this place was
I cried out in horror
A ten foot tall monster
Saying my name
as my mom let go
I clenched onto her
She pried my fingers off her shoulders
Was everything else a dream
Long walks with my mom along the ocean
Baking cakes with her, I missed
How could she leave me here with these strangers
There she left me in this terrifying place
With pink flowers and lady bugs on the wall
This was a prison

Lauryn Wilson, Grade 5
Coeur d'Alene Avenue Elementary School

Ode to My Hand Sanitizer

O, cleansing hand sanitizer,
Thy power of healing heals my hands in an instant
From any evil that has befallen them.
When in need of it I yell
O, cleansing sanitizer
And all my qualms subside.

What a sight it is
To see my hands cleansed of dirt,
Pain and despair.
When I first saw thee I thought
I had breached the heavenly Borders of Elysium!

The shining beauty of your being
Is too heavenly to behold.
Methinks thou art magic water
So mysterious and virtuous.

As thy bright clearness flows over my hand.
I fear if ever thee left me,
My heart would break like dropped china.
Thou art worth the whole world to me
Everything I own and so much more.
O, hand sanitizer, thou shalt be my lifelong companion!

David Plant, Grade 5
La Jolla Country Day School

Effy Obasi

Effy
Smart, helpful, and beautiful
Lover of a big family.
Who feels happy to be alive.
Who needs her music.
Who gives effort in her work.
Who fears getting chased by dogs.
Who would like to see her grandma again.
Obasi

Effy Obasi, Grade 5
Kentwood Elementary School

Daddy

Daddy's there at the door
coming home from people who are hurt
to be cured
Pain from work
I run down the hall
and daddy catches me in his arms
Swings me in circles

I cling to his arms
closing my eyes and screaming with little joy
He puts me down as I try to get away
He wrestles me on the couch
Tickles me until I laughing call out for mercy

Sophia Lambrecht, Grade 5
Coeur d'Alene Avenue Elementary School

Autumn

As green turns to gold
Leaves fall into a descent
With unearthly grace
Piling up into mounds of red
Many a legion of trees
Lose their coats of emerald
While the wind dashes through branches
A brief warning of winter
As signs mark the coming of
Autumn

Devon Rieckhof, Grade 5
Wagon Wheel Elementary School

I Love to Paint

I love to paint,
And I would love to paint all day,
I paint to many things I like
That I like to paint a lot,
Paint, paint, paint,
I love to paint
I can't stop painting so help me stop,
Paint, paint, paint
I love to paint,
I don't know where to put my paint,
So help me look for a place.

Alexa Gallardo, Grade 4
St Pancratius Elementary School

During Midnight

It is midnight
The moon is like light
There is rain and heavy wind
But there is a small, shaking cloud
Staring at a window
Because it wants
To get in to sleep

Paulina Gonzalez, Grade 5
Henry Haight Elementary School

Dads

Dads, dads, dads
are fun to play
and be with!
Dads, dads, dads
take you to
lots of places.
Dads, dads, dads
take you to
baseball,
basketball,
tennis, and
hockey games!
Dads, dads, dads
We Love You!!

Annalee Martin, Grade 4
St Pancratius Elementary School

Fading Love

If one day
you wanted to say
 you're truly sorry
from your heart of glory
 then please know
that I still love you so
 open up
your day of cup
 and let me in
once again
 through your dream
where fantasy gleam
 full of plain white
where you and I were only in sight
 feathers falling from the clear sky
the clouds rolling in up so high
 and open your eyes
and know that these are not lies
 but is our last memory
in this handwritten story.

KaBao Yang, Grade 6
Clayton B Wire Elementary School

Springtime Garden

Flowers are blooming,
Springtime is booming.
Chicks are being born,
So feed them lots of corn.

Butterflies are everywhere,
And spring is in the air.
There are colors all around,
And flowers on the ground.

Flowers look up to the sun,
And birds sing their song.
Children laugh and play.
They eat their juicy apples,
Then plant the tiny seeds.
They watch the butterflies,
As they flutter among the flowers.

Katrina Yap, Grade 5
St Linus School

Playing with Clay

What I like to do
Is some beautiful art
That is my way
Of showing my part

There is always time
To use some clay
Wherever, or whenever
I can just play

Erika Garcia, Grade 5
St Pancratius Elementary School

Las Vegas

Sitting, sitting and waiting
Sizzling, sleepy and dull
Wishing I wasn't there
Stuck in this blazing hot car
Awww, what a drag
Torrid wind rushing through
My sloppy hair
Watching the dirt devils
Chasing the scorpions
Falling asleep
To dream another dream
Of my frigid icy pool

Khyra Black, Grade 5
Clover Avenue Elementary School

Fishing

Mom and me on the busy docks,
Boats sailing around,
The sun is going home,
Birds flying around,
Movements flicker underwater,
But nothing on my rusty hook,
The sun's heat burns my back,
Yet a chill enters my body,
I am losing interest,
But I don't give up the hunt,
Suddenly a tug starts and ends,
A fish has lost the battle.

Samuel Cai, Grade 5
Clover Avenue Elementary School

Basketball

Basketball is fun.
You need to have potential.
Then you will play well.

Nirosh Mataraarachchi, Grade 5
Theodore Roosevelt Elementary School

Roses

Roses in a park
Flowing freely with the wind
Bristling in the sun

Karina Vescio, Grade 6
St Anne School

Music

A wonderful warmth of sound
That makes my little heart pound

It makes me sing
As the music rings

I know this poem should rhyme
But music takes some time.

Gabrielle Ribeiro, Grade 5
Sundale Elementary School

Shopping

I know…
The thrill of buying something new
Deciding what shoes would go with my outfit
The taste of sensation when I see a sale sign
I know…
The feel of silk shoes on my feet
The exploding smell of perfumes in the store
Dragging my mom along when she says she can't go any further
I know…
The anger when someone else gets the last sweater
Trying to convince my mom that I NEED those shoes
The touch of different fabrics as I walk through the aisles
I know…
The anticipation of getting to the next store
The breeze through my hair as I rush to get the last jacket
The weight of bags in my hands
I know…
Constantly explaining to people that it IS a sport
The impatience of waiting in the check out line
The adrenaline of hearing the credit card swipe
I know shopping!!!

Emily Chiem, Grade 6
Francis Parker School

Green

Green is like a leaf dropping from a tree.
Green is the color of eyes looking at me.
Green is the jello I eat.
Green is a big sheet.
Green is the ocean waves swishing up and down.
Green is seaweed drifting to the sea.
Green is that beautiful color looking at me!

Elizabeth Meda, Grade 4
Stanton Elementary School

Shrouded in Christmas

Standing alone in a snowy meadow
silent there are no bird calls
no neigh of a far-off horse
just the soft falling snow
like angels pattering silently
along the forest floor
the sky a warm cotton blanket
draped over you
and the rest of the world
sleigh bells jingle in the distance
jerking you sharply back into reality
your family and relatives
are waiting for you,
waiting for you to come in
so the food and dancing can start
the celebration of being together and warm,
the atmosphere of joy and love
warding off all unpleasant thoughts.

Tess Jagger-Wells, Grade 6
James B Davidson Middle School

Look Outside

At dawn my friend was sleeping.
I told her to wake up but she did not want to.
So I said it is so beautiful outside.
Smell the pretty flowers.
You will feel much better.

Asia Ridley, Grade 4
Garden Grove Elementary School

Respect

You should respect everyone
Respect your teachers
Respect your parents
Respect your elders

You should respect everyone
Disrespectful students get calls
Home to their parents
Receive consequences from teachers and parents

You should respect everyone
Your parents would be mad
If you come home with complaints
They will discipline you for your
Rude behavior in class

You should respect everyone
Even if you hate them
Be friends with your worse enemies
So you will be in fewer fights

Jonathon Lay, Grade 6
Ramona Elementary School

My Mama's Story

Every night my mama told me a story
of her life as a girl
I heard so many times
Sometimes I would gently drift into sleep
trying to hear her story
but my little ears were too tired to even think

One story always brought a tear to my eye
and my mama was always there to wipe it from each eye
Mama had a way with stories
too many for a girl like me
Time through time
Mama wasn't there at times
Doing important things

I was empty without any stories
Mama said sorry but to make it up
Mama told me more stories

There was a problem
My mama is my story

Danielle Asenas, Grade 5
Coeur d'Alene Avenue Elementary School

More Than a Sister
My best friend
That makes me laugh
And will always be there
No matter what happens
Through thick and thin
We stick together
Holds a special place in my heart
And always will
I tell her my secrets
And she tells me hers
Trustworthy and sweet
Funny and lovable
She's like a sister, but more…
Jaiden Alba, Grade 5
Theodore Roosevelt Elementary School

Erika and Jericha
There once was a girl named Erika
Her best friend was Jericha
They always hang out with each other
And they both had a little brother

One day they got into a fight
Erika said she was always right
She said Jericha was always wrong
And they both thought they were strong

The fight went on for a week
Jericha called Erika a geek
Why did Erika call Jericha weak
But finally they both speak

The two said they were sorry
Then found a girl named Corrie
Now they're all friends
And go shopping on the weekends
Frances Esquivel, Grade 5
El Monte Elementary School

If I Were in Charge Of…
If I were in charge of my home
I would have dessert every night,
No fighting with my sister, and
I would have my own room

If I were in charge of my school
It will start at 10:00 and go till 12:00
We will have no homework,
School will be only on three days a week

If I were in charge of the world
Kids could vote for any election
There would be no wars and,
Everyone has a home and lots of food.
Emma Johnson, Grade 5
Duveneck Elementary School

Heaven on Earth
The closest place to Heaven that I have found on Earth is the beach,
There I always feel God is in reach.
The warm sand beneath my toes,
The water comes up the sand and back it goes.

The salty smell in the air,
The blowing of my hair.
A calmness washes over me,
I am so thankful for Thee.

The ocean breeze clears my spirit,
The sound of the waves I just love to hear it.
To me the beach is Heaven on Earth,
So when I'm there it is God's and my turf.
Theresa Taylor, Grade 5
St Louis De Montfort School

Green Is Enormous
I know green.

Green smells like a fresh minty leaf from the gentle mint plant,
the aroma when you finish mowing the emerald lawn,
or a pinch of fragrant chives.

Green feels like a smooth surface of an interesting book filled with wonderful photos,
or the fuzzy moss lying upon a rough rock,
and the tender stem of a blooming iris.

Green looks like sprouting peas emerging from the fertile, nutritious soil,
the bright neon green, on a graceful frog,
and the shady green riding on the dazzling rainbow.

Green sounds like the whistling leaves on a maple tree,
the chomp when you nibble a sweet and sour green apple,
or the light splashing of the shallow algae filled water.

Green tastes like the luscious lime green grapes,
the garden-fresh lettuce and cucumbers,
and silly green eggs and ham, sitting on a sparkling plate.

I really know green.
Lauren Zhu, Grade 5
Dingeman Elementary School

Milky Ghirardelli Chocolate
When you open the golden wrapper it smells of carmel.
You take a bite and you feel the soft crunch against your teeth
As the chocolate gives way and the carmel leaks out.
The carmel is liquidy and sweet.
You wonder how it is made from a seed to a sweet, milky, bitter chocolate.
As you chew, the chocolate melts in your mouth.
When you finish it the desiring taste stays in your mouth.
Bits of chocolate stick to your teeth.
You can still smell the chocolate on the wrapper. Mmmmmm
Josh Teincuff, Grade 5
Morasha School

The Red Fern

Planted by the hands of an angel,
According to Indian folklore.
Guarding a young boy's best friends,
Who sadly are no more.

God's way of helping
The boy understand
Why they died months before.

Fanning out like fire
Over the little mounds of earth
A gentle reminder of the good times,
Of the joy and laughter and mirth.

Oh, the boy will always hurt
At the sight of the mounds of dirt.
But the small red plant from legends and lore
Will make his sorrows hurt no more.

Lucy Womack, Grade 6
Morse Avenue Elementary School

I Am Fever

I am Fever
I wreck lives of many
I kill like war
My malicious, dispatch will do you no good
Life may seem precious to you
But to me you're another target to hit
I'm the culprit of the crime
I'm a heart breaking illness
I leave no leeway for living
Your eyes resemble in my presents
I am not an elusive thing to catch
I generate fear and depression to many families
I will remain until the frost
But soon later I will return once more.

Hanna Kirk, Grade 6
St Andrew's Episcopal School

The Deep Sleep

Dreams are what life is about
With either happiness or doubt
Mine are filled with darkness and hate
It has nothing to do with happiness or fate

Nothing can stop this nightmare from spreading
There's nothing I can do to stop this sweating
Crazy out of my mind
These demons aren't so kind

Seeing things with my eyes
I think I should start saying my goodbyes
I wake up in the middle of dawn
And finally in my room the lights turn on

Damian Uribe, Grade 6
Cimarron Education Center

A Friend

A friend, a friend
A trustworthy friend
A good, great friend

Someone to tell
Your secrets to
Someone to tell
Your feelings to
Someone to tell
"You're a great friend!"

A good friend is kind
A good friend is caring
A good friend is loving
A good friend is loyal
A good friend is great
A friend, a friend

Rachel Min, Grade 4
Mayfield Jr School of the Holy Child Jesus

Ever Thought to Take a Walk?

On the soft warm sand that sinks between your toes
The steaming sun that brightens up our day
Cool waves spread ripples every direction
Seagulls send calls, calling us to come play

Glorious seas turn dark blue and dark green
The sky turns pink and orange and blue
The sun sets, the sky fades, the day is at end
We go to bed as stars glow and moons shine

Miranda Freeman, Grade 5
Merryhill Country School

Opposites

Jungle
Tangled, humid
Raining, hissing, slithering
Vines, quicksand, cactus, sand
Burning, scorching, hiking
Open, dry
Desert

Megan Clancy, Grade 4
Mayfield Jr School of the Holy Child Jesus

The Ocean

I hear the waves crash
along the rich brown sand
the wind blowing in my ear
the waves are dancing upon my feet
my hair is swaying back and forth
I smell seaweed
I hear dogs barking
the sound of the boat's horns blow
and the beautiful sight of the whales

Mykaila Fontes, Grade 4
Coeur d'Alene Avenue Elementary School

If I Were…

If I were the Eiffel Tower,
I'd shake my iron frame until all of the pestering people were off of me
I'd bask in the sunlight and soak in the glory of being free at last

If I were a balloon
I'd float and glide away into the cloudless sky to explore a new place
I'd look down at the poor people and smile knowing I wasn't trapped in that dark, lonely world anymore

If I were a book
I'd love the tingling feeling of my pages being turned by a reader so addicted to my story they couldn't put me down
I'd be read only by people who were intelligent, inquisitive people; people who just wanted to escape their troubles for a moment and I would be proud of myself for knowing I had helped them

If I were a color
I'd be a neon, vivid orange
I'd show off my vibrant shade by spreading myself over a sidewalk and infuse my tint into spectators' minds,
not letting them overlook me

Sarah Whittington, Grade 5
Aviara Oaks Elementary School

The Garden Through the Day

In the morning
The sun shining on silver dewdrops atop slender leaves look like glittering snow
The leaves, long and thin, are so slick they are soft
The smell of fresh rosemary and natural mint lush in the garden
The harmony of hummingbirds humming, bees buzzing and birds singing pass the ears of everyone who enters the garden

In the middle of the day
The intense afternoon sun beating down on the lavender bush in bloom
Short, fat, choppy leaves so soft on my fingertips
Lavender scent floating strong through the midday heat
The afternoon breeze rustles the leaves on the trees making the baking heat bearable

In the evening
The bright setting sun casts its glow on the calla lily turning its white blooms to a warm orange
The single petal bloom slick yet strong, the silky soft pollen in the middle of the blossom
Damp earth sending fresh aromas from the ground
Crickets chirping from mysterious places

During the night
Spider lilies glow eerie silver in the bright light of the full moon
The blooms smooth and silky in my hands
The smell of dewdrops settling on the plants crisp in the fresh night air
The sheer silence of midnight is a sound in itself

Sydney Gilman Dye, Grade 6
James B Davidson Middle School

The Ocean

As I dipped my foot into the water,
I felt the cold and icy touch send a small tingle through my body.
I listen to the sharp sound of the crashing waves,
but get distracted by the sound of the squawking seagulls.
The beauty of the setting sun draws my attention away from the birds.
I watch it as it sinks into the water like a giant light bulb growing dimmer and dimmer.

Brianna Aznar, Grade 6
John Muir Elementary School

Home

Don't outrun the world
You will find you are going too fast
Don't run behind the world
You will find it to be rather lonely
Don't go with the world
You will find it to be crowded
Find the place where you belong
Not the place where you feel alone
Or the place where you feel squished
But rather the place we all can call home
A home where you can come home to
A place where loved ones greet you
A place where you will never be lost
A place where you will be encouraged
A place where you are loved
A place with family
Home is a special place

Gabriella Morales, Grade 6
Round Valley Elementary School

Small

Small is not the big cheese.
Small is like a baby hand grabbing a
Small bottle.
Small is like a baby duck swimming
In a large pond.
Small is like a great white's tooth
Sinking to the bottom of the ocean.
Small sounds like a little rain drop dripping
Down off a leaf.
Small sounds like an ant crawling over
Mount Everest
Another word for small is tiny
One thing about small is that it can get bigger.

Dustin Michael Williams, Grade 6
Big Springs Elementary School

Mission

I am mighty
Soldiers protect me
I am the center of attention
I am the biggest thing around
I am home to Indians, soldiers, and Spanish people
I get new people every day
Indians work in my farms and shops
I hold church every morning
I call to all around
Inside I am protected
I hold farms and animals
I am the center of trade
If I am lost there will be nothing left
If I am lost everyone will lose hope
I am mighty
I am a mission

Noah F. Marx, Grade 4
Stone Ranch Elementary School

My Grandpa

Those eyes that were as black as the night
Were filled with never-ending love.
But when those eyes shut,
There was only tears and sadness.
My mother and father were crying,
But I could only stare.
It was the pain and sorrow I felt
That was the key to my silence.
No more will I be able to slip my hands in those warm hands,
And walk to the candy store,
And be so stubborn that I would get what I wanted.
No more will I be able to experience the comforting hug.
I would give up all my stubbornness, just for one of those hugs.
I will slowly start forgetting him,
But I will always look at the memories in my album.
When the eyelids actually shut,
I wasn't able to see those black eyes
That shone like stars in the dark world.
Today, he is one great influence,
As he was one who was always encouraging.
He is what I envision as one of God's angels.

Sakshi Choudhary, Grade 6
Parkmont Elementary School

Onion

The pink-brown onion, crunchy like dead leaves
but moist under the dead-like skin.
Without skin, a white-green apple
sits on the desk instead.

Clear covering coats the onion
like cellophane.
The white onion
smells up the room
a strong smell
an almost bitter smell.

The white onion now the size of
a large strawberry
tempts me to taste it —
a sharp taste, almost spicy.

The white onion,
finally shaved down to two small slivers,
looks like two onion fangs.

Genny Thomas, Grade 5
Carlthorp School

Tornado

I wish I were an unpredictable tornado,
Ginormous and jostling,
Twirling like a vicious top,
Whirling like a ruinous hurricane,
Destroying everything in my path.

Lauren Haller, Grade 5
Lake Forest Elementary School

My Heart
My heart is a river
that flows towards the sea.
My heart is a mountain
that touches the sky.
My heart is a cloud
that embraces the sun.
My heart is as bright
as the stars that shine.
My heart is an iceberg
when it comes to
Kyle.
Catherine Rose, Grade 6
Corpus Christi School

Ready
Approach the plate.
Load your power,
Bend your knees.
Keep your hands back.
Ready?

Pitcher takes his time,
To mess you up.
Pitcher takes a windup,
And throws.
Ready?

Could be a fastball,
Could be a screwball,
Could be a curveball,
Could be a change up.
Ready?
Nick Welter, Grade 6
Bernice Ayer Middle School

My Mother
Our bumpy tongues searched our
Mountainous spoons,
Like pirates scanning for treasure,
We explored for ice cream,
Running,
Trying to get away.
As we sat in the sun,
Boiling,
Like butter melting in a hot pan,
My mother and I smiled,
This was our time together,
No brother, no sister,
No father, no friend,
Nothing was there to separate us,
We'll stick together,
For the rest of our lives,
Mother and daughter,
Together in the world.
Bella Rivera, Grade 5
Clover Avenue Elementary School

This Is Where I Want to Be
In the middle of a meadow,
for miles all you can see is grass,
perfectly cut with longer grass
in the distance.

The wind is blowing to the east,
each blade of grass bent to the left.

Here is where I am,
in the middle of the meadow,
arms widespread,
standing.

The sky is blue,
the sun beating down on me.

I hear crickets in the distance
playing their sweet, soft melody.

This is where I am, this is where I stay.
Sabrina Foster, Grade 6
John Muir Elementary School

The Seed
As if a bolt of thunder had just boomed,
As if a blast of lava had just erupted,
The little seedling sprouted,
From its little cave of doom.
If it were not for the burst of liveliness,
And the sting of hope,
The seedling would have been trapped,
In its shell to mope.

The life to look forward to,
The joy of the sun beaming,
All these possibilities to come across,
And all these things to do.
Time to decorate the Earth,
With its beauty.
Time to feed the starving,
And give people oxygen,
Because this is its duty.

Take life as a gift,
And appreciate what you possess,
Because the path to achievement,
Is ongoing.
Dania Pagarkar, Grade 6
Islamic School of San Diego

Tree Climbing
Climbing trees is fun
I climb higher and higher
Soft landing below
Keelan Aponte, Grade 5
Caryn Elementary School

The Beach
The beach is fun
You can play in the sun

I love all beaches
there are no leeches

Beautiful waves crashing
little kids splashing
Ashley MacAskill, Grade 6
St Charles Catholic School

Special
I am so special
I am great at homework
I am great at sports
I am good at making friends
Thomas Vallejo, Grade 5
St Raphael School

Grandma
Ida,
Kind, funny, nosy,
Relative of Kira,
Lover of Christ,
Who feels the need of fairness,
Who gives advice,
Who fears pit bulls,
Who lives in San Jose,
Smith
Kira Sevor, Grade 4
Ladd Lane Elementary School

Bobcats
Running fast
Even when they're small
So cute
Soft skin
Skin feels like a pillow
On your skin
Then you'll love them
But don't touch
Because they'll bite you.
Angelica Castaneda, Grade 6
St Alphonsus School

Sleep
Tired of a long day's work.
just waiting to go home.
Rest peacefully in my bed,
until the day comes to an end.
Another day of work,
but no worries I have,
because yesterday I slept
peacefully throughout the whole night.
Claudia Serrano, Grade 5
Clayton B Wire Elementary School

Springtime

Sunny springtime comes in
Warm and rainy weather
Wash winter snow and coldness away.
Butterflies wandering around,
Ladybugs flying over our heads,
And caterpillars getting ready in their cocoons.
Winter fun changes into springtime fun
With pool parties and water balloon fights.
No more snowball fights and hot chocolate,
Wintertime is off duty
While springtime keeps us nice and cozy.

Alejandra Parra, Grade 4
Ladd Lane Elementary School

My Favorite Season

The wind is whistling, and the air is cold.
Kids rush to school, shattering the quiet.
Days are shorter, and nights are long.
As if it was a colorful blanket on a bed,
Leaves from the trees cover the ground.

The new season will soon knock at the door.
As the leaves dance and spin through the air,
The children stare out the wide window.
Nestling in the cozy warmth of the room,
Listening to the teacher and nodding.

As the wind howls like a wolf in the night,
As the endless rainbow of colors twirl,
This cycle of the year is moving fast.
This season will soon by past.
Can you guess what season it is?

Anna Chan, Grade 6
Dorris-Eaton School

Dreams

The sun has set so low
And the moon rose so high
Children getting ready to sleep
And to dream
As they doze away quietly
They dream…

Dreams
Peculiar or sweet
Dreams
Sometimes even scary
When they dream they question what will happen
Will they have nightmares or dream of a fairytale?
But very soon their dream ends
Children opening their eyes slowly
Starting a new day
Waiting desperately for their bedtime
To dream

Salma Soliman, Grade 6
Islamic School of San Diego

Spring Fever

Birds chirping in the morning light
Clouds scattering in the sky
Sun shines and wind blows
Blooming flowers adorn creation
Emotions are carried on the breeze
Passion takes wings, awakening hearts
Spring is a symphony flowing with harmony
Sunny weather puts a smile right on my face
Spring prepares us for fun surprises —
Here I come, spring!
It's giddy spring fever!

Rachelle Tanega, Grade 6
Corpus Christi School

A Blazing Light of Poems

In a blazing light, poems are always there
I walk in my dreams in a blazing light of poems
My heart is blooming with love when I look at you,
Oh blazing light of poems.

Whenever I'm feeling blue I look at you
And I feel happy again
Your flame is a gentle ball of light that warms my heart
You bring hope and happiness to my life
You are made of love
You are compassionate,
Oh blazing light of poems.

Sam Krutonog, Grade 4
The Mirman School

Bobcat

Big, tough
Prowling, eating, watching
Scary and pretty big

Yves Martinez, Grade 4
Mayfield Jr School of the Holy Child Jesus

Giovanni Da Verrazano

Giovanni Da Verrazano lived in Italy,
But Giovanni sailed for France, totally!
The New York Harbor was his find, finally.

For this voyage, King Francis I did pay.
However, the king wanted gold his way.

Verrazano's accomplishment
was finding the New York Harbor.
Giovanni used the stars and a compass
to accomplish his labor.

Unfortunately, at the
end of Giovanni's success,
the cannibals ate him,
without too much mess!!

Nick Kessler, Grade 5
Chaparral Elementary School

Blue Blue

Drip drop…Drip drop…
The sky is crying.
First just a few drops,
then more and more.
Pools of water collect,
making rivers, oceans, and lakes.
The sky is dark,
and the air is heavy.
The wind is strong,
blowing rain in my face.
I thank that,
for they hide the tears I cry.

Jessica Lee, Grade 6
John Muir Elementary School

Water

Water is peaceful
Forming beautiful waves
Settling silently

Dylan Radovic, Grade 6
St Anne School

Daddy I Love You

Daddy you were always there,
you always showed how much you care.
Even though things were rough,
you were always there and always tough.

You tucked me in bed,
and kept a roof over my head.
I was blessed by your love,
which I hope I'm worthy of.
I love you more than words could say,
in my heart you will forever stay.
GET WELL SOON!

Suduf Khan, Grade 6
Barstow Intermediate School

Lion

A lion hides from humans
Colored orange
Living in the jungle
And some lions live in the zoo
He is the king of the jungle
And can climb trees.

Joey Duran, Grade 6
St Alphonsus School

Dessert

Dessert is like heaven
Creme Brule is like the Earth's crust
Sundaes are whirlpools of goodness
Chocolate is as black as the night
Dessert is nice

Nico Conrad, Grade 4
Charles Armstrong School

I'm the Ocean

I'm the ocean.
I'm bright, beautiful, and so peaceful.
I have fun with my friends every second I have to live.
I'm the saltwater goodness.
Fire is my enemy and my weakness.
I'm friends with the surfers and skydivers.
I get mad when the pelicans come and eat my fish.
I have dolphins, sharks, fish, crabs, sea turtles, octopus and whales.
My ocean lives every second there is to live.
The motion is slow in the morning
And fast at night.
I wish I was the queen of seas!
That's how much I love, love, love, love…
Did I mention…*love* my ocean!
I just love being with my friends,
The waves,
And most of all my ocean.
I'm marvelous!

Madelyn Wordelman, Grade 4
St Joseph Parish School

Always Remember Me

Always remember me when flowers bloom early in the spring.
Always remember me on sunny days in the fun that summer brings.
Always remember me in the fall as you walk in the leaves of gold
And, in the winter time always remember me in the stories that are told.
But most of all always remember each day right from the start I will always forever
For I live within your hearts…forever.

Che Thao, Grade 5
Clayton B Wire Elementary School

Musical Talent

Music is the life inside of you.
Music is very important in life.

Music is a way to communicate to people.
Music is difficult to understand sometimes.

Music shows feelings most of the time.
Music cannot only heal you when you are sad but help you when you are in pain.

Music can provide you energy when you are weak.
Music is something you can sing along to.

Piano is something that I like to play.
Piano is something that I have a lot of experience in.

I have been playing the piano for at least four years.
Music is something that is part of my life.

I love to listen to music.
It is something that people around the world listen to.

And I am very happy that I have the ability to play an instrument.

David Rivera, Grade 6
St John's Parish Day School

Fever 1793

My name is Fever, killing is my game
Every year I cause more than 100 deaths
These are not fatalities, these are my doings
At night you are filled with fright
In the day you want to stay away
But it is no use, I will follow you
I ride on the back of my mosquito friends
If you happen to catch me
You will need to be immersed in water every hour
You will know whom I am with
You will hear their screams of horror
I am very widespread, I am everywhere
I am a very gory sight to see
You do not want to be with me!
You may think I am your own assailant
Well you are half way right
The truth is I am not a person
I am not an animal, I am a thing
I am a disease, I Am The Fever
So watch your back, Because you might see me
I Will Destroy You

Bethany Springs, Grade 6
St Andrew's Episcopal School

The Seagull

One cloudy afternoon
While walking on the beach
Something kept on bugging me
So I looked back and saw it was a seagull
It stared at me with its cold eyes
And squawked once,
Then twice
To me it seemed as if it were
Trying to tell me something
It squawked twice more and then looked up
And saw some clouds and
Squawked once again
But this time much louder
I wasn't sure what it was trying to do
So I walked away but just as I turned around
Something feel on me
It was rain
I looked back expecting the seagull
To squawk once more
But it had disappeared

April Banda, Grade 5
Jackson Elementary School

Books

Books! They are full of adventures, mysteries, and facts.
They help you learn as you grow.
The more you read the smarter you are.
The smarter you are the better the grades.
The better the grades the more successful you are.

Bryan Palomino, Grade 5
Kentwood Elementary School

I Am

I am curious
I wonder if the Loch Ness monster is real
I hear the sound of enormous dinosaurs stomping
I see very many aliens surrounding me
I want to be a star student
I am curious
I pretend to be in a dimensional world
I feel the heart of a butterfly
I touch an alien's friend
I worry about my grandparents
I cry when I see pictures of my dad when he really isn't there
I am curious
I understand why my great-grandpa died
I say the wind in my house is actually ghosts
I dream about having a better life
I try to reach up to my dad
I hope to be a peace-builder
I am curious

Jasmine Hunt-Silva, Grade 4
La Presa Elementary School

My Doll

I have a fragile and pretty doll
The name I gave her is Miranda
For a doll, she is quite tall
My best friend's doll is Amanda

Pia Montanez, Grade 4
Mayfield Jr School of the Holy Child Jesus

Black

Black is horrifying darkness
If it's inside of you, you're heartless.
If there's enemies in your soul
Kill them; that is your goal.

Trapped in a dark cell
It's like being in the dark depths of hell.
If black is with you there is no white
So you have now harmed the innocence of your inner light.

If black's beside you, you've been touched by the devil
Now you have reached a whole new level.
God has now let out a great sigh
Repent, repel before you have to die.

Alexander Correa, Grade 6
Vista Verde Middle School

Love Doves

Love is like white
And is also like two white doves flying together
It soars swiftly through my body
It reminds me of the time I went to a wedding
It makes me feel peaceful like watching a sunset
It makes me want to smile

Julia Machuga, Grade 6
St Anne School

Spring

Spring starts the new life
refreshes the old
throws away what's not needed
brings the future
brightens the day
makes it colorful
makes it nice
    nature is nice
    once it leaves it comes back
    spring starts the new life.

Nebil Youssef, Grade 5
New Horizon School

Chloe

Little baby
With the big brown eyes.

Giggles happily.
Smiles brightly.

Cries loudly.
Eats messily.

Grasps so tightly.
Pulls delightfully.

Please don't cry!

Little baby
With the big brown eyes.

Dillon Rosenblatt, Grade 5
Carlthorp School

My Big Sister

My Big Sis
Who is the life of the party
She is very energetic
And is an attractive hottie
She is smart and fashionable
Also, cute and considerate
She is small and tiny
And, a little whiny
Shelana is loving and funny
She likes carrots like a bunny
My big sis is very funny
And makes me laugh
When I laugh it cracks me in half
She is very talented in photography
She likes to take picture of my family
Shelana is sensitive
Also, she is very friendly
My sister has a unique charm
She is very nice
My big sis

Eryn Boyd, Grade 6
Century Community Charter School

How to Eat a Present

The yellow wrapping paper is thin lemon flavored fruit roll up.
The red ribbon around it is red licorice.
The blue bow on top is little blueberries all clumped together.
But the present inside is a big surprise with a taste different every time.
But if you eat it all up, you won't have a present to open anymore.

Aili David, Grade 5
Kentwood Elementary School

Love

Love has beautiful brunette hair that waves down her back
and sways like the sea on a calm breezy day when she moves.
She wears pretty pink dresses and gowns with white-gold jewelry,
meant to wear to a royal ball.

Love will cover you with sweetness, and demonstrate trust and hope.
She will make you float and daydream,
but one day may break your heart in unbearable ways.

She will flit into your heart and mind to make her magic happen;
it is then when she is like a fairy at work.

You may think you see her, but it is an easy mistake to make.
If she is truly there, Love will make her presence known,
for she is like a ballerina dancer in a music box, graceful and pretty.

Love is as close as any person will get to
real,
true,
magic.

Emily Allen, Grade 5
Wagon Wheel Elementary School

Buddy, Mackey, and I

On a cold and blistering day
My sister and I were skiing at Nome
We were on a high snowy mountain
Far away from home
We zipped and zigzagged
Past an Iditarod trail
I suddenly stopped and my sister wondered why
But I heard a really scary wail
Lance Mackey's dog turned left and fell
And got ran over by his sled
I took off my skies and scurried over
And just by taking one look, I knew immediately that it was sprained
So I put on my red skies and took the dog, even though his leg pained
I skied him along the Iditarod run
And the spectator said, "Thanks for your help and for getting the job done."
I got a reward and was the hero
And when I told my tale, my heart beat pure satisfaction
This is my tale
Of Buddy, Mackey, and I
The lesson is to keep a look out
For those who need your helpful eye

Samhita Palakodeti, Grade 6
Francis Parker School

Alone

I walk along this long stretched road,
to find that I am all alone.
Just waiting for someone to save me.
I feel like I am on a balance beam
with no one to catch me.
At least with someone near me I could feel comfort,
but I am alone.
I am now falling through the air
because I have slipped just thinking of you.
Memories of what I have seen and done
are flashing through my head.
Once again I am on this long stretched road
but now it's real you are with me.

Bailey Durnin, Grade 5
St Louis De Montfort School

Love Forever

I made a vow, to no one but you
I pledge my love to forever be true
I'll fed you and guide you and clear a path
I'll protect you and shield you from an angry man
I will listen to your problems and help you solve them
I'll make a rainbow and let the sun through.
I will take your side even if you are wrong.
Just to prove our love is strong
I'll plant a flower and make them grow
They'll be a symbol of love that we only know
I'll whisper your name so low that you can hear me
You will feel my love even if we're apart.
You know, we are in one heart.

Holly Vang, Grade 5
Clayton B Wire Elementary School

Summer

I run, I jump, I splash, I play
This often takes up most of my day

The warmth of the air blows my cares out the door
With no work to do, could I even ask for more?

Flowers, all sorts, that had bloomed in the spring
Now turn into fruit as sweet songs we do sing

We sing of happy times and fun
And we do not stop 'til a new day's begun

The nights, they are warm, with brightly-lit fires
As we dream of jumping off ropes tied to tires

Biking and hiking, don't want this to end
Within all the laughter I've made a new friend

But then we go buy some new pencils and things
And soon enough rush to class as the bell rings

Francesca Scotti-Goetz, Grade 6
James B Davidson Middle School

Cheetah —

The violent cheetah
Has long legs
Running fast, catching his prey
The cheetah swims if it has to bathe or find food
Decorated with black spots
They are despicable
Very protective of its prey
They like to fight
The cubs drink milk from their mom
Cubs always play
As if they are in a fight with another animal.

Alanie Ramirez, Grade 6
St Alphonsus School

Five Sisters

I am the only boy who lives with five sisters
I wonder if I'll ever get into the bathroom
I hear them talk about guys
I see them shaving, yuck!
I want to get out of this house
I am the only boy who lives with five sisters.

I pretend to be nice
I feel pain every day
I touch their diaries when they're not around
I worry when my parent aren't around
I cry when I have to play dress up
I am the only boy who lives with five sisters

I don't understand my sisters
I hope they'll leave me alone
I dream of having a little brother
I want to leave this house
I hope I get a new family
I am the only boy who lives with five sisters

Ibraaheem Agaba, Grade 6
Horace Mann School

My Saturday Morning

It was a silent morning
overlooking the water
Watching tall sailboats go by one by one
The air is chilly
with no moving wind
Eagerly waiting for the bright orange sun
creeping over the trees at the park on the other side
The sky pours with colors of yellow and soft pink
The water is still
practically sleeping
The very next moment all the pieces of nature click
the birds sing their innocent tunes
and the sun is up
and changed into a bright yellow
flamboyant circle of life and light

Ali Reedy, Grade 5
Coeur d'Alene Avenue Elementary School

Pink
Pink is a rose
With delicate petals
A carnation
That makes me feel mellow
Pink are erasers,
Cherry blossoms and more
Strawberry ice cream
You buy at the store
Bold and shimmering
Earrings on your ear
Puffy and light
Is the swirly cotton candy
The tutu of a ballerina
Who is always dandy
Pink is content a pearl too
Pink can be
A very pretty shoe
Pink is a heart
So big and bold
Pink will warm you
When you are cold
Nima Usha Chatlani, Grade 6
La Costa Heights Elementary School

Skateboarding
Out the door
To the skate park
At the skate park
Throughout the park
On the rail
Up the ramp
Down the half pipe
Through the cylinder
Over the volcanoes
Put the cone by the ramp
Thomas Waldenberger, Grade 6
St Anne School

Christmas Eve
Children running through the snow,
Plowing down plants as they go.
Screaming and yelling,
"Snowball fight!"
There won't be any sleep tonight.

"Santa's coming!" they all cry.
Get to bed early and he'll stop by.
Madeline Enmark, Grade 5
Merryhill Country School

Beach
Going to the beach
On a great hot summer day
On a lot of sand
Christian Lowance, Grade 6
St Anne School

Filly…At the Mission
The fuzzy filly snuffles
at the grass.
Her big brown
eyes search my hand
to gobble more.
Her horsey hay smell
reaches my nose.
Achoo!
The cute chestnut filly
blows her nose all
over my shirt.
Paige Thompson, Grade 4
Carlthorp School

The Pine Tree
Reaching, reaching up
Green needles pointing skyward
Dew glistens on them
Jacob Roll, Grade 5
Solana Pacific School

Blown from a Dandelion
The wind is picking up
Maybe today will be my day
Stronger, stronger, stronger still
Until…

Free, finally free
I see my brothers and sisters
Dancing in the wind
I see my mother swaying to and fro
I jump, leap, turn, fly

I see a green meadow up ahead
I am hopeful
All I ever wanted was to extend roots
Into fertile soil
And raise a family of my own
Swaying back and forth in the breeze
Ever more
Megumi Nakamura, Grade 6
James B Davidson Middle School

A Sunshine Day
Hip hip hooray
let's cheer for
the wonderful day
all sunflowers and daisies
bloom and blossom
on this wonderful day!

We sing and dance all day
until the sun goes down
and wait for another day!
Marilyn Mageno, Grade 5
St Pancratius Elementary School

Oh Montana
Oh Montana oh Montana
How I love you so
Fun games
Play dates
Jet skiing
Me singing
Water
Seeing Harry Potter
Boating
Hosing
Hamburger perfectly cooked
Beautiful views wherever I look
Oh Montana oh Montana
Tucker Moses, Grade 4
Charles Armstrong School

Aurora Borealis
I wish I were a radiant aurora borealis,
Phenomenal and colorful,
Flickering and flowing in the frosty night,
Illuminating like a daylight sun,
Gently fading into the midnight sky.
Jennifer Lo, Grade 5
Lake Forest Elementary School

Amazing Sea
Wind swooshing blue sea
Big sea whispering to land
Land dry as desert
Alyssa Echevarria, Grade 4
Ladd Lane Elementary School

The Stone Church
The great stone church
at Mission San Juan Capistrano
stands in ruins like a
wrecked old mansion.
The famous white walls
of stone remain from long ago.
Tiny pieces of sacred black rock
jag out of the walls
like sharks leaping
toward their prey.
Nobody ever forgets
the earthquake that
ruined the giant church.
The ghost of Magdalena,
a young woman killed
in the earthquake,
floats near the only window
on dark nights.
The great walls of the ruined church
stand today to remind people
of the stories from the past.
Charlie Thompson, Grade 4
Carlthorp School

High Merit Poems – Grades 4, 5 and 6

How to Be a Chicken
Never go near a butcher
Never cross the road
Lay a rainbow of eggs
Be the closest living relative of the Tyrannosaurus Rex
Celebrate in September
Get exercise 50 times a day
Become stressed, become cold
Always remember the chicken dance
Katie Guthrie, Grade 6
Big Springs Elementary School

I Need a Place
I need a place
Where love will never rust
Where the land completely is filled with trust
What we live in now
Is played by the cards
You can feel the pain
Of a thousand broken hearts
As fear in the crowd
Turns the love to mold
I need a place where joy is never old
And love is worth even more than gold
But I'm in a place
Where love is worth coal.
Will it ever change?
How will I know?
Spencer Waters-O'Mohundro, Grade 6
Grant Elementary School

Lolly
A cold day,
A "date" with Dad,
Italian in Santa Monica.

Ate tons of strings of spaghetti,
Rich red tomato sauce blanketing it.
Ice cream oozing from a bowl.

At the end a special treat,
Big blue lolly coiled like a snake,
Chocolate bar sweet and creamy,
Melting like butter.
Lucky lolly saved for later, said "good bye" to chocolate,
Disappearing into the dark tunnel of my greedy mouth.

The rest a kaleidoscope: blur of noises, sights, sounds.
Checking if my lolly lollipop's safe.
Not there, nowhere.
A hot damp face appeared,
But Daddy's hands wrapped around,
A flower of happiness opened up.
And I realized lollies you can replace,
Daddies, no.
Yi-Ling Loo, Grade 5
Clover Avenue Elementary School

CAS Stories and More
I can make a rhyme anytime
Because rhyming is mine

CAS is where I'm at
And no one can stop that

We are all different from one another
So say thank you to your mothers

This is my first year until the end
And I've made so many new friends

There are so many electives like wood shop and art
So come to CAS and START

There is lunch and recess, and a lot more
And all you see is trees galore!

This is a story for me to send
Now that's all I got, and that's the end!!
Tara F. McCarthy, Grade 6
Charles Armstrong School

The Color Red
It smells like the scent of cherries,
It sounds like the swish of a gentle breeze.
It fills my heart with happiness,
Since it's like the summer.
It is the color red,
Which belongs only to me.
Gurjeet Warraich, Grade 6
John Muir Elementary School

What Ifs
When I got to bed,
I lay down my head,
When I sighed,
And closed my eyes,
I saw "what ifs" in my head,
What if I saw my dogs talking?
What if I saw a fish walking?
What if I became a horse?
What if I was forced to run a course?
What if I saw a palm tree dancing?
What if I saw a caveman prancing?
What if I saw a log as a human?
What if his name happened to be Trueman?
What if my homework ate me?
What if the rocks hit my knee?
What if I had smelly flowers?
What if I had super powers?
When I woke up,
The "what ifs" time was up,
Now it was time to do "maybes!"
Katreena Adams, Grade 5
St Barbara School

Memorial

As the sun
rises over the
graves of
soldiers
we think

As the moon
comes out and
shows the
everlasting flame
we think
we think

Lorenzo Ortiz, Grade 4
Carlthorp School

Music

I am music
You know me
for the music in dancing
the people clapping
for the people stare
I dance with people
for the hard breath
and I'll hold your hand.
I have one enemy
She dances in her dress
a color of bright
She dances on stage
when it was dark
everybody leaves.

Ariel Saephan, Grade 5
Clayton B Wire Elementary School

The Ghostly Wind

Beating wings,
  dreams wrecked,
    stillness all around.
      No way to get out.
        Stuck in the hands,
          of a winter day,
        frozen cold,
      until your heart shatters.
    Then you fall.
Everything is
        lost.

Maddie Souther, Grade 4
Sierra Oaks K-8 School

Panda

The Panda is cute.
A Panda climbs trees to eat.
The bear eats bamboo.
The bear has black and white fur.
The tourists see the Panda.

Nickolas Meyer, Grade 5
Gustine Elementary School

Holiday

Entertaining and joyful holiday,
Wrapping paper being torn apart,
Joyful families being together,
Families putting up their stunning Christmas trees,
And astonishing decorations,
Smelling mouthwatering chocolate chip cookies in the oven,
Children presenting their magnificent gifts,
Sleigh bells ringing through the atmosphere,
Some outstanding children not receiving any sleep at all,
Magnificent little elves making marvelous little toys for children of all ages,
Santa becoming plumper than ever.

Nina Gardner, Grade 5
Highland Oaks Elementary School

The Storm

You're inside the room and the lights are out
You look outside and it's dark and murky
One second it's trickling the next it's crashing
You feel the cold drift through the window
And it sends shivers down you
The thundering and booming noise is so loud
It feels as if the room you're in protects you from the fierce winds
You're stuck in here cowering in fear
The electricity is out and you can't see about
You want to go outside and play in the rain
Because inside here you're going insane
You sit down in your cozy chair
And feel the wind rushing through your hair
You sit down with a pretty big frown
Because you know in your head that no one's around
Then you hear a moaning sound
And then you quickly look around
Nothing is there yet you're in for a scare
Then the storm passes and goes away
Now you can go outside and play all day

Matthew Liang, Grade 5
Duveneck Elementary School

Winter

Come and go the winter days
Of throwing snowballs and wrapping gifts
You are bright against the sky of gray
But with all the work to be done, you try not to throw a fit

Christmas morning comes and goes like the howling storms of snow
Hurray! Hurray! It's Christmas Day!
We run downstairs, get out our new sleds, and off into the snow we go!
"Thank you Santa!" we all say

I love Christmas like I love my birthday
What's a dream for me? Christmas Day!

Mom yells, "Come on! Wake up! We're going to the bay!"
I wake up from my dream and realize it is only the 25th of May

Michelle McKee, Grade 5
Solana Pacific School

High Merit Poems – Grades 4, 5 and 6

Night Watch

Nick has come to wake my crew for our watch
to learn what it was like for sailors
way back when.
We grumble and groan
as we put on our things.
We trudge upstairs at
two in the morning
as the wind starts to moan.

The bitter cold greets us as we take our places
on the *Pilgrim*'s deck.
A fisherman stares at the weariness on our faces.
For two hours we stand
watching the uneventful water.
The sails are damp with dew.
Diamonds fall onto the grey silk and
move forward while we stay still.
The stars seem like nails that hang
the black velvet curtain that will lift only
for the brightness of the day.
For now we wait to welcome the next crew
into the cold.

Jenna Thompson, Grade 5
Carlthorp School

Fire

I am angry, on a rage,
Every thing I touch gets destroyed,
Exploding with energy,
Bursting with flames, wood crackles beneath my fingers,
I dance and twist with myself,
In a deadly tango.
After I leave the scene of my wrath,
I clean out the old,
And give new life to blossom again.
People fear me,
But they have the wrong idea.
If you can look closely I am beautiful,
I am that anger and adrenaline that you feel,
But also a wonderful mystery.
I glow with brilliance,
And do a ballet that is unsurpassed,
Under my dancing feet, however,
Is a barren and scorched soil.
I consume everything around me,
And burn it until it's gone.

Hannah Eherenfeldt, Grade 6
Francis Parker School

Moms and Dads

Moms and Dads are so fun, sweet, and playful
Moms and Dads are so understanding and respectful
Moms and Dads will always be loved in my heart
Moms and Dads will be with me until death do us part.

Shanice Daniel, Grade 5
Main Avenue Elementary School

World Concern

I am concerned about the world
it is so bad I almost hurled
but now that Obama is our prez
we can all sit back in our shezz

All the wars I wish would stop
or else our men will fall and plop
killing is so ruthless and pointless
so many of our troops come home jointless

Global warming is such a shame
actually we are to blame
we really need to turn it around
fix the skies heal the ground

Look at our economy
there'll be nothing left for me!
We're losing our jobs and losing our homes
don't try to call us we can't afford phones

Don't give up hope
Obama's the man
if we all pitch in
"Yes we can!"

Alexander Freeman, Grade 4
Sonoma Charter School

Candy

Candy, Candy how wonderful it may be.
It melts in your mouth just like the sea.
Its colorful wrappers bring joy to your heart.
Look there it is, right in the cart.

As the wrapper opens, forcing you in.
You cannot regret, that it will win.
Your mouth is a vacuum sucking it in,
right onto the tongue, now that's a win.

Sucking, Sipping, or Crunching away.
Its got you trapped, no time to play.
Quick spit it out, there's no time to waist.
Oh no, you've swallowed, now it's paste.

Fariza Ahmed, Grade 6
Vista Verde Middle School

That Little Mouse

That little mouse so quiet and sneaky,
Come from their home sometimes creaky,
They steel your food,
That is for you,
They make a mess,
What a pest,
Really silent,
That little mouse is in your house!

Kayley Serna, Grade 5
George Washington Charter Elementary School

Life!

What is life? Is it a speck on a flower? Or is it an apple in a tree? Some people take life for granted, but others set goals and take care of their life. Some of these goals are simple, like getting good grades in school. Others include finding true happiness or finding true love. So, what is life? Do you think of yourself as a lonely star shining the brightest you can? Or are you a small, sad, lonely fish in the empty sea, just looking for a friend? Think about it. What does life mean to you?

Delaney Cooney, Grade 6
Bernice Ayer Middle School

I Am From

I am from a home,
Where fish pace back and forth waiting to be fed and I hear often remarks that our house looks like an old Mexican restaurant.
I am from a yard,
Where four wheelers zip around the tracks on weekends and a creek flows during fall, winter, and spring.
I am from a family,
Where my sister will never give her cellphone a break and where excitement rolls around the house when my oldest sister or brother calls from out of town.
I am from a holiday tradition,
Where enchiladas are steaming on the stove every Christmas and every Easter we head down to the Bay Area for the family picnic.
I am from memories,
That are stored in scrapbooks, frames, and on pictures in the computer.
I am from a home,
Where I love my life and wouldn't trade it for anything.

Ariana Gonzales, Grade 5
Notre Dame School

I Am

I am a large tree, outgoing and vibrant, but sometimes I am a small sprout, shy and timid.
I am a fantasy book imaginative and enjoyable, but sometimes I am a history book, boring and plain.
I am a monkey, athletic and energetic, but sometimes I am a turtle, lazy and slow.
I am a swan, graceful and nice, but sometimes I am a woodpecker, loud and annoying.
I am a rock star, crazy and fun, but sometimes I am a boss, strict and serious.

Kelsey Adair, Grade 5
Wagon Wheel Elementary School

Fear

Fear is a six-legged dragon that flies around the world scaring adults and children alike.
Breathing fire and intimidating you with her size, the dragon hunts you down until you are backed into a dark cave.
Cornering you until you face your fear and look into her bloodshot eyes, she backs away.
After she leaves, you think what would happen without fear? You now understand that we need fear to keep us alive.

Zach Mikus, Grade 5
Wagon Wheel Elementary School

If…

If I were a habitat, I'd be the tundra. I'd test your skills of survival by releasing an avalanche of solid snow and ice. I'd send a gust of Arctic winds across my barren plains. I'd let all plants wither in the freezing weather.

If I were an animal, I'd be an eagle. I'd soar and swoop high above the clouds with ease, then dart back down onto my cliff causing rocks to tumble below. I'd stun America with my six foot wingspan. I'd be known by everyone across the country as a symbol of strength.

If I were a planet, I'd be Saturn. I twirl slowly on my axis. I'd dance around the sun as skilled as a graceful ballerina. I'd be the showoff of space with my beautiful rings of rock, ice, and cosmic dust.

If I were a flower, I'd be a rose. I'd be a sign of true love. I'd have the sweetest scent out of all the flowers ever known to man. I'd have the beauty and the tenderness of an infant child. I'd create smiles on every face that sees me.

Maddie LeMasters, Grade 5
Aviara Oaks Elementary School

High Merit Poems – Grades 4, 5 and 6

Ukulele Know-how
I know that cutting out the body is no easy task
I know that routing out the sound hole is harder than it looks
I know how much trouble it is to sand the back of the neck
I know that it takes a long time to drill the tuner holes
I know it will be a hard task coating the ukulele with lacquer
I know it will all be worth it when it's done
Charlie Bullard, Grade 6
Francis Parker School

Croatia
C alm and very peaceful.
R oam many beautiful sights.
O ver the cliffs lies the sea.
A lways hot in the summertime.
T all beautiful trees surround me.
I slands are everywhere off the coast.
A ll the natural beauty I love to see.
Anthony Becerra, Grade 4
Mayfield Jr School of the Holy Child Jesus

Friends and Family
They're always there when you need them,
They never leave you solo,
They're people you can trust,
And never ever bust.

But why are they so important,
That's an easy question,
They always have your back,
And never let you crack.

Could we live without them?
We would never know,
To try the experience,
I'd rather let that go.

Thank God we have these special people,
In our lives forever,
When people ask, "Will you forget them?"
We always answer never.

There's a place in your heart,
For each and every one of them,
So never let them go,
Hold on to them tight.
Natalia Escobar, Grade 6
St Dominic Savio Elementary School

Blue
I see an ocean glistening in the red orange sun
I hear sweet sounding bells ringing and making music
I taste juicy and yummy blueberries
I smell the morning air after a night of rain
I feel soft clouds lifting me to a wonderful dreamland.
Janet Hwang, Grade 5
Andasol Avenue Elementary School

Falling Leaves
falling leaves from the sky
so graceful as can be
so very high
upon the tree
yellow, green, even red
it is fall
raining leaves over head
bare tree branches
dark brown trunk
the tree is in the ground sunk
fall is gone and the tree has faded way
Candice Hemphill, Grade 5
George Washington Charter Elementary School

The Ghost
Sneaky, white, spooky and pale
walking though walls when you see him you'll wail.
Soaring across rooms go in if you're brave.
Floating in air he's back from the grave.
He's clear and invisible you'll hear him go "OOHH"
and watch out he might even say…boo!
Micah Ramos, Grade 5
George Washington Charter Elementary School

My Puppy Lily
Lily shines, like the stars in the sky.
Lily is cute, like the clear blue sky.
Lily is bright, like the shining sun.
Lily is black and white like the color of night and day.
Lily is my 9 month old puppy, who is beautiful just like you.
Evelyn Barrera, Grade 6
Blessed Sacrament School

The Coming of the Moon
In the ends of the light
   its rays will still fight
To show off their glare,
   instead of an evening stare.
But in the end, the dark will prevail,
   as the orange light begins to fail.
The last flares of bright are seen no more,
   and the fires of day go out with a roar.
Apollo's fury howls in defeat,
   while blackness rages at its opponent's feet.
Finally all of the glow disappears into the night,
   after a long battle, dark finally finds delight.
Next comes the reviving power,
   the stars begin to endlessly flower.
In the midst of the flurry,
   as the silver stars scurry
Artemis' spirit, her image of power,
   the item with which all power she can devour,
From nothing comes arising,
   glaring as much as it is shining.
Eric Sirott, Grade 6
Dorris-Eaton School

Volcano
Filled with hot lava
Danger and very frightening
Deadly and scary
Ger Yang, Grade 5
Clayton B Wire Elementary School

The Midnight
The mist midnight sky
danced with the glittery lilacs
on an island of diamonds
Alexandra Macatangay, Grade 5
Henry Haight Elementary School

Cony
My mom's name is Cony
Her sister's call her Concha
But at her home in Guadalajara, Jalisco
They call her concheta
At home she's lazy
But sleepy

When my mom is mad
She is cruel and cold hearted
She likes to shop and cook
But is bossy and busy
My mom gets annoyed
Because she's angry

My mom is mostly
Nice and caring
But is mostly carefree
She's fearless and mysterious
Brave but is embarrassed

My mom is
Nice and caring
But is also cruel
And clumsy
Melani Hernandez, Grade 6
Century Community Charter School

Softball
The ball was pitched
I swung the bat
I ran to first base
And lost my hat
I kept on running
The ball was hit far
It rolled and rolled
'til it hit a car
I rounded third
I had hit a homerun
I love this game
Softball sure is fun.
Bailey Rall, Grade 5
Eastwood Elementary School

United States
There are lots of states
Our class has to learn them all
It takes a long time
Kora Verhoeven, Grade 5
Packinghouse Christian Academy

The Sun Tells
The sun tells us to wake up,
The sun stays until its shift is over,
But it will come back again.
In the morning, the sun
Waters my heart with joy.
I love the sun and it loves me.
Will Fortin, Grade 5
Bethany Lutheran School

I Remember…
I remember
when my dad
would put me on his lap

He'd stand me up
and hold on tight
and start to sing a song

Then he'd start
to make me dance
and I'd start cracking up

I remember
the best of times
of my childhood
Rachel Reyes, Grade 5
Theodore Roosevelt Elementary School

Feelings
happen like a lion.
Always uptight
it roars and demands space
pacing back and forth
mad as can be
hurting inside
not knowing how to express its rage
pretending to be a kitty cat
acting like everything is fine
while it eats you inside.
When you look around
everything is in slow motion
life starts to stop
the world crashing on you.
Facing the mirror
emotions spill.
Look back at the hollow mirror:
it cracks.
Ashlyn Warren, Grade 6
St Timothy School

Jeff Hardy
J umping and getting pumped up
E ager for a great challenge
F un with friends and family
F ights like a true wrestler

H as has a great experience
A true role model to children
R eally likes a good time
D oes special flip moves
Y ells for the crowd to cheer for him
David Tran, Grade 5
St Barbara School

My Head Scarf
What I wear
On my hair
Is for my honor and dignity
For Allah with intense sincerity

It's a command from Allah
To cover from head to toe
As believers we obey and follow —
I deem it's for my good benefit
And no one can state the opposite

I feel inner peace
With much integrity and bliss
When they ask about this scarf on me
I say so modestly and proudly —
A command from our Lord
That will never be ignored
Salma Hassane, Grade 6
Islamic School of San Diego

The Knight
There once was a knight
Who only rode off at night
To ride to his fair maiden
Whose name was Haden
And rode till morning light.
Mary-Catherine Mello, Grade 5
Sundale Elementary School

Sour Milk
In the refrigerator
Past the expiration date
Like poison
Between the chunks
Inside the carton
From the grocery store
With the dairy products
Below sanitary
Without a pleasant smell
Out in the trash
Jay Schuyler, Grade 6
St Anne School

Basketball

Basketball is my favorite sport.
I like to dribble up and down the court.
When I get the open shot,
you know what I'd want to do.
I'll take that outside J
and make it every day.

As I run the fast break,
and have the opportunity to pass,
I dribble and dribble until I reach half-court,
and do it behind the back like Steve Nash.

Basketball is so addictively fun,
and is a favorite sport worldwide.
It doesn't matter if you are short or stout,
as long as you stick with your team
and never foul out.

Noah Viray, Grade 5
St Pancratius Elementary School

Blue

Blue is the pastel of the sky,
Over a sparkling hot spring.
It's the color of shadows over ice,
Of marble on a table.
Blue is sad — a tear jumping off my eye.
Eyes can be blue.
Blue is a ribbon that won 1st place,
It's the saddest in the box.
Blue is a surfboard riding an ocean wave.
It's a car zooming by.
It's a house with flowers and birds.
Blue is a marker,
It's jeans,
Last of all, blue is Ice Paradise!

Sarah Zweerink, Grade 4
Stanton Elementary School

Camping Trip

The first time camping
In the dark night
No light in a tent
Animals in the wild so scary
Not being with my mom
It's not the same waking up not being with her
I miss my mom
Going to the beach
Cooking pancakes
Camping food horrible
Wanting to be with my mom
Her beautiful blue eyes
The camping people watching whatever you do
Crying in the night because I'm not with my mom
Living in peace back at home with my mom

Taylor McCowan, Grade 5
Coeur d'Alene Avenue Elementary School

Waiting

Waiting
Just waiting
A ballerina
Next to her mom
On a bench
Her mom tells her that
She'll be great
She says that ballet comes naturally
To her
But this is such a big show
That the ballerina can't stop the butterflies
That dance in her stomach
They dance better than she can hope to tonight
She's nervous,
Anxious,
Waiting
Just waiting
Then they call her name and her mom watches
As she steps onstage,
Ready to dance,
Done waiting.

Nicole Blackwood, Grade 5
Theodore Roosevelt Elementary School

Sloth

A sloth is eating. Chomp, Chomp, Chomp!
His heart is beating. Bomp, Bomp, Bomp!
His eyes are black. Stare, Stare, Stare!
I take that back. Glare, Glare, Glare!

He climbs a tree. Shimmy, Shimmy, Shimmy!
He grabs a bee. Gimme, Gimme, Gimme!
He starts to slip. Glide, Glide, Glide!
He can't get a grip. Slide, Slide, Slide!

He hits the ground. Whap, Whap, Whap!
His grave is found. Snap, Snap, Snap!
I am so sad. Weep, Weep, Weep!
The sloth's not mad. Sleep, Sleep, Sleep.

The zoo ain't happy. Argh, Argh, Argh!
Sloth's skin is flappy. Larg, Larg, Larg!
I'm in trouble. Bop, Bop, Bop!
That zoo busts my bubble. Pop, Pop, Pop!

Aaron Marcus-Willers, Grade 4
Sonoma Charter School

Eagle

Oooh! Oooh! Big eagle soaring in the sky
golden browns, big talons as mini as a fly
over the big wood
I want him to pick me up and have me found
lift me away from the ground
away from the land I've never understood

Lucy Houghton, Grade 5
Sonoma Charter School

My Favorite Shoes

A shoe is footwear
One uses for walking
A shoe is man's buddy —
Wherever man goes,
The shoes are always ready
Sports shoes, orthopedic shoes,
Dance shoes, work shoes,
Shoes of various colors and designs,
Shoes of various materials and heels
Canvas cloth of blue and green,
Shoelaces of blue and green,
Those are my favorite shoes —
My Converse shoes
High-cut sports shoes
Painted monkey's face and
Space Ace on either side —
I love my favorite Converse shoes
My favorite Converse shoes
I personally chose
I really love to wear them
From day to day to day today!

Roland Theo Capulong, Grade 6
Corpus Christi School

My Best Friend Diana

Diana is very funny
Like a nibbling bunny
I always call her DD
And she always calls me Mini
Diana loves the word wow
She taught how to milk a cow
She loves to tap her two knees
She is allergic to bees

Kaitlyn Ung, Grade 5
Eastwood Elementary School

Jealousy

I'm jealousy
You can't stop me
I make people mad
I make people sad
People always hate me
For what I do
That's why I hate you
I'm like a witch or devil
Or has a poem or riddle
I hear people crying
I don't know why
I feel the feeling that they have
I taste people tears
I just can't help
My enemy is happiness
I hope it doesn't trap me
Or you will be sorry

Ilana Sibony, Grade 6
Horace Mann Middle School

Cruel

Cruel is not pleasant
Cruel is vicious
Cruel is heartless
Cruel is being a savage
Cruel sounds like the cry of a boy when a school bully is taking his lunch money
Cruel sounds like a child being teased for his differences
Another word for *Cruel* is hate
One thing about *Cruel* is that it never ends in a positive way

Joseph Stanley, Grade 6
Big Springs Elementary School

Spring

Flowers sprout from the damp earth,
Colorful and fascinating flowers grow among the grass and trees.
The sweet smell of dew lingers in the cool air —
Bees and butterflies fly between the soft petals —
Children play gleefully outside their houses with the sun on their backs —
The sounds of their footsteps startle the hummingbirds —
Their loud screams scare away the robins —
And they fly away away away.
Over the horizon more children amuse themselves with youthful games,
Their footsteps in rhythm with the sound of the inadequate raindrops.
Soon summer will come —
And the sun will dry up all the luscious flowers.
But for now the air is still breezy,
And tiny animals still walk on the moist earth.

Samantha Wixon, Grade 6
Seven Hills School

My Mom

My mom is protective
When I do something bad she acts like a detective
Her birthday is in December which is kind of hard to remember
When I am sick she makes me tea
My mom is loud and she is proud
That I am her daughter
She likes my father too
She is very sensitive when she cries I know why

She loves to sing and always wears rings
She hates her hair but she has a certain flair
When she goes to parties
She is always happy
My mom is caring
She teaches me to be sharing
I love that she cares
I love that she is there

When it is nine
I go to bed
She gives me a kiss
She turns off the light
And says goodnight

Karla Peña, Grade 6
Century Community Charter School

High Merit Poems – Grades 4, 5 and 6

The Forest
Rabbits hop on by
The red fox, so sly
The relaxing forest, quiet

The old toad croaks very loud
The falcon buzzes off into the clouds
The relaxing forest, quiet

The doe and fawn drink from a stream nearby
The bear hibernates in a cave, on a cliff up high
The relaxing forest, quiet

Sydney Becker, Grade 6
Bernice Ayer Middle School

Gizzard
Have you ever seen a Gizzard?
If you haven't, a Gizzard lives
In a forest or jungle near a volcano!
Gizzards HATE the cold.
To find prey Gizzards dig underground and try
To feel its vibrations. Once it feels the vibrations,
the Gizzard launches and Snap!
The Gizzard then sinks back into the hole.
If a volcano erupts the Gizzard flies to a different forest.
Whoosh! They aren't silent fliers like bats and birds.
When they find the forest, they get lower and lower, until Crash!
If you believe it or not they crash land.
As they move on, they need to find a new nest.
Thud! Boom! Slap!
These are the sounds of a Gizzard making a new nest.

Alexis Orloff, Grade 6
Big Springs Elementary School

Wake Up! Enjoy It with Me
Hark, Hark, Hark!
See the sun stretch its arms.
Watch the cherry blossoms bloom bright.
Taste the pizza dancing up to your taste buds.
Come enjoy it with me.

Eddie Hernandez, Grade 4
Garden Grove Elementary School

A Magical Morning
Gorgeous shapes of raindrops falling from the gray clouds
Birds calling out to each other
Zimba whining at the front door
Waiting to be taken on a walk
Leash on, bag tied, as I open the magical door
Rain in my face as I jump in the sparkling puddles
I watch Zimba as she sniffs around
All those thousands of smells
Soon getting numb in my fingers
I go back inside
Having hot cocoa with a book full of dreams in my hands

Helene Miles, Grade 5
Coeur d'Alene Avenue Elementary School

Spring Fling
Spring is a time for fun,
Spring is also a time to see the sun,
Spring is the end for some animals' hibernation,
Spring is the time for happiness,
I hope I'm not the only one celebrating spring,
That would be sad,
Spring is fun with happiness,
But spring is not sad.

Fernando Alvarez Jr., Grade 5
St Linus School

My Garden
There's a key to the garden gate,
That only I have.
There's a whisper between the elves and fairies,
That only I can hear.
Imagination turns into roaring flame,
Because I have the spark to light the fuse.
Swing on the rope of dreams afar,
Not your everyday place,
That you can drive in an ordinary car.
In my garden I am safe,
When I hear someone coming,
I lock it up, and come back tomorrow,
And it's always more beautiful than before.

Katie Buss, Grade 6
Coastal Academy

Sitting with the Butterflies
I am sitting under an apple tree
with the butterflies talking to me with their beautiful wings
I close my eyes and say to myself
"What if there is such thing as blue and orange butterflies"
I opened my eyes and looked at them
there was what I had wished for

I started walking toward the river
the fish are dancing with each other
slipping when they dance
jumping over the river I fall into a path of flowers
looking at the clouds floating in the sky
I fall asleep with the flowers singing a lullaby

Ariana Miles, Grade 4
Coeur d'Alene Avenue Elementary School

Dogs
Dogs come in many sizes,
Some are small some are big,
Some are clean and brushed,
Some are dirty and dig,
Some like it cold and mush sleighs,
Some like it hot and swim all day,
Some are cute and eat neat,
Some are scary and chew your feet.

Joe DuBeau, Grade 5
George Washington Charter Elementary School

Scared

When you're scared,
You feel all black,
Like shadows on the floor,
Or when someone got shot by a gun,
And you run to the corner and hide,
Scared is when you get a big blanket,
And hide in the closet,
You pray and hide in the closet,
Scared is all black.

Richard Vu, Grade 5
St Barbara School

The Sun

As the sun is blazing down,
the shadow dances lovely.
It's still daylight but soon no more.

Erik Vang, Grade 5
Clayton B Wire Elementary School

As I Sleep

I have nothing to do,
And nothing to say,
I close my eyes,
And drift away.

I had a dream,
Of one of my thoughts,
But everything in it,
Is not what I sought.

Helen Bui, Grade 5
St Pancratius Elementary School

My Dad Rocks

My dad is stocky and bald,
Because he used to be a boxer,
And he is still strong,
And tries not to be wrong.
He explains things clearly,
And is understandable,
He has a big vocabulary,
And loves the power of words.
And he is caring,
That is, thanks to church.
He is the best of the best,
Thank God that works.
He cooks good food,
Because he used to be a cook.
My dad is also funny,
And likable too.
But he can be strict, or
He can be flexible,
And what he likes he likes,
And what he doesn't like he spites
MY DAD ROCKS!!!

Ashley Sims, Grade 6
Century Community Charter School

St. Patrick Mush Day

One year we had St. Patrick
brunch
With St. Patrick mush to
munch

Mush feels all slimy to the
touch
It smells like skunk so
pinch your nose

I don't think you'd care for
such
We didn't like to munch mush
much

Jade Le, Grade 5
Merryhill Country School

Leaves

In the big forest
the red leaves are floating down
in the late noon time

Logan Veloff, Grade 5
Santa Fe Springs Christian School

Fall's Glory

As the leaves fall from their trees,
I wonder…what is the glory of fall?
And when the sun gleams
behind the clouds I wonder
the exact same things
but then I see…
All the things that make me wonder,
those things, are the glory of fall.

Aly Refaat, Grade 5
New Horizon School

Skipping Rain

Raindrops
skipping softly
on my bedroom window
always
beats like an even tempo
on a metronome
I can do nothing
except
sit on my bed
and read my book
it's God's sadness
for the world
pouring out on us
raindrops change
I look out my wet window
seeing not raindrops
but a sun and a rainbow.

Casey Smith, Grade 6
Bethany Lutheran School

What's a Friend

Happy and playful
Doesn't yell at you
Never talks behind your back
Helps you when you are hurt
Goes through good times and bad
Always by your side
Never fights with you
Always tells the truth
Someone you can trust
A person that stays with you all your life
That's a friend

Sabrina Dow, Grade 6
Aliso Elementary School

I Am

I am special
I wonder if ghosts are real
I hear a beautiful waterfall
I see a pretty teacher
I want to be a sign language interpreter
I am special
I pretend to be in the Olympic games
I feel very stupendous
I touch beloved God
I worry that my mom will die
I cry when I read very sad books
I am special
I understand life is not perfect
I say good things happen to you
I dream of a sweet paradise
I try to follow my dreams
I am special

Sewit Tesfamicael, Grade 4
La Presa Elementary School

Mom

Her eyes bright with joy
She has that loving
Look in her eyes
Every time
She looks at me
She has a smile
On her face
She is my every need
She says
I love you
And will give me
A kiss good night
And say
Have a good sleep
Good night
I tell her
I love her
Too

Ariana Lester, Grade 5
Bethany Lutheran School

Fall

As dawn turns to dusk
As green changes to yellow and orange
Fall has arrived
The beautiful princess flows through the sky
Her hair streaming through the meadows
She dances with a prince, happily for months on end
Not knowing the prince she frolics with is winter
Though she feels his body is icy cold
She is blinded by his handsomeness and charm

As months pass, she gets weak
Not strong enough to hold off the prince
From taking over her kingdom
Her time has come and she falls to the ground
Her face pale as a ghost
As it lurks in the underworld slowly, hunchbacked
Winter digs an abyss, then throws the princess in
The abyss black and never ending

He gets back to the castle, icy in his presence
He sits in the throne in the sky
Now, the prince, winter, is the ruler

Brianna Goldberg, Grade 6
Francis Parker School

How Earth Was Made

It was beautiful in the starry night sky
Gaia was happy, for another star was added to the others
She sighed a sigh so huge that the gases came together
And created fire, and with it, Earth's core
Then, she had an idea
She took a thread of her long, thick, wavy hair
And covered the flames with it
Afraid it would catch fire, she packed on soil
Then, just to be on the safe side, poured water on top
She threw on seeds, animals, and man for entertainment
Her mighty breath causes wind and weather
While her face glows with pride
And her smile lights the sky
Appearing as the sun and moon today

Cole Tretheway, Grade 5
Rancho Vista Elementary School

Laying Like a Starfish

Laying lonely like a starfish
sitting on a glistening rock

When all of a sudden
I saw a swarm of fish
and swimming up while I lay on the beach

When I look up all I see
are dancing stars
and I see a beautiful sky

Grayson Alamango Shapiro, Grade 4
Coeur d'Alene Avenue Elementary School

Bees

Buzzing bees
Singing buzzing bees
Making lovely honey
Every day with roses daisies and buttercups
They work together for winter to come
Little bees with their black and yellow stripes
Along with their sticky feet.

Alexandra Peterson, Grade 4
Stone Ranch Elementary School

Ice Cream

Have you heard
the sound of
great ice cream:
    the slurp-slurp of kids licking
    the crunch-crunch of kids eating cones
    the ha ha of kids laughing
Have you heard
the sound of
great ice cream?

Cami Christopher, Grade 5
Theodore Roosevelt Elementary School

The Ocean Waves

My life is like the ocean waves
    Taking me through rough and calm.
    Yet most of the time it is stormy.
    Not knowing where I am going
    But where I want to be
    And fighting to be there
    I look for the lighthouse to find my destination.

Aja Two Crows, Grade 4
Coeur d'Alene Avenue Elementary School

Seven Years of Bad Luck

The rain knocks gently on my window,
I hear the breeze coming through,
In the distance the clouds are thick,
And I wonder if the sky will ever turn blue.

How I missed the sunshine,
Bright as ever can be,
Now there's been seven years of rain,
No sunshine for you or me.

Oh — how these dark days will go,
I do not know,
But I do wish that this rain,
Will stop slapping on my window pane.

Now this day is gloomy, dark, and stormy,
And filled with mud and muck,
I cannot stand this weather,
It is just raining bad luck.

Emily Gao, Grade 6
Alvarado Middle School

Wonderful Presents Just for You

I am going to send you a beautiful flower
of happiness
to honor
your one precious life.
Here is a magic sea
of appreciation to let you know
you'll always be loved and cared for.

Catherine Pham, Grade 4
Dingeman Elementary School

Are You an Elephant?

Are you an elephant?
No, I am not.
Of course, I am not.
In fact, I would rather live in a pot.
And besides,
my body is not
the right shade of blue.

And then,
right at that moment,
he sneezed, "Achoo!"
The houses fell down
and the buildings did, too
and then that poor boy
was the right shade of blue.

Allison Taylor, Grade 4
Charles Armstrong School

Surfing

Atop the wave
Down the face
In the barrel
Up in the sky
Before I feel I can fly
Around the white water
Among nature
Beyond understanding
Toward the barrel I turn
Until I catch another

Jake Fast, Grade 6
St Anne School

Long

Long was too far
as I could see
Made me too
sad when my friend
moved away.
Long took days then weeks but
still long was too far
Long long still was too far
But what do I see
Oh, my friend comes back to me

Ryan Kroemer, Grade 4
Montessori Center School

Green All the Time

Mowed, sweet scented grass lightly swaying side to side with the breeze,
Hideous, overgrown weeds generously protecting bugs and insects from predators,
Tall, trimmed oak trees shading humans for superb picnics,
Petite, light leaves dangling rapidly throughout the horrific rain storm,
Spiky, jagged cacti slowly sucking water from the moist ground after a rainy day,
Spotted, fat frogs leaping high onto another lily pad,
Bent, skinny flower stems sagging to the ground
Desperately pleading for sunlight.

Jenna Chapton, Grade 5
Highland Oaks Elementary School

Fountain of Marvels

Oh Fountain of Marvels, you rain hearts of love
and happiness every day.
Oh Fountain of Marvels, your details make clouds blossom
and make winds blow flowers to trees.
Oh Fountain of Marvels, you are my dream come true.
Oh Fountain of Marvels, you tell me a teal story
of how rivers and lakes came alive.
Oh Fountain of Marvels, your crimson soul
is connected to mine by ropes of silver.
Oh Fountain of Marvels, you speak of a blossoming tree
that started as a seed and then grew wings of hope.
Oh Fountain of Marvels, you sound like a bird
saying tweet tweet, tweet tweet.
Oh Fountain of Marvels, you are a treat to everyone's senses especially mine.
Oh Fountain of Marvels, you tell what lies within the Earth.
Oh Fountain of Marvels, goodbye, goodbye, goodbye.

Cady De Camara, Grade 4
The Mirman School

Fishing in a Spring, Pont de Cliché*

The man who sits upon his boat feels the tranquility of the stream
The water dances swiftly from one end to another
The man sits and listens
He hears the forest singing
She was singing him her song of the wind
He will listen closely as she lures him to stay
He sits and watches
The flowers and the grass sway in the gentle breeze
The forest has decided to sing
The stream is as peaceful as a long nap in a field of flowers
The man feels the summer water lapping
Against his cold, hard hand while he reaches into the river
Wishing he had made better choices
Hearing his thoughts loud and clear
Thinking back upon his innocent days
Shoving out the thoughts, trying to relax and live the moment
He likes coming here
He likes to put out all the thoughts and just sit and realize the beauty
He will come again, soon
He doesn't want to leave
...not yet

Madeline Ottilie, Grade 6
Francis Parker School
*Inspired by a Vincent Van Gogh oil painting

Forest Pines
All dark green and pure white
Are the forest pines in the winter night
All covered with fluffy white snow
Bright, bold and standing tall
Sofia Raptis, Grade 4
Mayfield Jr School of the Holy Child Jesus

My Bratty Nosey Sister
When my bratty little sister makes me mad, mad
My head feels like splitting up
My eyes turn red like red chili peppers
My face turns red and feels like it's on fire.

People yell and scream at me, not that I fail to listen,
It's only that I don't hear them
When I get mad, mad, I want to be left all alone.
This separation from others helps me calm down
And keeps me from doing something I would regret later.

I wish I didn't have to feel like this at any one time
But I am learning to be patient with myself and others
Especially my nosey bratty sister
Who never seems to get in trouble like I often do.
Ruben Solorio III, Grade 5
Joseph M Simas Elementary School

I Am
I am stupendous
I wonder how butterflies fly
I hear love calling
I see Van Gogh
I want a good career
I am stupendous
I pretend to be an angel
I feel my parents' love
I touch a star
I worry about my family members dying
I am stupendous
I understand my mother's feelings
I say people should not be treated wrong
I dream of being a vet
I try to be the best I can be
I hope my baby sister grows up to be perfect
I am stupendous
Sofia Velazquez, Grade 4
La Presa Elementary School

Sweets
I like sundaes, sorbets, shakes
Cookies, candy, muffins, cakes
I don't care 'bout getting chicken pox or flu
I want floats and chocolates, too!
Desserts are the best part of a meal
Sweets are so good they just can't be real!
Ariana Acosta, Grade 4
Mayfield Jr School of the Holy Child Jesus

Colors
Listen to the colors
they'll talk to you.
They sound like music.
They sound like a trumpet and violin,
red, green, blue, yellow, the colors sound
like dancing raindrops in my head.
Izzabella Dieteman, Grade 5
Henry Haight Elementary School

Words of Kindness*
Etch simple words of kindness in my head
Put shapes of joy in my mind
Let the paint fly off my pallet
And onto that blank canvas gleaming
With hope.
David Aaron, Grade 4
The Mirman School
*Inspired by paintings viewed at the
Norton Simon Museum in Pasadena, CA.

Yellow Is…
Yellow is a bitter lemon
sweet, sweet jelly beans
and a squishy banana
Yellow is a bright sun all day
a beautiful sunflower
to go with a cup of lemonade
Yellow makes me smiley, happy and mellow
Yellow is…
Megan Stevens, Grade 5
Caryn Elementary School

My Beautiful Mommy
My mommy is sweet as pie
She cheers me up
She loves to hug and kiss
Mommy is special to me
Also she is pretty how she looks
Mommy is pretty and skinny
She keeps secrets because she is trustful
Mommy is special to my family and me
She likes to help me and people
My mommy cares and plays with me
She is joyful and likes to share
She keeps me healthy and safe
Mommy loves to eat and lose weight
My mommy feeds us good
She plays a lot and we call her Sporty
When my mom is sad or cries she hugs me or my bear
My mommy is happy, she sings and dances
She has fun with me and my family
My mommy buys me things
And gives things on holidays
My mommy is special
Ana Tovar, Grade 6
Century Community Charter School

Another Day at the Beach
Sun shines on the beach
the sparkling waves crash wildly
on the rough tan sand
Halie Lasken, Grade 6
St Anne School

Winter
Rain falls,
Sidewalks slick,
Gifts arrive,
Christmas comes.

Sledding down a hill,
Tumbling in the snow,
Splat goes the snowball,
There it goes.

Here comes the new year,
School's taking over,
January, here I come!
Young-Kyung Kim, Grade 4
Montessori Family School

Sweet as Candy!
She is so sweet
she's loving and nice
she makes me think twice.
The one that is so loving and kind
she makes me happy
my mommy I love!
Mason Adams, Grade 6
Coastal Academy

Ice Cream and the Sun
I used to be an ice cream
until the sun came along
I used to have chocolate syrup
until the sun came along
I used to have sprinkles
until the sun came along
I used to have a cherry on me
until the sun came along
I used to have a cone
until the sun came along

Now I have a bad cone
when I was thrown out back
James Bloom, Grade 4
Upper Lake Elementary School

Flowers
Growing from the ground
Petals falling and growing
Different colors
Hannah Fox, Grade 6
Charles Armstrong School

Gray
The moon in the sky
A car in the parking lot
Shirts hanging inside my closet
Inside the classroom, a desk
I have my shoes with me
Lucero Gutierrez, Grade 6
St Alphonsus School

Wonderful Mom
My mom is giving
And also caring
She is my guide
To the future line
She is complacent
And full of excitement
She is loving
And also funny
She's always dedicated
To my family and I
But sometimes she's also my spy
I love her responsibility
Because she brings unity
To the rest of my life
She is my teacher
She is my friend
And she thinks of me
Inside her head
My mom is a glowing star
And she always leads me
To the head start
Isabel Magallanes, Grade 6
Century Community Charter School

Swing
I'm swinging in the breeze.
My hair blows in my face.
My eyelids droop
and I close my eyes.
I'm flying
holding on to
silver chains.
The chains I am holding
feel like ice.
I hear
a squeak each time
I swing back.
I open my eyes to a
different world.
Wind paints my face.
I jump off.
The swing is still moving,
as if there's
a ghost riding the breeze.
Maybe his eyes are closed.
Evelyn Taylor, Grade 4
Carlthorp School

The First Years
I remember…
My first birthday
And all the words I got to say
"Paint, cake, dress, dog,
Duck, mouse, crayon, and frog."

I remember…
Little Shadow, my first pup,
When I drank from a sippie cup.
My first play day with Kate
We played and swam and ate.

I remember…
My first day of school
I thought it was really cool
I went the next day
After 4 years I went away.
Katie Hobson, Grade 5
Theodore Roosevelt Elementary School

Butterflies
Butterflies float in the air
Butterflies are graceful
Butterflies are perfectionists

Butterflies make people young again
Without butterflies there is no Spring
Butterflies are perfectionists

Butterflies have a mind no one can sense
That makes butterflies so questionable
Butterflies are perfectionists
Sophia Spralja, Grade 6
Bernice Ayer Middle School

Sunflower
S uper tall
U nlike no other
N ot a weed
F ound in a patch
L oves to be tall and mighty
O pens its petals wide to the sun
W ide stem
E volves from a seed
R uler of all flowers
Mariella Sullam, Grade 6
Charles Armstrong School

Pyramids
Pyramids
Impressive, ancient
Towering, satisfying, forbidding
Honor for deceased royalty
Tombs
Tyler Mould, Grade 6
Big Springs Elementary School

Red
Red is the taste of a fresh picked sweet cherry.
Red is the look of an original cherry pie, ready to be bitten.
Red is the stench of a fire burning into ashes.
Red is the feeling of a bird gliding to your shoulder.
Red is the taste of a lion gorging the flesh of another animal.
Red is the sound of someone running from a fire in a house.
Red is the look of extremely puffy cheeks.
Red is the sound of a person skateboarding on a skateboard.
Red is the color of some of my shirts.
Red is the feeling of love and fire burning together.
Ryan Alexander Toulouse, Grade 4
Heather Elementary School

My Mom Is My Life
My mom is the best
She pays the bills on time
She has a lot of friends
Like a tree with leaves
When she cooks chili
She wants to make it best
When we make a challenge
She always wins
She cleans our home
Like it was spring
She may be small
But she is smart
She is caring
Like a gardener with her plants
She helps my brother on math as a teacher
She jokes on us
Like she wants to play with us
She is tired
Like a mother doing all the work
She likes to shop in the mall
Like it was Christmas day
Jahiro Salmeron, Grade 6
Century Community Charter School

My Pet
My beloved pet,
We had great times together,
Laying in the sun,
Or watching you chase the laser pointer.
You were the joy in my life
Until you had to go.
I remember that day all too well.
I woke up, and it was silent.
I knew what it meant.
I could not believe it though.
I know you will have eight more tries to make people happy,
But neither person nor pet could ever replace you.
You were by my side when I was sick,
And after I had my operations.
I loved you, and I could not have asked for a better pet!
Elijah Barsky-Ex, Grade 6
Parkmont Elementary School

Our Country
America is a place where there is happiness,
Where everyone is free,
A land with no violence or hatred,
There are new generations to be started,
Although years ago there was slavery,
And a war between the North and the South,
there was segregation in our states,
Now there are no color barriers,
This is why we are lucky to live in the United States.
Skylar Doss, Grade 4
Canyon View Elementary School

I Live in Basketball
I live in basketball is this where you live
I live on a wood basketball court
uniforms all blue
with a white and gold stripe on the side
basketball team pumped up and ready to play
hot gym because of the packed house
fans on their feet jumping up and down
dribbling up and down the court shooting the ball
drinking icy cold blue Gatorade during a timeout
is your dream to play in the Olympics one day mine is
before playing basketball I want to attend
the University of California Los Angeles
and play basketball there
then play in the NBA
I will try my best to do what I want to do
Jayson Williams, Grade 5
Franklin Elementary School

I Am
I am whoever I wish to be,
You know me for who I am.
My mother is the vast sky and the blue ocean,
My father is the blazing sun and the towering mountains
I was born in this planet, my home.
I live in this small world that you and I share
My best friend is happiness,
For it makes me feel well.
My enemy is hate and envy,
Yet I cannot ignore these feelings, for they make me who I am.
I fear death,
For it takes takes all I love.
I wish this were a happy and peaceful world.
Theo Schroder, Grade 6
Ranch Hills Elementary School

Red
I saw the red moon in the night of the eclipse.
I heard the crackling red fire in my burning ears.
I tasted the ripe red strawberry oozing down my chin.
I could barely smell the red apple because I had a stuffy nose.
I felt the little hairs on the red raspberries.
Sean De La Espriella, Grade 5
Andasol Avenue Elementary School

Soup

Soup, soup, soup you make me feel better when I'm sick. You remind me of my family's traditions and culture. Every slurp I take it reminds me of past times that I have had with my family. You can't use a fork, only a spoon. Soup, soup, soup you are a very important part in my family's history.

Debra Wexler, Grade 5
Kentwood Elementary School

Hope

She is wrapped in her blanket, the fringe being frayed and thin
Behind her forlorn figure there is a green trash bin
That is drenched in rain
The girl feels rejected, lonely, and emotional pain.
The dismal girl remembers her past.
She looks around her to see the only remnants of before that seemed to last.
All those things she used to buy at any desire.

What had that done except help the poor person's life have consequences so dire?
She hadn't the vaguest clue
All she could remember was giving up her last Prada shoe.
She also vividly remembered losing her job
Her hand leaving her house's doorknob,
Now she was in the gutter
But she decided that after what she'd done she deserved nothing better.

She felt disconsolate.
She knew that when she was successful many had waited for her to blow it.
Tears in her eyes, she looks up into the sky of cloudy gray.
Her eyes rest on a store window that reads "Help Wanted" and she seems to find hope in herself, a tiny ray.
She decided that tomorrow would be a new day.
She would fight back until she had nothing to give.
She would try as long as she would live.

Megan Verma, Grade 6
Big Springs Elementary School

Books

A hushed library.
Sunlight filters through glazed windows —
Sparkling dust floating in the air and dissolving into nothing — like the memories of those who had once come.
Click.
A single sound — not heard in a time that seemed forever, reverberates through the silent room.
The grand wooden door — once lovingly cared for, creaks painfully, its unoiled hinges threatening to break.
A moon pale face peeks around the corner of the massive slab of oak,
Followed by arms, a slight waist, and a dainty pair of feet. A girl.
The girl pads silently across the faded carpet and looks up at
The long-forgotten masterpieces towering above her like skyscrapers.
The books watch as she hesitantly approaches,
Carefully-placed fingers brush against well-worn shelves and slide down the bookcases.
The books feel as her fingers caress their cracked spines as she moves to each ancient work,
Wondering what mysteries each might hold.
A slight scrape is heard as she takes a single book out of the shelf, holding it like a fragile diamond.
She slowly walks back to the center of the chamber and quietly sits down.
The books crane to hear the faint rustle of paper and as they do, they lie back in their shelves, contented.
Unaware, the girl immerses herself into the book, sinking deeper and deeper
Into the portal leading to the book's inner soul.
She reads.

Alexandra Wong-Appel, Grade 6
Francis Parker School

My Grandfather

I love my grandfather with all my heart
He really means the world to me
He was always happy and outgoing
I always called him Papa Billy
We used to laugh while watching TV
I miss him so much but he's in a better place
Every time I think about him I want to cry
My mom always tells me I have to be strong
I just miss the things we used to do together
I dream for my grandfather who was never mean
I just want him to be very proud of me
Although he was old he was like my best friend
Every night I try to pray and wish I'll have him again some day
I was a little girl when it all happened
As I get older it seems I miss him more and more
I wonder who was his father
From time to time his memories are stuck inside my head
It's hard to hold it all inside
When you just want to let it out
I love my grandfather with all my heart

Asia King, Grade 6
Century Community Charter School

Music

Music is the thing that touches people's hearts.
It surrounds everyone, everywhere.
People in an orchestra play their individual parts.
Music fills the air.

People and flowers dance to the tune.
Music is so versatile that
People play music while looking at the moon,
Music is made even when you chat.

Birds chirp, cats meow — music is made anyhow.
Loved by everyone from east to west,
Music influences, I want to know how,
Music is considered as the best.

Variety of instruments create a melodious sound,
Music builds the passion for dance.
Great musicians are commemorated and crowned.
If you have the talent, give it a chance.

Sharanya Agarwal, Grade 6
Parkmont Elementary School

The Time Traveler

I am a rock falling through time
Kings, tanks, temples, and cars
But those are all things of past
Falling, falling through time I hit the bottom
And there on my left I see in the distance
The city, the only light in the dark world
A citizen of the village has picked me up

Thomas Lunday, Grade 5
Charles Armstrong School

Keeping Warm

I love the snow,
I do indeed,
There are special garments you will need,
They'll help you keep nice and warm.
Stay in shelter from a snowstorm,
Drink lots of hot cocoa get a quilt too,
If we didn't have these things what would we do?
Now that I've told you this you should know,
Ways to keep warm from the snow.

Caleb Calderon, Grade 5
Jackson Elementary School

Flowers

The seed sprouts as the sun is shining hard.
The soil is rich and fertile,
I pour water and day after day I watch it grow.
Soon it is all grown,
But in winter it lies down for a long winter nap.

Sonia Clinkinbeard, Grade 6
Bernice Ayer Middle School

If I Were

If I were a dolphin,
I would swim faster than a great white shark.
If I were a dog,
I would play with my owner after dinner.
If I were a bed,
I would hear children pray before bedtime.
If I were a mouse,
I would eat a hotel made of cheddar cheese.

Jasmin Islas-Chavez, Grade 4
Elder Creek Elementary School

Eric Gomez

My Papi is…
A really loving buddy
Who is always there for me
I love it when he's happy
But, dislike when he's angry
My daddy is…
Really active
He is also really confident
When it comes to playing the Wii
He gets really tired and mean
My cookie monster is…
A cookie lover
who could be smart
And also full of advice
Which is really awesome
My Danny is…
A jealous daddy
Who could come to his brave moments
Once I annoyed him
But at the end he was a caring cookie monster

Erika Gomez, Grade 6
Century Community Charter School

The Lizard

Green lizard,
Prickly and spiky,
Poisonous and scary,
He runs, sleeps,
Plays with friend the gecko,
The lizard mad and sad,
Lizard loving the cold air
Senor lizard says good bye.

Sergio Chavez, Grade 6
St Alphonsus School

The Life of a Snowflake

they fall through the clouds
they glide through the air with wind
then land on the ground

Nick Valverde, Grade 6
Francis Parker School

Life

Life is like a rolling train.
Life is like a game to play.

Life is like a long trip.
Life is when you truly get tripped.

Life is like a waterfall.
Life is when you really fall.

Life is like a wishing well.
Life is really hard to tell.

Andrew Lona, Grade 6
St Charles Catholic School

Dolphins

Dolphins of the sea
Taken to its depth
Underneath the waves
Fighting, fighting for its breath
Feet splash out
Coming upon something smooth
A Dolphin's song is heard
You are soothed
They carry you up
To the top
You suddenly wish
You could live down there —
Dolphin Child.

Guadalupe Rodriguez, Grade 6
St Alphonsus School

Thunder

Loud as a lion's roar
One thousand bolts in the ground
When heard crying starts

Alec Dardis, Grade 6
St Anne School

I Am

I AM Matthew
I wonder if I will go into the Hall of Fame
I hear sounds in the distance telling me to do it or not to do it
I see a 70-mile an hour pitch coming straight at me
I want to be a major league baseball player
I AM Matthew

I pretend to be extravagant in life
I feel like I can't fail
I touch my bed when I'm tired
I worry about my Mom or Dad getting hurt
I cry when the Red Sox lose
I AM Matthew

I understand that every team loses but maybe not like the Padres
I say baseball is life
I dream of being a major league baseball player
I try to do well in school
I hope to be the best
I AM Matthew

Matthew Blake, Grade 5
Aviara Oaks Elementary School

Halloween Horror!

Scrumptious, luscious candy waiting for us to consume,
Horrific, amusing costumes showing what Halloween is all about,
Pragmatic accessories frightening numerous innocent citizens,
Phantasmagorical house designs fascinating our minds,
Tiresome homework keeping our minds away from Halloween,
Wicked witches showing off their hideous features,
Haunting celebrations giving the goose bumps to all the invited guests.

Ryan Pan, Grade 5
Highland Oaks Elementary School

I Am the Ocean

I am the ocean…
In every crashing wave, throwing itself upon the rocky shore,
every salty drop of spray making up both the mysterious and majestic azure deeps,
every coral reef teeming with creatures, built over centuries by minuscule polyps.
I am the ocean…
In every school of silver anchovies, darting this way and that in giant schools,
every pod of spraying whales, emerging to spout fountains of water,
every single barnacle on the sandy shore, lying in wait of high tide, and its lunch.
I am the ocean…
In graceful manta rays, soaring through the sea,
delicate sea horses, clinging to the seaweed and devouring morsels of food,
scuttling crustaceans, scampering to the safety of their homes, away from danger.
I am the ocean…
In every shelled clam, producing precious pearls from plain sand and rocks,
every anemone, its transparent tentacles flowing the direction of the waves,
every tiny hermit crab, lugging its durable shell home along with it.
I am the ocean…

I am life.

Samantha Tsai, Grade 6
Lindero Canyon Middle School

Purple

Purple is that jubilant feeling you experience
It is the boost on your first day of school
The reason you finished the race

Purple is like jellyfish at the bottom of the sea
An unintended grape juice stain on your shirt
It is the plum in your lunch you refuse to eat

Purple is the mysterious dream you could not remember
Purple is jaunty and rebellious
Distinct, the odd one out.

Cassandra Vogel, Grade 6
James B Davidson Middle School

The Joy of Poetry

The joy of poetry
brings me to a world of creativity.
The joy of poetry
pinwheels in my mind.
The joy of poetry
floats in my heart and soul.
The joy of poetry
makes hope flutter around the world.
The joy of poetry
nourishes us with a fantasy dream of happiness.
The joy of poetry
will stay in my heart forever.

Iris Cong, Grade 4
The Mirman School

Tiger

T rembling with power
I ntense red and gold eyes
G reat leaps and jumps through a field of flowers
E ats great amounts of meat
R uns extremely fast to catch its prey

Halli Jacobson, Grade 5
Joseph M Simas Elementary School

The Sky

Space, space
A depressing place
Nothing to hear, nothing to see
Nothing special to me

Night, night
A pleasant sight
With billions of stars that scar the sky,
It goes on for miles, and miles high

The moon, the moon
As white as a cocoon
It's the only face in the sky,
I see the sun rising, and the moon saying "good-bye"

Anthony Folsé, Grade 6
Cimarron Education Center

My Dog

You are the one who makes my day.
You keep me smiling through out the years.
Without you I would be in tears.

Madeline Garcia, Grade 6
St Timothy School

Jason

You are the bright color of orange
that puts me in an excited mood.
You're the last note of a
rock 'n' roll song.
You are the cheese that melts on my pizza.
You're the cherry on top of my Shirley Temple.
You are the soft cotton
that makes me feel comfortable.
You're the last blade of grass
that makes Dodger Stadium
just a bit better.
You are the feeling
when I get up from bed
and find out it's Saturday.
You are the soft feeling
when I brush my hands
on a dog's fur.
You are the excitement
when I find out I got an "A"
on my math test.
You are my amazing brother.

Adam Sraberg, Grade 4
Carlthorp School

If I Were…

If I were a green popsicle,
I'd have delectable sweet and
Sour green apple tang and the kids
Would adore me

If I were a red popsicle, I'd have a rich luscious
Red color to lure in my prey, and
Then I would attack them with my delightfully
Sweet strawberry flavor

If I were an orange popsicle, I'd have
A tangy, sweet, orangey twist with
Just a drizzle of my secret flavored secret frost

If I were a yellow popsicle, I would be a light bulb
On a stick with my bright, luminous yellow
Color and I would have the most
Delicious taste out of all the popsicles.

If I were a purple popsicle, I'd be sad and lonely
Because nobody would want a popsicle
That tastes like medicine

Jason Levy, Grade 5
Aviara Oaks Elementary School

Parenting

Something told the lions
It is time to feed their cubs
Run and catch a zebra
For the cubs to be full

They finally catch one
All lions and cubs trying to get a piece
First cubs
Then lions
Now every one is full
With a warm mane

Time to wake up
Looking at the sky
With light coming into their prides
Time to hunt again.

Abdirahman Mohamed, Grade 6
Islamic School of San Diego

Pain

Pain is bad
Pain is heart broken
Pain is not fun
Pain does not make people happy
Pain is not love
Pain kills people
Pain is boring
Pain is not the best
Pain hurts people's hearts
Pain is without love
Pain is worthless
Pain is like a book
that has been torn apart
Pain is like a dead flower
Pain is like a burning tree
Pain is like a dead desert

Kong Thao, Grade 4
Clayton B Wire Elementary School

California Poppy

Golden poppy
Yellow and floppy
With petals all around
Planted firmly in the ground

Chloë H. Combes, Grade 5
Ecole Bilingue de Berkeley

Wake Up

Dear friend, dear friend!
Arise from your sleep.
Flowers are blooming and
Breakfast is waiting for
You to come outside.
Take a breath of fresh air!

Veronica Castillejo, Grade 4
Garden Grove Elementary School

Baseball

Baseball
The game of Heroes
Play it!
You feel the pressure and nervousness coming toward you
The sweat from your face is coming as fast as a jaguar's sprint
You hold the bat in your hands like it's a threatening weapon
The pitcher whizzes a 90 mile per hour pitch past you for strike one
Not to worry, you're just warming up
Another meatball,
Your swing is short and quick,
The ball rockets into the sky like an eagle's prey
Home Run!!!
Your team wins!
Baseball
The game of heroes

Joshua Yuen, Grade 5
Duveneck Elementary School

Beaches

Beaches look like waves crashing against the sandy shore.
Some surfers wiping out, others riding the waves in.
Beaches feel like the soft wind blowing against your face.
You also touch the dead jellyfish with your shoe and feel them jiggling!
You smell all the salt in the ocean and the food in your cooler.
You hear the waves going CRASH! CRASH! CRASH!!!
You also hear the wind blowing through your ears.
But to me, the things you taste is the best part of all
Because my dad makes the BEST BEEF JERKY *EVER*!!!
When you taste it it tastes like all the spices you never had!!!

Taylor Benson, Grade 4
Daves Avenue Elementary School

What Heartless Fool?

I am Fever.
I bring pain and heartbreak.
I have no regrets.
I am swifter than an arrow,
I strike harder than a hammer.
I relish the heat, flourishing in burning sunlight.
I devastate thousands of peoples' lives — sparing few to mourn for them
I have stranded the great, the strong, and the proud
I am the eerie nightmare of the waking world.
The goodhearted cringe in fear of me,
The empty hearted worry for themselves,
The cold hearted idolize me for they thrive with me.
The deaths are fast but the pain of the area is enduring.
Many flee me — they are wise.
Their attempts are in vain for though you can run, you cannot hide.
Those that stay are either very brave or very foolish.
It is pointless to fight me.
You can only watch, or die.
Feel the cold.
Rejoice like you have won the lottery prize of thousands of dollars.
For it means I am gone, but I will be back.

Jonathan Choi, Grade 6
St Andrew's Episcopal School

A Walk Down Memory Lane

I'm in my room lying in my bed,
Waiting for my mommy to
cook me some noodles and some bread.

While I'm waiting in bed,
I sit and wait for time to pass.
Thinking of those memories
when we both used to laugh.

I get out of bed anxious to
go eat my food.
When I see Tracy and Mark
come running up to my room.

I'm very happy to see my family
and friends around me.
I realize there's no point looking in the past,
when all I have and need is right beside me.

Mariah Contreras, Grade 6
Blessed Sacrament School

If I Were Random Things

If I were an instrument, I would be
an elegant piano so I could scream
out my piercing beauty to gratify the outside world.

If I were a magazine, I would be
The New York Times, giving
people never ending interest about America.

If I were a planet I would be
Earth, so I could be filled with
exquisite waters, with playful children splashing around.

If I were a car, I would be a
Jaguar, so I could pounce onto the
glistening road, lying in front of me.

If I were a scent, I would be
coconut pine, shaking into those
tunnels of hairy goop.

If I were a drink, I would be a
slick smoothie, slithering down
twisted throats.

Taylor Thomason, Grade 5
Aviara Oaks Elementary School

Blizzard

I wish I were a stormy blizzard,
Freezing and furious,
Blowing like an air conditioner,
Whipping snowflakes everywhere,
Finally coating the ground with a carpet of white.

Kevin Ralda, Grade 5
Lake Forest Elementary School

Hate

Hate is such a powerful word.
Hate shouldn't be in our vocabulary.
You should know the meaning of hate
Before you use it.
When you say you hate someone,
Deep inside,
You really love them.
A person wouldn't
Tell someone they hate them,
Out of the blue.
When you say you hate your parents
You really don't mean it in your heart
For in a little while,
You will forget what you were hating them about.

Tiara Brown, Grade 4
PLACE @ Prescott

Ears

The sea listens to me
She listens to the sound of my feet
Thudding
On the sand
She listens to me and my friends
Build sandcastles
On her shoreline
She listens to the sound of rumbling engines
She listens to the sound of my air
When I blow bubbles inside her
She listens to me splash into her
She listens to me
And watches over me

Sarah Machetta, Grade 5
Bethany Lutheran School

Waves

Waves are crashing onto the shore
Trying to fly and then falling
Sand crabs are getting washed away
Surfing the waves and then crawling

Fish are swimming then getting caught
From people ocean fishing
Seaweed is swaying along with the tide
Getting caught into kids in the water

Seagulls are picking up fish in the water
Then gliding away through the air
Fish are biting while sharks are fighting
As dolphins jump and do tricks in the air

Life guards run wild, sandcastles are falling
Making sand fly into everyone's eyes
Rafts are flipping as well as boats
And the waves keep trying to reach the sky

Julia Kappes, Grade 4
Stone Ranch Elementary School

Art

Art is a sculpture
Art is a painting
Art is a dance
Art is a song
Art is a book
Art is a feeling
Art is a flower
Art is nature
Art is music
Art is anything
You want it to be!

Ryan DoyLoo, Grade 4
Carlthorp School

Fish

I love fish
They are such a great dish
They slip and slide
and always say hi
They're great on a plate
and fun in the sun
so give fish a shot
you'll like them a lot!

Zabela Olascoaga, Grade 5
Sonoma Charter School

School

School is fun
School is the best
In summer I wait for school
I love school as much as you
Hate it.
In school you do projects,
You read, you write, you play,
You even get a desk to draw on.
I love my teacher
She doesn't give us any homework
She does everything for us
We do nothing
It's like a real teacher
That's why I love school
You'll love school too.

Kristie Campos, Grade 4
Oak Grove Elementary School

Furious

I'm so FURIOUS
I could cry
I'm so FURIOUS
I could pout
I'm so FURIOUS
I could scream
I'm so FURIOUS
WHY DID YOU LEAVE

Vanessa Givens, Grade 5
Kentwood Elementary School

Artist's Idea

I am pen
I am a written curve
I am painter
I stroke, I swerve
I am brush
In wet paint
Writing down a line so faint

I am a sculpture
I am tall
I am curved
I am not built to fall
I am hand
I am fingers
Coloring with paint that lingers

Not to destroy
But to build
Making pots
Heart so filled
Happy thoughts
Back round screen
Red, orange, yellow, green

Aubrey Van Dyke, Grade 6
Woodland Park Middle School

Ballerinas

At Susan's Dance Factory
Near St. Anne
Among the novice ballerinas
From pointed slippers
To jazz and tap shoes
Like beautiful birds
Into the air
With full confidence
Inside their hearts
Throughout their lives

Heena Gujral, Grade 6
St Anne School

Spring

Spring is stunning and colorful
Bees are buzzing around
Kids frolic in tulips
Kites hover in clear skies
The green trees are sprouting
How wonderful spring is!

Kyndal Rodriguez, Grade 5
Merryhill Country School

Ants

The ants march around,
in and out of the ground,
without making a sound…

Ian Chow-Ise, Grade 6
James B Davidson Middle School

The Book

One day I read a book
it was really bad
it was like a rusty hook
it made me really mad

I bought it for twenty bucks
it made me mad because
it killed a duck
my mom told me to try it out,
but I wouldn't 'cause

It hurts my eye
I don't know why
It's weird
I think it's growing a beard

Colin Nicholson, Grade 5
Sonoma Charter School

Painting

Art
Paint
I move my hand
Back and forth
Trying to do my
Best brush strokes
Smooth
Rough
I blend my colors
Twirling and twisting my brush
In my hand
Making a masterpiece.

Crystal Arias, Grade 5
Duveneck Elementary School

Purple Is Everything

Purple violets blooming in the spring,
Plump grapes growing on vines,
Purple pens, with purple ink,
The birds chirping,
The bouncing of a purple hand ball,
A purple bow,
Sitting upon a little girl's head,
The patch of the quilt,
That your grandma sewed,
An amethyst ring,
Beets in the kitchen,
So round and plump,
Grape juice and figs,
Pansies in the field,
Lavender, relax,
Peaceful and proud, too,
See the purple sunset,
Jump with delight,
Purple.

Ellie Berglass, Grade 4
Carlthorp School

The Devil's Lair

"Into the Devil's lair," he said.
Then I knew what was happening. I knew I was dead!
I tried to run. I tried to escape. I did not succeed.
Even though I begged to be freed,
he did not stop, he did not heed,
he kept a fast pace dragging me along.
I was scared not knowing what I had done wrong.
We got to where he was leading me
when I saw it I dropped to one knee.
I saw the flames and I felt the heat.
He dragged me because I would not stand on my own feet.
Shivers ran up and down my spine
and I knew I was running out of time.
I was scared
but nobody cared.
I knew where I was.
I knew where I lay on the floor,
I had been slain.

Sarah Ferral, Grade 6
Foresthill Divide Middle School

The Sun and the Moon

Sun
Bright, hot
Burn, scorch, sear
Star, heat, rock, cold
Glow, beam, glisten
Full, half
Moon

Andrew Wilmot, Grade 4
Mayfield Jr School of the Holy Child Jesus

Water's Life

Water everywhere
Rushes through the sky like birds
It flows over rocks in lakes
Eroding the Earth over time
Like a human getting old but never dying
Yet staying young running and falling like small children
Water is soothing yet harsh at times.

Margaret MacVean, Grade 6
Francis Parker School

Earth

The waves' rhythmic heartbeat is a lonely lullaby for
the midnight sky.
The wind's hushed whispers flutter through the
weeping willows' long, spindly fingers.
The evening sun ends its routine journey over Mother
Earth's quilted shawl.
The moon's salty tears fall upon the sea of dancing
petals amid the stars' bright spotlights.
The white-capped mountains whistle a synchronized
harmony into the thick blanket of mist.

Claire Nussbaum, Grade 6
Francis Parker School

Mittens

I have a cat with six nails on each paw
I have a cat without any flaws
Her eyes are as green as fresh cut grass
She runs like a cheetah so very fast
Her meow is as strong as a lions roar
She loves to eat kitty snacks and always wants more
She acts like a person who needs love and attention
She acts like a dog who always needs affection
Even though she is different I love her so
Even if she has six nails on each finger and toe
She will always be my little kitten
My little kitten whose name is Mittens

Taylor Rose Camacho, Grade 6
Oak Hills Elementary School

My Wormy Life

Name: Stinky Joe
Home Address: Fungus Toe
Working Hours: NEVER snooze
Special skills: making holes and curly cu's
Hobbies/sports: playing hide-n-go-seek with my friends
Favorite food: 2 week old, moldy leaf ends
Favorite band: Down in the Dirt
Favorite song: "Earth Worm Alert"
Enemies: people's feet and the neighbor's dog
Favorite subject: going under logs
Occupation: helping the Earth
My dream: to surf
Next of kin: my cousin, a million times removed, the dragon fly
Appetite: to try something new — never too shy

Remi Mooney, Grade 6
Francis Parker School

Time

Swift as a dust storm
Regular as tide
It soars in the wind
Like a bird in the sky
It flies by quickly
No time for despair
But sometimes you wonder
If it's even there
It is a dusky cave
That you must enter to exit
You can never come out
The way you went in
It hunts you down
You cannot hide from it
It grabs you and pulls you
Through various frameworks
It takes you through many different emotions
Moods cannot define it
Its passing is unrecognizable
As the morning flees from the night

Flora Park, Grade 4
Stone Ranch Elementary School

Losing a Loved One

She is gone now,
And she will never be back.
How terribly I miss her,
But she will be alive in my heart.

The day I walked into her room,
I thought she was asleep.
I tried to wake her up,
But she would not move.

I was frightened and scared.
I thought this day would never come,
But I was wrong.
Then I started to burst into tears.

Forever I shall remember her.
I have to forget this moment,
But I will never forget my grandma.
Judy Pham, Grade 6
Parkmont Elementary School

The Sun

A large hot heater
It is a big fire ball
Helping plants to grow
Skyler Martinez, Grade 5
El Monte Elementary School

Sunset

Every evening I look up,
And I see the sunset in the sky,
I see the colors very bold,
Shining red and shining gold.

The setting sun must be so proud,
Peeking from behind a cloud,
Now the colors are not as bright,
And soon it will be as dark as night.
Madeleine Bray, Grade 4
St Pancratius Elementary School

Baseball

Baseball is the best
It is fun to hit and run
I love to play it
Joey Kuhn, Grade 5
Theodore Roosevelt Elementary School

Violin

The rhythm flows within me
It touches my heart deeply
I cannot forsake this lovely instrument
The tunes are so forgetful
The soft sound has its own expression
Salena Yang, Grade 5
Clayton B Wire Elementary School

Pancake

Yummy delicious **P** ancakes
"Pancakes **A** re ready" I shoot out of bed
Batter is poured onto a flat pa **N**
Forming a round shape like a **C** lock
A mazingly springy and poofy
Very ca **K** e-like
No syrup or butt **E** r for me!
Kate Morse, Grade 4
Daves Avenue Elementary School

Unhappiness

I am War.
You know me for destroying peace like paint on a beautiful picture.
My father is World War I.
My mother is World War II.
I was born between two countries rebelling against each other.
I live in Gaza but I move around.
My best friend is Hurricane.
My enemy is Peace.
I fear agreement and peace.
I love revenge.
I wish I was really tough.
I dream of smelling horror in the air.
I destroy happiness.
I can be very strong at times, or a bear attacking a human.
I look like two armies attacking.
I smell gun powder in the air.
I feel like swords and shiny armor.
I am War.
Mayan Maryamian, Grade 6
Horace Mann School

My Babolat Tennis Racket

Better than Fisher's, Yonex's, Wilson's and Penn's
Babolat's the best, no doubt about it
Rafael Nadal, the world's best, uses my racket, during the test
Cramped in my locker, taking it out, I can't wait to start playing
When I step on the court, smelling the balls, I hear people rallying, back and forth
The sun beating down, on the courts, grabbing my grip, ready to play, on and on
Anthony Yabuki, Grade 6
La Jolla Country Day School

Change Is Gonna Come

Right now the United States is ample,
full of food and water to share.

But we also gotta think about the countries around us,
who are meager that have less than enough to survive in this world.

We have to cease that!
What we gotta do is reconcile and help each other.

And finally form as one.
And that is how change is gonna come.
Jonah Davis, Grade 6
Francis Parker School

Struggle
Challenge showed on the young dog's face,
Thus he was banned from all freedom,
Yet he still had hope in his challenged mind,
He was in turmoil;
To accept his horrible defeat;
Now he has a chance to escape from capture;
But with the courage he stays;
The future is in his paws.
With loyalty
And selflessness he will survive
Change has come.

Mia Jones, Grade 4
Canyon View Elementary School

Mrs. Slingerland
Mrs. Slingerland is my teacher
She has many great features
My teacher Mrs. Slingerland
Is always grand
She really loves to read
When we work on our garden she lets us plant seeds
She likes to work at Eastwood School
She is definitely not a fool
Even when she needs a rest
She will not rest she is the best!

Katie Babbitt, Grade 5
Eastwood Elementary School

Family
My family is fun
They love to play in the sun

We love to go to the beach
And my favorite snack is a peach

The adults play volleyball
While the kids build a sand wall

Then it's time for lunch
Can I have some peaches please, give me a bunch!

Alexis Loaiza, Grade 5
Theodore Roosevelt Elementary School

Trash Can
It's a trash can filled with garbage.
There is garbage everywhere, you name it.
It is dirty and it will sting your eyes.
If you see it leave it be.
If you come in you can barely see.
But wait, this is my room, it's true.
The health department will probably sue.
I'd better clean up before mom comes in,
Or she'll put me in the stinky trash can bin.

Justin T. Pham, Grade 5
St Barbara School

Ode to My Imagination
May imagination gives me anything I desire.
Even if it's a full head of fire.
I think my imagination is cool.
If other people don't then they are such fools.
I could pretend I am a king in a palace,
or even a priest with a chalice.
I could pretend I am a computer technician,
or a writer for a petition.
The best thing about my imagination,
is that it is my own creation.
There are some parts of my imagination that are bad.
They make me really sad.
I try not to imagine those things,
I'd rather imagine a bird that sings.

Quade Benson, Grade 6
St Dominic Elementary School

The Rainbow
I love the colors of the rainbow.
I follow my imagination through a colorful exploration.
That's how I dream big and colorful.
I draw with my imagination, though it is not really true.
I love the dreams going through the rainbow inside my mind!

Wendy Ruiz, Grade 4
Garden Grove Elementary School

In and Out a Tree
It's been around since ancient times.
It's been through good and evil.
In fire it burns,
And in water it molds.
It has many different sizes.
It has the power to let you breathe.
You probably couldn't live without it.
It seems old but that's just its rugged skin.
Maybe there is one in front of you right now.

Leopoldo Magana, Grade 6
St Vincent Elementary School

Annoying Siblings
Annoying siblings can be brothers or sisters
In my case it's my brother
He gets on my nerves because he's not a listener
His brain is about as thin as a feather.

When he drives me crazy
I go insane
At home he is so lazy
It hurts my brain.

He pushes my buttons all of the time
He's an acrobat trying to make me break
I hope he would get out of this room of mine
I wish he would wither away when I wake!

Analyssa Sanchez, Grade 6
Barstow Intermediate School

The Sun

```
           hot  we  see
      very                it
   is                        every
  sun                          day.
 The                             And
   away.                         I
     sweat                   always
        keep              put
           to          the
            down   sunroof
```
Alyssa Franco, Grade 4
St Pancratius Elementary School

Tank Eel

Tank eel roots about
Down in the gravel below
Keeps the gravel clean.
Sam Winglewich, Grade 4
Tomales Elementary School

Clouds

Clouds are like small cotton balls,
floating across the ocean.

Some days they are lost under the sea,
but rise back up in motion.

I see these cotton balls every day,
no matter day or night.

Yet I do not see in darkness,
I always see in the light.
Thomas Rodgers, Grade 6
St Charles Catholic School

Moon/Sun

Moon
Bright, white
Moving, orbiting, listening
Craters, astronauts, orange, rising
Surprising, spinning, exciting
Fire, blaring
Sun
Joseph Halsell, Grade 5
St Louis De Montfort School

Abyss Places

In those dark abyss places
I wonder if I see faces?
Are those creatures mean or nice
I wonder if they'll spare my life
Their long claws lurching towards me
I wonder if I'll fight or flee?
In those dark abyss places…
Shaun Hall, Grade 6
Lockeford Elementary School

Chimpy

You are the one that keeps me going
your black coat warm to the touch
your bright eyes shining in the dark.

You are the reason I am happy
when I come home, brightening my day,
filling my heart with laughter.

You are the center of the house,
king of our domain,
not a witch's minion on Halloween.

Without you
my life would be an empty swing
longing for a companion.
Jade Cook, Grade 6
St Timothy School

Apricot

Apricot is the color of suntanned skin
A plump peach sitting on a branch
A manila folder full of mysteries
Apricot is the color of the shore
The soft fur of a puppy
The shiny hair of a supermodel
Brown sugar in my cookies
Apricot
Brooke Smallson, Grade 6
Kadima Heschel West Middle School

Not a Snail

No, I am not a snail
I don't have a shell or a tail,
I don't live in a pail,
I don't smell like a snail,
And I don't leave a trail.

I don't hide under a leaf,
Or eat dead plants which is a relief.
I'm sweet as a bee.
Tall and slender like a tree.
I am Soline, that's me!
Soline Gauthier, Grade 4
Charles Armstrong School

Mother Earth

I am an otter.
I nourish on fish.
I depend on the sea.
My friends and I need our fur.
We are innocent, so don't kill us.
We need water, air, food, and safeness.
We are part of Mother Earth.
Save Mother Earth!!!
Morgan McIntyre, Grade 4
Ocean Air School

Diana

Diana is my cousin
She always says what's buzzin'
She's pretty and smart
And she likes to go to the park
Diana is young
And she likes to stick out her tongue
She is very cool
And likes to play pool
Diana is neat
Who likes to play with her feet
She likes to cheer people up
But she doesn't like to drink 7-Up
She thinks she's all right
But everything is not tight
She's a great lifeguard
And she thinks everything is cute
She is very confident
And wants to become a lawyer
She also wants to be a respectful person
Who doesn't curse
Marlene Martinez, Grade 6
Century Community Charter School

Sister/Brother

Sister
Girl, Smart
Jumping, teasing, laughing
Veterinarian, kind, athlete, funny
Running, pouting, snoring
Boy, active
Brother
Jackie Thompson, Grade 4
Heather Elementary School

Chocolate, Oh Chocolate

Chocolate, oh chocolate
How can I resist
Crunch, creamy, soft, or hard
Lingering in my mouth

Always so sweet
Never smells like stinky feet
Dark chocolate, milk chocolate
Making my mouth water

Chocolate, oh chocolate
How can I resist
What's that I hear
You want me near

I'm coming, I'm coming
Running faster than a race car
Munch!!!
Oops I guess it's the end
Camille Hope, Grade 5
Solana Pacific School

Nation of Peace

Walking for miles across a dirt road
Turning into freedom mode
Needing an escape
From all that they know

Forming a more musical nation
Taking a "mini vacation"
Discovering themselves
By having a musical sensation

Fans desiring a hopeful sign
Wanting everything to be just fine
Wishing for the rest of the world
To reach for the divine

Hendrix, Joplin, and the Who
Light and sound shining through
The darkness of difficult times
Sharing dreams under the skies that were blue

No one cared what time was on the clock
For here and now
People had freedom
Freedom at Woodstock

Emma Berson, Grade 5
The Mirman School

Lost to the Wind

My dearest.
My soul mate.
You treat me harshly.

Do you really want to lose me to the wind?

You laugh when I talk.
And scowl when I say

Do you really want to lose me to the wind?

My love.
My time has come.
I see you weep as I bid farewell.

You lost me to the wind.

Sarah Kirste, Grade 6
Orleans Elementary School

Golden Poppy

Gold is on my favorite color list
Poppy is on my favorite flower list
But does that mean I love California's flower most?
Because if I put the word gold with poppy together
I get golden space poppy.
It's the California state flower.

Allegra Sasser, Grade 5
Ecole Bilingue de Berkeley

Baseball

Baseball.
Throw it.
The ball zips past you like an angry bee.
You field it and throw it.
At the bench, you sit wide eyed watching your team bats.
You're up.
The balls are a blur but you manage to hit one.
Wham!
It flies into the air.
You dash all of the bases except one.
Home.
The word echoes in your mouth as you slide into the base.
Tiny grains of brown dirt fly all over.
You're safe.
Everybody cheers and shouts as you walk off to the dugout.
Baseball.
The game.
Hit it.

Ethan Khoe, Grade 5
Duveneck Elementary School

The Ocean

The ocean is green and blue,
I wish you were here too,
The sand gets stuck between my toes,
It might blow towards my nose,

The ocean seems so calm,
Waves just come and go,
So many shells come ashore,
It was fun to watch them by the sun's glow,

The sun is going down,
It is time for me to go,
Here comes the sunset up it goes,
How beautiful to see it going down low.

Joanna Maniti, Grade 4
St Pancratius Elementary School

Tick-Tock...
Ode to a Busted School Clock

My life goes tick-tock,
Just like a clock.
When a test starts,
It just stops.

At the end of school,
Life is just too fast,
Like I can't even breathe.

Thank goodness, we're back to school,
And time is normal —
Well, except the clock.

Reggie Hernaez, Grade 6
Corpus Christi School

Purple

When I see purple I see small violet flowers. The sound I hear is mellow when I think of purple.
When purple is near I taste vitamin water. The smell purple reminds me of grape juice.
Relaxed is how I feel when I think of purple.

Savannah Muenzenberger, Grade 5
Andasol Avenue Elementary School

I Am

I am cougar. I wander from places to places waiting until my prey comes. I just eat and sleep. I wait and wait day and night. When the victim comes, I chase it. I catch it. Then I eat it. I can taste the blubber but not the booger. I sleep to regain my energy. I sleep in a place that is beneath the ground. I am cougar. I am scary because my fangs will show when I'm angry. When I'm chasing the prey, I'll become fierce. I am cougar.

John Yang, Grade 5
Clayton B Wire Elementary School

James "Jim" Arthur Lovell, Jr.

James "Jim" Arthur Lovell, Jr. was born in Ohio, an American state on March 25, 1928.
When he was young there was no mystery to unravel how much he really wanted to make a space travel.
It was President John F. Kennedy's inspiring speech that gave NASA the money to get to the Moon within reach.
Lovell was certainly not a buffoon because he was the first to orbit the Moon.
He also saw the Moon's far side an American dream that was known far and wide.
However, the expedition that was quite a mission was the one called Apollo 13 that caused quite a scene
Two fuel cells suddenly went dead. "Houston, we've had a problem," was what Lovell said.
Would the astronauts come home alive? They had to think fast in order to survive.
Lovell was the one who rescued his crew by having his team climb into the lunar module.
Although they didn't land on the Moon, they knew they had to get back to Earth soon.
Because their oxygen was going out fast they had to make decisions or they, themselves, wouldn't last.
The astronauts made a filter on their own with a water bag, hoses, tape, and a sock alone.
For mission control, it was very stressful. Fortunately, their invention was very successful.
The astronauts then had to make the reentry to Earth. Lovell manually controlled the thrusters and engine for all their worth.
After 6 days in space they finally arrived. Rescued in the water, Americans were happy to hear they were alive.
Then President Nixon gave them an award. The Presidential Medal of Freedom, that is much adored.
Lovell, who is now retired from NASA will, in the year 2010, have a naval facility named after him.

Michael Santiago, Grade 5
Chaparral Elementary School

A Blizzard of White

I know white.

White smells like the light, puffy wisps of sweet whipped cream, an odorless sheet of blank paper,
and the sour sweet scent of drizzled ranch sauce

White feels like the thousand-knived frostbites of solid winter ice, the ticklish, feathery and sleek plumage of a gyrfalcon,
and the liquid, gooey feeling of oozing spider web-like glue.

White looks like the gently floating puffs of clouds, a single delicate droplet of milk,
precariously balancing on the glass rim of a cup, and a plastic spool of impossibly thin white thread.

White sounds like the thunderous roar of a raging blizzard, the shrill screech of a soaring seagull,
and the depressed sighs of a sad being, sitting in a gloomy corner.

White tastes like a gently drifting snowflake on the sensitive tip of a person's rosy tongue,
the desirably sweet creamy marshmallow puffs, and the disgusting, slimy, and sickly taste of the despised sunscreen.

I really know white!

Janie Kim, Grade 4
Dingeman Elementary School

High Merit Poems – Grades 4, 5 and 6

Ocean Creatures
The ocean is teeming with creatures
Like peering down from a New York skyscraper
At the people passing by
These creatures have different features
Spots
Speckles
Stripes
Freckles
Some slimy
Some rough
Puffy
And very tough
Most are big
Sometimes small
They are unique
I love them all

Matthew Crockett, Grade 4
Sierra Oaks K-8 School

A Great Mom
Magda is a great mom she is kind and respectful
Ma cannot last very long without cleaning
She is always there for me never can she let you down
Ma always thinks about others' needs
Ma has curly black hair and brown eyes
No matter what happens she is always there for me
Even though she has a lot of responsibility
She always makes room for me Ma is never selfish
She is an important person for me
She always puts food on my plate
Ma is smart and strict
Sometimes she goes overboard with things
She is like a shopaholic in malls
Ma always works hard for she has more than one job
Who is there when I am blue never does she let me loose
She is the one that always helps with things
Ma always brings me up when I am down
Ma you are the only one for me no one can replace you
For you are the one and only

Jazmin S. Gutierrez, Grade 6
Century Community Charter School

Thunder and Lightning
It is a dark and cold night
You are breathing the fresh air
The clouds soar at such great height
And you are not aware
That thunder and lightning is in our territory
You listen to the crashes and bangs
You listen to the terror
And hear all the clangs
But you can do nothing
But listen to the mess

Gabriel Raulet, Grade 4
Montessori Family School

Magic and Love
A little boy went walking,
he found a golden sock.
But when he went to try it on,
he turned into a rock!

A little girl went walking,
she found a golden toy.
But when she went to pick it up,
it turned into that boy!

Those children went a walking,
they decided to go faster.
When they grew up together,
They got married and lived happily ever after!

Sarah Gardner, Grade 5
Floyd M Stork Elementary School

Awakening Seasons
When sparkling dew settles on grass blades
Dawn arrives and darkness slowly fades away
Stars vanish while morning light decides to stay
Hearing the rush of falling water from a cascade

Flowers start blooming in the fresh air
Brilliant-colored blossoms appear everywhere
As rain showers fall onto the Earth
Glory and activity come with mirth

Wildflowers grow in some peaceful meadow
With butterflies gliding happily around
Millions of sprouts and buds come from the ground
Watching a swift, clear river smoothly flow

Green leaves hang on trees of any size
Animals crawl out into the warm light
Unlike some creatures hide in disguise
Until they awaken quietly during the night

New days arrive in joy and pouring sunshine
Of enjoying nature, this pleasure will be mine
Listening to birds chirp and sing
Wanting to watch the beauty of spring.

Caroline Chang, Grade 6
Challenger School – Ardenwood

Aqua
Aqua is very nice
Aqua is the color of ice
Aqua is the color of love
The color aqua is sent from heaven above
Aqua is the color of the sea
Aqua is the color of a bluebird in a tree
Aqua is the color of many places
It puts smiles on many peoples faces

Danielle Downing, Grade 5
Eastwood Elementary School

My Bedroom

My bedroom
every day
sunny and rainy
afternoon
bright and gloomy days
rain
kids laughing
the bright color green
my closet
cookies baking
rainy concrete
write
read
relaxed
happy

Madison Hubbard, Grade 5
Theodore Roosevelt Elementary School

My Mom, Dyah

My mom is talented
Head full of knowledge
Isn't tall
Is clumsy so she falls
She is a shorty but she is funny
And scrunches her nose like a bunny
She is sweet and she is very neat
She is beautiful and very neat like me
She is talkative and she is very active
She isn't selfish
But doesn't know how to cook fish
She is understandable
And is really workable
She hates things that are furry
Likes noodles
That taste like curry
Her name is not Lia
So that makes her
My Dyah

Lilian Salino, Grade 6
Century Community Charter School

Rain

Quenches our earth's thirst
Brings life, food, and happiness
Our world needs water

Trevor Bowen, Grade 4
Marian Bergeson Elementary School

Sports Time

I like to steal
and sometimes when I get hurt I feel
to shoot I jump
to bounce I pump
to prove that I am good I deal

Josue Jimenez, Grade 4
Clayton B Wire Elementary School

I Like…

I like to take hard tests,
But I don't like to be distracted.
I like to surf,
But I don't like to pearl*.
I like to play chess,
But I don't like to make stupid moves.
I like to swim at swim meets,
But I don't like to lose.
I like to be with friends,
But don't like when my mom picks me up.
I like video games,
But I don't like having to stop playing.

*Pearling is where the tip of your surfboard gets caught in the wave,
Shooting you from your board to the beach.

Koby Taswell, Grade 5
Morasha School

My Hero

My hero is a happy soul wherever he goes,
he runs and plays games all day,
he teaches me how to be a better athlete in every sport.
I look up to him in all he does, I want to be like him when I grow up.
Thank you Patrick Christopher for being my hero.

David Barta, Grade 5
Theodore Roosevelt Elementary School

Blue

Blue is the color of the sky miles above our heads.
Blue is the color of the high ocean waves crashing onto shore.
Blue is the color of the water that quenches our thirst.
Blue is the color of a Blue Jay soaring through the sky.
Blue is the color of really, really cold ice freezing.
Blue is the color of a kite flying through the sky.
Blue is the color of a beautiful violet flower just sprouting.
Blue is the color of the moistness in a blueberry on a hot summer day.
Blue is the color of the ice cream that we lick on a scorching day.
Blue is the color of a colt card that symbolizes achievement.

Samuel Perry, Grade 4
Heather Elementary School

Fever

I am Fever
I kill without remorse
I leave children without parents, parents without children
I am great blight; I have killed a hundred million people
I am a partner with Death, doing his every bidding
Mortals try to fight me, but they cannot defeat me
I thrive in warm weather, but die in the cold
The more people talk about me, the more my presence is felt
I am like an assailant, injecting fear into my prey before waylaying it
I steal minds and memories, kill loved ones and friends
I am a living nightmare that you can never wake up from
I am Fever and I will get you too

Benjamin Lewis, Grade 6
St Andrew's Episcopal School

Forest

The forest is a calm rustling body of green
Some are ancient, while some are still young
Rings circle in to their core
Rough bark covered in green silky moss
Speaking to each other
Their voices carried in the warm breeze
Rooted deeply into the Earth
When a sapling sprouts
They tingle with excitement
For their new family member
And they wave their arms until dawn breaks
And when a tree leaves them
They mourn for their lost friend
They stand very still with their needles wilted
Trees, while they may seem still
Are living spirits within themselves.

Haley Cloyd, Grade 6
Francis Parker School

The Animal Family

I have a horse, I named him Fred
He does not sleep in a bed
If he did, he would want his sheets to be red
One day, Fred decided to play with Ned
Ned unfortunately had a giant head
Ned is a cat and he wanted to play with a bat named Ed
The bat said a big hello
But the cat knew he had just made a new foe
The bat hid in the wall
Then he had no trouble at all
After that, the bat met a mouse
The mouse was wearing a lacy blouse
The bat fell deeply in love
He thought she was sent from up above
Then they decided to marry
In the home of Larry and Garry
The bat decided to invite the cat
The cat was delighted and decided to wear a festive hat
After that, the cat invited the horse named Fred
Fred got all dressed up in red

Sophie Misshula, Grade 6
Charles Armstrong School

Wind

Wind blows in your face
It is the month of September
You feel the breeze as you go down the hill with your bike
Next thing you know, you see a sunset
The sun is going down beyond the horizon
You stop at the beach to walk in the sand
Then you look up; you see the sky is bluish-purple;
You can see the birds flutter in the bluish-purple sky
The clouds are almost crying from all the beauty
A beautiful day has come

Kyara White, Grade 5
Juarez Elementary School

I'm Inside of Everyone, Realize Me!

I am courage.
You know I'm really important.
I was born inside of people.
I live in people's hearts.
My enemy is weakness.
I fear you not believing in yourself,
As much as ants fear being killed.
I love when people rely on me.
I wish no one would ever give up.
I'm a hole that you have to dig down to find.
I hear people talking about me.
I see weakness on people's faces.
My nightmares are when people lose me.
I try to keep people aware of me.
I touch and squeeze people's hearts,
I yell, and try to keep people noticing me,
I try to make people take me with them everywhere they go.
Realize me, because I'm courage and you need me!

Negin Houshanian, Grade 6
Horace Mann School

I Am

I am sly and sneaky
I hear the roar of the crowd
I see a huge stage in front of me
I want to be a famous rock star
I am sly and sneaky

I pretend I am a rock god
I feel the nervous chill going down my neck
I touch the guitar of gods
I worry about messing up
I cry that I am not good enough
I am sly and sneaky

I understand I might fail
I say I will make it
I dream of a band of my own
I try my best to learn about rock
I hope I will be the best,
I am sly and sneaky!

Kenneth Howard, Grade 6
Barstow Intermediate School

Late

My alarm clock goes off with a beep, beep, beep
while staying in bed when I fall asleep.
Mom wakes me up to get ready for school
so I get out of bed and move like a mule.
Getting ready but moving slow
while my mom is telling me that I have to go.
In a hurry, I have to get there by eight
It doesn't matter because I'm already late.

Johnny Knowles, Grade 5
Eastwood Elementary School

Spring
Sun shines in sky
Flowers sprout in golden soil
Creatures dance along
Isaiah Moreno, Grade 5
Ladd Lane Elementary School

The Earth and Me
The Earth is spinning around me
Like a bulb that never stops
Although I wish it could somehow stop
I'm just fine the way it is

But just for ten minutes
So I could catch my breath
But then again that wouldn't be the Earth
That would be
A big round still ball
Kayla Day, Grade 4
Montessori Center School

Basketball
Basketball,
The game,
Feel it,
The sweat on your face,
Your mind rushing with what to do next,
The duck under your opponent's arm,
The ballet like shot,
The praying,
The cheer of the crowd,
The graceful slip in,
The solo slip in,
The accomplishment,
Basketball,
The game,
Feel it.
Logan Drazovich, Grade 5
Duveneck Elementary School

I Am
I am a mountain,
standing tall through the trees,
I am a seal,
loud and happy,
I am growing,
every minute, every day,
I am purple,
sometimes calm, sometimes relaxing,
I am California,
bright as the sun,
I am a flag,
waving through the air,
I am joyful,
happy as the sun.
Maddie Froomer, Grade 4
Carlthorp School

The Dancers*
Oh dancers,
how you glide
freely like doves
in the sky.
You fly on your
toes like birds fluttering
all over the place.
You bring joy
to all the world
and all the people.
Please, dancers, bring joy
to the whole universe.
Saba Amid, Grade 4
The Mirman School
**Inspired by "Dancers in Pink"*
by Edgar Degas.

Rain
Morning rain comes down
Slowly renewing nature
Carrying the fog.
Taylor Plett, Grade 4
Marian Bergeson Elementary School

Change
Change is what makes life different
Change is something new
Change can be bad but also
Sometimes good

Things can change in an instant
Or sometimes very long
Change is sometimes a historic time
Sometimes it is not

On the 20th of January in 2009
Change was made by a man who
Never will be the same
He was Barack Obama
Kian Bagheri, Grade 6
Francis Parker School

Underwater
Mystical colors
Underwater coral reefs
Fish drifting calmly
Austin D. Valinoti, Grade 6
Lockeford Elementary School

Poems
I'm writing poems
This poem is called haiku
They are fun to write
Sam Chew, Grade 5
Theodore Roosevelt Elementary School

The Amazing Desert
I am the amazing shining desert.
I am as shiny as the sun.
My sand is like gold.
I am dry like the moon.

I hear the leaves blowing in the air.
I also hear the sounds of animals.
I can hear the snakes slithering
And I can hear the sand shifting.

I feel the animals moving.
I feel the cacti.
I also feel the wind blowing on me.
I feel as dry as a waterless lake.

I feel as hot as fire.
I see plants in the ground.
I see the animals on my face.
I feel the cacti on my body.

I am hot like the sun.
I am as sandy as a sand pit.
At night I am as cold as the snow.
I am the amazing desert.
Stephanie Simon, Grade 4
Sinai Akiba Academy

Beach
B eautiful place that is
E legant with an
A mazing horizon
C ool on summer days
H ow I wish it was really true
Annabel Chick, Grade 4
Charles Armstrong School

Life
Kids
fun, excited
playing, screaming, laughing
cute, pretty, cool, handsome
working, driving, hardworking
bills, jobs
Adult
Idalis Topete, Grade 5
Jackson Elementary School

Poker
P lay all night
O n the button, it's your turn
K ings beat queens
E ven the pot out
R oyal flushes are the best
Thomas Caldwell, Grade 6
Charles Armstrong School

Summer Fun

Family laughing
Willow trees waving like lightning striking
Little kids splashing
Elders telling stories
Suddenly
Little drops of rain
Nobody runs for shelter
Everyone rushes like a pack of tormented bulls
Toward the shimmering water
Suddenly darkness takes over the beautiful light
Party's over
Time to go home.

Carlos Ramirez, Grade 5
Clover Avenue Elementary School

What Is Green?

Green is the grass waving in the distance.
The limes blooming on many trees.
Trees whirling in the far distance.
Green is the smell of the fresh air blowing.
Green is the sound of the forest.
Green is an alligator moving through the swamp.
Green is a parrot flying around the world.
Green is a butterfly going on his journey.
Green is a beetle flying in the distance, disappearing in the sky.
Green is an eraser that erases your mind.

Braianna Martinez, Grade 4
Stanton Elementary School

A New Season

The wind whooshes as it whistles by
And travels like a great big sigh.
Sparkling snowflakes silently soar and sway
Each like a present from Christmas Day.
Something new is coming.

A blanket of frost covers the ground,
As the snowflakes dance all around.
A snowman gives happiness to all who pass,
As people gather for Christmas Mass.
A new time is coming.

As we warm our toes and gather together,
We still have holiday spirit despite the weather.
All houses alike are covered in ice,
And inside the warmth, a family of mice.
A new time of year is coming.

All of the animals go into hiding,
Not us, we just start sliding.
The Christmas spirit is in the air,
As we open our presents so rare.
A new season is here.

Mariel Salem, Grade 6
Dorris-Eaton School

Inauguration

Uproarious cheers of excitement
As Barack Obama becomes the 44th President.
History is being made,
The first African-American man
Becoming the President of The United States.
With Michelle at his side,
Barack bids Bush a friendly good-bye.
A hearty lunch awaits the Obamas,
And then a long parade.

Smile after smile,
That is all I can see.
Next to the winter coats and hats, that is.
Tears and tears of joy,
When people see Barack,
Walking to the podium,
To start his lovely speech.
I see happy faces,
And sets of teeth.
All those teeth belong to
Happy people all here
To see the 2009 Inauguration.

Kate Abed, Grade 5
Duveneck Elementary School

Mom

My mom is caring
She makes sure I am okay
She knows how to cook she knows how to make crambulay
She buys me whatever I want
And whatever I need
And when I am nice she buys me golden earrings
She is busy
But still patient
And she is strict
She wants me to be perfect
She makes me tea
When I get sick
Sometimes she is mean
When she wants my room to be clean
She is sweet
She is neat
I love her and
She loves me

Ashley Mercado, Grade 6
Century Community Charter School

The Banana

The banana was walking down the street,
And then realized he had no feet.
He wanted to walk on the street so bad,
That he soon started to become sad.
You might think bananas have no feelings
Imagine what is felt when you start the peeling.

Tai Stratton, Grade 6
Bernice Ayer Middle School

My Walk

One day I took a walk down a road
when I thought I saw a toad
I followed it
down a big pit.

It led to a cave
I had to be brave
to finally find,
what was inside.

Its eyes were as big as dinner plates.
It blew bubbles as small as snowflakes.
It had two heads
I thought to myself, I am dead.

Then I thought I heard it say,
"Please stay!"
So, I sat down on a rock
and it started to talk.

It asked if it could come home with me
he said he would give me a golden key.
I said if you don't make a mess
then I will say absolutely yes!

Frebrenie Dale, Grade 5
Sonoma Charter School

The Rainforest

The rainforest
Monkeys screeching
Bushes rustling
Twigs breaking
Parrots squawking
Leaves crackling
Snakes slithering
The rainforest

Sean Prior, Grade 6
La Costa Heights Elementary School

Playing

Playing in the park
Playing in the dark

Playing at your house
Playing with a mouse

Playing in the playground
Playing all around

Playing in a train
Playing in the rain

Playing in Delaware
Playing everywhere

Carlos Maciel, Grade 6
St Charles Catholic School

My Mom

My mom is like a rose blooming in the spring
My mom is like a beautiful bird flying south
My mom is like the sun bright and caring
My mom is like an artist creative and fun
My mom is like a penguin trying to get food for its young and keeps on trying
My mom is like Mother Earth very nice and donates as much care as she can
My mom is like a falcon wise and full of beauty
My mom is like a bouncy ball keeps on bouncing
My mom is like a mother bear fights for her life to protect her cub
My mom is like a cherry nice and sweet
My mom is like an eraser erases 'til everything is gone
My mom is like an everlasting board game it goes on and on and on

Pascal Sy Costa, Grade 4
Spring Hill Advanced Elementary School

What If…

What if roses bloomed during the night, instead of in the morning?
What if storybook characters, fairy tales, myths, and legends came to life?
What if animals could talk?
What if the future was now?
What if the Earth was a different shape?
What if people weren't people?
What if a person you loved came back when they've passed away?
What if I would always stay a kid?
What if I was famous?
What if I was the last person on the Earth?
What if the Earth was made out of candy and cookies and other goodies?
These are questions I ask about every day
And they always begin with…
WHAT IF?

Amanda Rowley, Grade 5
Theodore Roosevelt Elementary School

Hardworking Girl

I am a girl who is charming and hardworking
I wonder where life will take me
I hear success calling my name
I see the future through my eyes
I want the best in life
I am a girl who is charming and hardworking

I pretend there are no obstacles blocking me from reaching my destination
I feel that god will help me achieve my goal
I touch my teachers hearts with my wonderful work
I worry that there is someone out there trying to stop me
I cry when I get awful grades
I am a girl who is charming and hardworking

I understand the concept of working hard
I say that I will reach my goal someday
I dream that all I want will come true
I try my best to work as hard as I can
I hope I will be able to make this achievement
I am a girl who is charming and hardworking

Shauna Sarshar, Grade 6
Horace Mann Middle School

Remembering a Great Friend

I watch as my friend's house burned down, the site of this still makes me frown.
I think of my friend's bad luck as I waited for the ambulance and fire truck.
I kept on watching the eruption of fire as the flames on his house roof just went higher.
The scorched stoop's vapor smelled like burnt wood and paper.
The house looked like it had been lit by TNT, if you were there you could really see.
This event was scary and tragic, the only good thing was the fire was put out like magic.

As you can see it was a big loss to everyone including me.
My friend was like a brother to me, not only me, but also my family.
If you could only see how nice he was to me.
My friend is in heaven where no one can bother him.
My great friend's death will never be forgotten
Because when he sits up in the clouds that feel like cotton
I will make sure everyone remembers him.

Jeff Oney, Grade 6
Big Springs Elementary School

If I Were…

If I were a slice of cheese I'd be flavorful cheesy cheddar
I'd lure people in with my cheddar and tangy flavor

If I were a chocolate I'd be creamy Hershey's
I'd taste so luscious and soft like silk

If I were a tooth I'd be strong and healthy
I'd be shining more than the sun and twinkle more than the stars

If I were a diaper I'd be a Pull-Up
I'd be springy and flexible and potty train the young child

If I were a shoe I'd be a speedy Nike
I'd mesmerize people with my astonishing speed and dash through the finish of every marathon

If I were a color I'd be a deep rich sparkling blue
I'd be a deep ocean and be brighter than a light bulb

If I were a car I'd be a streaking and slick Ferrari
I'd race through the streets and win first in every car race

If I were a book I'd be *The Adventures of Sherlock Holmes*
I'd bewilder people with my brain boggling mysteries and allure readers so they can't put the book down

Roshan Ahmed, Grade 5
Aviara Oaks Elementary School

I Am From…

I am from a home,
   Where dogs run around outside, where moms and dads delicious food is being made in the kitchen.
I am from a yard,
   Where my family swims in a big pool and a large rock to jump off of. Where sometimes my brother and sister are annoying but also sometimes nice.
I am from a neighborhood,
   Where there are creepy cats and where there is a ball swishing through a net.
I am from a family,
   That keeps memories in lots of photo albums.

Giovanna (Gigi) Chiotti, Grade 5
Notre Dame School

Lawn Gnomes
Lawn gnomes are
ugly lawn ornaments.
What do you suppose they do
at gnight?
Maybe they come alive and
eat people.
They can't be happy —
they must be evil.
Gnow what shall we do?
We should gnot buy
lawn gnomes
anygmore.
We must destroy the lawn gnomes,
all of them —
should we gnot?
Richard Dimarucut, Grade 6
Corpus Christi School

My Mother
My mother is sweet like candy,
She is a nice cook,
She is very cautious,
She is a friendly person,
She gives me confidence,
She helps me get over my fears,
She taught me to be kind,
She is very busy,
She taught me manners,
She is a good person,
My mother is braver than me,
My mother disagrees,
My mother is honest,
My mother is caring,
My mother is very sentimental,
She is responsible,
She is respectful,
She is unselfish,
She is very mature,
She is my mother.
Danny Duarte, Grade 6
Century Community Charter School

Spring
Spring, spring, oh spring
Kids playing in the sun
Flowers blooming
Grass growing
Spring, spring, oh spring
Baseball, soccer, all the sports
Yes, of course, spring break
Beach fun
Sun tanning
Yes, I love spring!
Matt O'Sullivan, Grade 6
Grant Elementary School

Nile
Large, cold
Flooding, fishing, swimming
Provides water for Egyptian people.
Zaira Bonilla, Grade 6
Big Springs Elementary School

Thanksgiving
Thursday is Thanksgiving
A day to love and share,
I love my family
And share my happy times with them
Even my food,
I would give to my friends some turkey,
Because Thanksgiving is a wonderful day
A day to love and share.
Kirsten Hernandez, Grade 4
St Pancratius Elementary School

Every Season
Summer, spring, and fall,
All sorts of gorgeous seasons,
Winter's best of all.
Riley Lemons, Grade 4
Anderson Valley Elementary School

Stars
Stars are small and bright
they give us light

Stars are yellow
but don't play the cello

Stars are in the sky
I watch them go by

Stars are cool
I watch them while I'm in the pool

A star is not a possum
that's why this poem is awesome
Jannelle Mendoza, Grade 6
St Charles Catholic School

Poker
Take your cards,
Play them well,
Make a pair,
If you can…

Have a poker face,
Don't show emotion,
Bet low,
And you'll win.
Christopher Chiong, Grade 6
Corpus Christi School

Sunset
The wind is blowing
The clouds are racing
The light is disappearing
Orange and pink paint the sky
The birds are flying to their tree
Then everything is silent,
Absolutely silent
Alexandra Sexton, Grade 4
Daves Avenue Elementary School

Christmas
Christmas! Christmas!
It's almost here.
Christmas! Christmas!
It's time for fun.
Christmas! Christmas!
It's time for presents.
Christmas! Christmas!
It's time for love.
Christmas! Christmas!
It's time for Jesus' birth.
Stephanie Cano, Grade 4
St Pancratius Elementary School

Today
Today
January 20, 2009
is very special
to me.
Special to others.
Special to everyone.
Today made great history
and I will always remember it.
Barack Obama, African American,
sits in the White House
as President.
Years ago, people of different
cultures, colors, and religions
were enslaved and imprisoned
because of their differences.
I am very proud of my country,
the United States of America, today.
Freedom and justice
for all.
Miranda LaMere, Grade 5
Theodore Roosevelt Elementary School

Wagging Tail
My dog has a wagally tail,
We should put that tail in a jail.
It hits things all around,
They fall straight to the ground.
My dog has a wagally tail.
Jamie Iverson, Grade 6
Big Springs Elementary School

The Colder Seasons of the Year

The rustle of leaves captures my soul,
The color of the trees red and gold.
The leaves crunch as I step in the middle,
I'd like some pie now, just a little.

Go and ring the dinner bell,
The turkey tastes as good as it smells.
The gravy drips down over the food.
My family's in a lovely mood.

The trees look as cold as the chilled icicles,
No more people on their bicycles.
The pitter-patter of snowflakes dance on my roof,
I hear the prancing of a little deer's hooves.

The people are playing in the snow,
Oh how much fun, I really do know.
With winter almost over, I want to feel the sand,
As the last snowball melts softly in my hand.

Bridgette Venezia, Grade 6
Dorris-Eaton School

The Earth's Doomsday

Drought
Smog
Thunder, lightning, hurricanes
All over the Earth,
Clouds turn to gray
Hailstones falling
Windstorms through the trees
Tornadoes
Earthquakes destroy the land
Are these just natural disasters?
Or are these natural disasters the end of the world?

Jemm Magaling, Grade 6
Corpus Christi School

Thinking

When you are bored,
And don't have anything to do,
Thinking is the cure for you.
Your mind races and paces,
Back and forth,
Going places,
South to north.
Let's go to the ocean,
Let's go see the sea,
Where the ocean sends out messages,
To every person like me.
Swim in polluted seas,
And end up in treachery.
Then waters stand still,
But no one is free.

Nellesha Bettis, Grade 4
One Hundred Eighty Sixth St Elementary School

Softball

S lide to the base, are you out or safe?
O h, yes, she's safe
F ast as you can steal the base
T eamwork is all it takes
B atting up next is one of the best
A s she runs she tries her best
L ook at her go, as fast as day
L ike the feeling of winning, don't be ashamed if you don't

Ilene Sanchez, Grade 5
Jackson Elementary School

Falling Nowhere

Imagine falling nowhere seeing nothing
But a dark hole
Never know when to land
Never know what angle
You will never know how long it will take
Falling on water

Josh Nowikow, Grade 4
Coeur d'Alene Avenue Elementary School

Fruits

Fruits are sweet and sour
And has many colors.
It has so many tastes,
That I can't even discover

I love sweet tastes like
Strawberry and melons.
I also like sour tastes, too, like,
A raspberry, a lemon, and an orange too.

My favorite fruits are
Berries and melons
And bananas too
I love others too I wish to gobble them too.

June Park, Grade 5
Theodore Roosevelt Elementary School

Nightmare

I am in a corridor
being chased by a monster
he lunges for me
he misses
I run to the river like a jet moves
the monster trapped me
I go back closer to the river
the monster makes me go closer
I'm at the river's edge
I jump I go down the river
then I disappear
the next day the townspeople could not find me
to this day I am lost in the shadows of the dreams

Greg Fisher, Grade 4
Charles Armstrong School

Ocean

O ceans
C reate an
E cosystem worth saving
A nd a world of wonder that
N ever ends.

Carolina van Keulen, Grade 4
Marian Bergeson Elementary School

Way of Nature

A praying mantis
A fly sitting on a leaf
"Zap!" there goes the fly

Christian Vuceta, Grade 6
St Anne School

Love Is…

Peaceful like a river
Unfailing like Jesus
Always from the heart
Never ever selfish
Truthful and never lies

Steven Hughes Stubbs, Grade 5
Santa Fe Springs Christian School

Snowflake

I wish I were a beautiful snowflake,
Delicate and dazzling,
Floating like a fairy,
Flying down like a bird,
Lying down on the ground.

Michelle Zheng, Grade 5
Lake Forest Elementary School

I Am

I am silly and caring
I wonder what I will be when I grow up
I hear a mermaid's soft voice
I see a fairy
I want a great future
I am silly and caring

I pretend I am a princess
I feel a unicorn's hair
I touch the brightest star in the sky
I worry about global warming
I cry when my family gets hurt
I am silly and caring

I understand that my family cares for me
I say money isn't everything
I dream for a war free world
I try to get the best grades I can
I hope for a wonderful life
I am silly and caring

Marisa Rodriguez, Grade 6
Barstow Intermediate School

Roller Coasters

I love roller coasters.
I like looking ahead at the trails
Seeing what is up next,
If it is a giant circle or a sideways turn.

I love roller coasters.
I like the tingling feeling in my stomach
When I hang upside down,
Or when there is a trail that goes down toward the ground

I love roller coasters.
I like hearing the people screaming of excitement
As I go along with them
Trying not to scream too loud.

I love roller coasters.
I like tasting the fresh air,
As it goes into my mouth
Running through the back of my throat, as the coaster goes at high speed

I love roller coasters,
And I like smelling the foods' scent,
As it is floating in the air,
Reaching my nose from the park's meals, at the top of the coaster.

Naomi Meave, Grade 6
St John's Parish Day School

Yellow

Yellow looks like the blistering summer sun beaming through a window.
Yellow looks like the stars in a dull empty sky.
Yellow sounds like a juicy squash being plucked out of the ground.
Yellow sounds like a dandelion rustling in the wind.
Yellow smells like the pollen on a spring day.
Yellow tastes like lemon gumdrops.
Yellow tastes like delicious lemonade.
Yellow feels like an active school day.
Yellow feels like possessing enjoyment in the sun with a frosty ice cream.

Dylan Samuel Yanovsky, Grade 4
Heather Elementary School

Storm in Seconds

As I am waiting the clouds are forming,
Turning my waiting into rapidly shaking,
I decide to walk home in the rain,
Walking faster and faster,
Now jogging, as I am trying to keep warm,
The rain changes to a storm,
I start running, thunder strikes, and quickly it turns to night,
I run faster, now sprinting,
The storm keeps forming, while I cry out my legs are aching,
Finally I collapse, my legs stop aching,
The storm stops forming, the night turns to morning, the thunder stops,
The storm changes to a small drizzle,
Then my shaking stops and everything clears…

Paulo Cruz, Grade 6
Francis Parker School

My Dream

A dream such as mine
Unreal, but gives me a smile
A dream where I have my fantasy
May be fake, but keeps me asleep

My dream is a light in my window
With only hopes and no fears
Where everything I want happens
And I can find the me that lives inside

My dream is my door closing on the world
And is opening to something different
Somewhere I don't have to hide
When I'm cheerful, I know I've found a dream

Then a morning comes
The bright sun becomes a dull moon
Again, I'm forced to look happy
Until I have my next dream

Airelle Javelosa, Grade 6
Cimarron Education Center

Birthdays

B irth of someone close
I ce cream, all you can eat
R unning kids screaming all around
T he different laughing of many children
H aving your friends and family to celebrate with you
D uck duck goose, and many games
A cake with candles and a wish
Y ou getting a year older

Shatu Shali, Grade 6
Aliso Elementary School

Forest

Light peeps through the emerald green trees.
The branches like hands that reach out to me.
The sun is so bright it lights the blue sky.
The animals are hiding for they are so shy.

Clovers and grass lie in my path.
The river is flowing like an aqua bath.
Forests are beautiful. It is easy to see.
My favorite place, I like to be!

Tommy Attwood, Grade 4
Mayfield Jr School of the Holy Child Jesus

Hurricane

I wish I were a destructive hurricane,
Fast and frightful,
Terrorizing like a horrifying nightmare,
Blowing winds like speeds of race cars,
Flooding the shores with my streaming rain.

Patric Schoen, Grade 5
Lake Forest Elementary School

Columbus

Columbus…
was an Italian from Spain
waited ten years so that he can go on his trip
lead three ships called the Nina, the Pinta
and the Santa Maria when he went on his trip in 1492
witnessed three miracles on the ship
found a new world, and through it was Asia
loved the Lord but didn't always obey Him
put gold in front of God
was a poor leader because he loved gold
gold became his God when he found it
confessed his sins and went to heaven

Leo Covarrubias, Grade 5
Santa Fe Springs Christian School

Fall

Leaves came falling down on my face
  Like raindrops in the late summer days.
    When the leaves gently tapped my face
      It seemed to me in slow motion at a slow pace.
        I smelled the smell of apple pie
          And felt a gentle breeze I do not lie.
Then a leaf fell on my head
  And when I looked I saw it red
    I stood there looking at the beautiful fall day
      And thought I should enjoy it while I may.

Ilona Krasnodemsky, Grade 4
Sierra Oaks K-8 School

Blue

Blue is the color that makes me feel bad,
Blue is the color that makes me feel sad,
Blue can also make me feel mad,
And sometimes blue can make me feel glad.

Blue can make me feel bad,
Blue is the color I wish I never had,
When I see blue it turns my smile upside down,
It makes me want to mope around.

Blue also makes me feel sad,
It reminds me of the life I never had,
Blue makes me cry all day,
Blue reminds me of the color gray.

Blue makes me feel mad,
When blue gets me mad I start to do bad,
Blue turns my face all red,
It makes me want to pout in bed.

Blue can make me feel glad,
Only the ocean blue will have me not do bad,
The ocean blue I can have a lot of fun in,
It will make me smile a big grin.

Luke Wright, Grade 6
Francis Parker School

The Happiest Place on Earth
One day at Griffith Park, a dream sprouted in Walt Disney's mind
He would make his own amusement park, one like no other of its kind

They called him goofy, crazy as a loon
They called it Walt's Folly he should stick to cartoons

Walt needed dough for this extraordinary dream so much that he sold his Palm Springs home
ABC television gave him the means and in turn he gave them their top rated show

Work was begun by the Imagineers 108 acres of orange groves were cleared
And 17 million dollars and one year later everyone in Anaheim put on their Mickey Mouse ears

On opening day, it was terrible ladies in high heel shoes sank into the ground
The stifling heat was unbearable ladies in bare feet running around

The Mark Twain Riverboat sank like an anchor and counterfeit tickets filled Disney with rancor
Since that day, though, filled with much stress Disneyland's had half a billion guests!

So when he wished upon a star Disney's dreams definitely did come true
When his only wish was to create mirth Disneyland became the Happiest Place on Earth!

Freddy Mulbarger, Grade 5
The Mirman School

If
If I were red I'd be a hot sizzling fire burning in the fireplace.
If I were green I'd be long tall grass bristling from the wind blowing in every direction.
If I were blue I'd be nice cool waves crashing on the ocean floor letting every surfer ride me.
If I were yellow I'd be a nice ice cold cup of lemonade gushing down someone's throat.
If I were gray I'd be a dark lonely man walking down the street having nothing to do.
If I were purple I'd be a raspberry popsicle sitting in the refrigerator just waiting to be eaten.
If I were orange I'd be a fresh orange coming back from the store waiting to be eaten.
If I were white I'd be a seagull high above the ocean waiting to find a fish in the ocean depths.

Grant Holve, Grade 5
Aviara Oaks Elementary School

Mom
My mom is as sweet as candy, and as brave as a lion. Loving like kitten and as cuddly as a pillow. She has a voice so loud like a horn, but it's soothing. My mom feeds me with love and watches me with care. The love that she gives I will always be strong. When I become an adult she will have to let go, inside she will cry but on the outside she will be proud. As I grow up, I'll remember the wonderful things my mom did to keep me alive and going. I love you mom. I will always love you.

Adam Raber, Grade 6
Aliso Elementary School

Drabear
My animals is part dragon and part bear that has a lot of hair.
It has wings so it can fly, but when it does it will cry.
Swish, it's high in the sky when people wave goodbye!
Roar it goes when it is mad and sad. Yippee, when it's happy.
It walks on a path covered with leaves to get to its tree house, crush, crush go the leaves.
Splishy, splashy drabear goes when it plays in the rain while licking a candy cane.
Another thing about my drabear besides that it likes to eat berries is that it likes to go to the fair.
It likes to go on the train and buy a candy cane.
Her and her friends like to sing a lot of songs and play ping pong.
As you can see drabears are very interesting animals.

Nathalie Vazquez, Grade 6
Big Springs Elementary School

Raindrop

I wish I were a gentle raindrop,
Clear and splashing,
Falling like a soft feather,
Sparkling like a crystal gem,
Helping the plants and animals wherever I fall.

Stephen B. Tadena, Grade 5
Lake Forest Elementary School

Skiing

Riding up the chair lifts is for a hardy few,
In the early morning when the trees are frozen with dew,
A lake viewed to the side, the city of Reno behind,
Courage deep inside is hard to find,
I can't believe this is fun for people to do.

Arriving at the mountainous, steep cliffs,
I think I am crazy to enjoy all this,
My group reaches the pinnacle of the run,
The trees and drops will leave you stunned,
I can't believe this is fun for people to do.

I can see the lake now with a better view,
It is an inviting blanket of dark blue,
Swishing, sliding, down the steep slopes we go,
The park has jumps and complimentary rails as well,
Now I can believe this is fun for people to do.

Trenton Shore, Grade 6
Dorris-Eaton School

Green

Green feels like the soft grass on the summer morning
Green is as tasty as a Granny Smith apple
Green looks like the most soothing color ever
Green sounds like the crunching of lettuce
Green smells like freshly made guacamole

Devaughn Blount-Singletary, Grade 5
Kentwood Elementary School

Snowflake

I wish I were a delicate snowflake,
Sparkly and soft,
Falling like a freezing flower,
Twirling like a spider web,
Finally reaching the floor like a gentle leaf.

Shawdi Tarzjani, Grade 5
Lake Forest Elementary School

Shadow in the Night

It will be midnight soon
The dark, cloudless sky and yellow moon
Maybe one, or two clouds
I think I see a shadow now
Maybe not a shadow I found
Wait, was that a sound?

Isaiah Simmons, Grade 5
Henry Haight Elementary School

Catastrophe

Walking into my messy room,
You see the sight of ultimate doom.
Sports equipment laid all over the ground,
No wonder nothing can be found.

My disgusting, catastrophic desk is a mess,
There doesn't seem to be a bit of progress.
My horrible test papers are all mixed,
Clearly, nothing here can be fixed.

Torn pillows and blankets all around my bed,
This place looks like a terrible dread.
Ripped holes in a couple shirts,
I always make sure there are no skirts.

My brother's bed an ultimate mess,
Dirty lizards all about his dress.
Smelly cloth all over the place,
There is absolutely no free space.

Bats, spider webs, and monsters all around the ceiling,
There is always a terrible, horrible, and awful feeling.
This is my room you like it or not,
This is how I am and I like it a lot.

Mahdi Nafisi, Grade 6
Dorris-Eaton School

I Like and I Don't Like

I like nachos,
But I don't like when they put a bunch of hot cheese on it.
I like ice cream,
But I don't like when it spills on me.
I like tigers,
But I don't like when they eat me.
I like games,
But I don't like when I start over.
I like dogs,
But I don't like when they fight each other.

Christin Rajsombath, Grade 5
Elder Creek Elementary School

Hope

Courageous as he was
He felt scared
For he knew this day would come
But he didn't know it would come so soon
He watched
Astonished
As all his fighters went down
He knew it was his turn to be brave
He grabbed his greatest weapon
Hope
And that was all he needed.

Reese Savoie, Grade 4
Canyon View Elementary School

Water
Moisture on leaves,
Running through sprinklers.
Thunder Boom!
Lightning Crash!
The storm is over.
Calm rivers,
Rushing rapids.
Rising waves,
Explosive geysers.
Small wells,
Dirty ponds.
All are water,
All are life.
Corryn Knapp, Grade 6
Francis Parker School

Mother Earth
I am a shark.
I nourish on animals of the sea.
I require animals to live on.
We need sea, water, sky, oxygen, and air.
We need Mother Earth.
I can't help global warming, you can.
We must see trees, we must hear frogs,
We must feel safe and blissfulness.
I am part of the wonderful Mother Earth.
Save Mother Earth.
Sarah Sek, Grade 4
Ocean Air School

Summer
Far
different country
much different summer
much more different winter
but eating there…
feasting memorably
swimming

Swimming
cold water
diving in nervously
in a different world
getting out sadly
had fun
eating

Eating
very fancy
tastes so good
more than one fork
yum yum!
full
Niamh Tangney, Grade 6
Montessori Family School

Cold Night
Cold, damp, rainy skies
The wind howls in the air
Chills go down my spine
Madison Clark, Grade 6
St Anne School

Celtics
In Boston
With a basketball
Inside the stadium
Between the city
After dinner
On the seat
Down the stairs
Toward the court
Above the green
Throughout the state
Spencer Golanka, Grade 6
St Anne School

Pranked
I've been pranked all my life
I want that to change
My brother is pranking me
So I will prank him back
Whoopi cushion on his chair
Oh don't forget the bucket
Splash, poof, ha, ha, ha, poof
I've done it to him
I've pranked him
Nothing like a little fun
Pranks are pretty fantastic
I have a feeling
He is going to prank me back
Uh-oh I see an unusual object
What is it an encyclopedia
In a sling shot snap
Well like they say
What comes around goes around,
Dohh
Austin Alley, Grade 5
Merryhill Country School

Paper
I am in a dark room,
Why wouldn't anyone use me?
I am just an old piece of paper,
Would people write on me?

Color, write, and draw on me please,
The family wouldn't use me,
Does anyone need me?
Now let's do activities with me.
Matthew Nguyen, Grade 5
St Pancratius Elementary School

There Once Was
There once was a boy in Alabama
Who liked a girl named Hannah.
They fell in love,
Near a dove.
And they both moved to Montana.
Julia Talgo, Grade 4
Heather Elementary School

City of Dreams
I close my eyes,
To view heaven.
To seek clouds,
And imagine angels.

In this place,
I am better.
My vision is clearer.
I see beyond the fence.
I reach the stars.

Back home,
Lies my skeleton.
The empty bones that kept me,
Kept me locked up from myself.

Here,
I am what I am.
I've stripped myself of all poison robes.
My true body is revealed.
Now, I'm free to heal.
Heal and dream…

Like the phoenix, I've become new.
Alexis Holman, Grade 6
Cimarron Education Center

A Grand Winter
Winter arrives as a swell greeting
Soft snow blankets the ground
Adults drink hot chocolate
Kids dash outside in coats and in scarves

Kids laugh and make angels in snow
And sling snowballs down field
Families holler and sing
That's what a grand winter is like
Madeline Snider, Grade 5
Merryhill Country School

A Day at the Beach
A day at the beach
Enjoying the sun and surf
Calming peaceful day
Alexandra Heinen, Grade 6
St Anne School

High Merit Poems – Grades 4, 5 and 6

My Snapdragon World

Snap, snap
Pop, pop
Now they're starting to talk
I enter my world
Of peace and quiet
I sit in my garden
Then I heard a little quiet voice
It's my yellow snapping friend
He is bright like the sun
Yet soft like a puppy
Next to the yellow one, there was a tiny pink one
She was small and sweet like a mouse
And as pink as one's nose
Then the yellow one said his name is Mr. Sunshine
Then the pink one said she is Minnie
We played and played for the longest time
But, then it was night and I had to go
I will see you tomorrow I told them
And I went home

Olivia Raff, Grade 5
Mayfield Jr School of the Holy Child Jesus

Fever

I am a thief in the night
A filthy evil thief in the night
A thief that is also a killer; I am Fever
I am the culprit of fatality
I home in on my victims like a hawk to its prey
I break a thousand hearts a day; I am Fever
No one is ready when I attack
No pacifist can restrict me
No heart can take the pain I bring
No one can survive my wrath
I have no warmth for comrades
Only ice cold hate for enemies
I have no heart for love, I feel no shame
Only need to slake my thirst for despair
I will never die, I will always be there
Those who are lucky die quickly
And only experience my fury for a short while
Fever, Yellow Fever
A dark cloud on a summer day
A man in black at a wedding
I am Fever

Katie Watkins, Grade 6
St Andrew's Episcopal School

Snake

S lithering on the forest floor
N o legs to walk or run with
A lways on the prowl
K illing mice
E ating mice every day

Bridget Garrity, Grade 4
Mayfield Jr School of the Holy Child Jesus

Death

He stares at me in pain,
Then suddenly a surge of eternal agony rips through him,
Causing him to thrash around unceasing,
Abruptly he loses the thrashing momentum,
Then slowly the light of life in his eyes fade away,
He closes his eyes,
I feel his scarred chest for his heartbeat,
His heart has completely stopped,
Peace restores his face,
As his soul departs for heaven
He is gone for eternity,
Then I cry in despair for the loss of my friend,
My heart will be forever filled with woebegone and sorrow.

Tony Liu, Grade 6
Solana Pacific School

Fire

I am fire. I have bursts of flames.
If you get too close to me you will burn.
"Ouch!", you will say out loud.
You can use me for useful things,
You can use me to cook or light stuff.
I roam around the world.
I have one enemy and it kills me when I get too close.

Eduardo Romero, Grade 5
Clayton B Wire Elementary School

If You See a Red Penguin

If you see a red penguin, be careful.
For they are smart,
But have no heart.
They are strange creatures
With unusual features.
Their eyes shine like rubies
And they can swallow a polar bear with ease.
Although these penguins are rarely seen,
They can be very mean.
Approach them with caution you may,
But you better STAY *AWAY!*

Matthew Bea, Grade 4
Mayfield Jr School of the Holy Child Jesus

Water

Water's clear water's tasteless,
Water's liquid water's faceless.

Water's matter,
It can't shatter.

Water's not mash,
But it can splash.

Water's awesome but what makes water nice,
A burning hot day with water and ice.

Angelo Camargo, Grade 5
George Washington Charter Elementary School

Summer

S unny days
U nreasonable fun
M arvelous music
M eadow of sunshine
E xciting events
R omantic season

Emily Tran, Grade 5
Clayton B Wire Elementary School

I Wonder

I wonder what it feels like
To run through a field of flowers
I wonder what it feels like
To fun in a herd for hours
I wonder what it feels like
To have a fabulous pasture
I wonder what it feels like
To never have a mean master

Danyelle Ceresola, Grade 6
Lockeford Elementary School

Ode to Earth

Ode to Earth
Who gives life
To all people

Whose uniqueness
Makes her home

A small blue marble
In the vastness of space
Like a gem

Ode to Earth
Whose water
Is the backstop
For life as we know it

Whose mountains
Make our time here enjoyable

Whose deserts
Make the rest of her
Seem even more special

Ode to Earth
Thank you for being here

Sam Weinstein, Grade 6
James B Davidson Middle School

Beads

Smooth dark brown table
Beads glitter in the sunlight
The secret is love

Laney Richardson, Grade 5
Theodore Roosevelt Elementary School

Exciting

Exciting is playing in the Little League Championship game.
Exciting is winning the Little League Championship game.
Exciting is getting Derek Jeter's autograph.
Exciting is playing in the NJB Basketball Championship game.
Exciting is seeing a game at Fenway Park.
Exciting is playing catch with a football with a friend.
Exciting is seeing the New York Yankees in Yankee Stadium.
Exciting is watching a shot at the buzzer.
Exciting is seeing a game at Citizen's Bank Stadium in Philadelphia.
Exciting is touching a shark.
Exciting is going to the top of the Empire State Building.
Exciting is getting Shaun White's autograph.
Exciting is catching a ball at a baseball game.
Exciting is playing on the Little League All-Star game.
Exciting is…just exciting.

Donovan J. Kelley, Grade 6
La Costa Heights Elementary School

My Great Grandfather

My great grandfather playing the piano like when he was a teenager
Not knowing that it will be one of the last times
Just dancing
Singing
But still unaware

Ajna Revelle, Grade 4
Coeur d'Alene Avenue Elementary School

If…

If I was famous I could meet a lot of people like Gwen Stefani or Jen Gufani,
I could meet Akon or LaKeShone,
I could go to Hollywood with my dog Pollyhood,
I could walk the red carpet with a lollipop in my pocket,
I could meet a rapper on a ladder falling off with a clatter.
It would be amazing!

Nayeli Anahi Jimenez Mendoza, Grade 4
Anderson Valley Elementary School

If…

If I were a dog, I'd be a speedy border terrier running around a beach.
If I were a surfboard, I'd be a shortboard being ridden every day.
If I were an animal, I'd be a dolphin swimming in a wave.
If I were a sport, I'd be a baseball the best sport ever played.

Kyle Davis, Grade 5
Aviara Oaks Elementary School

I Know the Beach

I know the beach
The waves crashing down with the force of a thousand lightning bolts
Sand the size of grains, being filled up into a bucket
People running, screaming, and splashing water
Everyone is having fun, playing horseshoes and volleyball
Lifeguards patrolling down the beach, swimming out to save lives
Dogs playing with Frisbee, having the time of their lives
I know the beach, and I know the ocean

Caroline Harari, Grade 6
Francis Parker School

High Merit Poems – Grades 4, 5 and 6

Anger
Anger is like black
And is also like darkness
It crawls through my body
It reminds me of the time I felt like the world was spinning
So fast that I couldn't catch up
It makes me feel helpless like sinking in quicksand
It makes me want to hide in a hole and never come out

Cole Henriksen, Grade 6
St Anne School

Lightning
I wish I were a radiant lightning bolt,
Brilliant and beaming,
Zigzagging like a maze,
Flaming like a wildfire,
Striking the ground like a snake's tongue.

Reese Davis, Grade 5
Lake Forest Elementary School

Starbucks
As I walk in through the door, I see the happy faces
That the customers have as they receive their orders.
Everyone with a different drink. Everyone's full of joy.
I see everyone in a group of wonderful friends.
I can hear the people talking about all kinds of
Different things. Each group of people talking about
Current events and people they know. Each person
Talking about their weekend and their adventures.
I can smell the freshly brewed coffee. The exotic
Smells overwhelm me. So many smells all so good.
As I receive my caramel frappucino, I can feel how
Cold it is. On a hot summer day, it is perfect because
It is refreshing. The second I taste it, my taste buds are
Blown away. I am reminded of the reason it is my
Favorite drink. My monthly trip is always better than the last.

Ivanna Cano, Grade 6
St John's Parish Day School

My Cat Toby
Cats nice, calm, friendly
These words describe him.
He's brown, white,
and the nicest guy I know.
He's full of hair and fluffy
and he is rather puffy.
He won't claw or bite
but he'll occasionally get an ear mite.
His ear will itch
so we give him his ear drops.
He can explore or be lazy
and just lay on his bed
but he'll get right up when it's time to be fed.
After a long day of play and exploring
he jumps on his bed and goes to sleep.

Josh Smith, Grade 5
St Louis De Montfort School

I Have a Book
I never thought about doing this in my life
'Til one book changed my life
Reading is like cartoon in your head.
You can take it anywhere you want.
'Cause it is in your head
'Cause it's stuck in your head.
You can bring it everywhere you want.
It makes you learn a lot more than live TV.
I got this book that I can't stop thinking of
I think I will bring it everywhere I go
It is a little scary but not as scary as live TV action.
It is also in your head so you can see it your own way.
The colors of the scary parts are like
Someone squeezing red colored markers of real blood.

Maya Lin, Grade 4
Charles Armstrong School

The Sky
The blue feels like a smooth surface.
I smell the blue and it smells like a fresh ocean.
The blue sounds like waves to the surfer.
The blue is the sky.

Errin Lyton, Grade 5
Kentwood Elementary School

I Know Ballet
I know ballet
The tingling of pain as I stretch
The feeling of nervousness as I'm about to go on stage
The smell of brand new point shoes
The beautiful, bright-colored costumes
The sounds of girls chattering in the dressing room
The graceful, peaceful music that I'm dancing to
The applause after everyone takes their bows
I know ballet

Anna Wilson, Grade 6
Francis Parker School

My Life
My life is like a tree.
I stand in silence.
Nothing around me but wind.
I stand without saying a word
In a world with one life and one tree.

Joshua Krishna Ciup, Grade 4
Coeur d'Alene Avenue Elementary School

Knowledge
Responsible people bring success.
Courage in doing new activities
helps you have more knowledge to make good decisions.
Sometimes you have to sacrifice things to get what you want.
You have to have courage and strength to meet a challenge.

Jacob Groll, Grade 4
Canyon View Elementary School

Purpose Driven Dreams
Dreams are more than thoughts
Dreams are like a secret passageway
That take me to a separate place
Every single time I close my eyes
I start to think of my dream.

My dreams store away
precious memories to keep.
Memories that affect me deeply
Thoughts that can spook me
Or others that soothe me.

Now,
I am forced to ask myself…
Are dreams more than just dreams?
Or are they a sign?
But a sign of what?
A sign that I'm not sure of?

But
What I do know
Is that my dreams
Can lead my
PURPOSE DRIVEN DREAM.
Jasmin Flores, Grade 6
Cimarron Education Center

Night of the Stars
The moon hangs low
In the sky
One by one,
The stars pop out
From beneath
The dark cloak
Of night

The trees sway
To a silent breeze
Their branches reaching out
To caress the stars

A screech owl alights
On a nearby tree
Its voice resonates
Through the air

Now, in the dark hours before dawn,
Nature's beauty
Is unhindered by man

The stars wink merrily
And in the distance,
A wolf howls
Joanna Liu, Grade 6
Bret Harte Middle School

The Forest Winds
The forest winds hit me hard
Harder than possible
Too strong to live through
Must run away
Must give up
Give up
Home
Need home
Energy
I can do it
I have to go now
I am going to start
I can do it, I did it
Brendan Russ, Grade 4
Stone Ranch Elementary School

Bunny
By the grass
In the bushes
Between the branches
On the grass
After Easter
Outside my door
Over the hill
Toward the fields
Concerning carrots
Around the pink flowers
Chloe Zakhour, Grade 6
St Anne School

Mom's Cooking
The sky is blue
The sun is yellow
My mom loves to cook
And I love to eat Jell-O
Katherine Estrada Linares, Grade 4
Clayton B Wire Elementary School

How We Have Grown
Look how we have grown
From slavery to freedom
From friends to foe
Many lives were sacrificed
One man changed our thoughts
With only four words
"I have a dream"
Elizabeth Jackson, Grade 6
Francis Parker School

Clouds
Clouds live in the sky
As lovely birds passing by
Clouds are large and wide
Alysa Gomez, Grade 5
Joseph M Simas Elementary School

Grandfather
Grandfather I miss you.
Why did you go?

I never got to tell
You the things I feel inside.

You played with me so
Much and I had fun.

But you went bye, bye
And now it's done.

Now I have my family
But you are missing.

Why did you go?
I miss you so much.
Evelyn Gomez, Grade 4
Oak Grove Elementary School

Dreams
Dreams flit through the air
They are the moon and the stars
Golden sunsets
Waves coming in and out
Misty clouds hanging above
Morning dew
Dreams in the wind
They are colors
Wishes
Shady forests
Shining lights
Hope
Dreams are life
They shine on you
Diamonds in the night
Tinted bubbles
Silver mist
Falling dusk
Dreams come
They go
Remember
Sophia Yang, Grade 6
McGrath Elementary School

School/Summer
School
Recess, P.E.
Boring, reading, studying
Tests, science, cool, sports
Playing, running, jumping
Beach, fun
Summer
James Cruz, Grade 5
St Louis De Montfort School

High Merit Poems – Grades 4, 5 and 6

Sleeping Wonders

I would dream of a simple play
of my life itself
with a melodic rhythm I drift
I will dream of music
for when a piano plays
a routine of tap and lean
forgive me for this dream

I have dreamt of monsters, ghouls, and goblins
but a good dream never told well
a figure, a sign, a witch, a spell
is always but a memory
for good dreams I have had, still unknown to some
is a reason for lack of fear
forgive me, forgive me for this dream

I have dreamt of demons, death, and blood
as fear strikes my brain
darkness ascends, though still afraid
of a nightmare uncovered before
until I embrace courage, forgive me for this dream
when courage overlooked me
forgive me for this dream, forgive my sleeping wonders

Asia Smith, Grade 6
Cimarron Education Center

Ode to Love

Love, perhaps an attraction between two,
Two magnets working together,
Two forces, joined still more than one,
Working together, family and friends,
Two, sitting next to one another,
A flame of scarlet,
As the color of affection,
scorching heat, raging inferno, burning within,
Like the sky, insane colors of the air, a life that's crazy,
A life before love,
Turns calm, as the colors of the sunrise,
A life including love,
Like a tidal wave, it pulls at emotions,
Like a great wave pulls its bounties out to sea,
Concluding,
Love reveals the true beauty in everyone.

Olivia Nelson, Grade 5
Wagon Wheel Elementary School

Joy

Joy is like yellow
and is also like a day in spring.
It jumps through my body.
It reminds me of the time my BFF and I were together.
It makes me feel ticklish or fearless.
It makes me want to laugh like crazy.

Niloo Fathollahi, Grade 6
St Anne School

My Tousled Room

Open the door slowly and peer in,
Surely the owner is full of chagrin.
The horrible room is full of doom,
Believe me, you don't want to see the game room.
Slowly but surely looking towards your desk,
Soon to be saddened by it looking grotesque.
On your desk, there is a monster of mess crawling,
Clearly this room is terribly appalling.
The squeaky floor is wet and soggy,
Then you realized you stepped on a froggy.
My homework is spread out all over my wall,
It is certainly not going to fall.
My cluttered bed is soon next to see,
And on it is my week old iced tea.
Under the covers, there are bugs galore,
When you sleep you can't possibly snore.
Quickly you run out of your room,
Hoping no sudden mishap will cause you doom.

Anna Chan, Grade 6
Dorris-Eaton School

Hope*

Hope, hope is in the air
Hope is beautiful,
Hope gives me joy and laughter.
Hope, there are many ways to describe it.
Hope makes me think of pink!

Kelsey Shoemaker, Grade 6
Grant Elementary School
*Dedicated to Sheri Spurgan

If I Were in Charge of the World*

If I were in charge of the world
I'd cancel school,
Homework,
Bedtimes,
And vegetables.
If I were in charge of the world
Video games would cost no money,
You wouldn't have chores,
And there would be no goalies in hockey.
If I were in charge of the world
There would be no forgetting to feed your pets,
Never cleaning your room,
You would have dessert all day,
And parents would not get mad at you for getting bad grades.
If I were in charge of the world
You would always be with friends
And for Christmas you would get everything you wanted.
If you never said please or thank you
Or if you didn't have manners I'd still be
In charge of the world.

Griffin Kaminskis, Grade 6
St Raphael School
*Patterned after "If I Were in Charge of the World"
by Judith Viorst

Papa Joe

He told my mom
he would never
make it
to my birth.
He said he would
never make it to my
brother's birth.
He told my grandma
he would never
make it to my 10th birthday,
but he did,
and now he is gone.
All I have left
is his
smile.

Tiffany Buss, Grade 6
Bethany Lutheran School

My Hamster*

Sitting on the couch
My hamster in
My arms
Dying of disease
Breathing deeply
Then lighter
And lighter
And lighter
Then he
Closed his eyes
And never
Ever
Opened
Them
Again

Mia Gamberale, Grade 4
Westwood Elementary School
*In memory of Crouton the hamster

Silver

Silver, a metallic hue
Like the sleek dolphins
In the gray sea

Silver, the color of snow at dusk
On mountains with peaks so sharp
In wonderful, white winter

Silver, like the sardines
Swimming in tight schools
In the deep ocean

Silver, the color of my dreams
The sweet color of sleep
weaving in and out of my imagination

Maddy Tervet, Grade 6
James B Davidson Middle School

Ode to Books

A wide variety of books,
containing information we need.
Adventurous, mystical, and mysterious —
those are the books I like to read.

Filled with excitement,
as you turn every page.
A truly enjoyable object
for people of all age.

You enter a new world
and leave reality behind.
You go to a place you've never been
and meet new friends you can find.

Join in on a great adventure
to a mystical, magical place.
Or maybe ride on a rocket
and travel to outer space!

As you can see, books can be wonderful and fun,
making you laugh or smile, inspiring your mind with creative ideas, more than a ton!
An ode to books! Ones with pages filled with imagination,
filled with adventures and moral lessons. Books — a spectacular creation!

Isabeau Reyes, Grade 6
St Dominic Elementary School

Blue

Blue is the feeling of my smooth, fluffy pillow every night.
Blue is the sound of rain striking the ground going, "drip drop."
Blue is the look of the enormous sky in the afternoon.
Blue is the stench of a giant pile of blue cheese at a restaurant, YUCK!
Blue is the taste of freshly picked blueberries, plopped in my mouth!
Blue is the sound of blues music at a concert or church.
Blue is the smell of water brushing up against the seashore.
Blue looks like my fish waiting for me to come home every day.
Blue is the feeling of light on a hot day.
And blue looks like a waterfall at Niagara Falls.

Thomas Morey, Grade 4
Heather Elementary School

What Is Happening to the American Dollar?

My name is Bill, but George works too. I'm freshly printed, I'm crisp and new.
From New York I'm shipped away, to California! What a day!
Into Wells Fargo I march with pride. A clumsy hand drops me, and down I glide.
Next thing I know, I'm in a fist, and shoved in a purse with a shopping list!
I'm used in Safeway, buying yeast, but now I'm crinkled, and I'm creased!
A few days later, I'm folded down, and shoved in a suitcase, I'm out of town!
Across the world, to Cairo, Maine, and up to Russia, down to Spain!
Stop in Bangkok, I buy some beans, and then I'm stuck in a washing machine!
I'm swapped and moved from hand to hand, and end up back in my own homeland!
Wait a sec, I know this house! I lived here once, with my spouse!
But someone else is living here, Barack Obama, "Prez of the year!"
Now I'm proud, he's holding me! I'm the best "Change" you'll ever see!

Charlotte Constantin, Grade 6
James B Davidson Middle School

High Merit Poems – Grades 4, 5 and 6

The Circle of the Past

The past teaches us
What we should do better next time
And what we should do again.
The past makes us better people
The past lets us learn how to fix our mistakes
And that leads us to more friends and success in life.
The past can teach how to speak and read nature's ways
And have a good life.
The past teaches us the rights and wrongs of life
The past teaches us how to live
The past teaches us of love and family
The past teaches us our way of living
The past is part of us.

Adam Goodwin, Grade 4
The Mirman School

Yeslek

Squeek, swish, squeek, swish
Is the sound of the Yeslek as it walks by.
But be quiet it is awfully shy.
It's got two big eyes and a turkey tail,
Yet so small it can fit in the mail.
It's got Curlew legs and dinosaur arms,
yet so sneaky it won't sound any alarms.
It's hunting sound, Yi Yi Yi
Is so loud that it will make you cry!
It's feathers: pink and blue and his body: green.
Although, don't be scared it's not mean!
It goes Eh Eh Eh when it's happy!
But if he's mad he can be a little slappy!
The Yeslek has very soft fur.
When he falls asleep he goes Pur, Pur, Pur.

Kelsey M. Enos, Grade 6
Big Springs Elementary School

The Dream

One night I woke up in a dream
and looked up to see the ugliest thing
with a white face and eyes green
finding out it was a clowny fiend!
It chased me around as I screamed
through lots of junk and through smokescreen.
All of a sudden I saw a sheen,
spectacular, lightning, zapping machine.
I aimed the machine at the fiend,
and pulled the trigger which shot out a beam
which turned the ugly nasty thing
into a tiny pinto bean!
I squished the bean (which was kind of mean)
and saw the weirdest thing you've ever seen.
It started to twirl, it started to scream,
it turned red, blue, black, and green.
When I sprayed it with gasoline,
I suddenly got out of the terrible dream.

Gabriel Sanvictores, Grade 6
St Charles Catholic School

Imagination on a Rainy Day

I have a weird imagination…
When I look out of that window,
You may see rain, and trees blowing,
But when I see it,
I see kings and queens dancing in the rain,
Knights, princesses, castles, and dragons all together.
Whoosh…
I will go through the galaxy,
Between planets and beyond.
Boom! Bam!
A band is coming through,
Making sounds of thunder.
Nothing will stop my imagination,
Not even the cruelest thing.
Then I hear my name,
The teacher calling on me, and
My flight of imagination has ended.
But I hear the good-byes of my imagination,
Saying, "See you again soon!"

Anabell Gimena, Grade 6
Corpus Christi School

Questions

What if?
How would you know if you don't say what if?
Questions color our world; they paint pictures in our mind
Swirling images in endless space
What will you do?
Where will you be?
Questions guide us, opening a door of infinite opportunities
How would you achieve if you didn't know?
How would you learn if you didn't understand?
Just ask.

Anh Cao, Grade 6
James B Davidson Middle School

Fly Me to the Sun

C'mon everybody let's fly to the sun
You know it's going to be a lot of fun
We'll build a rocket and paint it red
Complete with a snack bar, bathroom, and bed
When we land we'll all climb out
To see if there are any aliens about
We'll look out into the sky
And see Earth as small as a fly
Soon it will be time to go
We'll want to stay but we'll have to say no
When we get home everyone will be so proud
They'll scream and shout and be so loud
C'mon everybody let's fly to the sun
What do you mean it's not all fun?
Fine, then we'll fly to the moon
We're going to leave really, really soon

Erika Jensen, Grade 6
James B Davidson Middle School

Friends

Friends are forever
They are there whenever
Friends love to talk
They really rock
Sometimes we get in fights
They last through the nights

But we know it will be ok
The very next day
Friends love to shop
A lot a lot

Friends are sweet
They are really neat
Friends have style
They are not just for awhile

Friends aren't just he and she
Friends are like you and me
They will never part
That's why friends have heart

Taylor Rivera, Grade 6
Barstow Intermediate School

Shopping

Around the corner
Inside the store
Behind the counter
Above the shelf
Across the street
In Los Angeles
About the style
At the mall
Concerning clothes
For the best

Emily Klein, Grade 6
St Anne School

New Year

Mom said, "Dinner!"
I go to the kitchen,
Today is New Year,
My presents and cousin
All waiting for me.
"The dinner is rich!"
My uncle said.
Everybody eating and talking
Many foods in my dish
"Thank you!"
"Happy New Year!"
Gift money from my uncle,
Everybody is happy,
Me too…

William Wang, Grade 5
Clover Avenue Elementary School

Mother Earth

I am a Bengal tiger.
I pad quietly to jump on prey.
As a stalker, I move like the ocean.
I like to face challenges and stay full.
I pretend that I am a ruler.
I always like to be intra-personal.
I feel like I'm the best of the best.
Save Mother Earth.

Amanda Yuan, Grade 4
Ocean Air School

When You Smile

When you smile, it shines
like the sun
your smile is unique
and different
from everyone

You don't have to do or
give any big thing
you just show your
wonderful smile
and be happy,
day by day!

Stephanie Cervantes, Grade 6
Corpus Christi School

Girls/Boys

Girls
Sweet, pretty
Loving, caring, nail painting
Pink, perfume, handsome, cologne
Racing, hunting, sleeping
Nice, cool
Boys

Skyler Addamo, Grade 5
St Louis De Montfort School

Laguna Beach

Chirp, chirp
Hear so early in the morning
Delicious breakfast burrito
Stares me in the eyes
Gazing out at the gorgeous sunrise
A sudden boom of the breaking waves
Breezes zipping past my hair
Waves carrying me to shore
My boogie board
A little friend of mine
Water splashing my face
Constructing intricate sandcastles
Playing with my cousins
Great time at the beach

Trevor Amer, Grade 5
Clover Avenue Elementary School

A Fierce Tiger

A fierce tiger hunts for water.
Then smells an angry animal.
Forest green trees climb to the sky.
An aggressive tiger
Drinks from the waterfall.

Aaliyah Garcia, Grade 6
St Alphonsus School

On the Beach

A cold silent beach
A couple of waves crashing
People are happy

Daniel Gallagher, Grade 6
St Anne School

Snow

The droplet of snow
Irritates my soft, cold, nose
Oh how I hate snow

Donya Gharineh, Grade 6
St Anne School

Flying Turtles

Fly turtles, fly high
Flying turtles making clouds
Safe flying turtles

Cody Herrero, Grade 5
El Monte Elementary School

They're Listening

They just stand there
with their roots
stuck to the ground.
My backyard
is full of palm trees
and even a Japanese maple.
They all have robins
and humming birds
that sing to them.
Even when my bird goes out
she warbles too.

I think the trees listen
because the wind and the birds
talk to them so much,
they get used to it.
The wind makes the branches sway
and they make a calming rhythm
like a jovial song.

The trees listen
to their surroundings
and to people passing by.

Melissa Brunkal, Grade 5
Bethany Lutheran School

High Merit Poems – Grades 4, 5 and 6

My Grandfather

Your warm, kind smile fills me with joy
never will I forget
the times we had
the little things now seem big
like the chewing gum always stored in your breast pocket
the trips to the pool on roasting hot days
where I would cling to your back
as you glided smoothly through the clear water
cling, and never let go
you had a sparkle in your eye
a fire that would never burn out
you could vanish the gloomy clouds
and make the bright sun reappear
those days I clutched you so desperately
I knew I could never let go

Eden Avery, Grade 5
Coeur d'Alene Avenue Elementary School

What If…

What if the Earth wasn't round
What would we do?

What if aliens invaded
How would we act to that?

What if the war in Iraq became World War 3
How many people would die fighting for us?

What if global warming overtook the Earth
What would happen?

What if this happened
How much would this poem mean?

Samantha Hebri, Grade 5
Theodore Roosevelt Elementary School

Cloud

I wish I were a mellow cloud,
Calm and peaceful,
Hovering and hanging in the sky,
Floating like a balloon that never touches the ground,
Cooling and condensing until I start to cry.

Jaydlin Vahid, Grade 5
Lake Forest Elementary School

Music

Music is the best noise you can hear.
The day where there is no wind is like music.
The day when it is just a little warm is like music.
There are ten billion bands.
Music is awesome with the base drum.
Boom! Boom! Boom!
Music is the best noise you can hear.

Garett Huston, Grade 6
Barstow Intermediate School

Nature Grows

I look inside a rose,
though the only thing I seem to see is my nose.

I lay there and wait until I see it move a pinch,
but the only thing I see is a finch.

It slowly blooms in the sun,
until it is completely done.

Even though it can be very slow,
now I know that nature grows.

Lindsay Berardi, Grade 4
Charles Armstrong School

The Qur'an

The Qur'an is gold,
Its meaning is beauty,
It teaches us more about the words from our Lord,
Whom we worship and cherish,
And will always remember.

The Qur'an is a guide,
That helps us in our time of need,
It tells us stories about brave prophets
Like Moses, Jesus, Abraham, and Mohammed.

The Qur'an is a reminder,
Just like a mother
Who prepares for the big day,
The Day of Judgment.

Ayan Jama, Grade 6
Islamic School of San Diego

Splendid Spring

The cool breeze
blows
the Gardener mows,
the children play,
almost every day.
The ocean mist
wanders off.
the sprinklers go on,
and then,

We sing, laugh
and play.
I enjoyed the day,
but I have learned
We shall not only play,
but see what the earth and God provide,
You shall learn from them,
In order to survive:
Protect, Conserve, Respect

It's the season of
beauty and love
the skies above
are blue and white
filled with birds
day and night.

Asiya Madha, Grade 5
New Horizon School

If I Were an Animal

If I were a tiger, I'd creep through the undergrowth, looking for my cubs
Then I'd stop with my ears pricked, alert, tense
I'd hear the sound of small tigers playing together in the lush forests of Asia.
If I were a copperhead,
I'd slither silently, stalking my prey, moving through the bushes,
Lacking noise, the mouse stops, but only for a moment; I'd pounce! One bite, then two, all gone.
If I were a dolphin, I'd swim through the ripples, gracefully following my brother as he leads me away from the pod.
"Where are we going?" I'd ask. "Over the waves, into a cave, the place where we've always belonged."
If I were a kangaroo, I'd jump up into the sky, reaching, reaching, can't reach.
I'd bounce around Australia, past a koala, next to a ranger station.
Then I'd race home, as if a pack of dingoes were chasing me, another mile, then half a mile, then I'm home.
If I were a panda, I'd wander around China, eating bamboo
I'd climb through the bushes, over the rocks.
Then I'd waddle over to my cubs. Time to go home! Back to the den we go.
If I were an eagle, I'd soar through the skies, over the treetops, next to the mountains.
Flying far, far, away on top of the world, across the oceans.
Then I'd fly home to my nest, swooping through the open skies, just a little farther, a little bit more, then I'm home.
If I were a polar bear, I'd dig my den deep into the snow, ready to wait out the winter storms.
Then in the spring I'd wake up from my sleep and make my way towards the ice flows.
Just when I'm so weak that I will die if I don't reach the ice flows soon. Suddenly, I'm there and I begin to hunt.

Sarah Coffey, Grade 5
Aviara Oaks Elementary School

I Am From…

I am from
A house with my friend's piano against the wall, where a wood stove sits against a brick patio and wall, where a picture made by my mom is always going to fall.

I am from
A yard where a hot tub sits always making sound and a fenced dog area where cats always abound.

I am from
Neighborhoods where a hairy black cat is as skittish as a bat.

I am from
A family where "Andiamo Weasels" is said when we have to leave, where "ergo" makes every one pleased.

I am from
Traditions where Eggs Benedict is served for breakfast on the day of my mom's birth and dinner arrives every night with great mirth.

Celeste Wilson, Grade 5
Notre Dame School

Someone I Know

Someone I know is…my cousin Joshua. I love him very much and he means a lot to me. I barely get to see him, so when I do get to see him, I make the most of it. During the summer we go to a water park called the Ravine. It has big water slides and cool stuff. I also go to his house or we both go to our grandma's house with my uncle and sisters. We also jump and flip on his trampoline. Or we play with his cat named KOALA! This is someone I know.

Lillian Gates, Grade 5
Theodore Roosevelt Elementary School

Blue

I love the color blue, it's the color of the sky. Blue is the color of the nice cold ocean in the summer. I think about the ocean when I see blue and the nice, cold and relaxing sound of the waves. Blue is the relaxing sound of the raindrops hitting the roof at night. Blue is relaxing and soothing. I love the color blue.

Tyler Howard, Grade 5
Kentwood Elementary School

Nature

It is all around me
It is my joy.
I am a flower.
I am a bug.
I always come back to it because it is calming.
Mother Nature brought it to me and nature is my goal.
It is very moving.

Nature is my heart.
Nature calms me down.
It is the best!
I will never rest to find new things in it.
And when I find new things in it
I am very, very excited.

Now, I hear the sounds of birds,
The rustles of the leaves
The whoosh of the wind
The sun is beating down on me

So, as you can see
Nature is a wonderful thing.

Rebecca George, Grade 4
Charles Armstrong School

Am I a Plague?

I am Fever
I can kill you when ever I please
I am invincible and global
I will not give pity on pathetic people
You can run from me but you can't avoid me
There is no escaping me
I put the hole in your heart
I kill like there is no tomorrow
I make you miss your loved ones
Loved ones will miss you and be devastated
You will be like a trunk when I get you
I create immense darkness
I am a great enigma

Chris Velez, Grade 6
St Andrew's Episcopal School

A Friend

A friend is not just a person who happens to be there
But a friend is somebody you can depend on
Sometimes a person is only there when you want them,
But a friend is there for you, no matter what
A friend is somebody who is special,
Somebody who is always there to listen,
Somebody who won't ever leave you
When you need them most
A friend turns your whole world around
And makes your whole life better
A true friend will be yours forever

Roni Nievera, Grade 6
Corpus Christi School

Color

Red is the color that is in my sight
I can hear the sound that the red drum makes
I can taste the red apple on my tongue
I can smell the red roses in the air
I can feel the red scarf across my face

Bruce Claiborne, Grade 5
Kentwood Elementary School

My Cat Peanut

On an expedition to find her mother
My mom found her in the gutter
Sitting there forgotten and alone
Mom's instincts told her to take her as one of her own
Now Peanut's safe and sound
As she romps and tromps all around

She is filled with relentless energy
Though I knew the cat was right for me
When her energy finally depleted
We knew just what she needed
Some food and water would be just right
And love and care all through the night

Then one day I went to school
To tell how my cat was so cool
When I cam home waiting to be greeted
By a cute kitten which I would've treated
I stood sulkily waiting for the kitty
Then an eruption of tears, it wasn't so pretty

Steven Sherden, Grade 6
Big Springs Elementary School

Summer

You know me for being hot.
I make people get hot and go to the pool.
You sometimes don't like me because I'm too hot.
Some kids like me because I make them not go to school.
Adults don't like me because I make kids not go to school.
My greatest enemy is the greatest holiday, Christmas.
Sometimes I never go away in Mexico.
When people stay outside too much I burn them.

Adolfo Gonzalez, Grade 5
Clayton B Wire Elementary School

Morning

Startled by the birds' melody
Blinded by the sun
A whole new world again
The aroma of bacon, eggs and sausage
Lingering in my nostrils
And throughout the house
The sizzling of the bacon and sausage
Tapping on my eardrums

Ariana Stuhaan, Grade 5
Coeur d'Alene Avenue Elementary School

Wolf Howling Wind

As I lay in bed wide awake
I hear a scary sound
A howling, growling, wailing sound
That keeps me wide awake

I kept on wondering again and again
About that scary sound
Was it a wolf or a bear?
I wondered again and again

Suddenly the window bursts open
And a breezy wind comes through
I laugh at myself for being so crazy
When the wind came rushing through.
Kimmy Dovan, Grade 5
St Barbara School

Grandma

Roaring up the stairs
Sprinting towards Grandma
"Just a little bit further"
Tipping and falling
Banging my head,
But I did not care —
Grandma was right there.

The guardian over,
Blazing hot, pushing me away
From the treasure that awaits:
Extraordinary cookies and cake

Fighting my way up past this monster,
Crawling my way up
No need to worry,
Grandma is right here.
Adam Chaarawi, Grade 5
Clover Avenue Elementary School

Leaves Poured Down Upon the Earth Like Drops of Colored Rain

looked outside my foggy window

big leaves
small leaves
fat leaves
skinny leaves
glide
slide
slip
zip

all fall
upon the
ground
Catherine McClure, Grade 4
Sierra Oaks K-8 School

The Small Brown Seed

It started with a seed, a small brown seed that was planted in the ground
And this seed turned into a sprout
With delicate, green leaves and a wispy stem
With time, this delicate sprout turned into a tree
This tree, this long awaited tree stood in the middle of the backyard
And was admired by all who had the chance to see
This majestic tree lasted for many generations
   A little boy's first step…
   A new dog's first home
   A girl's first kiss….
It weathered the seasons
Winter
   Spring
      Summer
         And fall…for every year of its being
It was a significant tree to those who had the pleasure of sharing in its life
If I were this tree, I would be grateful for the joy I could give
If someone was frightened, I would provide protection
If someone wanted quiet, I would provide a place of solitude
It is all thanks to the one who planted the seed
That one small, brown seed
Samantha Suman, Grade 6
Valley Beth Shalom Day School

If I Were

If I were a blanket I'd make someone warm on a cold, snowy day,
I'd wrap around somebody's body and bundle them up while they sit by the fire.

If I were a forest I'd have tons of lumbering trees,
I'd have creeks flow rapidly throughout me and have flowers blooming everywhere.

If I were the color white, I'd be the dazzling clouds in the sky,
I'd be a clean sheet of paper and a smooth tissue to blow your nose in.

If I were a rose I'd smell similar to scrumptious apple pie,
I'd be as beautiful as a waterfall with the sun sparkling upon it
And have scarlet petals as smooth as a round pebble.

If I were a koala I'd climb the highest trees to touch the sky,
I'd chomp up crunchy leaves and swing from tree to tree.

If I were me…
Claire Harelson, Grade 5
Aviara Oaks Elementary School

I Am from Tradition and Love

I am from a house with a long kitchen table and a double-sided fireplace.
I am from a yard with a pirate ship tree house and handmade brick patio.
I am from a neighborhood that was once John Bidwell's ranch.
I am from a family of great grandfathers that lived very old.
I am from a family that reminds us to "Eat your salad."
I am from a family that gathers around pancake breakfast and homemade pizzas.
I am from a family that keeps their memories in photo albums and shoe boxes.
I am from a family of tradition and love.
Dante Specchierla, Grade 5
Notre Dame School

Loud

Loud is not a baby sleeping
Loud is a train coming down the railroad
Loud is a D.J. at a party
Loud is a fire truck coming down the street
Loud sounds like a party
Loud sounds like ambulances
Another word for loud is noisy
One thing about loud is that it's everywhere

Brooke Sullivan, Grade 6
Big Springs Elementary School

Red

Red, blazing and scorching
like the fire in the sky
burning and energizing a new sunrise

red, strong and courageous
like a dragon's steamy fire
ash flying everywhere

red, vibrant and deadly
like blood in battle
yelling in fury and confidence to take over

red, soft and juicy
like a jalapeno dipped in sauce
bringing fire to a person's mouth

red, independent and sovereign
like the United States of American flag
waving in the air seeking justice and freedom

Ruth Cho, Grade 6
James B Davidson Middle School

Me (In a Funny Life)

I am kind and funky in a funny life,
I wonder if I ever will get a dog for my own.
I want to find my missing things,
I see me reading by a bank,
I am kind and funky in a funny life.

I pretend to own a home of animals,
I feel my hair waving in the wind,
I touch an island of my own,
I worry I will live a lonely life,
I am kind and funky in a funny life.

I understand that people need friends,
I believe I will have a good life,
I dream to have whatever I want,
I try to make a lot of friends,
I hope to go to parties galore,
I am kind and funky in a funny life.

Libby Fish, Grade 5
Sundale Elementary School

The First Day

In kindergarten
I miss my mom
her dark brown hair
Her lotion and perfume
that she has on all day long
I help my cousin wash glue off his hands
I miss my mom
but it's okay
my mom put her lotion on me

Dwight Murray, Grade 5
Coeur d'Alene Avenue Elementary School

The Iditarod

It's a tough dog race with a quick, quick pace,
　Where rest is best it's a very tough quest,
　From a dream to a very important team,
It starts in March and ends at the Burled Arch

There are many good breeds with lightning speed,
　Some will be on the trail and some will fail,
We saw a frightening moose that was on the loose,
　It ran onto the ice but that was very nice,
With so much action there is much satisfaction

It's a tough dog race with a quick, quick pace,
　Where rest is best it's a very tough quest,
　From a dream to a very important team,
It starts in March and ends at the Burled Arch

Alec Morgan, Grade 6
Francis Parker School

My Bro

My brother is named Ryan
But I call him Bro
He liked my bird named Bow!

He plays soccer
And basketball
And he used to play football!

He has curly hair
And it is brown
And he is never down!

He is very tall
Taller than me
And taller than a baby tree!

Emily Roberts, Grade 4
Charles Armstrong School

The Winter Tree

Trees in the winter
Winter greens will never die
Beautiful always!

Jordan White, Grade 4
Mayfield Jr School of the Holy Child Jesus

Sakura
Pink, pretty
Smelling, growing, blooming
Pretty flower, pink petals, sweet color
Standing, picking, flying
Sweet, happy, peaceful
Cherry blossom
Christine Lam, Grade 5
Eastwood Elementary School

The Sound
I am sound
The birds singing
Like petals of joy.

I am sound
The water rippling
Like a universe of solace.

I am sound
The hawks flying
Like branches of strength.

I am sound
The sound,
The majestic sound of nature.
Jenna Brandt, Grade 4
The Mirman School

Cloud
I wish I were a wonderful cloud,
Small and soft,
Flying like a fairy,
Floating like a sailboat,
Flowing through the sky.
Kimberly Osorio, Grade 5
Lake Forest Elementary School

Blizzard
I wish I were a blowing blizzard,
Freezing and frosty,
Swirling snowflakes around,
Blinding people like fog,
Covering everything in snow.
Joshua Huezo, Grade 5
Lake Forest Elementary School

Fear
Behind the mask I am.
I hide myself when I fear.
I fear snakes, spiders, and bears.
But that is perfectly fine because
I am not perfect and neither I
Nor anyone ever will be.
Natalie Sanchez, Grade 4
Garden Grove Elementary School

Sun After Rain
The sky is blue
With fluffy white clouds
It was raining
Yesterday
And all night long
But now it's
Sunny

Everything
Was washed
Even the sky
Was washed
All the colors
Are especially bright and beautiful

The sky is blue
The clouds seem to have
Crisp edges, they seem solid
But fluffy, soft
Against the clean blue
Sky.
Natalie Boyer, Grade 6
Montessori Family School

O Captain, My Captain*
You're awkward.
You're experienced.
You have long hair and glasses.
You drink hot coffee.
You drink iced coffee.
YOU LOVE COFFEE.

You teach us.
You tell stories.
You're anxious.
You're soothed by your own voice.
You're helpful.
You like a clean deck.
You have plates in your head that rattle.
You punish.
You yell.
You command.
But most of all you get
us through the night
safe and sound.
Robbie Lowe, Grade 5
Carlthorp School
**Inspired by Walt Whitman*

The Perfect Raindrop
The raindrop comes down
Not too fast, but not too slow
It comes down just right.
Austin Rego, Grade 5
Joseph M Simas Elementary School

Something Told the Lioness
Something told the lioness
It is time to return
Though she didn't hear it
Something whispered "turn"

Something like the sun
Red and orange it was
Covering the fields
Running toward her cubs

As fast as the wind
The mother raced
Her mind panicking
Thinking of her defenseless cubs

Something told her "stop"
It is time to be calm
No fire had reached them
And safe they were
Rayyan Aburajab, Grade 6
Islamic School of San Diego

Guitars Are So Cool
Guitars are so cool
They make nice deep sounds
This is why guitars rule
It takes a lot of practice
It's a little like school
I like that guitars make music
When you strum the strings
Guitars aren't like most things
Edward Chavarria, Grade 5
St Louis De Montfort School

Track
The sport.
See it.
Orange whizzing by
In a blur at your feet.
Flashes of cream-colored paint
Recede as you pass.
Time and time again
Around the track.
A shadow.
Someone catching up.
Your legs pump harder.
The shadow backs away.
A lap to go.
The finish.
The vision of rubber against face.
Track.
The sport.
See it.
Eric Foster, Grade 5
Duveneck Elementary School

Poor, Little Snail

I am only a little snail
    Who sees some grass across the trail
To get there quickly is a feat
    To get some tasty grass to eat

I may be a little, lonely snail
But I am hungry for the grass
    So I look upon this winding trail
To find an easier, shorter pass

Wait! I see a giant being
    These monsters can crush you, it is said
No! Crush! Splat!
    Oh great, I'm dead

Taylor Kong, Grade 6
James B Davidson Middle School

Cookies

I love cookies they're my favorite snack
I love them so much they're always what I pack

In my room there is a stash
My mom tells me throw them in the trash

I eat them in the morning I eat them at night
But when it comes to the last one there's going to be a fight

Kayla Daou, Grade 5
Theodore Roosevelt Elementary School

Dream, Dream Away

I wish I could be a bird —
a peaceful, little white pigeon.
I would fly over all regions.
I'd inspire hope to people in vain.
I'd bring joy to people in pain.
People see me, there's no more war!

I wish I could be a star,
a shining, bright shooting star.
I'd pierce the darkest souls
to rescue them from deep, devil holes.
All dreams would come true
every time I'm dashing through.
People see me, their minds recharge their power!

I wish I could be a flower —
a sweet, fragrant velvet rose,
a symbol of beauty and loyal love.
My thorns remind me I'm strong.
I'll keep fixing what I do wrong.

People's lives don't last that long.
So why would I stop dreaming?
I wish I could be…

Cameron Trando, Grade 4
Dingeman Elementary School

Bugs

Bugs, bugs they're everywhere
Some on the ground and some in your hair
Bugs, bugs they're quality is high
Some up, some down, some in the sky
From the caterpillar eating leaves off the tree
Who is constantly dreaming that someday he will be
A butterfly soaring high and free
Doing airborne stunts limitlessly
From the centipede and his thirty-odd legs
To the average fly that carries her eggs
From the red and black one they call the ladybug
To the spiders, bees, and wasps who you don't want to hug
(Except the mosquito and the bunches of blood he can chug)
Oh, I wish I could be a bug!

James Hatch, Grade 5
Mayfield Jr School of the Holy Child Jesus

The Elements

Wind, Fire, Earth, Water
Are what is needed to survive,
Now and again creating chaos
Yet typically keeping serenity.

Fire licks the air, gasping for breath,
For to survive, it must consume
The heaven's air to stay alive,
Just as you and me.

The wind is majestic like a proud stag,
Using its speed to travel in the blink of an eye.
Yet, its story is no more than an enigma
To you and me.

Water has the power to be a mere mist,
Yet without notice a Tsunami strikes.
Its personality is a mystery never to be revealed
To you and me.

The earth is home to you and me,
As well as everything which surrounds us.
The elements work in harmony,
Trying hard to keep tranquility.

Zareb Razvi, Grade 6
Dorris-Eaton School

The Blade of Grass

Spikey, jagged, light
As a feather
Swaying in the
Fields they sense
Kids stepping on
Them and having
A blast

Mac Carey, Grade 5
Mayfield Jr School of the Holy Child Jesus

Dance

As you move side to side
With every step and glide,
You're acting very bold,
But it is just the way
The story is being told.

With a blink of an eye,
Or a look at the sky,
Maybe just a small glance,
But all across the world
You see many types of dance.

For a dance can be shared,
Whether it's here or there.
When you would like to dance,
You add musical notes,
Then dancers begin to prance.

With your face and your arms,
You give off a charm.
With your legs and your feet,
All will come together,
And you will dance to the beat.

Marissa Madan, Grade 6
Parkmont Elementary School

Destroying Star Destroyer

I'm sorry I broke your
Giant Star Destroyer
I was jumping on the bed
Until I landed
On your magnificent creation
I gave my best effort to miss
But it just wouldn't do
I hope you can finish it again
With some of my help

Kieran Cabezas, Grade 4
Montessori Family School

Sun/Moon

Sun
fiery, bright
shining, burning, warming
sky, rays, night, dark
lighting, twinkling, dazzling
cold, white
Moon

Sabine Rizvi, Grade 4
Heather Elementary School

Rain

Falls like gloomy tears,
dampens my day, all is fine,
a rainbow appears.

Isaiah Guerrero, Grade 6
St Charles Catholic School

The Road I Travel

The road I travel is dusty and dry as skeleton trees lurk nearby
But still I ride and still I roam in hope of finally getting home.

My horse keeps trotting, my breath still short and soon I see the old sea port
The soil is now mud, my horse starts to slow the moon reminds me that I'm not alone

The road I travel is murky and wet the light of the sun still not up yet
But still I ride and still I roam in hopes of finally getting home

Beyond the dock are the farming fields full of wheat and ripe corn ears
The rain begins, plummeting down I continue on without a sound

The road I travel is rather frightening with beads of rain and bolts of lightning
But still I ride and still I roam in hopes of finally getting home

Around the corner, through the gate a frightened, lonely family waits
The rain still falls, the moon still shines I've left that long and lonely path behind

The road I travel is soft and warm where nothing is broken and nothing is torn
I have ceased to ride and ceased to roam because I have finally made it home.

Rachel Brownell, Grade 6
Bernice Ayer Middle School

The River's Coming

Oh town, you live by a volatile river,
Soon the flow, if not stanched,
Will consume your crops and livestock.

Valiant you are but no foe is there to be stopped,
You're vulnerable in the face of this rush.

You have stature yet the river is robust. It is strong, you are not,
But, you will stay as the river consumes your people.

Withstanding the river is no simple task,

I would make a blockade stopping the river's course,
Yet a wall takes time and of that you have none.

I suggest your people run!

Lena Foellmer, Grade 5
The Mirman School

Pink

Pink is the color of a new-blossomed flower.
Pink feels like a soft comfortable pinkish pillow.
Pink smells like a sweet bubble gum scent.
Pink looks like a new dazzling sparkling dress.
Pink tastes like yummy fluffy cotton candy.
Pink sounds like a brand new car cruisin' down the street.
Pink looks like a newly sharpened pencil on the first day of school.
Pink is the sound of a tiny fairy's shoes clicking together.
Pink is the color of a squishy starfish in the clear blue sea.
And pink tastes like pink sprinkles on a frosty ice cream sundae on a sunny day.

Talisa Castro, Grade 4
Heather Elementary School

Drimventor

If I was the greatest inventor,
I wouldn't need a mentor,
I would create a machine that could make animals talk,
Really not like parrots who just mock,
I could make a machine that could help with the farm,
And a battery powered car that would do no pollution harm,
Maybe a cat feeder that fed cats gar,
Or a CD that taught me guitar,
I'd make a better metal detector,
But from digging up the yard, from my mom I'd get a lecture,
Maybe a dino bone finder that I could do lots with,
But I can't and I'm not, that's only a myth

Julia Brock, Grade 4
Anderson Valley Elementary School

If

If I were a bird,
I'd be a dove, white as the moon,
I'd soar high over the silent clouds,
And rest on the highest, greenest tree in sight.

If I were a time, I'd be morning, when the sun is up
And the sky is bright,
I'd listen to the songs of the birds,
And feel the heat of the big, glowing sun.

If I were a foot, I'd be a bare one,
I'd feel the squishy brown mud as I ran outside on a rainy day,
And I'd feel the cool air between my outstretched toes
On a nice, breezy afternoon.

If I were a plant, I'd be a tree, calm and still,
I'd be a home to many fuzzy
And feathered critters,
And would never do any harm.

If I were anything, I'd be music,
I'd bounce through the air, and sing my song,
Becoming louder and softer,
Faster and slower, never having a care.

June Hasty, Grade 5
Aviara Oaks Elementary School

My Cat

Merlin what were you thinking of
when I pet your soft black fur
I sit next to you scratching your chin
Merlin I wonder of you
I wonder what you are doing Merlin
I will see you Merlin but I don't think I will see you soon
Merlin I remember when you would sleep on the end of my bed
I remember when you would jump off trees
Merlin I miss you so

Francesca Mujic, Grade 4
Coeur d'Alene Avenue Elementary School

Branches

Branches come winding down
    And they go their own ways.
Big, small, all different sizes and shapes
    Up and down they grow.
Some look like little trees made out of bigger trees
    Some are bushes made out of branches.

Beatrice Williams, Grade 4
Charles Armstrong School

Summer

Oh summer, why can't you get here?
I'm ready to have some fun.
Also splash, and play in the sun.
I can't wait the whole year.
I won't fear!

Mikey Kelly, Grade 4
Mayfield Jr School of the Holy Child Jesus

It Breaks Comfort

waving candle
shining
shivering
you sing jagged warmth

despite weariness
you resist lonely darkness
causing sleeping people reassuring comfort

softly and delicately
you allow darkness
another chance
as coldness breaks in
and warmth turns into hurt

fighting darkness
you die

it breaks my comfort beside you
although your soul whispers

Megan Phelps, Grade 4
Hawthorne Elementary School

My Dream World

I dream of a world
Where people live in peace among animals and mystic people.
I dream of a world
Where there is no terrorizing and no dark war
And people do not kill other people.
I dream of a world
Where people ride in hovercrafts
And where people are loyal to their leaders
I dream of a world
Where people can love whomever they want to love
And have PEACE!!!

Hank Gaylord, Grade 4
The Mirman School

Sun
The sun is so hot
It gives light for the day
Enjoying morning
Mario Gonzalez, Grade 6
St Charles Catholic School

Water Lily
Water drips off of the crisp leaves,
So delicate, it glistens in broad daylight.

So lonely and calm,
It sits in perfect silence.

Still and serene,
From dawn to dusk.
Maddie Thomas, Grade 6
Grant Elementary School

Winter Night
Stillness
Of the cold night.
People sledding down slopes.
Sipping hot chocolate under the
Bright bright moon.
Sarah Euyoque, Grade 4
Marian Bergeson Elementary School

The City with Magical Hopes
My city
always has magical hopes,
caring whispers,
yells of truth.
The powerful rain
shouts sorrow in tears
truth in rivers
cries in the big salty ocean.
My city
has tourists running,
cameras blinking,
cars honking
loud crazy city laughters.
Maggie Cornwall, Grade 4
Dingeman Elementary School

Ice Cream
Great for a hot summer day
I just don't like to pay
Ice cream is the best
All for me and none for the rest
Ice cream is cold
Almost all of them are sold
I like eating ice cream
It feels like a dream
Derek Nguyen, Grade 5
Eastwood Elementary School

How to Shoot a Red Rider
First you point down range,
Then you load ten BBs,
In the stock and cock.

Next you aim and squeeze,
Remember not to breathe,
For if you do,
It will reduce,
Your accuracy and aim.

Follow these rules,
And you will get,
A bull's eye every time.
Jacob Marsh, Grade 5
St Pancratius Elementary School

Leaves
Leaves fall from tall trees.
They're from all over the world.
They are orange, red, or green.
They appear in parks and sidewalks.
In Fall they crackle and leave.
Miguel Reyes, Grade 5
Gustine Elementary School

Clownfish
Bright orange and white stripes
Swimming through the deep ocean
Always is salty
Alexandra Silva, Grade 4
Charles Armstrong School

Winter Path
Walking through the winter path
See snow falling
Hear kids laughing
Feel the cold
Touch the glass
Taste the water
Walking through the winter path
See the snowman
Hear the hiss
Feel the bliss
Touch the ice
Taste the bitterness
Walking through the winter path
See the trees white
Hear the kids fight
Feel the shiver
Touch the lake
Taste the snowflake
That's all I can say
On my beautiful day
Dhouha Abbas, Grade 6
Barstow Intermediate School

Night
Night swiftly calls
As leaves fall against the ground
To all the children
Sleeping soft and sound
Alexandra Freels, Grade 4
Placer Elementary School

Fall
Leaves falling from trees,
Full of color; red, orange,
Soon they shall be raked
Season will only come once a year
It is always a great time.
Justin Wellington, Grade 4
Stone Ranch Elementary School

Spring Is Here
Here is spring,
The flowers are blooming,
Like the wind that is zooming.
Birds chirping in the sky,
When they are very up high.
God made creation,
Against people's competition.
The blue sky with clouds,
Spring is so beautiful
Especially when you are not a handful.
Spring is the best!!!
Jacob Zavala, Grade 5
St Linus School

The Bunny
It's the bunny
Listen! Listen!
do you hear something nibbling
something that goes
munch
crunch
lunch
munch
crunch
lunch
do you hear?
It's it's it's it's
Bunny!
Bunny!
sloshing in the grass
with it's bushy tail
it's face snowy white!!!
and then I heard crunch!
he ha he ha
it's the
Bunny
Yovanni Flores, Grade 5
Sundale Elementary School

High Merit Poems – Grades 4, 5 and 6

My Mom
My mom is my best buddy
She is strong, concerned, and cheerful
She is confident, loud, and funny
Busy, bold, and calm
That person is my mom
An awesome person
That's who she is
Strong and brave
Day and night
My mom is always by my side
My mom is the person who gives me freedom
She is huggable
She is lovable
Overprotective, gentle, and timid
She is with me every minute
Neat, cautious, and caring
She's a person who is very daring
Fair, helpful, and clever
She will be with me forever
My mom is my best buddy

Blanca Sandoval, Grade 6
Century Community Charter School

The Kingdom of Rest
The fish, they like to swim in the sky
And the flowers, they think they can fly
The sun thinks that it is blue
And the clouds think they can change colors too
Everyone lives in the sea
But of course not me
All the animals think they can dance
And horses don't even know how to prance
Lions don't ever roar
And my dog thinks she can soar
All the plants come alive at night
And there's no such thing as light
TVs and computers were never made
And there was never a thing called an arcade
This crazy topsy turvy world of a mess
Is a place I like to call The Kingdom of Rest

Hailey Newton, Grade 5
Magnolia Elementary School

Mom*
I love her she loves me,
But I just need to obey her,
But I need to learn to listen,
She is like a butterfly going across a garden,
And a flower that just keeps growing,
But I should not do anything to her,
And I should grow up a little…
So I can make her pleased
And she will go to Heaven with me.

Samuel Barcelona, Grade 5
Theodore Roosevelt Elementary School
*Dedicated to Mom

Hail Stone
I wish I were an icy hail stone,
Rising and falling,
Bouncing like a falling ball,
Sliding like a penguin moving to the water,
To melt away when the sun shines out.

Lilly Orellana, Grade 5
Lake Forest Elementary School

Dawn
I wake up in the morning to see,
A blanket of dew drops on the lawn.
The dripping sun shimmers down on me,
Thus I see the break of dawn.

Birds are chirping in the meadows,
Making their nests in old willows.
The world looks as delicate as a fawn,
And thus I see the break of dawn.

Prathima Akella, Grade 6
Challenger School – Ardenwood

Big Brothers
Ten big brothers were having a good time
One went to the market and then there were nine.
Nine big brothers were eating a cake.
One got too fat and then there were eight.
Eight big brothers were in heaven
One fell down and then there were seven.
Seven big brothers were so sick
One died coughing and then there were six.
Six big brothers went to sky dive,
One forgot his parachute and then there were five.
Five big brothers were on the dance floor
One broke its leg and then there were four.
Four big brothers went to replace a knee
One was poor and then there was three
Three big brothers like Mr. Magoo
One laughed his heart out and then there were two.
Two big brothers went numb
One didn't wake up and then there was one.
One big brother went for a run
He ran too far and then there were none.

Theran Washington, Grade 5
Kentwood Elementary School

Dangerous Weather
Disasters tornado sucking up cars, animals,
Terrible lightning striking at trees,
Freezing snow burying houses,
Darkening clouds turning gray,
Leaking rain plotting itself to the ground,
Loud thunder pounding repeatedly,
Dropping hailstones hitting people.

Brandon Rahmanian, Grade 5
Highland Oaks Elementary School

God Loves You

It's raining outside,
And you're at home,
You're going to cry,
You're all alone.

You go on your knees,
And say a prayer,
You ask God, please,
"Are you there?"

God answers "Hello."
"Here I am,"
I answer below,
"May I stand?"

God says with love
Be kind to others
Don't push or shove
Your sisters or brothers.

God says we are all the same,
He knows that it is true
Whenever you feel ashamed,
Remember, God loves you.

Beverly Fontaine, Grade 5
St Joseph Parish School

A Boy Named Matt

There once was a boy named Matt
He was really good at bat
He hit a home run
Had a lot of fun
That was the end of that

Matthew Saad, Grade 6
St Anne School

The Water Cycle

The gentle rapids go down the hill
D
  O
    W
      N to the waterfall
D
  O
    W
      N goes the waterfall
It flows into a lake
The lake flows to the river
The river flows into the ocean
Then the water evaporates into the sky
The water forms a BIG grey cloud
Then it rains and rains and rains
It falls back to the hill where it started
And starts the journey all over again.

Nathan Wiggins, Grade 6
Francis Parker School

The Forest

The forest is a very old woman whose leaves are dark green,
Along with her ancient trees who are calm and not lean.
On her head she has a rushing river as her long, flowing, hair.
While on her face are many growing plants kept in good care.
And on her body is more plentiful trees and green grass,
While on her hands and arms there are flowers of all kinds in a huge mass.
Resting, playing, and grazing on her legs are many different forest creatures,
And owls rest on her toes looking like wise, old, teachers.
While finally on the tip of her toes is blooming white, frosty, snow;
This waits until winter to float up her body and layer the forest high and low.

The forest is a very old woman whose leaves are dark green,
Along with her ancient trees who are calm and not lean.

Olivia Fidler, Grade 6
Francis Parker School

The Deserted Road

I walk and walk through the thin arid desert
thinking of my dog that died
I cry and cry with an eagle eye
that watches everything nearby
I see him "Lone Wolf"
walking on all paws beckoning me to come
I find myself upon a road so extensive and a road so vacant
Lone Wolf calls beckoning to me to come on the one less traveled
I follow him and find myself and my life
changed forever

Matthew Arias, Grade 5
Coeur d'Alene Avenue Elementary School

I Am From

I am from a home
Where stained glass windows make the corner glow with beautiful colors,
Where the dining room walls are wrapped in grass cloth wallpaper.

I am from a backyard
With a 15 year old swing set that fills the grass,
With a pool to jump in to cool off in the summer,
With a magnolia tree that is perfect for climbing.

I am from a neighborhood
Where the old bad cat roams the street,
Where we walk to the corner store to get Ice-cream and a slice of pizza.

I am from a family
That has so many nick names such as Aunt Snail and Uncle Buck.

I am from a kitchen
Where Swedish Pancakes are the weekend breakfasts,
Where we have Eggs Benedict on Christmas morning.

I am from many memories
Where there is a dent in the door from my cousins,
Where we measure ourselves from the age of one until we leave the house.

Abby Anderson, Grade 5
Notre Dame School

High Merit Poems – Grades 4, 5 and 6

Me
There once was a leprechaun named, me
He had a glass of tea
Five minutes later
He turned into a gator
And played football on the WII

Joey Lemos, Grade 4
Charles Armstrong School

My Paradise
As I sprinted through the soft textured sand,
I glanced at the glistening sea.
Waves peacefully swooped to the moist sand
And "swooped" the sea's colored shells.
Chippering seagulls gracefully soared through the horizon
as it sank down.
Palm trees swayed back and forth.
Jumping, splashing, and squeaking, gray slippery dolphins
jumped in the moist air.
As I turned my back to the breezy ocean, I could not help but
to wonder how this nature came to be.

Danielle Klein, Grade 5
Wagon Wheel Elementary School

Kauai
Summer breeze floating through my hair;
The smell of fresh coconut playing through the air;
I'm running so fast no one can catch me;
If someone sees my face they will know I'm in glee;
A beautiful place with no worries at all;
I try to surf and sometimes fall;
A crazy rock did not scare me;
I took a big breath and jumped in the sea;
I sleep so well it really is not hard;
When you're living the life on a Kauiaan postcard.

Hannah Richardson, Grade 5
St Joseph Parish School

Loneliness
Loneliness is like a thunderstorm
with bright lightning crashing out of the sky.

Loneliness is not cheerful but depressing
as if you were lost in the woods.

Loneliness is like a gloomy, foggy, misty day.

Loneliness is a feeling you get
when no one is around to play.

Loneliness is when you are sick
and nobody is there to take care of you.

Loneliness is a lazy color gray, or black night.

Emma Barnes, Grade 5
Wagon Wheel Elementary School

Rain
Drip Drop, Drip Drop
The rain is beginning to fall
I run inside
So I won't be wet
The rain is coming from up above
But I think it's God's tears
I question God, "Why are you crying?"
He answers with anger
By making thunder and lightning
Rain falls harder and washes everything away
Then a rainbow comes out, and the sun is shining
I thank God for stopping the rain
A beautiful, fresh, new day has begun
With angels watching over me

Kimberly Cheng, Grade 5
Mayfield Jr School of the Holy Child Jesus

Penguins
Swimming fast through the sea
getting interested in whatever they see
they waddle with delight
over the ice of white

And they have fun playing
with their chicks who are saying
I'm hungry please get me food
the mother will fish even when not in the mood

They fish all day
sometimes when astray
they waddle around
on the snow white ground

They slide on the ice
and look really nice
so please say
they are the best today

Nico Sloop, Grade 4
Sonoma Charter School

Christmas Dinner
On Christmas day we eat and play,
We sit at the table and prepare our tongues,
The greens sit on the side steaming with smells,
And fresh muffins baked from scratch,
With every dish sitting so fine,

Soup from Grandma's,
And fresh boiled eggs from the chicken coop,
With every dish sitting so fine,

Through the night we drink mint tea,
And Russian tea cookies shining with glee,
With every dish sitting so fine.

Layla Chamberlin, Grade 5
Kentwood Elementary School

The Secrets of Green

I know green.

Green smells fresh, like the smell of washed, nutritious vegetables,
the tart fragrance of tiny green apples
and the newly grown grass in my small backyard.

Green feels like the slimy skin of a baby frog that lured me into falling in the cool pond.
It's smooth like the solid wax of my finger-sized crayons
and spiky to protect the beauty of a vain, lovely rose.

Green looks like the sparkling shine of valuable emeralds
and the graceful movements of the elodea in my empty aquarium.
And I also see green as the slit lily pads that carry beautiful pink lilies like a small raft.

Green sounds like the irritating squeaky noise that my inky expo marker makes.
I can hear green when my rectangular pencil box opens to reveal many things.
And green sounds like the rustling leaves of a pleasant spring morning.

Green tastes like the mint gum my dad buys me at the Korean supermarket.
Green is sour and bitter when I take a bite off my unripe banana.
I can also taste green when I take a small pinch of wasabi at the Japanese sushi restaurant.

I really know green.

Jennifer Bahn, Grade 5
Dingeman Elementary School

Love Is…

Love is when someone wears fluffy dresses with red roses all over. She waits for you perfectly. She has long blond curly locks with roses also too. She has little glass slippers that go click click click. Her hands are as soft as feathers on a yellow newborn chick. Her face is full of beauty; everyone falls in love just by looking at her. Love is when you get goose bumps all over your body. She dances oh so elegantly; nobody can dance as wonderful as her. She has a big smile that shows her happy feelings and the people around her smile back at her. She walks down the royal carpet with a little girl throwing flower petals in front of her. Love is the feeling you get when you care very much about someone. Love is a very special feeling. Love is a hard choice. Take your time. Choose what you really want. Be wise. Good luck!!!

Maya Hanaoka, Grade 5
Wagon Wheel Elementary School

Football

I love to play football
As I run down the field, the scent of sweaty armpits smelling like garlic onions
Clogs my nostrils and limits my smelling
I see helmets ramming each other like mountain goats claiming their territory
I hear "blue 42 down set hike"
I touch the football, as I jump for the catch
I taste and kiss the ground as I flop with a big thunder scoring a touchdown
Despite the scent of sweaty armpits smelling like garlic onions filling the whole field, I love to play football.

Anthony Reyes, Grade 6
Joseph M Simas Elementary School

Goodnight Daffodils

I often lay on a bed of daffodils slowly swaying in the breeze over valleys; imagining dances by the waves and trees. When I'm sleeping, I draw these daffodils and waves. The sunset comes up and says, "Goodnight little daffodils, waves, and humans. May we meet tomorrow." Soon the moon comes and says, "Goodnight and may we meet again." I slowly drift off as I think what a great world this is as I imagine again what happens around this wonderful world.

Noah Lev Schoolsky, Grade 4
Coeur d'Alene Avenue Elementary School

High Merit Poems – Grades 4, 5 and 6

I Am
I am intelligent and athletic.
I wonder about my life in the future.
I hear a soccer ball hit the back of the net.
I see David Beckham.
I want to be a professional soccer player.
I am intelligent and athletic.

I pretend I am a professional player.
I feel a hand pat my shoulder.
I touch a signed soccer ball.
I worry about where my future will take me.
I cry when I'm sad.
I am intelligent and athletic.

I understand the basics of soccer.
I say children are our future.
I dream about being a professional.
I try my best to make All-Stars.
I hope my future will be what I dream for every day.
I am intelligent and athletic.
Aryana Mahoney, Grade 6
Barstow Intermediate School

Speed
I run around the track all day
I am as fast as a gazelle
All the fans say I'm swell
Look out because I'm coming your way
Trejon Shelton, Grade 4
Mayfield Jr School of the Holy Child Jesus

The Garden
Like a warm, bright day.
Like playing with my dog.
Like reading a good book.
Like standing under a shady tree.
Like listening to my old grandma tell stories.
Like a hot, sunny day in my garden.
Ariana Tovar, Grade 5
Gustine Elementary School

Fever 1793
People blustering about the virus that kills many,
about the one that steals several souls.
Families fleeing headstrong from the homes they inhabited
Neighbors showing fidelity to their loved ones,
dead or alive.
People on the streets remorsing at the sight of their infants,
eerie and yellow eyes like mother's bitter lemon pie.
Everyone's stomachs ravenous eating the youth from inside.
Will this duration end!
Then when everyone just lost hope,
snow comes and defeats the awful disease…
Once and for all.
Stephanie Peyton Wallace, Grade 6
St Andrew's Episcopal School

The Moon Is
The scale on a mermaid's tail
A pearl with the universe for its oyster
A lotus in a pond of stars
An orb of silver and white
A feather from an angel's wing
A snowflake that never reaches the ground
An ornament on a tar black tree
A mirror in a dark room
Katherine Dhuey, Grade 5
Montessori Family School

Friends
Friends never break apart
Friends always have a true heart
Friends get into fights
But friends might come together
Just might
Friends always come through ups and downs
But then they turn around to see
The bright side of friends
Just because
Friends never break apart
Friends always have a true heart
Friends get into fights
But friends might come together
Just might
Friends always come through ups and downs
But then they turn around
To see the bright side
Of wonderful, grateful friends
Isabel Torres, Grade 4
Stone Ranch Elementary School

What Should I Put in a Box Marked "Summer?"
Ice cream, popsicles, sweets galore
Hamburgers, hot dogs, and so much more
Lemonade and smoothies are a refreshing treat
But watermelon and strawberries are still good to eat

Playing ping pong in the sun
And jumping off the diving board is very fun
Oh how I love beach volleyball
Or chilling at the mall

I ride the swan boats
While I sip ice cream floats
I go to the Red Sox game
But the Boston Garden is anything but lame

Bursts of color rapidly fly into the sky
Dads barbecue, while kids chase the fireflies
Oh I love 4th of July
But the summer just whizzes by
Ellie Chen, Grade 5
Duveneck Elementary School

Otter
Otters black and silver
Swimming on their backs
Noisy
Playful
Long and flat
They're round
With small eyes
In the sea most of the time
Living in the sea
And swimming on their backs.
Their fur so soft and smooth.
Kennedy Delgadillo, Grade 6
St Alphonsus School

The Dog and the Lark at the Park
Once I went to the park,
and my dog started to bark.
I pulled him aside,
and then asked him why
he felt the need to bark at a lark.
Alissa Poston, Grade 6
Aliso Elementary School

Fever Talk
I say no "hello"
and give no time for "goodbyes"
I come to many people
those people I surprise
At first I strike at leisure
but I prefer a deadly pace
When I come to visit,
pain contorts the face
I do not knock before I enter
instead I run right through
I am Yellow Fever,
and I've come to get you, too
Shannon Foody, Grade 6
St. Andrew's Episcopal School

Shining Night
The sky is as shiny as glitter
I lay on the grass
Trying to count them
As they flash on and off
Upon the bright blue sky
I fall asleep.
Nelli Petrovskaya, Grade 4
Sierra Oaks K-8 School

Danger
In the darkened sky
Danger is everywhere
Blinding lights flashing
Emily O'Neill, Grade 6
St Anne School

Dream Land
There is a lake of gold,
there are fish walking too.
There are a trillion people,
and there are cardinals made of blue.
There is no homework,
and the paper is edible.
They have tigers as pets,
and the food is incredible.
They are so very nice
they have cats on their wrists.
But I am so sorry,
none of this exists!
Seth Giambastiani, Grade 5
Theodore Roosevelt Elementary School

My Mom
My mom is so nice
She is there when I'm sick
She drives me to school
She gets me clothes
She is my mom
Matthew Krisik, Grade 5
Theodore Roosevelt Elementary School

Love
Roses are red
Violets are blue
I want to find a love
So do you.
Chang Yang, Grade 4
Clayton B Wire Elementary School

My Sweet Mommy
Mommy is always there
To cheer me up
Always kind
She looks fine
Helpful
A hard worker
Supports me
Nice and sweet
Like cupcakes
Helps others
Talks
Is always joyful
Keeps me comfortable
A trustful person
Cool and awesome
Is giving
Funny
Super mom
I love my mommy
Do you?
Leida Rojas, Grade 6
Century Community Charter School

Rainbow
I wish I were a colorful rainbow,
Reflecting and radiant,
Sparkling and shining like a pot of gold,
Arching like a bridge across the sky,
Silently fading away.
Julia Gionet-Gonzales, Grade 5
Lake Forest Elementary School

The Clock
It's the clock
listen, listen
do you hear?
it's telling you
your time is near
your time is near
tick tock
tick tock
tick tock
don't you hear
it's it's
it's it's
clock
clock
the face is white
and black its hands
are going back
the ticking all around
the Grim Reeper is abound
tick tock tick tock
CLOCK.
Joshua Kelly, Grade 5
Sundale Elementary School

The Tea Fire
The night was dark
and the wind did blow.
I looked outside
to see a red orange glow.

Burning hot fire
danced in the sky.
On the hills to the east
the flames rose high.

My cousins had to leave
their home and come to ours,
down streets of ash and smoke,
so thick it hid the stars.

Through the long night
the brave firemen fought.
They put out the angry fire,
they gave it all they got.
Isaac C. Kershner, Grade 4
Montessori Center School

Red

When I was red, I was pained, hated, unloved, so mad
So upset, so used up, so let down
So torn apart, as if nobody was around to help me
But I'm not the only one
Refusing to back down
So when I fall, I'll get back up
And love once again
My heart is still broken
My dreams have vanished
But I will dream new dreams
And sew my heart back up
And love once again
When I am red I love, but I am hated
But that's ok
Because I refuse to give up
And if I fall down
I will get up
My heart may be broken
My dreams may have vanished
But I will still love again

Adam Wright, Grade 6
Francis Parker School

Powder, My Dog

What do you think about
when I hug you
before I leave?
Feeling your warm soft fur
like the sun warming you up
did you like it?
Walks and swimming are your favorite things
playing with a tennis ball
where the tomatoes grow
you chased the scorpions
the way I love you

Leila Alamango Shapiro, Grade 4
Coeur d'Alene Avenue Elementary School

I Am From…

I am from listening to my dad Oscar and my mom
Eloina telling me to do my chores.
I am from taking care of my sisters Hannah and Maddy.
I am from celebrating Cinco de Mayo and dressing in
traditional Mexican clothes
I am from celebrating birthdays and Christmas and
getting presents.
I am from celebrating football games and talking
about the game with friends.
I am from eating my mom's enchiladas, burritos, and
sushi and getting full.
I am from going to places like Mexico, Acapulco,
Los Angeles, Arizona and having fun with my family.
I am Oscar Vargas Jr.

Oscar Vargas Jr., Grade 5
Duveneck Elementary School

Fever

I put people through grief and misery.
I am invisible.
I am no one's friend.
I am a blight that is very horrible and deathly to many people.
I devastate and setback many people's lives.
I cause fatalities and hardships.
I awaken people in the night, watching them
cough, moan, and writhe.
I make people unhappy forever.
I can find you as fast as a predator spots an enemy.
I can destroy many people as fast as
a forest fire destroys trees and plants.
I have the stamina to keep people famished, sick,
and ravenous for a long time.
I am like an assailant, trying to besiege an innocent person.
I listen to people as they despise my name.
I can only go away when the frost comes.
It is impossible to find me,
but I can find you.
I am Fever.

Kristina Fong, Grade 6
St. Andrew's Episcopal School

If I Were in Charge…

If I were in charge of my house
I would be able to eat anything I want at any time,
I would make sure my dad did all my chores for me.

If I were in charge at school
I would say no math for over an hour,
Everyone does three hours of reading each day,
And art every day

If I were in charge of the world
I would have a house the size of a state,
Make sure everyone has their basic necessities,
Allow kids to drive at the age of twelve.

Xavia Andrews, Grade 5
Duveneck Elementary School

Nature

I like the wind that flows like the water,
On a clear sunny day.
I like the leaves,
Small and light.
The rain is fair,
Cleansing the land,
All for free.
Most flowers are full
Of many bright colors.
While some are dark,
With shadowy tinge.
Nature is wonderful,
With its many surprises.

Davis Tse, Grade 5
Mayfield Jr School of the Holy Child Jesus

The Beach

The lambent sun staring at dad, and me.
Hugging us with all its heat.
Our bodies in the sea sensing water,
Like hungry animals finding food.
The sky blue sea,
Floating like oil at the top of your soup.
Our feet going through soft sand,
Miming our every move.
Sandcastles waiting to be built,
And waiting to be seen.
Washed by the ocean,
Never to be seen again.

Vivian Kong, Grade 5
Clover Avenue Elementary School

Cat

Pet
Fluffy, cute
Purring, chasing, sleeping
Most popular pet in the world
Cat

Eric Tsu, Grade 4
Daves Avenue Elementary School

Fontana

I moved away from a far away land
to a place called Fontanaland
it will be an adventure for everyone
in every land.

Joannie Snider, Grade 5
Caryn Elementary School

Gymnastics

Gymnastics is so great
Gymnastics is so fun
Gymnastics is so skillful
Gymnastics in the sun.

Gymnastics is my spirit
Gymnastics is my soul
Gymnastics is my championship
Gymnastics as we know.

Aylene Moreira, Grade 5
St Pancratius Elementary School

A Day at the Beach

I see a reflection on the waves
children playing in the
warm water and sand
I feel happy, relaxed, and calm
I feel like the warm sun
is beating on my skin
I would love to have
a day at the beach.

Mattie Motz, Grade 5
Theodore Roosevelt Elementary School

Shark Bite

It's night.
The sky is pitch black making the moon shine brighter than ever.
You're in the middle of the ocean, stranded by its waters.
The suspense is driving you crazy.
As the waves thrash you around,
You think of your last words, hoping they would just come quickly.
The water calms,
You are overjoyed even in this unfortunate event.
There is one more thing you begin to worry about.
You start thinking of your last words again.
The music that haunted your nightmares started playing in your head.
You knew that something was under you,
Waiting, hungry.
The suspense made you cry.
Screaming, you knew that your own horror movie
Would not end well like they were supposed to.
As you feel sudden pain in your leg,
You reach down and cannot find your right foot.
You could not think of your last words in time.
But you did have last thoughts.
Death. Not death, death from a shark bite.

Katelyn Kolb, Grade 6
John Muir Elementary School

My Brain Is Freaking Out!

I hear my brain screeching, "homework is torture!"
It completely breaks down when it knows that I have to do writing.
You know…it might even blow up!
Math makes my brain scramble.
I can't stand it!
My brain…is freaking out.

Nicholas Melton, Grade 5
Kentwood Elementary School

The Circus of the Sun (Cirque de Soleil)

I make my way to the front row seats, excited for the show to begin
Suddenly a man in a green body suit runs forward.
He does three nonstop flips in the air before he touches back on the ground
The excitement begins as a woman wearing a beautiful white shimmering dress sings
She sings in a whole new language, and yet it describes the mood perfectly
Then the music builds up and drums play as a trapeze artist swings on a giant swing
She leaps into the air doing flips and turns then gently touches the swing again
Then funny music begins as the clowns run onto stage
They do funny tricks, and we all laugh until our sides hurt.
Then before you know it, they have already gone
Gentle music starts when a boy comes down on a long curtain
He twists around rhythmically and then goes up again on the curtain
Then everything becomes quiet…
Suddenly loud booming music plays a man comes onto the stage
He is riding a huge black bike and doing all sorts of tricks
He turns himself around and we all stare in wonder
The finally it all ends and the trapeze artist and clowns each take turns bowing
We all smile and clap and wave
You never know what to expect at the Cirque de Soleil.

Tanuja Adigopula, Grade 6
Francis Parker School

Listen

I never like to listen
Not even one bit
If I start to listen
Then I'll throw a fit

I don't know how you do it
It takes up too much time
If you want listening skills
Then you can have mine

Alexandra Raff, Grade 4
Mayfield Jr School of the Holy Child Jesus

Sunny Day

On a sunny day
I like to get away to the beach, I play.
Laying flat on stomach then on back.
After that I like to go under a palm tree and relax.
When the sun isn't so sunny
I go home and drink some honey.

Rionna Jones, Grade 4
W D Hall Elementary School

Surfing

I love to surf it is really fun
my favorite thing to do.
I don't always stand up on the first time.
I think it is fun to fall because no matter how many
times you fall it does not hurt.
I love to feel the cool air in my hair.
I like how the board just glides through the water.
I love how it looks like it is a big wave but it is really not.
I also love how you go down on the wave.

Allie McCoy, Grade 5
St Raphael School

I Am

I am clever
I wonder what I am going to get for my birthday
I hear my heart pounding
I see the future
I want to be a star student
I am clever
I pretend to be Jack Sparrow
I feel protected
I touch my imaginary friend
I worry about when the world is going to end
I cry when my mom says something touching to me
I am clever
I understand that life isn't fair
I say I believe in God and the Holy Spirit
I dream about racing Joey
I try to be a peace builder
I hope to get a job
I am clever

Brandon Caprini, Grade 4
La Presa Elementary School

Destiny

Courage is our path to our destiny
To reach that destiny we need to restore honesty
We need to defeat our fear
In this generation
Hopes have been crushed
Through a fragile line
Our progress needs to grow
But we can do it
We can!
No matter our size or skin color
We have the right to be free
And freedom is just the beginning
Of our destiny.

Jen Levy, Grade 4
Canyon View Elementary School

My Brother

My brother is awesome.
But I barely get to see him.
If I could wish for one thing,
it would be to see my brother more often.
He works a lot, and goes to school,
and sometimes goes swimming with me in the pool.
I know he's busy,
but I still love my brother Danny.

Brianna Castillo, Grade 5
Theodore Roosevelt Elementary School

Christmas

Christmas looks like,
A whole crowd of people rushing in,
An exploding house of presents,
Kids running and playing, and parents talking,

Christmas feels like,
Joy from everyone,
Happiness from kids,
Tiredness from the boys, and love from everyone,

Christmas smells like,
Grass stains from the boys,
Grease from a Mexican buffet,
Perfume form the ladies, and cologne from the men,

Christmas tastes like,
Cheese from the quesadillas,
Chicken from the quesadillas,
Delicious cake and cookies, and my favorite punch,

Christmas sounds like,
Conversations from everyone everywhere,
Giggling from the kids,
Pouting from my dog, and ripping from opening presents.

Anne Kraus, Grade 4
Daves Avenue Elementary School

Tears

The radiant sun
emerges
from the darkness
veiled
in soft pink
gold
and caramel

Carrying a promise
of a dewy morning within which
America
may have the determination to
start
again

Morgan Hansen, Grade 6
Bethany Lutheran School

Shannon Sevor

Shannon,
Caring, loving, smart,
Relative of Domenick Sevor,
Lover of football,
Who feels joyful,
Who gives care and love,
Who fears mosquitoes,
Who would like to see Paris,
Who lives forever more,
Sevor

Domenick Sevor, Grade 4
Ladd Lane Elementary School

Snow

Snowing in the fields
Sparkling snowflakes drift gently
In the early morn

Emilia Mariolis, Grade 5
Santa Fe Springs Christian School

What I Like to Do

What I like to do,
Outside every day,
Is walk my favorite dog,
In the middle of the day.

What I like to do,
Is challenge my mom in chess,
If I always try my best,
I soon may beat the rest.

What I like to do,
Is to be in my little dome,
As I wait for the day to pass,
I say, "Home, sweet home!"

Andrew Narag, Grade 5
St Pancratius Elementary School

A Recipe

1 dash of cheerfulness,
1 drop of love.
2 pints of mysteriousness,
2 pints of smiles.
6 gallons of understanding,
7 handfuls of hugs.
1 dozen of caring,
plus a heart...
is the recipe for a friend.

Annie Ching, Grade 6
Purple Lotus International Institute

Frost

Frost freezes the air
It makes you huddle for warmth
Till its warm again

Olivia Blair, Grade 6
St Anne School

Gold

gold is the color of bright stars
in the morning sky
the sun rising
in the morning
daisies in the spring
a gold ring
shining brightly
touching the soft sand
at the beach
smell like sweet honey
gold makes me happy

Hiram Smith, Grade 4
Carlthorp School

Purple Streaks

Tadpoles swim
Fish glide
Cattails are abundant under
The glimmering moon's light
Their glossy golden scales
The water nymphs
Wade in eternal youth
With exquisite rippling waves
At their fish like waists diving deep
They flee but the wind prances with joy
With nimble pace the fairies of the deep
Come up and sing to me
But I know I must go home
When the stars shine on me
But I am sad to leave
For the water
With its baby blue face
Reflects purple streaks on me

Rachael Nunberg, Grade 5
Bethany Lutheran School

My Mom Is My Life

She is hardworking
My mom is funny and nice
You can trust her any time
She is LOVABLE
My mom is special because I love her
She respects me
And everyone else
She is happy even if she is stressed
My mom is happy
Because she is from MEXICO
She is honest
My mom is my best friend
She is kind whenever you need her
I love my mom
She is the best mom in the world
She doesn't get mad
If you get her mad
My mom is very talkative
She cheers me on when I am sad
I get very happy
She is number one

Henry Zelaya, Grade 6
Century Community Charter School

Diane Is...

Diane is...
Your best friend
Diane is...
A clever girl and
A very good dreamer
Diane is...
Loyal and careful
And always will be
Helpful

Diane is...
Daring and immature
Diane is...
Active, because she is
Skinny as a real life
Penny because of this
She is just so funny
She'll be there
Through thick and thin
Because Diane is your
Best Friend

Adriana Bragg, Grade 6
Century Community Charter School

Fishy

I see a fishy
The fishy makes me so mad
I cannot catch it

Morgan Pizaña, Grade 4
Tomales Elementary School

School

School is where you learn your ABCs
Some kids say, oh, help me please
School is where you learn to count 1, 2, 3
Sometimes it's hard to figure out
School is where you learn to write
Sometimes words look a fright
School is where you learn to play
Recess always saves the day
School is where you have phys. ed.
Getting hit in the head
School is where you have nutrition
The food is great ammunition
And
When school ends
Don't worry it begins again

Zoe Lovett, Grade 5
Jackson Elementary School

Rain

The steady, cold, spitting rain and gusty winds outside
Quick flashes of lightning and loud claps of thunder
A haze of gray storm clouds stretched across the sky
A relaxing rainy day around the warm fire with a book
Floods of water flowing into the gutter leading to the ocean
Playing in the puddles feeling a splash of icy cold water
Listening to the drip-drop of the heavy rain pelting the roof
Waking up the next day looking around at the fresh, damp earth

Ysabella Sawaya, Grade 6
Francis Parker School

A Bliss Drop

Dive into your raindrop
to make your appearance.
A raindrop is like a little glass ball
falling from the sky.
Seeing tall mountains, deep valleys,
blue oceans and lonely plains
just as if it were wearing glasses.

It's a drop of anything you make it.
While you look out of a raindrop
it's possible to glance upon little, tiny details
like an ant carrying a grain of sand
into its home,
a crack in a mountain.

A raindrop is a place
for all people to enjoy.
A raindrop is a glass ball
helping you to follow your bliss.
To be welcomed inside a raindrop
all you have to do is
dive in.

Maddie Oswald, Grade 6
Carlthorp School

Sunshine

I wish I were a dazzling sunshine,
Blinding and bright,
Glowing and gleaming,
Shining like a light ball in the sky,
Energizing the earth with its enormous power.

Sara Sadeghi, Grade 5
Lake Forest Elementary School

How to Be a Salt Water Crocodile

Never cries
Never lives on land
Able to see underwater
The babies come from eggs in nests on the ground
Lives on the hottest continent, Australia
Fights for land and mates
Can also live in the sea.

Justin Russell, Grade 6
Big Springs Elementary School

Good Friends

F riendly people to everyone
R eally nice to us
I have lots of nice ones
E veryone is nice to them
N ever will lie to them
D og friendly people
S ome people have a lot

Angelina Grego, Grade 4
Mayfield Jr School of the Holy Child Jesus

December 7th

December 7, Japan came in one swoop
A swoop that changed us forever
Planes bombing Pearl Harbor
An extraordinary explosion taking us by surprise
Yamamoto knew our weakness
Our rivals joyously heading back to Japan
This meant war

Pearl Harbor, vulnerable as a newborn
Planes, aircrafts, and ships destroyed
Grasslands blazing with fire
Pearl Harbor, shattered the people in tears
Our land, illuminated with the light of the fire
Smoke was all we could see
We had to save ourselves from another attack

Those who survived roused by anger
Anger beyond describing, resolved by action
Anger that brought us to World War II
Changing many people's views on life
Arousing vengeful impulses
Revenge was all we wanted
"A date that will live in infamy"

Jessica Wolf, Grade 5
The Mirman School

The Little Green Leaf

It hung from an autumn tree,
Far above the world to see
It was a little green leaf.

Time stole its color,
But did not make it duller,
The little yellow leaf.

Wind carried it away
And dropped astray
The little orange leaf.

As time nimbly galloped by
The forest heard the winter's cry
Frost covered the tree up high
And below it would forever lie
The little red leaf.

At last came the icy knife
That carved out the last of life
In the little brown leaf.

Saumitra Kelkar, Grade 5
Frank C Leal Elementary School

Pharaohs

Pharaohs
Smart, decisive
Commanded, attacked, ruled
Took over other empires
Kings

Gene Panferov, Grade 6
Big Springs Elementary School

Rain

Rain goes down
The opposite of up
It makes things really wet
So you better cover-up!
When you go outside,
Bring an umbrella
'Cause when you get soaked
You won't be a happy fella
If you are lucky,
It won't go all day
So that you can get out
Of the house and just play
And if you listen closely
At night when it's silent,
I'll bet you can hear
The rain on the roof
And maybe, just maybe
When you wake up next morn
The rain will be falling
Just as before

Camryn Choye, Grade 5
Central Elementary School

People You Love

I hear my family's voices with many colorful notes,
Those are the beautiful sounds that I love to hear in the mornings,
My mother saying breakfast is ready, while my father ties my shoes,
The delicious food that fills my tummy, makes for a beautiful day,
While my dogs are ready to have their morning meal,
They wait for me while wagging their tails all happy to see me,
I catch a few licks before I depart to one of my favorite spots,
Yes, my school where all my friends await my arrival,
What a wonderful morning greeted by the people you love.

Oriana Alejandre, Grade 5
Kentwood Elementary School

How to Be a Basketball Player

Never be lazy, and don't be late for practice.
Never disrespect your coach.
Always practice shooting, and dribbling.
Be ready for anything.
It is not about winning, it's about having fun and playing the game.
Always try to have fun in the game.
Practice, defense, and offense in order to win the game.
Don't be intimidated by the size of the other team.
Don't listen to the team when they tease you, they're just trying to distract you.

Mitchell Lou Mosley, Grade 6
Big Springs Elementary School

Community

I ride on my bike and I ring a bell, ring, ring, ring, ring,
Next I went to the store and the cash register went den, den, den,
After a while I went to the Staples Center and the players feet go squeak squeak.

Vytas Escalona, Grade 5
Theodore Roosevelt Elementary School

All the Little Things About Life

Life is as simple as the weather
As amazing as a circus
As sad as a tear
As upsetting as a baby crying
As creative as a painter
As unique as someone's idea
As graceful as a dove
As colorful as a parrot.
Life is full of life. Life is full of death.
Life is full of love. Life is full of change.
There are storms, ice, and fog.
There are oceans, cities, rainforests, and forests.
And there are so many small things.
People should stop and smell the flowers.
And they should go outside and play
Instead of watching TV when they have nothing to do.
Because even though there's so much going on,
You have to grab on to a little piece of life.
And when you think "I want more!" When you hate the gray skies,
You should think of the people who don't have anything.
Because life is a gift.

Sasha Kerievsky, Grade 4
Montessori Family School

High Merit Poems – Grades 4, 5 and 6

With a Listening Ear We Hear Waves Crashing at Night
This is Guadalupe
beautiful as can be,
most people think its foggy,
but the sun we always see!!!

The beach is down the road,
the dunes are just before,
watching snowy plovers
nest around the shore!!!

With so many stars the sky is really bright.
I live in this paradise, lucky for me,
see this is Guadalupe
most beautiful as can be!!!
Madeline Perry, Grade 5
St Louis De Montfort School

I Am
I am a caring boy who loves to help
I wonder how my dad takes care of me
I hear the sounds of people crying
I see people on the sidewalk asking for change
I want my dad to not have to work
I am a caring boy who loves to help

I pretend I could help everyone in the world
I feel happy when I help others
I touch the hearts of young boys and girls
I worry about how people will survive in years to come
I cry about the people who have died
I am a caring boy who loves to help

I understand how people feel when they are in need
I say, "sure I'll help"
I dream about people caring about one another
I try to change people
I hope one day everyone will have a job
I am a caring boy who loves to help
Michael Jurich, Grade 5
Lydiksen Elementary School

Unnecessary War
Screams and cries are heard everywhere.
Mothers and fathers are losing their children.
Thousands of people are losing their homes.
Bombs and shooting are going in the air.
Blood shining everywhere.
People saying "Stop, stop! Stop the shooting!"
But the people who are shooting never listen.
When the war is done, dead bodies are on the ground.
The population of orphans are beginning to grow.
Because their mothers and fathers are one of.
The dead bodies on the ground.
I think that is an unnecessary war.
Zinab Attia, Grade 5
Sierra Charter School

Fever
Do you know who I am?
My victims must be bled.
Most of which are already dead.
I follow you everywhere you go.
Until it starts to snow.
I am an eerie sight to see.
That's why you don't want to catch me.
I make your world filled with strife
Oh, what a horrible life!
You writhe with pain as I attack.
I'm this far now not goin' back.
Relish your moments while you can.
For you're going to need a good plan.
Have you figured out me yet?
I'm an enigma that you won't soon forget.
Fear me, don't be near me.
I am Fever.
Shannon Chance, Grade 6
St Andrew's Episcopal School

Books Are Full of Greatness
Books are full of greatness
They give our hearts much brightness
Each book is joy to us as we read them on the bus
You'll read some books aloud
And others you'll think about
Just don't forget your book
And quickly take a look
'Cause all books are full of brightness
Ashly Cobian, Grade 6
Fairview Elementary School

Permit Me to Tell You About Sadness
Permit me to tell you about sadness
For I have felt the sadness of losing
The sadness of getting bad grades
And I felt the sadness of doing something wrong
But the sadness I remember the most
Is when I lost a loved one
Very close to my heart
Vincent Grimaldi, Grade 6
John Muir Elementary School

Florida's Ocean
Lying on my bed, I stare at my teal blue wall,
thinking of snorkeling in the beautiful Florida ocean.
I see the schools of fish all over,
then suddenly I am swimming with dolphins,
lightning fast with outrageous strength.
Soon that is all over and I am right back in my room,
lying on my bed, with a grin on my face,
staring at Florida's seas and the dolphins
and the fish that live there.
Ana Marie Carvalho, Grade 6
John Muir Elementary School

Smoothie

S weet like the love of a person
M ushy like the big puffy clouds
O utstanding like a smart mind
O riginal taste of fruits
T reats you nicely like a human
H ealthy drink for a diet
I ncredible to drink on a Summer day
E nough Vitamin C to make you playful

Jade Luong, Grade 5
Clayton B Wire Elementary School

Shiver

One
Enormous peak
Every day waits for snow
Perching
Behind the trees
Waiting
Day after day
For flakes of ice
But one day
A cloud will rise
And the mountain
Will be attacked
By bright
Frozen
Raindrops
But the mountain
Will always
Shiver in the night

Harrison Paschal, Grade 5
Bethany Lutheran School

The Door to Nature

A slow wind blew from the south.
I hear little sounds of nature
going through my ears.
I hear chirping from baby birds
calling their mom.

I lay down
feeling little dark green sticks
tickling me
Big leaves that are all brown,
crispy,
fall into pieces when I hold them.

The sun will go down.
The stars come up.
I see the moon watching over me
I close my eyes and hear
the sweet whisper of nature
take me to sleep.

Miranda Psaila, Grade 5
Bethany Lutheran School

Focus

F ocus in a competition
O r one may lose.
C an you strive to be first place?
U seless talk is a waste of time
S o you choose.

Rebecca Karlous, Grade 4
Marian Bergeson Elementary School

God's Light

The sun comes up
It brings us
Dawn
If you wake early
Gaze upwards
Brilliant shafts of pink-orange light
Will greet you
As dawn turns to morning
Noon
Then night
The light is lost
Into a sea of shadow
But dawn with its color
Always brings morning light.

Weston Snyder, Grade 5
Bethany Lutheran School

Parrot

Parrot
Loud, color
Fly, stand, talk
Parrots are good talkers
Bird

Lisa Fang, Grade 5
Clayton B Wire Elementary School

Beautiful

The **B** is for beauty
The **E** is for elegance
The **A** is for awesome
The **U** is for unique
The **T** is for texture
The **I** is for individuality
The **F** is for fire
The **U** is for you
The **L** is for loveliness

Beauty is for big and small
It's also for the short and tall
Beauty is inside not out
Everyone should be
Beautiful
Your beauty is in your hands
Be confident

Kelsey Stevens, Grade 6
La Costa Heights Elementary School

Peace and War

War is loud, big and mean
Makes innocent people scream.
Peace is good, quiet and calm
It helps people get along.
So why can't there be no war
There would be so much to adore.
Choose peace and not war
I promise it will open new doors.

Isabella Fernandez, Grade 6
St Charles Catholic School

Loving Me, Loving You

In my eyes
I see your heart beat
In my heart
I feel your love
In my ears
I listen to your song of life
But in me
I feel so much more!
But in the days of hope
I feel it, I feel it,
I feel your *love*
Can't ya see?
Can't ya see?
Don't think,
Don't think,
Just love me,
Love, love,
Love me
Don't think
Just love *ME*
Like I love you!

Giselle Etessami, Grade 4
The Mirman School

Paragliding

Mexico
no rules for me
Flying high
soaring like a bird
So light in the sky,
like a feather in the breeze
Nerves racking up,
off the ground before I knew
Taking time to embrace
the sweet views all around
Dropping to the sea,
more fun than it would seem
Scooped onto the jet ski
holding the stranger by his shoulders
It doesn't matter —
it's all good...

Noah Slosberg, Grade 5
Clover Avenue Elementary School

Perfection

Perfection
Purity, peace, conqueror of darkness
The doorway to heaven it shines
Leading, guiding, showing the way
Ending evil, on evil it dines

Like the guardian angels at Heaven's gate
Like the beautiful birds above the never-ending sea
Like the true symbol for all that is right
Flawless beauty shines above me

It's the feather of justice
Elegant, majestic its sight
For when shadows creep in
Destroying all will be white.

Brian Perez, Grade 6
Vista Verde Middle School

Is It True…?

The moon does not know what to expect
When it first comes out
But neither does the sun
Are they afraid? Are they excited?

All the moon can think about
Is the music he knows
Not the music we know
But the music of nature
The wind whistling
The thunder roaring
The lightning as quick as a flash
The stars painting a picture in the pitch black sky
The owls whispering in conversation

The sun can't seem to think about
Anything but his music
The children playing, the grass growing
Waves barking, fires screaming
Rain trickling on the rooftop

We recognize different music than the sun and moon do
The sun and moon recognize different music that we do
But we all know our own type of music

Gabbi Paschal, Grade 6
Bethany Lutheran School

Being Hyper

Being hyper is like the color neon pink
And is also like a sugar rush
It rotates through my mind
It reminds me of the time I first learned how to play volleyball
It makes me feel jumpy like a trampoline
It makes me want to laugh

Tiffany Nolet, Grade 6
St Anne School

I Am

I get frustrated when I clean up stuff and it keeps getting messy
A peacemaker like a pearl is a characteristic of me
I'm a rip current going with the flow
To my brothers, I'm a volcano erupting when they speak
I'm a zoo manager; I love animals
When I feel pressured, I let people take advantage of me
Insects creep me out like ghosts on Halloween
I am a youthful, athletic puppy always needing food
A broken watch resembles me, always trying to fix my problems
I'm an ant wandering to new places, getting lost
Clouds remind me of myself, soft and kind hearted
I am Amanda Allessa Napoli

Amanda Allessa Napoli, Grade 5
Wagon Wheel Elementary School

The Squirrel and the Skunk

During the last weeks of fall,
The squirrel doesn't relax at all.
Getting food
Is her mood,
She says, "Hurry, hurry, hurry" while working
Never stopping, never shirking
For she knows she must prepare
Because in winter, she knows how she would fare.

As the squirrel worked, another creature stunk
That creature's name was skunk
For while the squirrel labored hard
The skunk didn't work a shard.
"Why should I," he would say
Not aware what would happen the next day.

There is a moral to this tale
"Procrastinate, and you will fail"
For while the squirrel laid snugly all season
The skunk was cold because he acted without reason.

Jared Knight, Grade 6
Barstow Intermediate School

Cat

Favorite Place: in a tree
Working Hours: whatever suits me
Occupation: professional snoozer
Weaknesses: NONE! I ain't a loser
Hobbies/Past times: roaming the 'hood
Special Skills: catching mice like I should
Favorite Snack: my special kitty treats
Best Music; phat cat beatz
Color Choice: lantern yellow like my eyes
Weight and Height: don't talk about my size
Things I love best: catnip rat
Things I hate most: my silly cat hat
Family: my owner, I love her a bunch
Best times of day: breakfast, dinner, and lunch!

Alexandra McColl, Grade 6
Francis Parker School

Happiness

Happiness is like lime green and is also like the red hot sun shining its bright light over the calm and quite blue ocean. It rushes through my head reminding me of the times that have been fun and crazy. It makes me feel speechless or like when the wild wind hushes over blossoming flowers. It makes me want to imagine about all the times that have been wonderful and amazing.

Haley Giddings, Grade 6
St Anne School

Discovery

Discovery wears a big and kind smile as warm and comforting as Grandma's kisses and Mother's cookies. His smile jumps from people to people it all depends on what they discover. It has a big blue robe moving in the wind that you picture when you discover something. He walks toward you skipping and smiling. Discovery is so important they made it a channel on television.

Garret Lee Shawkey, Grade 5
Wagon Wheel Elementary School

Groovy Green

I know green

Green smells like the aroma of freshly cut grass, the bulky, repulsive odor of swamp water,
and the scent of a newly bought, shiny Toyota.

Green feels slippery and scaly, as it flops up and out of the water, the rough, bumpy texture of a spring leaf on a tree,
and the smooth cushiony structure of a Boston Celtics jersey.

Green looks rutted and jolting, and crude all over its reptile body, the moist, thorn surface of a dew dripping rose stem,
and the half liquid half solid that jiggles, squirms, and squishes as a metal spoon digs into it.

Green sounds very faint, but swishes its tail back and forth as it dashes through a house's backyard, it sounds crunchy, when a long, wide food accidentally crushes the shell covered creature, and it sounds booming as it is hit or kicked at a wall or to each other.

Green tastes flavorful and luscious until the core is eaten, and the external layer remains, green is very frosty and saccharine, and served on a cone or in a cup, and the tangy saturated fruit added to a sugar filled glass of water as a final ingredient.

Ryan Ghassemi, Grade 4
Dingeman Elementary School

If I Were the Colors of a Rainbow...

If I were red I'd be an apple, juicy as can be
I'd be fire, clearing a path and setting new plants free

If I were orange I'd be the fruit, which gleams in the sun
I'd be a sunset mixed with purple, pink, and blue...yum!

If I were yellow I'd be the sun, glistening down on everything
I'd be a daisy, singing delicately and honestly

If I were green I'd be a tree, producing lots of fruit
I'd be the grass, blowing and growing very fast

If I were blue I'd be a waterfall, streaming down for all to see
I'd be the sky with birds flying across my face and flapping their wings gleefully

If I were purple I'd be a river flowing through the land
I'd be a plum hanging in a tree and when I'm picked, I am consumed with happiness in me

If I were pink I'd be a flower dancing in the sun
I'd be a leaf in the autumn and when I fall, I float right down, barely hurt at all!!

Katie Oberman, Grade 5
Aviara Oaks Elementary School

If I Were a Flower

If I were a flower, I would be a white daisy
I would watch children be gentle with me
My petals would be small and lightly scented

My scent would attract children's attention
I would watch them as they climb up many trees
The children would giggle, play and run around with joy

My leaves would be slightly blowing
My petals would bloom in the spring
My petals would drop off in the fall

My petals would sleep in the winter
Soon the process would begin again
My petals would come back and everything would start over

Alana Schall, Grade 6
Valley Beth Shalom Day School

Music Is My Life

What's the first thing you hear?
Music in your ear
The guitar is so loud
But it makes people proud

Singing is a pain
But you just got to get your head in the game,
Every time you walk down the street
You hear different kinds of beats

If you can't keep up with the beat
Try to use your feet
Hip-Hop, is like Pop
It will still make you drop

Music helps me pass time
From morning to bedtime
Nothing makes me more happy
Than a catchy tune that makes me start tapping!

Alex Avila, Grade 6
Cimarron Education Center

Fever

I am the Fever,
Widespread, yellow, strong,
I am unforgiving,
You won't last very long,
You could not, should not, will not hide,
I can blight you deep inside,
I'm in the river, the trickling stream,
I will dispatch you but with a big team,
You cannot find me I fly through the night,
Even if you tried you couldn't win the fight,
Once again, I shall warn you,
Recede if you want life to come anew.

Matthew Joseph, Grade 6
St Andrew's Episcopal School

Food Warfare

Tomatoes and coconuts fly over the street
Gooey messes pile up here and there
Many are in a crazed and wildly mood
Because today is the Food Warfare

All competitors enter food war territory
Armed with packs of different types of food
Many hide, holding baguettes, and others prowl silently
Even so, they are all pretty good

A man threw a tomato, the fire started
A clash of messy food, messing up the greenery
People take it as fun for everyone
But it's bothersome to the scenery

Alas, a whistle is blown and the war ended
The scene is glad that it's going to get cleaned
Some sad, but some are excited
Because next year's Food Warfare has beans

Andrei Badilla, Grade 6
Cimarron Education Center

Colors

Brown
Is the soil that grows our crops
Brown is the cane that holds up the old
It is the bread that we eat
It is the shovel that builds our home
It is the eyes of a newborn child that smiles at its mother
Brown

Gray
Gray is the moon that shines as our night light
It is the wolf that wanders the night
It is the sword that takes the life of a warrior
It is the mist on a cold rainy day
It is the cloud that covers the town
It is the tip of a quill that writes the poems of our world
Gray

Tal Toker, Grade 6
Kadima Heschel West Middle School

Friend?

What is a friend
   a companion
   a partner
   a savior
   a helper
   a comedian
   the first person you want to see in the morning
   the last person you want to see at night
   a person who brings you up when your falling down
That's a friend

Zoe Muratalla, Grade 6
Aliso Elementary School

My Dear Friend, Sports

Basketball, swimming, jumping,
tennis and skateboarding too.
Football, boxing and running,
sports are what I do.

Sports are exciting and fun.
They give me an exciting feel.
I love the feeling when I've just won!
Sports are like the best…for real!!

They give you a forward
they give you a past.
Sports are for everyone, even a nerd,
and after I play I can have a snack!!

So when I'm extremely sad
or oddly blue
not long will I be mad
'cause sports I'll turn to you!

Maximilian Perez, Grade 6
Cimarron Education Center

Ode to My Glasses

O, thee wonderful glasses,
You whom I saw in that store window.
Thou art sparkly and blue.
If I did not purchase thee,
My heart would be pierced through.
From the roughness of my palm
To the smoothness of my ears.
I loved the feel of thee
From that day on.
How thee shines in the hot sun!
Thy beauty is most excellent.
I thank thee for sight
Of moon, stars, and sun.
I can finally see all that there is to see!
Oh yes, what things have appeared
Because of your qualities:
The little branches bursting forth,
Birds flying in the distance,
The sunset in all its glory
All are gifts you have made possible.
To thee I give thanks, o glasses of mine.

Carlin Smart, Grade 5
La Jolla Country Day School

Love Is…

always determined to do what's right.
as patient as your parents.
peaceful like a quiet stream.
tough like the root of a tree.
gentle as a butterfly.
always loyal like your best friend.

Madison Huizar, Grade 5
Santa Fe Springs Christian School

Brr!!!

You know me for having an excuse to drink hot chocolate
My father is a blizzard
My mother is the queen of rain
My enemy is summer
My best friend is a snowflake named Doris
I wish I was as beautiful as a snowflake
I smell flowers blooming, that means spring is near, OH NO!!
I touch the people's faces when they go into their houses to warm up
I was born when the first blizzard occurred
I fear melting
I love when the clouds pour rain
I dream of being rained on so I can stay alive
I live on both ground and in the sky
When my friend Doris falls from the sky I grow bigger and bigger
Do you know what I am?…I am winter!!!

Emily Hoorfar, Grade 6
Horace Mann School

Red

Red is the taste of juice gushing out of strawberries.
Red sounds like lava bursting out of a volcano making everything into ashes.
Red smells like fresh, juicy, ripe cherries ready to be picked.
Red looks like a steaming hot summer day.
Red feels like the silky fur on a baby fox that was just born.
Red is the color of a fire in a chimney that is pleasant and warm.
Red is the taste of a cherry flavored popsicle.
Red is the smell of tomato sauce on pasta.
Red is the color of a beautiful fresh rose sparkling in the sun.
Red is the taste of hot, spicy salsa on your nachos.
And red is the color of blood that will keep you alive.

Ashley Herrero, Grade 4
Heather Elementary School

My Chaotic Room

A smell of stale fish is reeking in the air.
You are coming towards my room, so beware.
My pet leftovers are strewn all over the floor.
Maybe he should be trained a little more.
Video game covers are covered in layers of dirt.
Tripping on one will indisputably hurt.
Moldy, opened candy bags clutter the ground,
And they pile up in a gigantic, disgusting mound.
The grimy carpet is covered with dust,
And fills the room with a scent of musk.
Appalling curtains ripped in the shape of a banshee,
Presage you of death with much guarantee.
My wrecked auburn desk is a horrible site.
It will surely give you a fright.
I have a walk-in closet that will definitely make you yell.
A tsunami of stinky socks collapses, giving off a dreadful smell.
The covers on my bed are like a ball of yarn in a twisted cluster.
Everything just continues to pile up in a bluster.
Once you enter, you will meet your impending doom.
My acrimonious room will be your final tomb.

David Lin, Grade 6
Dorris-Eaton School

High Merit Poems – Grades 4, 5 and 6

A Woof in the Park
I see it! It's around the corner!
Across the street! We're here!
The park, with its bright yellow flowers,
Wonderfully yellow leaves on trees!
I can hear them, children laughing and giggling!
The sun is bright, up in the sky,
It truly is a sunshiny day in the park!
Just my dog toy and me!
(Oh, and my owner!)

Alexie Infante, Grade 6
John Muir Elementary School

Bigfoot
You know that the world thinks you are fake.
You know that hardly anybody believes in you.
Sure, you are out there, but according to the world,
you never existed. Bigfoot, you are on the same list
as the Loch Ness Monster, Godzilla, and little green men.
The world doesn't believe in you but I do. I know you are
out there. I still believe in you Bigfoot. I still do.

Carson Benjamin, Grade 6
James B Davidson Middle School

I Am
I am down to earth
I wonder if people are really who they say they are
I hear music all the time
I see jewels everywhere
I want my parents want
I am down to earth
I pretend to be a whole new person at home
I feel cared about
I touch my young siblings
I worry about if my dad's eye will get better
I cry when people die in my family
I am down to earth
I understand that life is not all about me
I say believe in your dreams
I dream that all people are good
I try to control my attitude
I hope good people don't die
I am down to earth

Faye Parkes, Grade 4
La Presa Elementary School

Change
He has the honor of planning peace,
His trust is being silent,
He is now powerful in the new age,
The planet will change,
He feels humble and free but with hard choices,
He has skill and determination,
He will help our country, the USA, change.

Christian Carrillo, Grade 4
Canyon View Elementary School

Ode to Candy
Oh, dear delicious cavity makers,
I love you so
We eat you at the movie theater
We suck on you when you are a pop

You're sour or sweet
Hard or chewy
And sometimes your insides are gooey.

Sweet Tarts, Dum Dums, Sour Patch Kids,
Twizzlers, Tootsie Rolls, Hershey's, Twix,
Butterfingers, Milky Way, Almond Joy and more
Eating candy is never a bore

I love the things that melt in your mouth
Or the things you chew
Don't forget the small little candies
That tickle your tongue with sour

So, if you see candy, eat it
Enjoy it, don't let it go to waste
Once it's gone, don't be sad,
Halloween is always coming.

Sheridan Constant, Grade 5
Wagon Wheel Elementary School

Oscar
Oscar is my friendly dog.
Although he eats like a hog.
I bring him in to show and tell.
But when he's tired he curls into a shell.

Sofia Bennett, Grade 4
Mayfield Jr School of the Holy Child Jesus

What Should I Put in a Box Marked Summer?
Oh hoorah! School is out!
It's time for fun without a doubt!
Windy days and flying kites,
Looking at stars, during warm summer nights.

Hot days, keeping cool,
Having fun in swimming pools!
Fourth of July, bright fireworks,
Enjoying the colors with no homework!

Eating ice cream, making cookies,
Playing baseball as rookies!
Having fun of all sorts,
Staying healthy, playing sports!

School is starting, getting ready,
Sleeping early, with lots of teddies!
Vacation's over, what a bummer,
At least I'll always remember this summer!

Andrew Lee, Grade 5
Duveneck Elementary School

Legendary

Legendary rarely seen
Seems like you're never there
I wonder what it might be like,
To have a legend,
I know what it feels like,
I have three.

Kassandra Murillo, Grade 6
Fairview Elementary School

Snow

Cold in the winter
Near the mountains or water
Snowflakes falling down

Morgan Goe, Grade 6
St Anne School

Blue

Blue is the sky
When the clouds aren't out
The ocean
Salty and strong
Fountains
Relaxed as can be
Hearing the birds
Flapping their wings
The taste of blue is cold
Blue is the ocean
Surrounding our world

Elizabeth Addas, Grade 4
Carlthorp School

Blue Is My Color

Blue is the ocean, dolphins, and skies
Blue is soothing
Blue is calming
Blue tastes like blueberries
Blue smells like violets
Blue sounds like the ocean
Blue feels like winter snowflakes
Blue looks like a blue jay
Blue makes me happy
Blue is the best color of all!

Aaron Gomez, Grade 5
Jackson Elementary School

Dawn Arising

Look at the dawn,
as beautiful as a rose.
Ponder through the eyes of God,
as the morning glories bloom.
Not a cloud in the sky,
like clear ocean water.
Come with me and discover light!
Come with me and discover being!

Corinne Elyse Dela Cruz, Grade 4
Garden Grove Elementary School

Ode to Dart

A sick weak cat, saved by my extremely lucky family.
Resisting the urge to pull the small stub of a tail he has.
Taking every chance I get to touch his soft fur,
to take a look or he just might vanish.
Feeling sick not to look at his beautiful angel face,
resisting to preserve every hair he sheds.
Looking at his grayish brown fur in the sun light.
Sharing every spare moment I have playing with the monster,
though I know my hand will be torn up.
Listening to his whisper of a purr trying to dignify himself.
The aroma of sage just barely making itself noticeable.
The brilliant and beautiful cat is and always will be a priceless treasure.

Sydney Wilson, Grade 5
Wagon Wheel Elementary School

My Nature

My nature is a blooming flower,
a fir tree growing as tall as a skyscraper.
The autumn leaves drifting through the silent wind.
The green grass growing as lush as a forest.
Mountains kissing the sky.
Blue lakes reflecting the suns rays.
Birds flying overhead, seems like they're waving to me.
My breath showing in the cold air, like a white blanket in the wind.
A single leaf alone in the dirt, untouched.
Smell the soil under my bare feet.
Moss covering each rock on the river's shore.
My heart beating like a drum in the summer heat.
My nature.

Sydney Carbone, Grade 6
James B Davidson Middle School

Gas Guzzler

Mrs. Fryman's Jeep.
16 miles per gallon on the freeway.
Inhales gas as if it were air.
Like a bottle with a leak.
Big supporter of our economic crisis.
Mrs. Fryman drives, and drives, and drives, and drives, and drives and drives.
The Jeep kills, and kills, and kills, and kills, and kills, and kills the environment.
No match for a smart car.
Don't get me wrong.
The Jeep has four-wheel drive, which only uses up 2x the amount of gas.
What a bargain, like spoiled milk for $20.
But it gets better, the Jeep's like a giant moving trash can.
When you climb out, all the money in your wallet is gone.
One road trip, from California to New York,
Will guarantee another ten years of work, without vacations.
If you end up behind Mrs. Fryman's Jeep,
Grab a bucket and catch your share of gas coming out of the pipe.
Put it to better use in your smart car which will go three times as far.
The best part is, it only takes a gallon or two to start the Jeep.
In the end, I hope Mrs. Fryman learns her lesson.
For your next car, don't buy a Jeep, buy a Smart Car.

Andrew Schiller, Grade 5
Mayfield Jr School of the Holy Child Jesus

Pro-Procrastinator

The level brown wood stands in front of a stool
Although she'd much rather recreate in a pool
She sits down to play a tune
Just her, the piano and quietude in the room
She looks outside and thinks to herself
I won't just sit here like a book on a shelf
So she plays a few scales and then a few more
She tries to persist, but she is so bored
Procrastination starts setting in
"Oh no!" She says. "I'm doing it again!
I've got to make this experience fun,
Before I know it, I'll be done
Maybe if I play amusing songs to get started
There'll not be an ounce more of boredom to be smarted"
She uses this piano theory every practice every day
And she learns to play piano in a new, more exciting way
Now she loves to play those smooth ebony and white keys
She procrastinates no more and practices with ease.

Kamilah Nall, Grade 6
The Mirman School

Dangerous

Dangerous is not cautious
Dangerous is crazy
Dangerous is wild
Dangerous is risky
Dangerous sounds like suspense
Dangerous sounds like someone's last words
Another word for *dangerous* is chancy
One thing about *dangerous* is not being careful

Christopher Munkres, Grade 6
Big Springs Elementary School

Life Bounces

Life is like a ball
Going up and down
Sometimes we make it go through the hoops
Other times, it just stays on the ground,
Waiting to go up again
Many times it just stays between up and down
Life is like a basketball, so
It's our job to make sure
That we all reach success
And not quit or lie any more

Nicholas Gordon, Grade 4
Charles Armstrong School

The Lovely Sunset

Relaxed is like orange
And is also like you're at a sunset
It rushes through my head and out of my brain
It reminds me of the time that I cried
It makes me feel relaxed like when I'm at the beach
It makes me want to see fireworks in the air.

Marissa Cariello, Grade 6
St Anne School

Sunny

The sun laughs quietly shining bright rays of peace
The clouds stir lightly
Weightless with no rain
The breeze giggles and smiles at the world
They are a team
A nation
The sun looks at a flower
His eyes smile
The soil is damp with last weeks rain
The clouds dance
The breeze tickles
Peace falls like a blanket covering the world safely
The breeze trips
The sun chuckles at his bountiful youth
The clouds are silent, thinking
The breeze is yet a child
The sun is a wise man
And the clouds are artists
They are a team
A nation
Always

Anna Barcellos, Grade 5
Montessori Family School

Yellow Fever Pennsylvania 1793

I am Yellow Fever
I spread terror and death like war
People fear me but know not of where I come
They try to run but I am in every corner
I am Death's servant, as people wither and die
People think me eerie
I feel no remorse when I kill
People vacate the areas I ruin
They don't know me
They can't know me
I am an enigma, one that will kill you
I am Yellow Fever

Chris Yavercovski, Grade 6
St Andrew's Episcopal School

Only One

One window is all I need
Break the ice, let go, be free
Be able to make my own decisions
To not feel trapped, like in a prison.
One window is all I need
To open the door, to find the key
To unearth the treasure that lies within
Your soul; it's a warmth under your skin.
LOVE, that's what it's called
It makes all your troubles feel vary small
Love is gracious, love is true,
But most of all, it comes from you.

Sarah Park, Grade 6
Heritage Oak Private School

Candles
Candles
Tiny torches
Glowing in the evening
Silently calling me over
Fire
Avalon Johnson, Grade 6
The Coastal Academy

Park
At last, last month,
a trip to the park.
With mom and dad.

Leaving home,
Walking,
Seeing stores —
A food store, a toy store,
Trees.

So tired,
But still walking.
At last,
The park!
Baseball,
Soccer,
Hockey.
But no time to play,
Time to return home.
Eric Kim, Grade 5
Clover Avenue Elementary School

Waterfall
Big tall waterfall,
That crashes in the river,
Be careful don't fall!
Rosie Guerrero, Grade 4
Anderson Valley Elementary School

Midnight
At midnight
the bell clangs in time.
In the rippling pool
there's a shadow.
The rain rains,
and there's music
in the window.
It's dark,
so you can't see
the clouds going away.
While morning is coming
The shadow was mist
tricking your eyes,
while sunrise is coming.
Jasper Chang, Grade 5
Henry Haight Elementary School

Forgive Us
We have taken over your world
Destroy what was once plentiful
Destroy the things that you have created
And probably destroying you

And which
Probably
Taking from
Your intricate design

Forgive us
We are a superior creation
Of yours
Sorry.
James Bartlett, Grade 5
Montessori Family School

The Flower Gardens
Here are the flower gardens,
With roses galore,
Colors pink, red, and white show up,
In the many gardens there is to explore.

Ponds with white lilies,
Patches of Queen Anne's Lace,
Sprigs of tulips set aside,
Ready to be put into a vase.

Sunflowers guard the path,
With delicate white daisies,
The bushes of lavender look quite good,
With the puny purple pansies.

There's much more to see,
If you ask me,
It's quite a bower,
So come see the flowers!
Ariel Pan, Grade 4
Palo Verde Elementary School

Freedom
Every man has a weakness,
every woman has a strength:
every human has a purpose,
even those who go unranked;
No one man above the other,
no one man that is armed;
no one man should take cover,
because of a man he never harmed;
I beg of you, do not do, the evil things
you want to.
And most of all, don't let the world fall,
when it all comes down to you.
Joseph Mendoza, Grade 6
Selby Lane Elementary School

Neat Freak
Neat freaks
They clean all day
And never play.
If you look at their place
You won't see a thing out of its space.
It's so boring
I start snoring.
Neat freaks.
Ethan Williams, Grade 5
Theodore Roosevelt Elementary School

How to Be a Turtle
Never travel by yourself.
Never eat an eel.
Glide through the deep blue sea.
Sandy beaches are great for laying eggs.
Don't forget you need your oxygen.
Your hard shell will help protect you.
Jellyfish are a scrumptious treat.
Stay away from humans!
Bethany Steffon, Grade 6
Big Springs Elementary School

Ocean Side Farm
I remember the time of play,
I remember the scent of hay,
I remember the ocean waves,
I remember the view of bays,
I remember the dirt paths,
I remember there were no baths,
I remember that big red barn,
I remember Ocean Side Farm.
Peter Polizogopoulos, Grade 6
Lockeford Elementary School

The Sea Shows…
The sea shows…
good hearted things,
the things you wonder about
the things you cherish
the things you hate.
It glows as bright as the sun,
But sometimes you wonder
is it delicate as a blanket?
Is it as cold as ice?
Is it loving and caring?
Is it hash and scary?
With the creatures that lie beneath
it might be a calm place
with salt water
with the clouds above its endless beauty.
It has feelings
just like you and me.
Sonora McClellan, Grade 6
Bethany Lutheran School

I Am From

I am from a home where my father is playing his piano softly into the night. Where my mom is always cooking and where pictures line the walls filled with family memories.

I am from a yard where sports equipment covers the grass like dew drops. Where a fish pond sits in the corner. Where a garden lay waiting to be watered, and where an old rope swing sways in the breeze.

I am from a neighborhood where kids are playing and laughing. Where bikes roam the cul-de-sac and where we have water balloon fights in the summer.

I am from a family where we are usually at sports events. Where we play board games together on the kitchen table. Where when we have relatives over we sit in our courtyard, and where every night I have dinner with my family.

This is where I am from, and I wouldn't trade any other thing for it!

Caroline Habib, Grade 5
Notre Dame School

Everything Changes

The earth is always moving, always on the go.
Nothing ever stays the same, even the tide's steady flow.
But it is not a simple fact that the earth changes, it must change, a simple word left out.
If things did not change, the cardinal wouldn't fly,
and the kitten would never learn to meow.
For things must alter, change at some time,
or things will never function right.
The cardinal must grow feathers,
and a kitten must grow older.
The world is always changing, this is essential for life,
or the wind would never blow, and the dog would never howl.
But the earth does change,
so the cardinal flies, the kitten meows,
the wind blows, and dogs will always howl!

Jess Jones, Grade 5
Coyote Ridge Elementary School

Black Burglar

Loneliness, like a quiet monster creeping up to surprise you. A very scary prospect within you suddenly you need a friend. I never pictured it dressed in all black like a burglar, creeping from shadow to shadow waiting to pounce. Swallowing every other feeling. Like a snake slowly making you coil before falling asleep. So strong nothing can come over you, no thinking is allowed when loneliness steals your mind, actions, and whole body. Beware and always have friends close.

When loneliness dwells it is very dangerous to try to get rid of alone. When a friend leaves, loneliness strikes. Putting on the black mask, beanie, pants, and sweater starting to creep from the different shadows. Filling up on all other things, watch out for this feeling, have options of friends and hold on to them. Otherwise get an alarm for this burglar, sly and stealthy. BEWARE!

Melissa McDonald, Grade 5
Wagon Wheel Elementary School

Love

Love is a time when red roses spring. Your heart pounding out of your very own chest. Love is when your toes are seeping into the cold sand, when you hear waves crashing against the shore, covered with shells, and when the sun is just setting, making those peaceful colors of joy. Dazzling, subtle, and satisfying, watching the sunset, slowly coming to an end, leaving the color of maroon all around you. But when nightfall arrives, the stars come alive. Shining bright above, giving you a wish to enter into your mind, all through the night. Midnight is a sigh of relief just around the corner. When you hear the word "love," you think of swans twirling their necks into a shape of a heart, nuzzling each other close. Love, o' love, it is the light that brightens your inner soul of calming peace.

Natalie Janett, Grade 5
Wagon Wheel Elementary School

Places

I need to find a place
Where everything is new

I need to find a place
Where there are cheers instead of boos

I need to find a place
Where happiness is in the air

I need to find a place
With no cruelty and despair

All I need to know is where to look,
Eureka I found it!
It is in a book!

Jenna Teagarden, Grade 6
Grant Elementary School

The Penny

I get spent in stores
turned in to banks
travel around the world
and sleep in people's pockets
I am the penny

Ryan Bockholt, Grade 5
Charles Armstrong School

Basketball

Basketball is my favorite sport.
Ten people on court,
five for each team.
Free throw, one point.
Slam dunk, two pointer.
Half court, three pointer…
Lots of teams in the NBA,
twelve to fifteen players
on each NBA team…
Why I like basketball is because
I like to dribble and shoot the
ball — Swish! —
And play with my friends and family.
There are so many sports,
but basketball is my favorite,
tops!

Genny Lhyne Parnala, Grade 6
Corpus Christi School

Sun and Moon

Bright, huge
Shining, energizing, nurturing
Light, Apollo, Artemis, dark
Sleeping, silent, resting
Small, reflection
Moon

Pietro Sette, Grade 6
Francis Parker School

If I Had a Zoo

If I had a zoo,
I'd invite everyone
I'd invite my mother, father, brother, and we'd have fun!
We'd take a special tour to where the jocular zebras stayed
And then go where the mountainous, antic elephants played
I would show them the alligator's dewy swamp
Then we would stroll to where the impish lion cubs romp
Next we would see the rhythmic hippos doing their dance
And after that, we'd visit the pandas, wearing their suit and pants
I wouldn't forget to walk us by the bloodcurdling snakes
We'd jump as we walked by the big hairy ape as he wakes
Then we'd take a picture of the orangutans playing on ropes
And gather everyone to see the bantam antelopes
Everything would be enchanting and new
If only, if only, I had a zoo.

Michelle Temby, Grade 5
Solana Pacific School

Leslie

My best friend Leslie means the world to me
I just wish people could see
I'm her Emo and she is my Elmo
She is great and barely ever says no
I call her my sister because we have the same last name
We are in sync which means the same
She is "punk rockish" and supportive
She is also tomboyish and active
We are both magical like darkness and light
We have also only gotten into one fight
She is full of peace and love
We walk around and look at birds above
She is lucky, pretty, and friendly
She is cool, weird, and funny
We both like a lot of guys
We both can see a lot about guys by their personality and their eyes
She is excited, silly, and awesome
I ask my sister to call her so we can hang out and have some fun
She is my favorite person in the whole world, I love her because she is like my sister
I miss her, she was Leslie, and we wish we can soon see each other

Angel Hernandez, Grade 6
Century Community Charter School

No. 1 Mom

Dear Mom,

You are number one, even though sometimes you spoil the fun.
You made lemonade for me when I came home from school,
It was even better than jumping in a pool.
Even though I may get in a dual.
You won't scream and yell "stop fighting you fool."
That's not all, you are also super cool.

Love,
Mark

Mark Newman, Grade 6
La Costa Heights Elementary School

Chocolate

Chocolates are the sweetest things
in the world for you to eat.
Only one piece can give you a ride to heaven.
As long as you are eating, your sweet journey continues.
Some have nuts, some have almonds.
That's even better.
People eat chocolate to feel better.

What is a chocolate?
It is a mixture of cocoa butter, sugar, and milk solids.
They normally come in three different ways.
Milk, dark, and white.

But, you need to limit it.
Because if you eat too much,
it's going to be bad for you.

Jake Lee, Grade 5
Solana Pacific School

Hike of Perseverance

The drops of sweat roll down my face
My skin is red hot to the touch,
This is the work of the summer Utah sun.
The pain in my feet, it pulses and pounds relentlessly,
Never ceasing like the seconds that go by,
This is the work of the hard ground beneath me.
And so, with these treacheries combined,
Time never seems to go by.

The rocks glare and laugh at me,
Mocking my miseries, laughing like hyenas.
Yet, surge after surge of perseverance floods into me,
My conscience instructing not to give up.
I gradually go faster, my heart beating quicker,
I finally start to put some miles behind me!

As I hike up the torturous path,
Closer and closer yet to my destination
My mind pushes me on.

Then, just like that, I arrive, sizzling and sticky,
Yet still alive.
I will never forget that hike in Bryce Canyon,
And the lesson I learned: don't give up!

Brian Frastaci, Grade 6
The Mirman School

Aurora Borealis

I wish I were a radiant aurora borealis,
Lovely and luminous,
Flowing as a river of light,
Appearing as arcs and bright streaks of green,
Showing a beautiful scene.

Rafael Tuazon, Grade 5
Lake Forest Elementary School

10 Little Puppies

10 little puppies running around the vine
one got out and then there was nine.
9 little puppies playing in the gate
one got out and then there was eight.

8 little puppies have an owner named Evan
One was adopted and then there was seven.
7 little puppies got in a fix
One escaped and then there was six.

6 little puppies played with a hive
One got stung and then there were five.
5 little puppies went to the shore
One went for a swim and then there was four.

4 little puppies went up a tree
One got stuck and then there were three.
3 little puppies chewed on a shoe
One got sick and then there were two.

2 little puppies had so much fun
One got tired and then there was one.
1 little puppy went for a run
It never came back and then there were none.

Nia Redd, Grade 5
Kentwood Elementary School

Butterflies

Fly off, little butterfly,
Take your place up in the sky.
Flowers are fragrant and very pretty,
But you know your place is above a city.

Your wings were not created to just stay on ground,
But created to circle sky round and round.

You're graceful, wings painted by God,
Meant for us mere humans to applaud.

So take off, little creature of wonder,
Make sure of your home of sky and you
Do not sunder.

Cara Sutherlan, Grade 6
Pinkham Elementary School

Freedom

Everyone has freedom,
Everyone has hope,
Everyone has something they want the most.
He is a humbled man in the USA,
He is a good man in the world.
He is the first African-American president,
He will help America today.
His name is Obama.

Matthew Qi, Grade 4
Canyon View Elementary School

Forest Green

Green, green
The forest of things
So sweet and so lush
It isn't all mush.

It stands for life
Which is a hard strife
The forest cut down
Makes the world go brown.

For green is like peace
Which stops the dark beast
That brings down trees,
Harms poor bees.

Green is energetic and calm
And great trees that are palms
Animals so rowdy and fun
Can't play without the sun.

Ian Hanson, Grade 6
Vista Verde Middle School

PS3

PS3 PS3 you are the best
I play you all day and even my guest
homework homework
when you are done
I play my PlayStation
it's much more fun
PlayStation PlayStation
you are the one
when I'm bored or sad
you make me laugh
Call of Duty, Call of Duty
my favorite game
but thanks to PlayStation
I get to play

Shane Colston, Grade 5
Wagon Wheel Elementary School

Ice Cream

Creamy
Cold
White as milk
Glistening under yellow tinted lights
Gleaming and sparkling
Like golden dew on plants
Add a pinch of happiness
Tablespoon of joy
With your family
Everything tastes great
Especially a cooling dessert
Of vanilla ice cream

Andrew Zhong, Grade 5
Clover Avenue Elementary School

My Cruel Brother

My cruel brother is a clumsy…
Lazy and a cruel brother
Who sometimes is…
A girl lover…
Who is always talking in my space
To other girls
And always pulls my ears
When he is angry in my room…
And could be very dangerous,
He could always buy…
Something for you but
When he does not have money,
He will ask me,
To give him money
He sometimes gets busy
He talks like if…
He was crazy,
The only thing and time he gets happy
Is when Jasmin his girl friend
Comes to the house and acts dumb

Juan Carlos Mejia, Grade 6
Century Community Charter School

Winter

White is snow, clouds, and moon
White is happiness
White is cool
White tastes like vanilla
White smells like roses
White feels soothing
White looks like cotton
White is winter

Fredric Silva, Grade 5
Jackson Elementary School

Rain

Somber clouds veil the dark sky,
Growing briskly and violently.
Thunder clamors in the distance,
Accompanied by
sporadic flares of yellow.
Rain strikes the ground
In an incessant beat.
Each raindrop falls delicately,
as if made of glass.
The gentle beat
transfers you to a place
of repose and composure.
Then a ray of light
Penetrates the veil,
growing gradually yet unequivocally.
And the world
is at ease.

Erik Riis, Grade 6
Francis Parker School

Mother Nature

The wind is blowing
Mother Nature is calling
Spring is coming soon

Courtney Crane, Grade 6
St Anne School

The Blue Boat

A blue boat sailing softly on the sea
The wind is piercing it, something I see.
And the only one who can drive it,
Is a captain like me.

Rohan Krishnakumar, Grade 5
Lydiksen Elementary School

Eel

Eel you are super
You don't sting any of us
A rock he sucks on

Bryce Bianchi, Grade 4
Tomales Elementary School

Navy Blue

I wish I were the
Navy blue
At a marine base
Fighting

Jonathan Applebury, Grade 5
Eastwood Elementary School

Lovely

My aunt my aunt
She is a caring person
She is there for my mommy
Nice and lovable
She is huggable too
You will see her peaceful
Then you will see her joyful
Awesome she will be

She is hardworking for her son
Patient and patient
She will be waiting
Love, love, love she will give us
You are so beautiful to me
Can you see far, far away
Still in my dreams
She is a seed
She will grow every day

She is a star
She will shine day and night
She is my aunt
What else could she be

Geraldine Renteria, Grade 6
Century Community Charter School

My Dog Is a Rottweiler

My dog is a Rottweiler,
He's a special dog,
He's my guardian and my friend,
And I'll love him 'til the end.

His name is Bruce,
And he's our big dog,
When I'm afraid, he's always there for me,
Because he's my friend.

My dog is a Rottweiler,
He's a special dog.
He's my guardian and my friend,
And I'll love him 'til the end.

Raphael Pizarras, Grade 4
St Pancratius Elementary School

Peace

I am a girl who just want peace, like a flower wants water.
I wonder what life will be like in 2000 years.
I hear about the war.
I see people hurt.
I want it to be over.
I am a girl who just want peace, like a flower wants water.

I pretend I am back home in Israel.
I feel sadness and sorrow.
I touch the wounded.
I worry about their lives, and their families.
I cry for God's help…but will he answer?
I am a girl who just want peace, like a flower wants water.

I understand the hate in the world.
I say everything will be all right.
I dream of peace and happiness.
I try to feel better and not cry.
I hope peace will come soon.
I am a girl who just want peace, like a flower wants water

Gony Idan, Grade 6
Horace Mann School

A Mother's Love

When a mother gives love
Through a whisper in her daughter's ear
That powerful love passes on through the future to their child
It keeps going endlessly
Just like the rain continuing to fall all over the world
Bringing beams of bright sunshine again after the rain
The love a mother gives to her daughter is more powerful
Than any other love whispered in her ear
For the power of that love
Is a symbol of the pride the mother
Gives the family
A mother's love is more powerful than anything

Angelina Ruiz, Grade 5
Juarez Elementary School

The War

Disagreements start it all,
And then the soldiers start to fall,
The war is happening, it is finally here,
There are those who fight and those who fear
And those who shed many a tear.

My people, my family torn in two,
The majority for them, but still a few,
Will fight for their homes and for their rights
They will not stop, they will fight and fight.

And here I stand between the two,
The majority, and those a few,
I watch them both, and I fill with dread,
Their faces white, their hands are red.
And all at once, they are all gone,
They have fought and someone won.

Disagreements did start it all,
And the soldiers did start to fall
There were those who fought, and those who feared,
And I shed many a tear.

Carly Lynch, Grade 6
Coastal Academy

Blue

Blue is the color of the ocean waves.
Blue is the feeling of raindrops falling on your head.
Blue is the sound of spiders creeping on the floor.
Blue is the feeling of sadness filling your body.
Blue is the taste of blueberries crushing up in your mouth.
Blue is the sound of a freshwater stream flowing on and on.
Blue is the smell of a high mountain flower in the breeze.
Blue is the color of your destiny just waiting there.
Blue is the color of the endless sky.
And blue is the color that is special and magical.

Florian Ruhstaller, Grade 4
Heather Elementary School

A Happy Yet Lonely Path

I stand there and stare
the divided road before me
which way to go, which way to explore
I begin to walk
slowly I walk toward a path,
not knowing what lay ahead
A path filled with yellow roses
and wet grass surround my feet
The happiness it brought
To be alone on a beautiful road
No one to see, no one to talk to
I felt alone in the happiest way
In the happiest way I could ever be

Carrington McDowell, Grade 5
Coeur d'Alene Avenue Elementary School

Ode to Amor

Amor, amor, amor
How could I ever live without you?
Love is the comfort of sitting by a warm, cozy fire,
Bundled in a fluffy blanket.
Through the tough times when I don't think I could
Go any further.
You come between us,
As a mother lion holds her cub until the cub cuddles in her arms,
Slipping into slumber.
Amor,
You're here in the brightest of days,
And darkest of nights to forgive and protect
While we wish for the true Amor.
You remind us of the sunset,
Rays of light flashing right in front of our eyes.
Crimson and amber glowing bright to show love and compassion
Just as our hearts glow with light.
Amor,
You come to us from the smooth blue of the ocean,
Swaying back and forth with the rush of your crashing waves,
Raging water rising up and falling back down, 'till you're eventually lost in your dreams!

Jodi Goldman, Grade 5
Wagon Wheel Elementary School

Indecision

Indecision is like a snake, coiling around your gut. He constantly questions you, "What if you do this?" Indecision has you thinking nonstop about the consequences of what you do. You struggle with him every day whether you're out shopping or at school. Indecision is like a termite, pesky and annoying. There is no easy way past indecision. All you can do is just choose and hope for the best.

Benjamin Siemens, Grade 5
Wagon Wheel Elementary School

The Shadow

It creeps in the shadows of the night, prowling, to cause much fright.
It stoops around like nobody's watching, and opens the door without even knocking.
I catch a glimpse of it and stare, I turn for a moment and no one is there.
Up the stairs it creeps loudly but calm, holding a box, it must be strong.
There's a creak in the wood, it came from upstairs,
I take a quick peek, but nobody's there.
All shadows are different, each shape and each size,
I see one that's moving and two beady eyes.
Each step is quiet and not at all loud;
It looks around quickly and takes the last step proud.
As the boards squeaks, it flinches, it sees me, will it run?
But instead it disappears, not a sign of it, not one.
What was that thing was it a ghost or a thief?
Or was it just my imagination, that would be a relief
I tell it's still here, I can feel it in my blood,
Could it be creeping up on me like any robber would?
Suddenly I feel it, breathing down my neck, I'm scared stiff, not knowing what to expect.
I tighten my body, and shut my eyes tight, next thing I know, I see a bright light.
It's the early morning sun shining down upon me; I realize I'm in the living room.
I must have fallen asleep! But how could that be, was it all just a dream?
Or was it more than it may seem?

Madelynne Long, Grade 6
St Hilary School

Special Memory

There was a time in the sky
The sun was up
I could smell the fresh scent of my mom's hair
The smile on her face lit my face up
Her face filled the room with wonderful sounds

She felt as happy as me
Walking down killing time
The hallway seeming to shorten
Time going by slowly
Step-by-step the clock ticking

The mall filled with talking and yelling
My mother's laugh, the only laughter
The day was ending happily
As we walked out
The sun went down
SLOWLY

Shazia Naqui, Grade 5
Clover Avenue Elementary School

Missing My Cousins

Every morning I look out the window,
Out to the chirping birds, the soft clouds,
And the children laughing.
I ask myself,
"What are they doing? Do they miss me?"
I know we see each other once a year,
But it is not the same as when we were younger.
I remember the laughs and the smiles.
I also remember the hugging and the tears.
"Goodbye, I'll miss you," and "I'll see you again."
We said our goodbyes with tears rolling down our faces,
And off they went.
Oh, how I miss my cousins.
Even though I don't see them physically every day,
I will always have their smiling faces in my thoughts.
I will never forget them,
And I will not forgive myself if I do.
My cousins are my best friends,
And they do not deserve to be forgotten.
I will love them forever.
Oh, how I miss my cousins.

Megan Miu, Grade 6
Parkmont Elementary School

Rainbows

Red, the color of my heart pounding as I run.
Orange, the color of the lantern I light on Halloween.
Yellow, the color I wake up to in the morning.
Green, the color of the fresh silky grass.
Blue, the color I see when I am feeling down.
Purple, the color I see on my walls when I fall gently to sleep.

Caroline Goldsmith, Grade 4
Center for Early Education

The Fairies

I lay in a field small and quiet
I listened for the flowers calling
As I lay among them
Talking to the butterflies
Fluttering around me
Suddenly I heard a flower talk, soft and sweet
It talked to a daisy
The daisy was talking to a daffodil
The morning glories were sleeping in the sun
As I listened to the pussy paws talk to the blue bells
I saw the butterflies land and become fairies
They made me feel like I could fly with them

Skylar Klembith, Grade 4
Coeur d'Alene Avenue Elementary School

Youthful Exuberance

Three faces appear, each with a grin;
Four more arrive, creating a great din.
Two at the seesaw, one on the swing,
All perfect examples of the gaiety of spring.

Cries of victory ring out as the ball hits the net.
Every player is covered in sweat.
All pant, "Good game!" as the teammates' hands shake.
Teachers blow whistles to signify the end of the break.

Beeps from text messages echo through the hall,
Recent gossip and rumors shock and enthrall.
Slamming of lockers and bustling of feet,
Into their classrooms the students retreat.

Anxious to escape once more, pencils are rapping.
Children await recess; toes keep on tapping.
Finally, the bell rings, and all kids are free.
Youngsters come out looking bright-eyed and dreamy.

People and notebooks and pens galore
Litter the hallways of the vast corridor.
In the far corner sits a small young girl,
Watching the middle school mystery unfurl.

Mira Partha, Grade 6
Challenger School – Ardenwood

Basketball

B ouncy, round ball
A stounding tall players
S hots from the three-point line
K eeping the ball from the opposing team
E xcited fans cheering their favorite team on
T ake the ball to the hoop
B all flying across the court
A ttack the ball in the air
L ay-up on an open lane
L et the ball make a swish

Alaena Logan, Grade 5
Joseph M Simas Elementary School

Fabian Hernandez

Fabian is…
A lazy and bossy cousin
Who could be funny and annoying
And is lovin'
Billy is…
An awesome cousin
Who could be a little too busy
Who could be caring and sweet
Also active with his doggy Missy
Fay is…
A caring kid
Who is intelligent and honest
Happy in the days
Fabis is…
A nervous friendly cousin
Who is independent and a hard worker
On his break he is adventurous
Disco is…
A mysterious lucky cousin
Who could be active at school
And a real fool

Suseth Fonseca, Grade 6
Century Community Charter School

Meeting My Grandma

An early, chilly spring night
Working on eye-popping puzzle.
Suddenly,
The door burst open
A chill up my spine
And —
There she was!
Finally,
My mysterious grandma
Running up, hugged her tightly
She came
Halfway around the world
From Ukraine.
We talked and talked that night
About family memories
Until our throats couldn't take it.
That exquisite night
In my mind
As if it were
Yesterday

Thomas Gosart, Grade 5
Clover Avenue Elementary School

Ocean

O ften waves
C rash against the shore.
E xcited people play
A nd surf in the
N ever-ending, salty water.

Spencer Bentley, Grade 4
Marian Bergeson Elementary School

Dreaming

Dreaming is when you…close your eyes and you're in your own world
Dreaming is when you…go wild with your imagination
Dreaming is when you…do stuff that is unbelievable
Dreaming is…

Amanda Rivera, Grade 6
Bernice Ayer Middle School

As a Tree

Red. Orange.
It's spring and my leaves are comfortable and just right.
The sun isn't too dark or too bright.
There is no one fainting or freezing in my sight.
Yellow.
Summer has come and I'm sweating like crazy. Water!
I need you, water! I need you! The sun seems to be getting hotter.
Green.
The third, a second to last season, is here at last!
Summer has made me go through torture. Fall don't go away fast,
I get goose bumps on the thought that winter will come.
I would need sunlight, not a lot though, only some.
Blue. Purple.
Oh! How miserable! Winter! I'm so sad.
I want it to be spring. I'm so mad.
All my leaves have fallen off and I'm so cold.
However, I've got to be bold.
So you see, it's a cycle of rainbow colors
Over and over and over it goes.
I hope this cycle flows.
Forever. It never ends. As a tree.

Amy Hu, Grade 6
McGrath Elementary School

What I Think Blue Is

Blue…
When this word comes to your mind, what do you think about?
Oceans, skies, light pastels, or even painted eggs on Easter?
Well I don't.
What about the storms, hurricanes, huge bolts of lightning
Terrorizing the average American family.
Fleeing from broken homes, the crazed rage of nature,
All the hurt in one blow and it didn't take much.
The notes of an electric guitar belting out noise,
But it begins to pull you in.
The deep cruel blue attracts you…
Then it all…just…stops…
Flashing blue lights flash off and on, pitch black for a second.
Then a bright blinding light back and forth, on and off.
So you run.
And then the light fades away,
And instead of the blinding light is a million stars in the deep blue sky.
You sigh.
For this is only a harmless trophy of the night sky.
It is what blue is for many
But, not for me.

Janelle Arguelles, Grade 6
John Muir Elementary School

High Merit Poems – Grades 4, 5 and 6

Heart Defect

A wondrous miracle,
A baby was born,
But a mom and dad were crying.
Their baby girl had a heart defect.
They were afraid she would die.
"She won't die," the doctor said.
"We will have to do an operation though."
The mom and dad were relieved.
Hours waiting for the doctors to mend her heart were worth it.
Soon their girl was asleep with her heart repaired.
The mom and dad could see the stitches on her chest,
But years later their girl was growing well.
She went in for a yearly check up on her heart.
She also had to go for MRIs when she was older
To make sure she wouldn't lose so much blood.
The mom and dad were happy that their girl was growing well.
The operation was worth it.
It was a wondrous miracle!

Jamie Chen, Grade 6
Parkmont Elementary School

The Rain Is Falling

The rain is falling in a drizzle
making little puddles on the cement
deep enough for leaves to float on.
When more rain falls on the puddles…
it makes little ripples along the surface.
You can jump and splash in the puddles.
You can open your mouth and try to catch some rain
even though it refuses to go in.

Jesse Nadel, Grade 4
Carlthorp School

Wind

The wind is flowing through open skies
Beyond the horizons, with each gentle stroke all is calm
The wind was strong, but all is now quiet
No trees are rustling, no dirt is moving from the wind
Wind whispers as if a spirit has awoken
Your bitter rage
Your anxiety is opening
Your inner voice
Now a new wind blows
Flowing with a new voice
Flowing with soul, hope, and destiny
It flies meaninglessly
Throughout long days
And long nights
It takes the world for granted
Because it doesn't know where to go
Or where to turn
It will just have to wait
And wait
And wait…

Lyric Quinto, Grade 4
Juarez Elementary School

Music

Beautiful melodies dance through my ears
Fills my heart with joy and no fear
From songs on 9.89 to 9.41
I don't like any genre better than another one
From such a simple beat
Can suit me sweetly
No one can tell you not to sing
Or start a band called the Pings
I do hope you enjoy music
Just not to the point it makes you sick
So don't hold back, let it all out
Show everyone what you're all about

Erica Parris, Grade 5
Juarez Elementary School

Amelia

My mother Amelia is the best
She's like a bird taking care of her nest
She's patient with me but also funny
Nobody can compare to her beauty
Her beauty spreads like cooties

She is kind to all she will even give you a ball
You can just give her a call
And she will be there to console
Her heart can never be compared
Her kindness can be shared

She is hardworking she's also heartwarming
She is never lazy she does chores like crazy
She is always to her top top nineties
She has the house to the tip top tidy

There is so much I have to say
Words are not enough to way
My mother is the best
She almost never take a rest
She does this all for my brother and I
She never give up and tries, tries, tries
All I have to say is that I love my mother

Heriberto Marin, Grade 6
Century Community Charter School

Mother Earth

I'm a snowy leopard.
I sneak up on my prey.
I romp with other leopards.
I'm an animal that walks like a ghost.
I quickly pounce on small animals.
I live in tropical mountainous Asian countries.
I'm an endangered species.
I live like superior hunters in mountains.
Save Mother Earth.

Vishnu Doppalapudi, Grade 4
Ocean Air School

The Blanket

The blanket is soft.
This blanket is elegant.
This blanket is warm.

I can curl up with it.
I can snuggle with it.
All day and night long.

It is gentle to my fingers.
It is oh so very white.
It is only in the mountains.
Which is oh so very high.

This blanket will cover everyone.
It is snow!

Anastasia Gomez, Grade 5
St Barbara School

Kites

As you lift your kite up high,
You give in a breath and take a sigh.
"My kite's colorful!"
"My kite's blue!"
Swish it around,
See a red one with a shoe.
Smell the fresh air, on the clean beach.
See a dog chasing one,
Strapped on its leash.
Laughing! Dancing!
Falling! Blowing!
One is soft.
One is shining.
Uh oh!
My kite is climbing!
Until next time,
I fly my kite,
I watch my kite go on its breezy flight.

Krystal Le, Grade 5
St Barbara School

In Bed

When I went
to bed
I whirled
and twirled until
I could not stop.
And when
I stopped
I curled up
like a drop.
And then I twisted
and circled up
like a bubble.

Tatianna Kelly, Grade 5
Henry Haight Elementary School

In the Sky

When you look up
at the sky
and see
the blue clouds
to sleep on,
it's like millions
of waves
splashing mist
on your face.

Andrew Zhen, Grade 5
Henry Haight Elementary School

Homerun Hitter

I'm a homerun hitter,
And when I go to bat,
The fielders start to jitter,
So I give them a tip of my hat.

I go step up to the plate,
Then the pitcher throws the ball,
I thought it would hit the gate,
But I hit it past the wall!

Ryan Nelson, Grade 5
St Pancratius Elementary School

Bed Bug

He sleeps in my room at night
He cuddles in bed real tight
Falls asleep with me
Behind my right knee
His name is Bed Bug, good night!

Giana Acosta, Grade 5
El Monte Elementary School

Who Are You Happiness

Who are you happiness
Are you pride
Or are you an inanimate object
Are you victory
Like a prize
Or a sports game
No
You are not pride
Not an inanimate object
You are better than pride
You are a feeling of complete joy
Complete contentment
Complete belonging
A feeling of bliss
You start on the inside like a breath
You fill me up like a laugh
Is that who you are happiness
Yes that is true happiness

Ryan Ward, Grade 6
James B Davidson Middle School

The Lemon Tree

On a vivid summer morning
Swaying in the wind
Was a bright yellow lemon
On a tree with ease
Birds flutter on the branches
The shiny leaves will be so perfect
I imagine it to be so
But I still cannot wait
For this lemon tree to grow

Alexandria Creasy, Grade 5
Merryhill Country School

Sunrise

When you watch the sunrise
You forget your feelings
All you feel is happiness
Because the sun is so beautiful
The sun is moving over the sky
As the day progresses
When it reaches the other side
It sets and makes a fiery sky
When it's dark you go to sleep
Until you wake in the morning

Brandon Lynch, Grade 6
La Costa Heights Elementary School

Families

F amilies are
A team
M aking a happy life for each other.
I nterested in making a goal
L aughing and talking
Y ou will never forget them.

Madison Hulse, Grade 6
John Muir Elementary School

Everyone Has Me

I live inside of you.
Everyone has me.
I like,
I wish,
I dream,
About people sharing me with everyone.
I fear nobody will have me.
I am wind that keeps you going,
I am water that calms you down,
You know me,
You want me,
You try to hide me.
My enemy, hate, is like me.
You hate what you like,
You like what you hate.
I, born inside you, I am love.

Hankyul Choi, Grade 6
Horace Mann School

High Merit Poems – Grades 4, 5 and 6

Halloween

The moon gives off brilliant white light,
Illuminating those who wander in the night.
Ahhhhh! The children scream with fright,
The white skeleton is silhouetted against twilight.

The bat screeches, the witches shriek,
While their cauldrons bubble and potions reek.
Then they ascend above the moon,
Sailing swiftly and speedily like a harpoon.

The candles reach out towards the door,
Their shadows dancing as the children explore
The glowing path leading to wonderful treats,
A pumpkin filled with succulent sweets.

Soon, children's shouts fade away,
Signaling the end of fun and play.
They have finished trick-or-treating for now,
With sacks full of candy, more than mothers allow.

Whoosh! The wind goes, as it sweeps past the light,
Blowing it out, finally bringing black night.
The happy children are waiting to rest,
The holiday of Halloween is truly the best.

Andrew Li, Grade 6
Dorris-Eaton School

My Uncle

My uncle playing his soft violin
The wind outside echoing his song
All my dreams of the past fading
like a myth
His eyes closing a little every second
Finally sleeping with me on the
warm couch.

Ellie Pearson, Grade 4
Coeur d'Alene Avenue Elementary School

The Pom

The Pom can fit into
the palm of your hand.
She is white as snow,
and has angel wings that sound:
Flutter, Flutter, Flutter,
as she goes around.
She is usually very polite,
but do not get her mad,
'cause she will make you oh so sad!
With a CLASH! BASH! and MASH!
The whole town will be down.
To make her happy again,
you must sound like a cow, and go Moo, Moo!
It will hopefully not be the end of you!

Madison Butler, Grade 6
Big Springs Elementary School

I Am Fever

I am Fever
I kill when times are hard and have no mercy
I do not care if you are good or bad
Happy or sad, serene or ravenous
I will kill you
Do you not believe that I can kill you?
If you don't, reminisce
That I have wiped out a whole city
Those people of those cities shiver at my name
Fever
I am Fever
I kill young, old, strong and weak
I am the culprit of death
I make people writhe with pain
Twist and scream in the dead of night
Most people
think they are safe at night, they open their windows
the truth is that a small crack from a window
a million fatalities will come
Beware, I am Fever

Christina Cherekdjian, Grade 6
St Andrew's Episcopal School

Vision

The hope was in the hands of one person.
We will trust that person
We the people have the power
America is one nation
Only an era of peace and
Kindness can settle America
Trust
People
America
Peace
Kindness
These are small words that can change America.

Andrew McCaw, Grade 4
Canyon View Elementary School

Clouds

When I see the clouds
I think of an old man with white hair
I think of a giant soft pillow
I want to sleep all night and all day

On stormy days the clouds cry of loneliness
On sunny summer days they're pearly white with happiness
The sky is the cloud's best friend
At night you can't see the clouds because of the darkness

Summer he is bright and happy
In fall he is sleepy
In winter he is sad
In spring he is joyous

Jordan Cantor, Grade 6
Francis Parker School

Baseball

Baseball
getting ready to fall
sliding, diving
running to the base
hit a homerun
so much fun
hear the crowds cheer
it is like music to your ear
steal home base
to make the winning run
what fun

Michael Ford, Grade 4
Marian Bergeson Elementary School

Rain

Rain falls as we speak,
Rain covers as we listen,
Rain will sometimes leak.

Luke Nevarez, Grade 6
Fairview Elementary School

Frog

Splish, splash
The frog jumps into the pond
Drip, drop
He trudges out slowly
Clip, clop
The frog hops along
Sudden silence
The frog stops

Nicole Finlay, Grade 6
Bernice Ayer Middle School

Coke Bottle

Coke bottle Coke bottle come to me
I am thirsty as can be!
I don't want water, I don't need juice,
All I request is you, you, you.

You are so brown and yummy
Your fizz just loves to fill my tummy.
Coke you're so tasty to drink,
You just make my heart complete!

Xochitl Ochoa, Grade 5
Merryhill Country School

Icicle

Snow falls lightly down the sky
Held up by the trees,
Looking, oh, so free
Dripping down drop by drop
Screaming with delight
Off the rooftop it will freeze
Forming an icicle I believe

Jessica Larson, Grade 6
Bernice Ayer Middle School

Blue

Blue is the color of the calm ocean
Blue is the sound of the salt water waves crashing against the sandy beach shore
Blue is the taste of a blue ice slushy
Blue is the smell of the blueberry muffins baking
Blue is the salty ocean water touching my skin

Dylan Sledge, Grade 5
Kentwood Elementary School

If…

It snowed chocolate ice cream!
I would go outside and make an ice cream snowman.
I would tell my parents I was going outside to play with ice cream!
My cousins and I would have an ice cream fight!!!
Rosie, Nayeli, Hanna, and I would make ice cream angels!

Daisy Ibarra, Grade 4
Anderson Valley Elementary School

Here

You head to school, not late, not early, right on time.
You go to your seat, get all of your books out and get ready to learn.
Instead…
You daydream, you play with your pencil, and you finally fall asleep.
While you are asleep your teacher takes attendance.
When she calls your name you're…absent?
You go home and your teacher calls to ask why you weren't at school.
But you were there.
Were you really there if you weren't focused and you didn't say here?

Hannah Hacker, Grade 4
Stone Ranch Elementary School

Colors

If I were red I'd be a slick Ferrari zooming down the highway.
I'd race in tournaments and smoke everybody by a long shot.

If I were green I'd be an enormous tree watching the world from above.
I'd watch over my city and protect them from the pouring rain.

If I were blue I'd be the salty ocean waiting for someone to leap in.
I'd crash into the shore and let all the surfers ride my swift waves.

If I were orange I'd be a mouth watering clementine.
I'd wait for someone to take a delightful bite and taste the juice of my fresh meat.

If I were brown I'd be the slimy mud upon us.
I'd wait and wait till someone slips and tumbles right on top of me.

If I were purple I'd be a beautiful flower.
I'd let everyone smell me and gently touch my silky petals.

If I were yellow I'd be the blazing sun.
I'd give everybody golden tans and hot red sunburns.

If I were black I'd be the slithering night.
I'd frighten and swallow up anything that came my way.

Nils Methot, Grade 5
Aviara Oaks Elementary School

High Merit Poems – Grades 4, 5 and 6

Rose

The rose is red
Its scent so sweet
I'll look at it when I get out of bed
I guess it can be called neat

Each pedal soft and silky, too!
It's nothing like a stinky shoe
I love roses red or blue
How about you?

What if I gave it a lot of water
Would it grow and have a pretty daughter
If I sang it songs
Would it sing along?

Two musical roses
Pretty and keen
They are so beautiful
I wish they were seen.

Christina Kim, Grade 5
Theodore Roosevelt Elementary School

A Lost Father

I loved my parents for who they were.
Apparently they did not.
They yelled, screamed and were mean.
I asked what happened,
And my mom became angry.
She asked me why I wanted to know.
I did not answer.
She said why — my dad?
My dad had been in jail.
I asked my mom, "Why?"
She told me about the split.
I was shocked.
"When did you become curious?" Mom asked.
"When Dad did not come home today," I responded.

This became the worst day of my life.
That day I sat in my room.
I had lost all emotion.
Cold, silent, sad — why did it happen?
It was as cold as death,
As silent as a graveyard,
And as sad as a lifetime living on borrowed time.

T.J. Hargrove, Grade 6
Parkmont Elementary School

Lightning

I wish I were a bright lightning bolt,
Striking and stunning
Hitting tree tops and lighting up the sky,
Causing thunder and frightening people,
Then disappearing when the glowing crack of lightning dies.

William Young, Grade 5
Lake Forest Elementary School

Puff

I have a cute, vivacious cat, Puff
She is as white as a snowflake indeed
She may be small, but she acts very tough
She ran towards my old grandma at full speed

In her little blue bowl I give her food
I give her the green package every time
Now I believe she is in a bad mood
Because this time her dinner tastes like lime

Oh no, she is going towards the double doors
Puff is going through her kitty door now
Her furry feet slide against our shiny floors
Puff jumps up and lets out a small meow

Puff sounds real, but she is a creation
That's all in my big imagination

Sajia Bidar, Grade 5
El Monte Elementary School

Red Is…

Red is the color or rosy red cheeks
It is the color of flamingo's beaks
Red is the color of blooming roses
It is the color of difficult poses
Red is the color of a hilarious joke
It is the color of Cherry Coke
Red is the color of a Valentine heart
It is the color of a strawberry tart
Red it is the color of delicious berries
It is the color of happy fairies
Red is the color of your favorite book
   A tomato is red
   A cherry is red
Red is the color of an incorrect mark
It is the color of a fun park
Red is the color of your nose when you're sick
It is the color of a dog's nice wet lick
It might just be your favorite
   COLOR!

Jennifer Rokhman, Grade 6
La Costa Heights Elementary School

Loud

Loud is not the sound of the night
Loud is the sound of a black shirt
Loud is the sound of the window open on a freeway
Loud is a baby crying
Loud sounds like an airplane taking off
Loud sounds like a concert
Another word for *Loud* is noisy
One thing about *Loud* is that a classroom is always
Loud never quiet unless they get in trouble

Alyssa Hartzheim, Grade 6
Big Springs Elementary School

Tiger Woods
On the eighteenth hole
Concerning the championship
Over the ridges on the green
Throughout the training
Within him
Past times of success and failure
From side to side
Down goes the ball
Along his line
In the hole
Alex Tatman, Grade 6
St Anne School

Salt Creek
During summer and winter
By my house
With big swells
Along the coast
Underneath the blue sky
At the beach
Near Strands Point
Behind the cliffs
With body boarders and surfers
Against littering
Jack Harris, Grade 6
St Anne School

Star
I am star
you know me
far up in the sky
I'm really tiny
for the hard stare
you have to use a telescope to see me
so I will be bigger
I shine on you all night
I have one enemy.
She lights up the sky
she rises up from the water
she is really hot.
Dominique Maestas, Grade 5
Clayton B Wire Elementary School

Jelly Beans
Colorful
Smooth
Tasty
Yummy
Small
Bean shaped
Rainbow of fun
Chewy
Lots of flavor
Sam Orr, Grade 5
St Louis De Montfort School

The Adventure
The Bold Adventurer,
During the silent night,
In search of His right
Sets out to seek His fight

Through valleys of shadow,
Into the dragon's lair,
And out to the fields of plenty
By guidance of His star

Through pits of fire,
He must endure the pyre,
And pass through the graveyard of souls,
In search of His battle

And at last He makes it,
The war begins,
He fights under fortification of his guide,
Wondering whether He'll live or die.
Carlos Leal, Grade 6
Cimarron Education Center

Pink
Pink is like a delicate flower.
It is a whisper in a gentle breeze,
Cotton candy in my mouth.
Pink is like a sweet aroma in the air.
It is a soft fluffy pillow in my sleep.
Kaylen Hiromoto, Grade 5
Kentwood Elementary School

Appreciate
Seagulls calling,
waves gently crashing
against the sandy shore
bringing new glorious shells,
the glossy surface
of the ocean.

Trees silently swaying,
whispering new secrets
to each other,
the sun hiding behind
the dense tree tops,
the sound of tiny paws
rustling through the leaves.

Nature can be so peaceful,
away from busy streets,
and crowds of people,
if we just took the time
to appreciate
God's wonderful work.
Mary Alexander, Grade 6
Bethany Lutheran School

Flowers
In every color
Above the ground
On a stem
Beside leaves
With other petals
For loving people
To my mom
Below the trees
From small seeds
Along the fence
Sophie Blair, Grade 6
St Anne School

Little Tea Leaf
Little tea leaf, you hold so much.
Yet you are so little; your friend,
hot water, will always be the one
who releases your inner secrets.
Who ever knew that you could
send out bursts of minty flavor,
hues of deep mellow maroon,
waves of citric scent?
Who could even guess
the aftereffects of
peace and tranquility,
strength and energy?
You, the maker of that
warm gentle liquid,
caressing the way the breeze
lifts a dove in flight.
You, the fuel behind the
cup of tea cooling on the table.
Little tea leaf, I ask you once more,
how do you hold so much
when you are so little?
Yu-Shien Ni, Grade 6
Carlthorp School

Music
Music to my ears.
Songs that make me happy.
Songs that make me feel.
Something too deep to reach.
Something I need to find.
I need to reach something I don't know.
Help.
Listen to the songs.
The music.
We can't find.
We can't reach.
Help.
It's too deep.
Music.
Staycee Lewis, Grade 5
Clayton B Wire Elementary School

High Merit Poems – Grades 4, 5 and 6

Down to the River I Go

Down to the river I go,
the birds call to me, the wind whispers to me.
The sky is clear and the sun is bright,
the weeping willow smiles.
Across the bridge I run,
passing flowers of the prairie,
till I reach my destination:
her body drifts along,
her beauty astounds me.
The willow dips his fingers in,
the wind ripples her surface.
The sound of her voice,
laughing and calm like the tinkling of bells,
fill my ears.
Her shining face soothes, her listening ears comforts.
She is forever singing, forever there.
Her unchanging shape flows on,
just as the sun rises each day.
I sit by her till sundown, then I depart.
The next day,
Down to the river I go again.

Emily Chen, Grade 6
Joaquin Miller Middle School

I Remember

I remember her smile
How much she loved me
Her soft voice
Her moist chocolate chip cookies
When she played cards with me
When she taught me how to spell my name
How she told me stories
The way she comforted me
How she helped me
Whenever she taught me something
Even though she left on Easter
She'll always be in my heart
She's just the same as before
Watching over me like a grandmother would

Briana Deahl, Grade 5
Theodore Roosevelt Elementary School

Ode to Chocolate

Rich flavor fit for a king
Coconut, raspberry, dark, milk
Giving the feeling of delight
Sensation reaches taste buds and stomach
Sorry, I love you, I'm hungry
Many ways to use it
Gooey delight
Chewing, chewing
Down my throat
Yum! I love chocolate

Justine Halas, Grade 5
Wagon Wheel Elementary School

Dreams Turn into Nightmares

Dreams turn into nightmares all the time.
Maybe not to other people,
but to me they do.
I can't help but to wonder why?

Dreaming one night, my dreams
turned into nightmares.
I woke up broken out in a sweat,
repeating no, no, no
I fell asleep again…

Starting to dream yet again,
this time, I slept longer.
Hoping to stay asleep, it happened again.
This time, I woke screaming.

Dream again, I told myself.
Again, it turned into a nightmare.
This time I woke up to the reality,
of the nightmare of real experiences.
Once again, I can't help but wonder why?

Damani Dean, Grade 6
Cimarron Education Center

My Mom

My mother I call her mom
Excitement and love
That's who I get it from
I see her getting ready for work
Such a pretty woman
She is different than all of us
But still just a human
Such a hard worker
Day and night
And still has time to be by my side

When she is not working
Or spending time with me
She is outside being active and staying healthy
She is loving, friendly and very protective
But still gives me freedom
To have my own fun

Just like my grandmother
I call her Mamita
They are both strong and wise
But now it's my turn to shine

Vanesa Delgado, Grade 6
Century Community Charter School

Butterfly

I wish I were a butterfly. A butterfly up in the sky.
Wandering around, up high in the sky.
Then landing on a beautiful tree that has green leaves.

Holly Crowell, Grade 5
Eastwood Elementary School

Family Fun

Sitting there quietly,
Feeling the breeze
Against my face,
Running around
Constantly catching fireflies,
Afraid of holding them,
The night twinkled
With bright star fireflies.

Blinking like cars in traffic,
Little dots in the air,
Circling around me,
Sitting with my parents
Saying "I love you"
And I'll always remember this,
Forever.

Sara Zemtseff, Grade 5
Clover Avenue Elementary School

Whispers

Midnight fire dance into music
Scattering millions of whispers into
Puddles and waters

Andrea Macatangay, Grade 5
Henry Haight Elementary School

America

A mazing things we can see
M arvelous things we can be
E agles fly high in the sky
R ich land spread far and wide
I ncredible mountains here and there
C aring for our country dear
A lways grateful for America

Karina Jacobo, Grade 5
Jackson Elementary School

The Music's Beat

Feel the beat,
Listen to the words flow,
Close your eyes,
Let the music fill your soul,
Block it out dance it out,
Move your body to the flow,
Release all emotions,
And lose control,
So slip away to the music's flow.

Alexus Fermenic, Grade 6
Barstow Intermediate School

Hawaii

Waters are flowing
As people are working hard
The sunset shining

Sepi Tuavao, Grade 5
El Monte Elementary School

I Am From

I am from a house,
Where family photos are everywhere and old china plates and cups
Are sitting quietly in the cupboard.

I am from a yard,
Where a pool is used all summer and an old play set is still standing
And also where a creek flows strongly all winter.

I am from a neighborhood,
Where my aunt and uncle live across the street
And where I see squirrels running up and down the trees.

I am from a family,
Where we are always loud but loving
And where we celebrate all holidays together.

Emily Erlendson, Grade 5
Notre Dame School

Alone…Again

I am alone again, my mind is racing,
My dreams are unfolding, right before my eyes,
I will break all of my boundaries, and I will tell no lies.
I am alone again, left to think about myself,
My morals, my dreams, my goals,
My mind is overwhelmed with all of the right and wrong I've done,
And I finally have a chance to look at how I've become the person I am today,
I am happy, and aware of the price I've had to pay,
For the good morals I have right now,
And because I know how,
To grow into the wise person,
I have always wanted to be
I'm not always proud of what I have done,
What I sometimes have to do,
But I know I have begun to learn right from wrong,
Even if I already thought I knew,
My mind is like an endless bookshelf,
With books that are like guides willing to help,
But, I'm just a kid so I shouldn't be so hard on myself.

Alyse Cronk, Grade 5
Walnut Canyon Elementary School

Yellow

Yellow is a lemon being picked on a sunny day.
Yellow feels like lightning running through your body.
Yellow is the color that brought people to California.
Yellow is the taste of a lemon being squeezed.
Yellow is the speed of a falcon.
Yellow is the sun rising high in the sky.
Yellow is the taste of lemonade being drunk.
Yellow is the taste of pineapple sherbet being slurped through a straw.
Yellow is a bumblebee buzzing to flowers.
Yellow smells like gold.
Yellow sounds like a pencil writing a word.
Yellow is the thing that answers tests.

Hunter Manter, Grade 4
Heather Elementary School

Dawn

Come, wake up, the sky is dark and dim.
Look at it, soon it will be gone.
Enjoy it while it lasts.
Its dark shade makes it seem like it's night.

Dalton T. Wiggins, Grade 4
Garden Grove Elementary School

Seasons

Spring birds are chirping, Tweet, tweet,
Spring flowers are blooming; red, blue, and yellow.
Days are growing longer, it's getting hotter.
Spring trees are growing green,
A child flies a rainbow kite.
Summer Splash! Splash!
Water hits softly upon the water,
Plip Plop Plip Plop
Hit, hit a baseball blast, into the air,
Run run, catch catch
Fall, Fall leaves twirling red, yellow and brown.
Days are getting shorter, Nights are getting colder,
Rain and more rain are trickling into the gutters.
Kids inside wanting to play, waiting for a clear day.
Winter snow is falling, kids are dressed in heavy coats,
Zip Zip Zip, snowballs are flying everywhere,
Snowman are stacked here and there
With a warm red scarf blowing in the cold air.
Now snow begins to melt away, the kids
Stop shoveling the sidewalks today.
Then it starts all over again.

Brandon Calk, Grade 4
Sierra Oaks K-8 School

Circle of Life

We start as a baby
As cute as can be,
Then we grow into a toddler
One, two, and three.
Next is a kid,
Five, six, and seven
And then when you're ten
you feel like you're in heaven
Teenagers are what you turn into next
Sitting around, starting to text.
Grown-ups are busy
And talk a lot
They make you do chores
That never stop.
Finally comes grandparents
Who spoil you like mad!
Then when they're gone,
Everyone turns sad.
But it's not over,
It's not the end!
Cause it will start all over again!

Harrison Burns, Grade 5
George Washington Charter Elementary School

Love Is in the Air

Love is like a red sunset,
And is also like having butterflies in your belly,
It runs wildly in my mind,
It reminds me of a time when my knees felt like jelly,
It makes me feel warm like fire,
It makes me want to tell her how special she is!

Alexander Gallastegui, Grade 6
St Anne School

Reading

When I slowly reach into the bookshelf I don't look.
I want the book to choose me.
I finally think I felt the right one and I pull it out.
I start reading, taking every word in.
I don't want to miss anything.
While I read about a ball I can almost hear the music playing.
I can see dancers right before my eyes.
And the King and Queen sitting on their thrones.
It was a magnificent castle with beautiful people in it.
With the stone columns and marble floor it seems unreal.
It feels like I am in the story.
As they describe the wonderful dinner after the dancing,
I can almost smell and taste the gourmet meal.
There was roast beef, baked potatoes, and for dessert
Luscious, moist chocolate cake.
Then the book is over.
And then I put my hand in the shelf once more
Hoping I can fall under the story's spell again.

Baylee Bakkila, Grade 5
Newport Heights Elementary School

Seasons

Winter and summer are like day and night,
Ice cream's for summer, winter's a hot chocolate delight,
While sitting by a fire, warm and bright,
Halloween's costumes are really dandy.
Oh, how great it is to have some candy.
Later the sweets may come in handy,
During fall, clouds weep until the sun stops the rain,
Oh, how sad it all looks, and what a pain,
Not to jump in puddles as they go down the drain,
Winter brings with it happiness and joy,
Anxiously, I'm awaiting a new toy.
Soon Christmas will be here, for all to enjoy.
Spring has come, and birds' voices boom.
Flowers everywhere are also in bloom,
While insects everywhere soar and zoom.
Now it is summer, where did all the time depart?
Fall is here and school has started,
And now once more, the seasons have darted.
Every time of year goes so fast.
Still it's all fun, what a blast.
Surprisingly, we all enjoy what has passed.

Arjun Sharma, Grade 6
Dorris-Eaton School

I Am From…

I am from a home where Mom and Dad are making something delicious in the kitchen
And where photos line the walls.

I am from a yard where a big black dog romps and little mountain quail
scramble into the bushes.

I am from a neighborhood where dirt roads lead to Rock Creek and old Indian caves and where
beautiful mountain scenes are waiting to be seen.

I am from a family that gathers for Christmas dinner each year.

Jon Ross, Grade 5
Notre Dame School

If

If I was an animal, I'd be a sleek cobra, rearing up ready to strike with my venomous teeth.
I'd take fang to anything that passed through my territory and I'd bite without warning. All would fear me.

If I was a habitat, I'd be the waterless, scorching desert. I'd sunburn anyone in my area and everything would die without water.

If I was a state, I'd be the golden land of California with the deep dark marine blue waves crashing against my shore
always letting anyone enjoy the beauty of them. I'd burrow my gold deep in the earth allowing no one to find it.

If I had a job, I'd be a construction worker. I'd build skyscrapers that scrape up to the heavens
and tower among the white gentle floating clouds.

If I was a shoe, I'd be a Nike. Swooping around the racetrack, I'd show everyone that I was the speediest
and mightiest footwear. I'd cross the finish line first and the gold medal would be mine.

Grant Matais, Grade 5
Aviara Oaks Elementary School

A Sky of Yellow
I know yellow.

Yellow smells like the tangy, miraculous aroma, of a trickling drink that refreshes your nostrils,
Like the astounding fragrance of a gorgeous sun on top of a stem,
And the repugnant odor of a golden yellow stone.

Yellow feels like an excruciatingly painful, spherical, scorching ball,
Like a metallic, molding mineral that feels smooth, sleek and polished,
And like a crunchy, gritty, salty snack, rough and crude.

Yellow looks like a gargantuan smile painted on a bubbly excited face
And like a glimmering, shiny, valuable gem with a puny, bright, white sparkle at the corner of its cut,
And a long, round cylinder with bumpy sides and broad, thin ears, covering its body

Yellow sounds like a sharp, pointed needle piercing a bright, inflated piece of rubber
A delighted, joyous yelp of a satisfied, miniature child,
And a gentle pop of an exploding kernel.

Yellow tastes like a tart, juicy fruit that gushes a savory drink down a thirsty throat
A cheesy, tasty noodle that is gooey and sticky and very flavorful
And a mouthwatering liquid, fluffy and sweet, icy and cold.

I really know yellow.

Lilah Blalock, Grade 4
Dingeman Elementary School

Saturday Morning
There I lie, in my bed
Staring at my eyelids
The room completely dark
Opening them, slowly
Walking to the kitchen
Sitting at the table
Relaxing my head
Standing up, watching my
Ice cubes flowing to the current
In my glass of water
Wishing I was one of those
Ice cubes, but in a warm way
Amber Perry, Grade 5
Coeur d'Alene Avenue Elementary School

Roller Coaster
We
   used to best friends,
well that's before she came in the picture.
   I think I made a bad alternative
     by selecting her over you.
But I assumed I could trust you
   and I could, just not back then.
     She was there when
   I needed a shoulder to cry upon
     a hug
       or a friend.
Out of nowhere she backstabbed me.
   She and I aren't friends anymore.
     Maybe you and I could go back
       to the former days.
We jumped in the pool,
     giggled until our sides hurt,
   stayed up all night
       just having fun.
So can we go back to those days,
     those best friend days?
Savannah Lindley, Grade 6
Bethany Lutheran School

Red as a Leaf
He died today
I don't know…
He probably was old
I remember the first day
I saw him,
His bright reds!
He was very beautiful
Like the red leaf in my hand.

Sweet dreams, Rocky,
My little crayfish
The red leaf reminds me of you.
Amaya H. Frutkoff, Grade 4
Coeur d'Alene Avenue Elementary School

Summer
A time of fun and dreams
Awesome jokes and times
Sports and tubing
Rain and sunny days
Friends and family everywhere
Water skiing and kneeboarding
Traveling and leaving
Sandcastles and waves
Movies and candy
Memories and a holiday
Michael Langenbahn, Grade 5
George Washington Charter Elementary School

Calm Waters
Calm is like deep blue
and is also like a river, weaving its way through a dark forest.
It flows through my very soul, leaving a light impression.
It reminds me of the time when the full moon rose
over the silent trees, casting its pale, silver light.
It makes me feel serene like a water lily
floating on a tranquil lake.
It makes me want to listen to the soothing sounds of music
echoing through the still air…
Courtney Nam, Grade 6
St Anne School

Fish
Fish are friendly. They do not usually bite.
They are smooth and nice. Fish murmur by themselves.
They are usually in a school of fish. Good for pets.
Kristy Khullar, Grade 5
Andasol Avenue Elementary School

I Know Ballet
I know ballet
The feel of the tights against my leg
The touch of the ballet leotard
The flow of the skirt as I jump
The fright of doing a solo
The pain of a fresh blister
The smell of feet and old shoes
The feel of sweat drippings roll down my back
The touch of the point shoe ribbon around my ankle
The flow of the movements to the music
The fright of messing up on stage
The pain of breaking new point shoes
The smell of the room full of sweat
The feel of finishing a class and being out of energy
The touch of the teacher correcting you
The flow of your body through the dance
The fright of the teacher saying you did something wrong
The pain of sitting in the splits
The smell of the musty air around you
I know ballet
Natalie Greenberg, Grade 6
Francis Parker School

Kids

Kids go out to play,
And after they've played all day.

They go to hit the hay,
They love it when it's a holiday.

When they wake up they are sad,
They know something is bad.

They have to go to school,
Which is very, very uncool.

Though they want to play in the pool,
They leave covered in their own drool.

Even if they feel a fool,
They always know kids rule.
Connor Tisch, Grade 6
James B Davidson Middle School

Love

Love doesn't stop
but through your heart and your soul
your love will always stay strong.
Love is like a passion
for something or someone.
Love is when you say I do
or saying you love your mom.
That is the meaning of love.
Lawrence Attaway, Grade 5
Clayton B Wire Elementary School

Cavities

The ride to his office was slow
At a snail's pace
Just my mom and I
Already I felt the pain
I arrived
He set me down
Slowly, like he wouldn't hurt me
A mask
Squeezed on my face
The bright light above
Blinding
The drill, slow
Painful
My mom in one hand
My other gripping the seat in pain
Pain was all I felt
A living hell that day
Brushing —
All I did when I got home
CAVITIES!
I hate the dentist!
Kian Farin, Grade 5
Clover Avenue Elementary School

I Am From…

I am from a home where instruments sing gaily,
Where a dog and two cats chase each other around the house,
And books line the walls,
Where family pictures speak like voices from the past

I am from a neighbor hood where coyotes howl,
Where Jackrabbits roam,
And Ranchero Airport stands alone,
Where an almond and walnut orchard supplies us with nuts

I am from a family that comes from Slovenija, Mexico, and Puerto Rico
That marks special days with special dishes

I am from a yard where a pool sits waiting for summer,
Where ivy lines the fence, and it begs to be fixed
Where the old hen house sits unused.

I am from a school where friends are many,
Where teachers are caring and kind.

This is where I live, and I wouldn't trade it for anything.
Joseph Simenc, Grade 5
Notre Dame School

Music Frights

Under comfortable blankets, hidden, I wait until sunrise.
Sounds from the downstairs piano, rising, climbing, into my room.
Frightened, I wait until the notes…silently, crumble apart.
Quinn Vu, Grade 5
St Louis De Montfort School

In Remembrance of Sara*

Sara Hirschy was gravely loved by all
She was a kind woman that wouldn't loathe anyone, tall or small
When I first met her, she was like an angel, and loved me
Never did she say bad things to me, as far as I could see
Sara was always a comrade and also very giving
I had good times with her; she made me happy, while she was living

Sara loved every single type of snack
Long as I could remember she would make delicious desserts, sugar they didn't lack
She was a friend and physical therapist partner with my mom
Even when terribly sick, she wouldn't miss work, and stay calm
Later she started to go to our church and our family got closer to theirs
I got to know her kids and they came to our house, sometimes with sugar pears

One melancholy day we got the bad news that she had cancer
In this seldom event, my family and church did all we could for her
Sara was relentless in her battle with the cancer, and wouldn't give up
Her kids were hoping she'd be as healthy as a pup
Then, on a fateful black Sunday night, she died
I was shocked and sympathized for her, and I just cried
Sometimes, I hear her voice right behind me; when I turn to look nothing is there
Kevin Michael Joslin, Grade 6
Big Springs Elementary School
*Rest in peace Sara Hirschy 1962-2008

Bob
There once was a man named Bob.
Who could not find a job.
He found a chick.
And a guy named Rick.
And they opened a restaurant called Slob.
Mingma Sherpa, Grade 5
Sonoma Charter School

Reminder of Sadness
Sadness is like turquoise
And it is also like the ocean dark and empty
It invites me into its embrace
It reminds me of the time I lost a loved one
It makes me feel empty like when I look at the ocean
It makes me want to sink into the ground
Gabriela Pattinson, Grade 6
St Anne School

Sea Glass
One day, in New York along the beach,
I took a stroll.
It was a nice day,
So I walked along the water.
Later when we were heading back,
I saw something shiny in the sand.
Clumped around it were seashells and some dead jellyfish.
I walked over to see what it was.
It was shiny, smooth and red.
It was sea glass.
What was so pleasing, was that I had lost a piece of sea glass
Earlier that day.
I brought it back home with me.
Arif Zamil, Grade 4
Montessori Family School

Why Did You Leave?*
Why did you leave?
Where did you go, that I couldn't follow?
Everything is different without you
All I know is that things will be okay
I still think about you every now and then
Of all the good times we had together
The jokes you would tell me to make me smile
Stories that would teach me a lesson in life
The words you spoke to me held such meaning for me
Those meaningful words will stay in my heart forever
You helped me achieve great accomplishments
By supporting me in whatever I did
I am grateful that you have been in my life
For some reason I can't forget you
I want to tell you how much I miss you
The question still lingers in my mind:
Why did you leave?
Montana Villamil, Grade 6
Corpus Christi School
*Dedicated to my grandpa

Far in the Ocean
Far in the ocean a sea creature swims;
slick, graceful, and black

Far in the ocean a sea creature eats;
gobble, gobble, smack

Far in the ocean the sea creature is bothered;
wait, ready, slap

Far in the ocean the sea creature stings;
pain, blood, collapse

Far in the ocean the sea creature lies;
pebbles, rocks, sand

Far in the ocean the sea creature's at peace;
waves, splash, splash
Anna Song, Grade 5
Wagon Wheel Elementary School

Caravan of Life
In life we encounter
Situations.
Many are alike, and many are very
Different.
By having the strength
From within, we can hope to
Make the right or reasonable choice.
If our choices are made with honesty
Though wrong, we can at least learn while
On this caravan of life.
Life's unpredictable,
Surprises at every turn.
We never know
What tomorrow brings.
But hope for the best and
Prepare for the worst.
Life sometimes is unfair
But there are oases,
And a joyous destination
On this caravan of life.
Belle Nguyen, Grade 6
Corpus Christi School

Determination
Hope flows through our veins.
Patriots man and women boys and girls sacrifice their only
Value so that America might be a better nation.
Peace to challenges to strengthen our country America.
Violence to humbleness but no matter what we are the
GOLDEN state California
And GOD is holding us in his hand and he will never
Give up on us!
Kyono Chantal Morin, Grade 4
Canyon View Elementary School

Leaves

Leaves are fall
                ing to the ground
Birds are tweeping all around town
Children's laughter fills the air
People raking up leaves
Kids climbing trees
1, 2, 3
Wee they scream
They are nowhere to be seen
Pop!
Out of the leaf piles they came
Their little feet running home
To find some delicious cider
Then they cry out loud
What a wonderful day!
Gracie Christensen, Grade 4
Sierra Oaks K-8 School

Time for Bed

O' omnipotent Moon, take my place
Twelve hours I have withstood
In my daily reserved space
Vulnerable, I have been waiting
For my time to come
Soon I will be waning
Behind the mountains
Where I'll soon come back from.
Nikita Bess, Grade 5
The Mirman School

Goal

Kicking the ball for a point
A teammate screaming "pass!"
Sprinting and passing
Everyone screams
"Pass the ball!"
"Hurry!"
"Pass!"
"Too late!"
Still sprinting
Doing my best
The goalie waits
I kick with all my might
As I flip it is a goal…
Joshua Taylor, Grade 4
Stone Ranch Elementary School

Rain/Sunny

Rain
Drops, Puddles, Wet, Water
Droplets, H₂O, Dry, Hot
Desert, Heat, Sizzling
Sunny
Savanna Walters, Grade 6
La Costa Heights Elementary School

Waterfalls

Water crashing down
Pretty sounds through the river
Clear water flowing
Gabriella Cortes, Grade 5
El Monte Elementary School

War Is Sadness

The sadness of war
Is just so poor
When will it stop?
When will it end?
We ask today

The sadness of war
Children do not know
If they will be alive tomorrow night
The sadness of war

The sadness of war
Injuring and killing
Children start crying
The sadness of war

The happiness of peace
Children playing in their backyard
Children going to school
The happiness of peace
Abdurashid Nour, Grade 6
Islamic School of San Diego

Blockade

Woe, woe, the blockade
Which we though so indestructible
Lost as sea
Forever, bless me

Too martial
Too warlike
Too powerful
Too greedy

Now lost at sea
Brave men
All gone
Lost
Ryan Bergman, Grade 5
The Mirman School

Tree

Used to make paper
People chop them down for fun
Used to make long boats
Oxygen
Esteban Paredes, Grade 6
St Charles Catholic School

We Can Change

We need help
hear me yelp
we have a chance
even in France

It's getting worse
like a curse
we're turning our world upside down
just look around your town

Where there was a flower
there is a tower
It's getting crazy
because some people are lazy

There is no fee
to plant a tree
I hope now you see
what the world means to me
Sarah Bell, Grade 4
Sonoma Charter School

Remembering Spring

Wake upon the rising sun.
Feel the warm morning breeze.
Winter's icy palms are gone.
No more snow on the trees.

Colored buds burst anew.
Flowers stretch in arrays.
Birds chirp alluring melodies.
Know this is a special day.

Walk along the wide brook.
Listen to the enchanting flow.
Where flowers bloom and birds sing,
Your happiness will grow.

On this first day of spring,
The change of these seasons,
We're all born again.
A new life begins.
Katherine Tsay, Grade 6
Parkmont Elementary School

Boy/Girl

Boy
Intelligent, active
Running, jumping, fishing
Brave, funny, helpful, bragger
Laughing, gossiping, playing
Wise, animal lovers
Girl
Jason Kuhn, Grade 4
Heather Elementary School

High Merit Poems – Grades 4, 5 and 6

Help Our Earth
Doing nothing is not an option,
You have to help our animal friends on Earth.
Go to your shelter to get a dog for adoption,
Or help a cat give birth.

You can also do something dramatic,
Like donating money to a needy cause.
Give freely to help the Manatees which are aquatic,
And help those with injured paws.

Cassidy Hopper, Grade 5
Central Elementary School

Rainbows
Radiant and majestic are rainbows to me.
They are ever so pleasant for eyes to see.
They bow over houses, mountains, and trees.
Showing off their colors red, yellow, and green.
There's an old legend of rainbows I'm told,
That at the end of a rainbow there's a big pot of gold!

Katrina Gallardo, Grade 6
Barstow Intermediate School

Desire
Desire is like gold
And is also like a magnet
Pulling you towards it
It runs through my mind
It reminds me of the time I went to Notre Dame
It makes me feel inspired like Rudy Ruettiger
It makes me want to go to Notre Dame!

Guy Malcolm, Grade 6
St Anne School

Calm Pastels
Positioning themselves in front of me
adding the environment which surrounds me
interlining a black white clear canvas

the artist is not done
but still anticipating the adventure
that falls ahead of her
exploring for new pastels;

through forests
to find hunter green,
deep down under great seas
to use indigo blue,
scrutinizing in mines
discovering silver and gold,
creating fire
to get true red,
many more adventures await her
to present a masterpiece.

Cassidy Lamphear, Grade 6
Bethany Lutheran School

I Wish
I wish I could see all there is to see —
To see into space
To see in the water
To see through the trees
To see the breeze.
I wish I could see all there is to see.

I wish I could hear every sound —
To hear my friend's thoughts
To hear the scamper of a bug
To hear a bird humming
And a guitar strumming.
I wish I could hear every sound.

But if I could see all there is to see
And if I could hear every sound
Would I really want to hear and see that much
Or would I want it the other way around?

Christina Duval, Grade 5
Carlthorp School

Sadness
One day I was as sad as can be,
I felt as small as a flea,
Maybe I'll see the other side of me,
Then I'll sprout like a beautiful tree,
To see birds fly up high,
And wonder why and how they fly,
Sadly, I hate to say,
Don't be a pain in my way.

Giselle Morales, Grade 4
One Hundred Eighty Sixth St Elementary School

Pencil
I sit on a table or a desk,
ready to write down ideas.
Using my pointy, sharpened nose,
I will create new worlds.
It takes your mind to guide my tip,
your thoughts say what I write.
Your hand helps me move around,
it helps me make new worlds.
Fantasy, adventure, action and more,
I'll write any genre you want.
I'll wait in a pocket on your shirt
ready, always ready to be used.
I feel pain when my point breaks,
and I must be sharpened again.
I am shrinking, slowly, shrinking,
soon I'll be no more.
I've enough left for stories or poems,
just like I am making now.
With my short, stubby body and my newly sharpened tip,
I will create new worlds.

Sanjay Mohan, Grade 5
Daves Avenue Elementary School

Dreams

In your mind
About the strangest things
With fact and fiction
Into a new world
From deep inside
Amid your waking mind
Near the end
Into a shaking place
Like a rocking ship
Before you wake

Brian Scott, Grade 6
St Anne School

The Sparkling Ocean

As the wind blows,
and the leaves rustle,
A shining blue mass of water,
just sparkling
for the world to see,
fish swimming,
a shark catching a fish,
A dolphin swiftly gliding,
and jump in the air,
water sprouting out of a whale,
the ocean,
Such a wonderful view,
just sitting on the top of the cliff,
and watching it,
Just the beautiful area to watch,
the ocean
and all this,
happens in the wonderful ocean.

Rabeeya Mayet, Grade 5
New Horizon School

Sharks

A deep sea predator
Fast, strong, and fearless
Hunts, captures
Eating its prey
Scary sharks
Fearless and mighty
They frighten boys and girls
And fish, too
These predators search for fish.

Jacob Guerrero, Grade 6
St Alphonsus School

Typhoon

I wish I were a deadly typhoon,
Dark and dangerous,
Venturing in the ocean and open land,
Slithering in a spinning pattern,
Leaving no traces of beauty and love.

Asir Savdharia, Grade 5
Lake Forest Elementary School

I Am From

I am from a home
Where newspapers collect in my driveway.
Where the air is filled with the scent of sweet almond blossoms in the spring
And the branches flow against the sky.
Where a 1936 Knaabe piano sits in our music room;

I am from a backyard
Where a not-very-often white dog takes a mud bath
Or drags dead creatures up from the creek behind our country-style home.
Where 4-H pigs wait in their pens under the shade of the olive orchard
For me and my sister to come and feed them.

I am from a neighborhood
Where neighbors turn mariachi music up on the weekend so everyone can hear.
I am from a family
Where Grandma Patsy once lived with us because she had breast cancer.

I am from a home
Where there are sayings like "It takes money to make money."

I am from a home
Where I have four dogs, three cats, two rats, five horses, and eight chickens.

I am from a wonderful family I wouldn't trade for anything.

Sutter Long, Grade 5
Notre Dame School

Geeky

Geeky is not those gangsters outside
Geeky is all about getting bullied
Geeky is very common around here
Geeky is those overalls on you
Geeky sounds like that party you are going to
Geeky sounds like your scream when a bully stuffs you in a locker
Another word for geeky is nerdy
One thing about geeky is that you are one

Justin Holmquist, Grade 6
Big Springs Elementary School

The Silent Killer

I am truly a silent killer
I will take life selfishly
I will bend you until you break
I am the nightmare your mind is to scared to dream of
I shall torment you like you never have been tortured before
I am the culprit; you have caught me but can you contain me?
I will turn your happiest thoughts to thoughts of agony and despair
I shall go down in history and I will take many with me
I can't be treated I can't be cured you will only have to wait me out
In time your numbers shall weaken
I shall prevail if I persevere
I am not planning on giving up
I am
Fever

Jon Michael Raasch, Grade 6
St Andrew's Episcopal School

I Am

I am intelligent
I wonder what I will look like when I'm older
I hear creepy noises when I'm at home alone with my sisters
I see shadows at night
I want to finish school
I am intelligent
I pretend to be a math wizard
I feel my mom and dad's love
I touch my parents' hearts
I worry if my grandpa is safe in heaven
I cry when a family member gets hurt
I am intelligent
I understand that my parents not only love me
    they also love my brother and sisters
I say whatever you get, be proud of it
I dream about my sister's future
I try to be a fun big sister
I hope people will live forever
I am intelligent

Jalissa Branstetter, Grade 4
La Presa Elementary School

Baseball

B ase runner running home
A nd now the ball is going to shortstop
S hortstop got the ball and made the play
E very base runner is moving to the next base
B all is in the air
A nd the sun is in the way of the ball
L eft Fielder sees the ball and he catches it
L eft Fielder became player of the game

Andrew Pinto, Grade 6
Aliso Elementary School

Friends

Friends are people,
Who care about you,

Friends are people,
Who will help you when something is wrong,

Friends are people,
Who will forgive you no matter what,

Friends are people,
Who will never lie,

Friends are people,
Who will not talk behind your back,

Friends are people,
Who will do anything for you,

I have friends and that's what they do.

Fiona Domergue, Grade 6
Grant Elementary School

Circle of Time

The future brings us tomorrow,
The past brought us yesterday,
But today is a day to enjoy,
To live.
We all live in the circle of time.
We all understand the circle of time,
For it brings us the gift of life, creation.
The Great Spirit created the circle of time
For us to live in.
We must respect the circle of time,
For it respects us.

Andrew Campion, Grade 4
The Mirman School

Gift Given to Man

Most beautiful aspect of Mother Earth,
Visualizing this appearance makes me feel mirth.
Magnificence of nature surpasses all other
Gorgeous creatures here and there hover.

Nature donates an incredible amount to humankind,
Thinking of its sacrifice boggles the mind.
We destroy the gift of nature,
Without thinking of its marvelous feature.

This wonderful gift has been given to man.
It is a blessing to the whole of our clan.
Flowers, plants, and birds swaying and chirping,
Catching my eye the butterfly's colorful wing.

Vibrant colors of season everywhere seen,
In summer and spring zesty green
In fall, red, orange, and yellow
Makes me feel so mellow.

Songbirds build their nests on the branches of a tree,
Likewise does the small gray chickadee.
Woodpeckers peck at tree trunks all day long.
Here is nature's lovely song.

Nishita Shetty, Grade 6
Challenger School – Ardenwood

Winter

The sugar cookies are as good as hot chocolate.
I am as jolly as my mom.
The elves are as busy as my grandma.
My sister is as colorful as presents under a tree.
The fog is as white as a ghost.
My Christmas tree is as big as my house.
My stocking as heavy as dumbbells.
The tamales were as hot as the oven.
The eggnog is as cold as ice.
My grandma is as beautiful as an angel.

Unica Garza, Grade 5
Jackson Elementary School

Dreamer
I am a dreamer
A dreamer in the clouds
I have a heart that can't be broken
I am a dreamer
A dreamer in the sky
Watch my words become my wings
So that I might fly…
So that I might fly down to Earth
So that I might mourn with the rain
Hannah Yi, Grade 6
Grant Elementary School

A Kitten
Meow! meow!
It's a kitten!
Prrr! Prr! When she sleeps.
Scratch! Scratch! When she plays.
Hiss! Hiss!
Boing! A mouse flies across the room!
Wshshsh!…
It's, it's,
A calico mini monster!
Sharp razor claws!
Scratching here and there,
Wshshsh!…
It's another flying mouse!
Kelsey Swall, Grade 5
Sundale Elementary School

Baby Doves
Baby doves
Who fell from the tree next door
Into our backyard.
Ever so delightful.
Little wings
That will be bigger soon
And they cry
"Help us help us."
When they have to leave
I miss them so much.
Today, they come to our house saying
"Thank you thank you."
And they are still here
To play.
Ryan Strausbaugh, Grade 5
Bethany Lutheran School

Raccoon!
Baby raccoons capture their prey
The mask is a disguise
Some colors gray and black
They are fast but scary
Also quiet and sneaky
Angel Guerrero, Grade 6
St Alphonsus School

My Mother Is an Owl
My mother is an owl
Seeing everything that I do
Whether I'm sleeping
Or causing mischief
Nothing can escape my mother's eye

My mother is an owl
Catching prey for me
Like hot dogs and chicken
Enough for everybody

My mother is an owl
Protecting me from danger
Seeing everything around us
Looking out for a stranger

My mother is an owl
I love her very much
Even though she scolds me
I cherish her with all my heart
Aisha Asif, Grade 6
Islamic School of San Diego

Golden Poppies in California
Poppies all over make California golden
That's why California is full of gold.
Gold poppies are golden,
and they grow in California.
That makes golden poppies.
Claire Bertrand, Grade 5
Ecole Bilingue de Berkeley

Snow
I love snow.
Take my hand,
And we'll make a snowman.

I love snow.
My hand, you will take,
And we'll catch a snowflake.

I love snow.
Zeque Goldsmith-Morgan, Grade 4
Montessori Family School

Bears
Soft fur covering his backside.
Fierce roars scaring animals away.
Smoky the Bear
Protecting children from fires.
Small cub sleeping with their mother.
The animal decorating
Our state's flag.
Noel Barrera, Grade 6
St Alphonsus School

Repetition
A dear runs by
The wind rustles the trees
The forest is so peaceful

A bunny scampers away
The dandelions float by
The meadow is so peaceful

A dolphin jumps from the water
The waves lap the shore
The beach is so peaceful

Forest, meadow, beach
All so peaceful
I am calm
Nash Taylor, Grade 6
Bernice Ayer Middle School

Spring Fun
My favorite time of year is here
The sun is bright the air is clear
Spring is here gone is fall
Now it's time to hit the ball

I put on my jersey, socks, and cleats
And run with a skip upon my feet
Sweat running down my face
As I run to the next base

1st, 2nd, 3rd almost home
I love running the base alone
The crowd cheers as I pass home plate
My coach tells me I did so great

As I walk back to the dugout
My teammates shout
I am the best there is no doubt.
Leticia Lara, Grade 6
Barstow Intermediate School

My Sister Is a Pain
Sisters are a pain
They annoy you
They get everything they want

They get to go wherever they want
They get on your nerves
They blame everything on you!

They think they are better than you
Just because they are older than you
Even though she does all those things
I LOVE HER!
Maria Valadez, Grade 6
Fairview Elementary School

High Merit Poems – Grades 4, 5 and 6

The Black Spotted Cheetah
The black spotted cheetah
Ran across the woods
As fast as lightning
In search for his dinner

He searched for his dinner
Up on a tree
He found it there
Laying so freely

The cheetah ran
With all his might
He finally caught it
And took a big bite

The next day
He was hungry again
So this strong beast
Went back for a feast
Ramzy Awad, Grade 6
Islamic School of San Diego

Old Willow Tree
I'm just an old willow tree
I sit and pretend someone cares about me
I know the truth, I am not loved
But I think someday, my turn will come
I'll be something beautiful, then someone will care
People will know how I got there
A stool or a bench, yeah that's it
That's what I'll be, then all of you will see
That I can become something
I see a man, he's coming my way
He's carrying some tools, I know it's my day
A day when I'll shine and be something new
Something used to help people like you
He's cutting me down, I'm so excited
But later I find, I'm going to be ignited
A plain block of wood is all I'll become
In a young man's fireplace my life will end,
But to that man my warmth I'll send.
Sapna Singh, Grade 6
Francis Parker School

Sleep
I love to be warm and cozy in bed,
While many things drift in my head,

I cuddle my teddy bear close to my heart,
I hope we will never be far apart,

I never want to be waken,
Until I smell the bacon.
Sydney Schwartz, Grade 5
Theodore Roosevelt Elementary School

The Best Mommy
My mom is…
An awesome person
Who I have confidence in
She is always thinking about others
She does not like messy stuff
She likes clean stuff
She helps me out in everything
I need help in
She is very energetic
She is an awesome cook
She makes everything very good
My mom is always worrying about my health
She is very fair to everyone
She makes me laugh about everything
She is always proud of me
Especially when I get good grades
She is sometimes moody
When I make her mad
My mom sometimes annoys me
But I still love her
From the bottom of my heart
Stephany Huitron, Grade 6
Century Community Charter School

Desolation
Desolation is like gray
And is also like sadness
It seeps in through my mind
It reminds me of the time where I felt no happiness
It makes me feel like a sun with nowhere to shine
It makes me want to cry out in terror and weep at my sorrow
Siena Hahn, Grade 6
St Anne School

Violin
Wandering into a mist of notes and treble clefs
Gliding, creeping, stumbling into a pit of two strings
The sound trembles through your mind
As if
In another world
Forte fortissimo piano pianissimo
Trudging up stairs of swerving scales reaching the top
The note saunters out
The piece is finished
I come out of my other world and into another
MacKenzie Kugel, Grade 5
The Willows Community School

Aurora Borealis
I wish I were a radiant aurora borealis,
Colorful and continuous,
Slithering like a multicolored snake through the moonlit night,
Swirling and twirling like an acrobat through the air,
Becoming lighter and lusterless until I'm gone.
Kaiya McCullough, Grade 5
Lake Forest Elementary School

The Day I Fell into a World Book

If I fell into a world book…
I wouldn't know how I would look
Maybe I'd look like Maryland
Oh I could see me stand
I may be Vietnam
I'm the huge dam
Or even the giant Amazon Forest
Or the plains in the Midwest
I would know everything that happened
Like the problem about global warming
A world book can be very interesting
Because I can be almost anything!
If I fell into a world book…

David Vo, Grade 5
St Barbara School

My Best Friend

My best friend
We have a lot in common
He likes to play video games
And his favorite food is Ramen

He has been to my house once
For a couple hours
We ran around a lot
Until we really dropped

We actually became friends in 5th grade
So we've been friends for 7 months
His name starts with an "M"
And we've had a lot of fun.

Mihir Desai, Grade 5
Theodore Roosevelt Elementary School

Fall and Spring

Fall,
Leaves, trees,
Windy, brown, crunchy,
Seasons, beautiful, mysterious, colorful,
Breeze, bright, green,
Flowers, fruits,
Spring

Ron Oppenheimer, Grade 5
Montessori Family School

Red

Red — roses
Resting in the garden,
An inky pen decorating the table
Red — the delicious strawberries
Waiting to feed the young boy
The long, beautiful scarf
Wrapped around a pole
And the look of blood inside you!!!

Jennifer Hernandez, Grade 6
St Alphonsus School

Fever 1793

I come without warning and I kill without mercy.
I see the fear in the eyes of many, and do not stop to give them even a penny.
I am the blood that stains all of your sheets, the fierce yellow eyes that cannot be beat.
I am the trouble you see everywhere, I am the reason for your discontent.
I never stop but to see, your pain and your trials,
All of your suffering, that reason is me.
I break many hearts, and the cart that pushes me.
No mortal man can see what I see, no famished mind can tell what I am.
The pulsing blood that runs through your veins,
The shattering screams outside of your windowpanes.
There is only one thing that can open the key,
The only one thing that can demolish me.
I am the irking nightmares that ruin your dreams,
the eerie death of rich, poor, black, and white.
I am a small creature…Can you guess what I bite?
You can scour the cities, you will never find me.
I am the one reason for your darkest dreams,
Do you know what that means?
There are precious few men that can endeavor,
The dark yellow eyes, the piercing, scared screams,
Start packing your bags…I am the Fever.

Eva Yavorkovsky, Grade 6
St Andrew's Episcopal School

My Edible Pencil Box

My pencils are stale, crimson red licorice.
The erasers are chewy, carnation pink gummies.
Inside is sticky, creamy white frosting used for glue.
Nothing at all really tastes that crummy.
They are all held in a delicious milk chocolate pencil box.
If I was allowed to eat as much sweets as I want, this would be my fifth.
However, this poem is just a myth.

Vanessa Nguyen, Grade 5
Andasol Avenue Elementary School

School Troubles

Oh my! It is the first day of school.
I am so shy, I even try not to act cool.
Oh no! I will have to go back to waking up early,
And eating a cereal brand called "Toe."
I will see many, bullies nabbing at my hair.
But I see no reason, to look at my hair so awkwardly, this is called stare.
Those who like so much treason, are the ones I mostly dislike.
Darn, I will be a loner with the season, for there is no one to like.
There is gonna be so much homework,
And with my luck it is gonna be math.
There is gonna be a new lesson called patch work,
While I'd rather be taking a bath.
Hey! I got the nicest teacher, Mrs. Lee who gives no work to do.
The one who gives you a really nice day.
It is the place that every fifth grader wants to go to,
I heard that she is really gay, (I mean the happiness, okay)
Maybe I am going to like school for once.
Since I am going today, I will give myself a chance.

Seyeong Min, Grade 5
Andasol Avenue Elementary School

Snow

Snow is a vast cold thing.
Good for skiing, snowball fights, snow forts.
It's that great hot chocolate after a long day
playing in the snow.

Erol Stevens, Grade 4
Montessori Family School

A Confused Poet

Frustrated, so completely frustrated,
Thoughtless, so narrow-minded,
The teacher tells me to write a free verse poem,
And I don't know what to write about.
Should I do it of a lost loved one,
Someone who I was really close to?
Yet, I have not experienced death.

Should I do it of a lost best friend,
Whom I used to talk with every day?
Yet, all my friends are still close to me.
Should I do it of my long dead pet,
The one I used to cuddle in my arms all the time?
Yet, I never had a pet whom I cared for.

Frustrated, so completely frustrated,
Thoughtless, so narrow-minded,
But then a thought comes to my head.
What if I write about not knowing what to write about?
So, I give myself a pat on the back,
"What a good idea I have,
That I am writing a poem about,
Not knowing what to write a poem about."

Pablo Solar-Sanchez, Grade 6
Parkmont Elementary School

Stars

High,
shining
in the big
dark sky above,
laying down seeing
they shine down on
the Earth, just glistening
up in space, waiting to fall down, so light
it brights up the night, can't see them
in the day, millions and billions, too
many to count, constellations
may occur, everywhere
you look in the
sky there's one bright
star just sitting there, up
so high out of the atmosphere,
if you see a shooting star
wish on it and it may
come true.

Alex Leventis, Grade 5
St Louis De Montfort School

The Summer Season

The sun shines on the radiant water,
As the day temperatures start to matter.
I wonder when summer days will reappear,
I'm eager to have the nights warm and clear.
Thoughts of days so long and nights so brief,
Engulf my mind with sublime relief,
The sun seems like a ripe orange to be gorged upon,
While I look around and see a lively fawn.

Away in a plane like a white bee soaring through air,
I vacation in a distant land with unusual flair,
Far from the rigors of daily work.
My family is busy without going berserk.
The basketball shoes slip onto my feet,
After removing my soccer cleats.
The basketball is gunned towards the hoop,
Alternating with the soccer shoot.
Gliding through the pool perfecting my stroke,
Keeping ahead of the nearest bloke.
I wish school would never will start,
As I hate to depart on life's next part.

Vishal Jain, Grade 6
Dorris-Eaton School

The Untamed Ocean

The ocean is wild
It cannot be tamed
People will try to tame it
But it will turn out the same.

From the creatures down below
They flow and they flow
Where will it lead?
No one will ever know.

From the ocean to the sea
Now I can see what is right in front of me
The oceans wild curves
Help me tame my wild nerves.

Cynthia Hernandez, Grade 6
Cimarron Education Center

Rainbows of Delight

Rainbows of delight shine through me
Rainbows of delight are in the world of violet
Rainbows of delight run around in a meadow of happiness
Rainbows of delight dance in the dreams of joy
Rainbows of delight play in the clouds of calmness
Rainbows of delight fly through my head
Rainbows of delight sing over the world
Rainbows of delight fly through my dreams
Rainbows of delight swish in my soul
Rainbows of delight glide through my mind.

Saba Amid, Grade 4
The Mirman School

Love

Love wears long and ruffled gowns in the most beautiful colors with a heart on the sleeves of every dress. She has gorgeous long brunette locks of hair. Love makes you get goose bumps, on your arms, butterflies in your stomach, and tongue tied when you feel her. She has porcelain white skin that she says she has to represent her purity. She knocks you down and then helps you up at the most unexpected times. Love carries a single luscious, big, and beautiful crimson rose in her soft hands. Love is bossy, outgoing, and destructive. While sometimes she can be sweet, innocent, and shy. Love is one of the most controlling and powerful feelings which is why she is queen and ruler over all. She is scary and yet wonderful. Love is the most gorgeous feeling ever. She is trapped inside your heart like a butterfly in its cocoon wishing to escape and let herself go out of control, but when she does nobody can stop her until she is broken or has gotten tired. Love knows that someday she will be set free from her prison, your heart.

Michelle McCann, Grade 5
Wagon Wheel Elementary School

Recipe for Marriage

Take half cup of love, one teaspoon of flower. Put a cup of kiss in water. Mix with a big spoon, until it turns really red like a big marriage heart. Pour in a big pan. Cook in an oven at 300 degrees until it looks like it's a marriage. You can tell it's done when it will be like two cute couples. Let stand until it is like a bright red heart. Cut and serve only one slice of marriage. Taste the only one slice of marriage.

Selina Thao, Grade 5
Clayton B Wire Elementary School

If I Were

If I were a state, I'd be Washington D.C. with national monuments and the White House on my streets.
If I were an animal, I'd be a cheetah with stealth, speed, and I would be able to run through tall stalks of grass happily.
If I were anybody besides myself, I'd be Wolfgang Amadeus Mozart,
Gracefully creating classical music for the enjoyment of listening to.
If I were a mountain, I'd be Mt. Everest with my snowy peak touching the very tip of space.
If I were a color, I'd be the color blue filling the sky with life and the ocean with crisp blue water.
If I were a musical instrument, I'd be a piano, able to make sounds like no other type of instrument.
If I were a plane, I'd be the Air Force 1 listening in on top secret things.
If I were a president from the past I'd be George Washington, who was able to sign the Declaration of Independence.
If I were a sea animal, I'd be a great white shark, the mightiest of all the sea animals.

Jordan Edgin, Grade 5
Aviara Oaks Elementary School

The Fever

Deadly, vicious, and fast are three adjectives that describe me. I make my victims writhe with pain. The more I spread, the more ravenous I become. I am the Devil's pet. Are the mortals smart enough to know where I am and where I am not? Almost everyone who confronts me dies in a matter of days. I am just a virus, yet I spread as fast as light. If I am correct, 1 out of every 100 people survive. Some gruesome things I do to my victims are making them cough out a black, murky liquid that will make a victim's loved one cry from the sight of the liquid. I can also make the victim's turn a dark yellow. I am like a 24/7 stalker/serial killer that is ready to attack at anytime. I watch you when you aren't watching me. That is what makes me so immortal. I will assure you. You can run, but you can't hide. I will hunt you down with my deadly, vicious, and fast moves. No matter how hard you try to escape me, I will always have one eye watching you. Beware, yellow fever is here.

Jason Chen, Grade 6
St Andrew's Episcopal School

Gym

Dear Kids
I am gym I can make people lose weight, I can make them athletic, I will make you do different stuff like dancing, soccer, baseball, basketball, volleyball and football. Some kids hate me because they think that I make them run a lot but some kids love running and that's why they love me, I am gym. I think dancing is the thing that kids hate the most because some people are not so good at dancing but some are good, I am gym. I am gym you know me for my wooden floor and my big walls I think people get very strong when they come to me they get strong by lifting weights and using running machines, also by hitting and punching bag real hard, I am gym. So remember kids I am good at making you very strong and athletic, I am gym.

Jesus Ramos, Grade 5
Clayton B Wire Elementary School

Scared

As I lay here at night
I feel a little fright

I pull the covers over my face
and feel as though I should keep it in place

I look underneath my bed
and it's just me in my head

Carlin Kinlow, Grade 5
Theodore Roosevelt Elementary School

Daffodils

I lie beneath the pale blue sky as I watch the birds pass by
It was springtime, I was walking
I glanced and saw some daffodils dance
It was like the whole world was alive

My heart was pounding with a wonderful beat
I went back home and fell asleep
Then it was dark
I woke up and looked at the sky

Emma Vollkommer, Grade 4
Coeur d'Alene Avenue Elementary School

Fever

I am fever
I have no mercy
I am the culprit for all fatalities
I am an assailant stalking you,
Preparing to dispatch you
I burn through life after life relentlessly
I am like a black rose in a colorful flower patch
You may want to depict me as a murderer,
But you are wrong,
I am death
I instantaneously have you in my grasp
It doesn't matter if you are rich or poor
I am coming, and you know it
The strong cower before me,
The weak beg for mercy but get none
Don't try to kill me for you will get nowhere
You can hand out a million vaccinations
They won't help because I am too strong
It's too late for you, and just the beginning for me

Lance Miranda, Grade 6
St Andrew's Episcopal School

Love

Love is the winding path that always meets at the end
The missing peace to some hearts
The warm wind on the beach
Yet love leaves the heart easily
But is so strong, always comes back

Katherine Corwin, Grade 4
Phillips Brooks School

Did I?

Did I clean up the kitchen?
Did I clean up my room?
Did I clean up my pet's business?
Did I clean up the trash in the streets?
Did I clean up my valuable collection?
Did I clean up my act?
Did I clean up my grades?
Did I help the older ones cross the street?
Did I help the community?
Did I do my essay?
Did I help my classmate with his homework?
Did I do my homework?
Did I accept the challenge?
Did I surpass expectations?
Did I skip school?
Did I forget your name?
Did I aspire to greatness?
Did I remember to pray?
Did I bring joy to my family?

Joshua Berja, Grade 6
Corpus Christi School

The Beach

Aquamarine waves crashing, soft sand gleaming in the sun,
tide pools glittering, lifeguard posts,
kids splashing in the shallow waters.

Grace Hammel, Grade 5
Our Lady of Assumption School

A Pink Carnation

A pink carnation
Emerald leaves
A sharp mint smell
Delicate petals arranged around the stem.
The flower resting short
In a green pasture.
In bloom
Its pink petals grow,
You can see its magenta color
From a mile away.
A gardener comes
To pick it up
And puts it in an exquisite bouquet
With other stunning, dazzling flowers.

Kristen Mascarenhas, Grade 5
Mayfield Jr School of the Holy Child Jesus

My Older Brother Robert Andrew

You are as buff as Gaston in *Beauty and the Beast*,
You're like a game of Stratego making sure of your every move,
You are the brains behind the story,
Your eyes sparkle like the stars in the sky at night,
You think as fast as a jaguar runs through the field,
You are like a John Deere tractor, you never stop moving.

Caroline D. Ricci, Grade 6
La Costa Heights Elementary School

Bunny
Big, fluffy, and floppy ears
Unable to resist carrots
Nobody can catch a bunny
Nose is red and damp
You'll be happy with a bunny
Kylee Spagnola, Grade 5
Joseph M Simas Elementary School

Oblivious Sea Anemone
Lying in the sea
So peacefully
Idle to its surrounding
Oblivious to the fish
Lying in the sea
So peacefully
Like the sun in midday
Oh sea anemone
May I lay
In the sea
So peacefully
Alongside you
Asmaa Deiranieh, Grade 6
Islamic School of San Diego

I Love You More
I love snow
But I love you more
I love rainbows
But I love you more
I love games
But I love you more
I love your love
But I love you even more!
Miranda Huntley, Grade 4
Upper Lake Elementary School

Earthquake
Earthquake
On a rampage
Rattling the mountains
6.8 on the Richter Scale
It stops.
Justin Beverly, Grade 5
Theodore Roosevelt Elementary School

Sun/Moon
Sun
Huge, light
Blazing, blinding, shining
Day, play, sleep, night
Glowing, glistening, brightening
Big, grey
Moon
Gabriela Pariseau, Grade 5
St Louis De Montfort School

Orange
Orange
Color, pretty
Honeysuckle and scarlet
My dad's very favorite
Golden
Emma Dodson, Grade 5
Sundale Elementary School

Nature
The little drops of rain,
the wild fur on a lion's mane,
the trees blowing in the wind
whispers to those who have sinned,
the sinned who cut the trees,
the trees who stand in pain,
the little drops of rain.
Shelsey Stephens, Grade 6
Bernice Ayer Middle School

Fountain of Faith*
My water slowly spills over you,
filling you with faith and happiness.
And those who are not worthy
shall suffer from the pain of hate.
My foaming bubbles represent all people
who are worthy and fair.
I let people embrace themselves
with faith and plenty of love forever.
As long as infinity is still going on
we shall stay happy
for the rest of our lives!!!
Milena DeGuere, Grade 4
The Mirman School
*Inspired by the fountain at Descanso Gardens.

Tomb
tomb
dry, art
crying, laughing, sleeping
looking for afterlife
coffin
Krista Mugnai, Grade 6
Big Springs Elementary School

Under
I wonder what is underneath
Under all the coral reefs
I wonder if there are sharks with light
Under all the schools of fish so tight
I wonder what's on the ocean floor
Under all the whales galore
I wonder what is under…
Sydney Walthall, Grade 6
Lockeford Elementary School

My Dog
I am so short
Compared to my family
And I look so different.
I always forget
How to sit and shake
I wonder why?
When they are eating
At the dinner table
I search for leftovers
Like meatloaf
Ahh meatloaf.
When I am full
I love to curl up
In Kiana's warm and fuzzy jacket
And go to sleep.
Kiana McCaul, Grade 4
Daves Avenue Elementary School

School Days
There are cliques,
There are groups,
You don't know which one to choose.

School can be a nightmare,
Who doesn't think so.

Sometimes people can be so low,
When you walk down the hallway
As the new girl, people stare at you
Like you aren't from this world.

You go to your class,
Sweating in fear
Knowing that the first day is here.
Katherine Gussman, Grade 6
Blessed Sacrament School

Blossoming
The days go by
I watch
The little sunflower grows
The sunlight towering
Over the innocent flower
The radiant yellow
Petals glowing in the sunlight
I watch the sunflower swaying
From side to side
In the breeze
Whenever I look at something like that
I am amazed
How one little seed
Can turn into something so beautiful.
Taylor Anderson, Grade 6
Bethany Lutheran School

High Merit Poems – Grades 4, 5 and 6

Prophet Muhammad

Prophet Muhammad came to the world of legacy
His humble and kind character created mercy
He was respected among his people
And treated everyone equal
Known to cherish for his honesty
Allah has chosen him for prophecy
The Quran was revealed to him alone
The final words to the Muslim world

Sarah Antabli, Grade 4
New Horizon School

Laughter

I laugh when something is funny
It makes me red as a tomato

I roll and burst all of the laughter in me
I hold my stomach and kick my legs like a windmill

Laughter makes my eyes water like rain
I like this feeling — it's like sunshine
Laughter is good for me

Natalie Magaña, Grade 5
St Barbara School

Love

Kiss hugs sweet adorable love
When I'm with you I feel happiness in the air
Boxes of chocolate and red roses
That's what love is about

Yvonne Bibriesca, Grade 4
Jackson Elementary School

Artichokes

Eeeeew! What's that smell?
Peeeeu! What's that smell?
On no!
My mom's cooking artichokes
Every time I eat an artichoke
it really makes me choke!
I hate, hate, hate
absolutely
HATE artichokes!!!
Ucky, yucky artichokes
are green like vomit.
Ucky, yucky artichokes
are nastier than gutter sewage.
I hate, hate, hate
absolutely
HATE artichokes!!!
No! No!
There's icky, icky artichokes on my plate.
I whine and whine,
but it doesn't work.
Oh well!

Robert Heriman, Grade 5
Jackson Elementary School

The Song of Life

I stand amongst the tall grasses of the plain
A wind flies by, whistling through the tall grass
And they bow down to the wind, adding their small voices
Their sounds ripple through them like a wave
That never ends its song

Bees sing in their soft and buzzing voices
Birds call out to their young
And mice squeak as they scamper on the ground
All add their strong calls
To those of the wind's
And even the trees, both young and old
Rustle their leaves in harmony

All nature sings as one song
As one orchestra, one harmony which sings forever
The music is all around us; all we have to do is listen
Listen to the one word it sings:
Life

Mira Huang, Grade 6
Alternative Family Education School

I Am a Fake, But I'll Be Real

I am a fake, but I'll be real
Don't be afraid, if you are brave
You have a world with friends
But if you fake them
Nothing will be real

I am a rake, but I'll be real
Think about it without fake
There is a place with happiness and love
But that place will be a fake
If you don't believe is a fake

I am a fake, but I'll be real
Inside your heart there is a fake love
If you fought for it, is real
Sometimes is always fake
But you would know that
Your heart would tell you if that real or fake
You would see…

Carolina Chu, Grade 6
Purple Lotus International Institute

Leaf

She gave me a leaf,
I imagine where this little leaf has been,
In the fire I suppose,
Its fiery red color shows,
The burnt colors make it look like coal,
I wonder if it misses its other leaf friends,
She gave me a leaf.

Tess Reinhardt, Grade 4
Coeur d'Alene Avenue Elementary School

Springtime

Springtime is here,
No need to fear.
There are birds everywhere
And clouds in the air.
All I hear are the sounds of the birds
Saying to me chirp! chirp! chirp!
I see many flowers in the ground
And many birds flying around.
This is the season to laugh and cheer
Because the spring season is now here!

Nicole Biley, Grade 5
St Linus School

Red Is Everything

Red is the blazing sun
Lying over the land
Red is a stop sign
The fine American flag
Symbolizing our freedom
Red is the siren flashing a
Blinding light
Red is love, kind sweetness of life
Red can be as hot as chili peppers
Burning in your mouth
Red jelly tickling your tongue
Red is everywhere and
Everywhere it shall be

Jaclyn Wittbrodt, Grade 4
Carlthorp School

Hurricane

I wish I were a dreadful hurricane,
Horrible and violent,
Twirling like a harmful tornado,
Lasting days and days,
Harming everything in my way.

Marcos Perzabal, Grade 5
Lake Forest Elementary School

My Favorite Place

Rock Beach
Wintery Saturdays
Crispy cold
Sunrise
Light breeze
Gulls talking
Boats roaring
A rainbow of rocks
Burning logs
Fresh rain
Running along the shore
Collecting shells
Happy
Free

Sasha Hellwig, Grade 5
Theodore Roosevelt Elementary School

High Desert

An Indian desert on a two-mile plateau,
In between the Himalayan Mountains,
The desert is fifteen feet below the snow,
The snow makes rivers in this very hot desert

There is nothing seen,
Unless your eyes are keen,
Then all is revealed,
In the sand there are desert snakes, lizards, salamanders, mice and fox

The cacti are fresh and juicy,
Hummingbirds are by flowers or fruits,
Desert hares down by the roots,
As dusk falls the elf owl hoots

The chunks of snow fall and make rivers,
While the snake slithers,
The kangaroo rat jumps,
And the small desert fox burrows

On the sand the snake lunges,
And the rat dodges,
In the river the crocodile snaps,
And the salamander zips out of the trap.

Alex Bistagne, Grade 5
Mayfield Jr School of the Holy Child Jesus

The Ocean

I love the ocean.
As the warm glossy waves come up,
the shells cling to the sand so they don't get pulled into the deep.
Dolphins dazzle as the sunset hits the water.
Fragile starfish glow as the sunset slips into the night.

Camryn Storvold, Grade 4
Stone Ranch Elementary School

Survival

Survival has a never ending fear,
But he himself is the bravest warrior of them all.
He has a unique imagination, with a sun hat on top of his head.
He roams around the tantalizing forest and the raging seas.
He only sips water from a nearby creek.
"Go forward, never go back," is his motto,
"There is a tiger ready to snap, if you turn around to look behind."
His knife is ready to kill when something comes near.
And when he has found his treasure and he thinks he is done,
Nature sits around the corner laughing and having fun.
With his bow and arrow he aims toward a tiger walking away.
Softly whistling and humming like a morning bird singing a song,
He tries to get the tiger's attention.
When the 2 eyes meet, he gently lets go, and misses.
The only choice now is to use his survival technique.
He plunges forward before the tiger could leap away.
The battle was over, survival had survived.

Caroline Batson, Grade 5
Wagon Wheel Elementary School

Ten Little Elephants

Ten little elephants wandered off fine
One got lost and then there were nine
Nine little elephants went on a date
One couldn't go and then there were eight

Eight little elephants all turned eleven
One didn't change and then there were seven
Seven little elephants were all playing sticks
One didn't do good and then there were six

Six little elephants all took a dive
One flipped over and then there were five
Five little elephants were all very poor
One got rich and then there were four

Four little elephants sang the note D
One didn't like it and then there were three
Three little elephants said it was true
One disagreed and then there were two

Two little elephants ate a big bun
One ate a small one and then there was one
One little elephant went shopping for a ton
He never came back and now there is none

Samantha Pallett, Grade 5
Kentwood Elementary School

We the People

Peace within our world,
Faith shined upon her pearly white smile,
Bold in the future of her freedom,
Humble, she is grateful for trust,
With peace, our challenge will be met.
Our world is changing,
Peace is a treasure.

Amanda Templin, Grade 4
Canyon View Elementary School

The Wave

When I am surfing I feel the wave catch my board
It swoops me up onto the wave
When I'm riding the wave it feels awesome
It feels so good when you
Drop
Into the wave
Being in a barrel is like heaven
Once you fall out of the wave
It feels
So
Good to know
That I
Caught
The Wave

Zak Sievers, Grade 4
Sierra Oaks K-8 School

Teachers

Teachers, what a wonderful person
Who takes their time
Cares for students
Giving them knowledge to succeed
Preparing them for college

Teachers are smart
They are helping, caring, and loving
Teachers will help you to do right
They will also make you bright
To give you education
To make you very smart
It takes a lot of studying
To get you to a good start

Good teachers will help you to succeed in life
They help you to grow
To grow in good education
And to help you to think right
Who was the one who helped you pass the test?
Who was the one who taught you all that you know?
With a little bit of time and effort
Teachers are the one

Amber Daughtry, Grade 6
Century Community Charter School

The Clouds

The clouds sway swiftly
In funny different shapes
In the dark night sky

Grant Nelson, Grade 4
Mayfield Jr School of the Holy Child Jesus

Survival

Survival, slithering alone in the wild.
Nothing to feed on, only using what lies around him,
and what lies within him.

He is feared and well known, avoided with every chance.
Survival has a hard life, adapting to every climate,
every place, every situation.

He can come in many forms.
Even as a rugged, torn up person,
who looks like that day is his last.

He lurks in the darkest caves, all alone,
or places unknown.
Even though he prefers the form of a cobra,
he may turn into whatever he pleases.

Sometimes in many different places at once.
Survival is the wild.
Survival needs nobody.

Justin Tropp, Grade 5
Wagon Wheel Elementary School

Annoyance
Some kids are nice
Some kids are mean
But there's one problem
They won't let you be
You will see

Let me be
You see little children
I'm trying to read
You won't do what I say
Just leave me alone
Be gone I say

So I dashed around
I jumped up and down
I made bird noises peek peek
I bounced on my head
I made sounds like bing or bebopidyded
Until they hollered stop!
We can't take the jumping the squeaking
The squawking and the bouncing
We're sorry we teased you
This we really dread.
Darren Chism, Grade 5
Merryhill Country School

My Favorite Place
Grandma's house
every day
any day
all the time
happy days
cookies baking
birds singing
fun movies
my loving grandma
orange trees
yummy food
watch movies
bake and cook
super happy
joyful
Milla Almaraz, Grade 5
Theodore Roosevelt Elementary School

Sadness
Sadness is like a cool dark blue
and is also like a dark night forest.
It flows through my imagination.
It reminds me of a petrifying rain storm.
It makes me feel alone or forgotten.
It makes me want to run and hide.
Corrina Thompson, Grade 6
St Anne School

Basketball
I like bouncing
I envy the rim
It hurts a lot
The fingertips
So soothing
The horn
So loud
Not the bag
So stuffy
So uncomfortable
I'm suffocating
Ryan Muirhead, Grade 6
James B Davidson Middle School

Don't Be Shy
Don't be shy
just get up and play
throw the chuddy ball around
kick it
throw it
do anything with it
just get up and play
Dalton Melgar, Grade 5
Andasol Avenue Elementary School

Molecule
M olecule is my dog
O ften sleeps
L ikes all kinds of food
E xcept ginger
C ute
U nder covers to go to sleep in my bed
L ikes every person he knows
E xciting all the time
Alyssa Kent, Grade 4
Charles Armstrong School

I Am
I am a rock,
sturdy and strong
I am a bear,
smart plus caring
I am young,
never grow older
I am green,
moldy and powerful
I am a coast,
peaceful and adventurous
I am a basketball,
jumps and bounces
I am creativity,
art, colors and structure
Abel Rossi, Grade 4
Carlthorp School

Camping
I prefer buying tents
But I only have 50 cents

I would also buy firewood
But only if I could

But that is okay!
My mom is here anyway.
And we are at Sports Chalet
"Thank you, Mommy!"
Jezelle Escobar-Lopez, Grade 5
Sundale Elementary School

Sky
I gaze at the night sky
I get lost in the many stars
I never want to leave
Hours pass
I awaken to the morning sky
Macy Drew, Grade 6
Bernice Ayer Middle School

Dancing
dancing
graceful, emotional
turning, kicking, leaping
as though no one is watching
expression
Taylor Britt, Grade 6
Barstow Intermediate School

A Best Friend
A best friend never lets you down
  or leaves you all alone.
A best friend laughs at *all* your jokes
  and calls you on the phone.
A best friend tries to make you happy
  when you're really sad.
A best friend *never* likes it
  when you're really, really mad.
A best friend always likes or tries
  to be friends with your dog.
A best friend never *wants* to grab
  or act just like a hog.
A best friend always loves your shirt
  and always likes your pants.
A best friend always sings with you
  when she prefers to dance.
She always wants to stick with you
  through every single bend.
And all these reasons written down
  are why you're my best friend.
Maricarmen Garcia, Grade 5
Dehesa Charter School

You

Even if you do not like the way you look,
That does not mean you should change,
Because you are you
And I am me.

If they do not like you,
I will always be there,
Because you are you
And I am me.

Many people judge others by their looks,
While I judge them by their personalities,
Because you are you
And I am me.

So, please — Oh, please,
Be who you are and do not change,
Because you are you
And I am me.

Tiffany Chen, Grade 6
Parkmont Elementary School

A Sticky Situation

Slimy and disgusting, that's what I am,
Attached to the bottom of the desk near your hand!
I think that they should set up a blockade,
So contact between us won't be made,

Stop, you vulnerable hand,
I don't appreciate you invading my land,
You won't be able to withstand my touch,
You'll wriggle and squeal and cry, "Oh, yuck!"

Nathan Lee, Grade 5
The Mirman School

Birds

Birds singing sweetly
On a beautiful tree branch
On a forest tree

Michael Sweeney, Grade 4
Mayfield Jr School of the Holy Child Jesus

Happiness

Two hazel eyes in a warm, soft bundle of luxurious fur,
This is happiness.
A sweet golden puppy smiles into the world,
She knows just when you need her.
Bounding gracefully,
She comes to take away your sadness,
Replacing it with the most pure feeling.
We seem to take her for granted,
And if we thank God for her presence,
Maybe she will come more often.
Maybe we would be in peace.

Shea Bishop, Grade 5
Wagon Wheel Elementary School

What Should I Put in a Box Marked Summer?

Ice cream, popsicles, and every cold treat,
Watermelon and peaches are yummy and sweet,
Lemonade and smoothies quench your thirst,
Gatorade refreshing me when my lungs are about to burst

Water gun fights and soccer in the hot beating sun,
Looking at stars in the pitch black sky is lots of fun,
Picking berries on a nice June day,
Then making pie is delightful and tasty, I must say

Seagulls, kelp, and ocean water galore,
Feet burning as they touch the hot sandy floor,
Finding shells like hidden treasure,
Endless beach days are such a pleasure

Parades and streamers on the Fourth of July,
Brightly colored fire works lighting up the night sky,
Pedaling down the street on a decorative bike,
You never know what summer will be like!

Lauren Feitzinger, Grade 5
Duveneck Elementary School

Lost in the Happiest Place on Earth

That was it,
Officially lost in one of the happiest places on Earth,
I saw a sobbing woman,
Crying the tears of the dark, black sea,
My mother.
Swimming to a far away island in the deep, blue sea,
Reaching my mother island,
I hugged her for a lifetime,
After, I said softly,
"I love you,"
And began sobbing,
The tears of the sweet, blue sea,
Tears not of sadness,
But of joy.

Sydney England, Grade 5
Clover Avenue Elementary School

Butterflies

Some days my thoughts are just like butterflies
Flying high and fluttering with happiness

The butterflies fly way beyond the clouds in my head

And other days my thoughts are like tornadoes —
Destroying everything in its path

Later I find the path that the tornado left behind —
All cold and lonely just waiting for the butterflies
To come back again

Rachel Dumiak, Grade 6
La Costa Heights Elementary School

Swim

S plash in the pool
W ith a friend
I n their pool
M others, too, in the deep.

Natea Stinson, Grade 5
Joseph M Simas Elementary School

Prophet Muhammad

Underneath the shade of the date tree,
He set many slaves free.
He invited all people to Islam,
And taught them how to read Quran.
He loves all people and he was kind,
Caring, helpful, fair and just.
Our prophet is the best one,
He always cares for everyone.
He is our great knight,
who gives us light,
and showed us how to live our life right.
Beloved of all,
He will never let us fall,
Always there for one and all!

Natalia Rawjee, Grade 4
New Horizon School

I Hear Yawning

When I wake up I hear yawning,
Everybody yawning,
The whole state yawning,
Every time I wake up I hear yawning.

Cameron Smith, Grade 5
Kentwood Elementary School

Sharks

Terror of the sea
Teeth crush down on fleshy meat,
Punishment is doom

James Delos Santos, Grade 5
Andasol Avenue Elementary School

Games Rock

A tari
B akugan **C** artoons
D uke **E** ntertainment
F ree **G** ames
H ard **I** mpossible **J** obs
K irby **L** ooks **M** ore **N** egative
O pponent's **P** rogress
Q uest
R aging **S** earch
T eams **U** nbelievable
V ictory
W inning **X** cellence
Y ou **Z** oom!

Thomas Kendrick, Grade 6
Aliso Elementary School

The First Day of Kindergarten

I cling to my mom's hand
as she reaches a cold, half-rusted gate
I remember crying unsure tears
trying to find their way past my cold cheeks.
My mama whispered that I would be okay,
I trusted her as much as I did before
I started school.
I wrapped her hair around my fist
as I whispered with my shaky voice, "Bye-bye Mama,"
as I slowly stammered into the classroom.

Time to leave, I didn't want to go
Leave all my old friends behind
"Will I see them tomorrow?" I asked myself out loud again and again
and no matter how many times I asked
Mama's answer was, "Yes, you will."

Sofi Zurek, Grade 5
Coeur d'Alene Avenue Elementary School

Love

Love is like a seed sprouting from the ground and the petals opening up slowly.
With good care, the flowers bloom and shine, and so is love.
When flowers wither and fall to the ground, beauty disappears.
Just like love left without care withers to the unknown,
Leaving hurt feelings of sadness, pain and loneliness on the hurting hearts.

Cristian Hernandez, Grade 5
Joseph M Simas Elementary School

The Room of Despair

Snakes and spiders, onions and green beans,
homework in the trash can along with worn out blue jeans.
Here and there, a startling cyclone of doom.
You guessed it, this is my room.

Mud and dirt cover my appalling doodles,
along with moldy take-out such as wonton and noodles.
Footprints of my terrier ride all over the ceiling,
and my fish tank is rather unappealing.

The fish are all dead, and there's even a skeleton,
there's bleach in the tank and some leftover gelatin.
My lizard's cage is piled with an immense mountain of poop,
there are beetles in the soil and in the water bowl, there is soup.

My closet will explode like a vicious volcano of revulsion,
almost as if there was a sudden convulsion.
T-shirts and jeans bounce off the walls,
jacket flow from the ceiling like the famous Niagara Falls.

Yes, I admit, it is a truly horrid sight,
to see my room in this condition can really offer a fright.
No matter how much I labor, it will never stay in full bloom,
after all, this is my room.

Rohan Savoor, Grade 6
Dorris-Eaton School

High Merit Poems – Grades 4, 5 and 6

Colors
Purple reminds me of tulips
I see a tulip as I eat chips
Yellow makes me think of the sun
Sunlight feels great while eating a hamburger bun
Red reminds me of blood
And sometimes a rosebud
Blue is like the ocean
Rolling in its wavelike motion
Black is how we describe midnight
It's not at all bright
Green makes me think of trees
Oh, no! Are those bees?
Orange reminds me of fruit
In one book they dressed fruit up cute

Amanda Wagner, Grade 5
Eastwood Elementary School

Kitchen Counter
You sit at the kitchen counter,
Wondering what life would be like
Out in the lush green garden
Where birds sing.

Sipping your morning coffee
Thinking about gardens
You wonder what would happen
If there were no gardens
What a poet's life would be like.

Andrew Eaton, Grade 4
Mayfield Jr School of the Holy Child Jesus

Mommy Dearest
My mommy...
She is very lovely
Yet she is also demanding
She is very thoughtful
Her scream is very awful
My hates it when we don't use commonsense
She wants us all to be independent
My mom is very impatient
But me and her both have a relation

My mommy...
She hates it when we call her a dwarf
My mom is very faithful
And for that she is grateful
She is very ambitious
She is very happy
Except for when she is snappy
She's a lady of five foot two
There's nothing in the world that she cannot do
She taught me how to eat and tie my shoe

Bree Wright, Grade 6
Century Community Charter School

The City!
The city is oh so very busy
So many people everywhere
Shopping and driving around without a care
All the cars "Beep Beep Beep!"
All the kids on the school bus "Weeeeee!"
Police sirens "Weeeeeooooooo Weeeeeeooooooo!"
People walking, people driving, and people biking
So many people in the city
That's what makes it oh so very busy!

Sophie Fortner, Grade 5
Mayfield Jr School of the Holy Child Jesus

Ice Cream
Ice cream is a tasty treat
just for you and me to eat
it goes in the freezer
you can tease your little sister
just eat it right in front of her
and go yum, yum, yum
just make sure you ask your mom
she might say no
she might say yes
Just remember ice cream is the best!

Coletta Vasquez, Grade 5
George Washington Charter Elementary School

Colors
Orange is the color of the sunset that's coming down on you.
Red is the color of love in a couple's eyes.
Black is the color of darkness at night with no moon.
Green is the color of the grass, swaying with the wind.
Yellow is the color of the sun in the summer.
Gray is the color of clouds when it starts to rain.
White is the color of a baseball coming at you: uh oh, swing!
Purple is the color of soap cleaning your hands.

Dylan Dodge, Grade 5
Joseph M Simas Elementary School

Peacefulness
Peacefulness is like bright blue,
And like waves crashing on the beach
It runs through my mind
It reminds me of the time I sat on the shoreline
It makes me feel peaceful like a cool day
It makes me want to sit peacefully and watch time fly by

Brittany Kamerman, Grade 6
St Anne School

Night Happiness
As slowly as the night moves
the stars spread happiness throughout the land
people sound asleep
grin while night moves
and the stars do dark magic

Samantha Valenciano, Grade 4
Sierra Oaks K-8 School

Ms. Gonzalez

Ms. Gonzalez is…
A nice and supportive person
Who is sometimes active
She is a very good soccer player
She is mostly very funny
And she is very intelligent
When she gets mad
She is also creepy
Since she is intelligent
She really knows a lot
She loves students
Who are good
She speaks clearly
And also is good at listening
When she gets mad
It is like a horror movie
She has a big pool
That she likes to swim in
She is one of the best teachers
Who is important to me

Augustin Cardozo, Grade 6
Century Community Charter School

Kitty

Kitten
Cuddly, cute one
Playing, brightens the day
Playing with yarn balls, eating mice
Kitty

Kaycie Hinds, Grade 5
Joseph M Simas Elementary School

Thunder

When I hear thunder go boom
It makes me want to go to my room.
Next comes lightning
Then it gets frightening.
Hopefully next comes rain.

When I think of rain
I see gray horses with white manes.
When I say I like rain
My sister says I am insane.
Which puts me in a lot of pain.

Demi Smith, Grade 5
Montessori Family School

Love Is…

Calm and peaceful.
Patient and kind.
Nice and helpful.
Good and loving.
Awesome and cool.
The best thing ever.

Elijah Bernard, Grade 5
Santa Fe Springs Christian School

The Winter Wonderland (1830)

The small cold flakes withered down to the ground.
A small kitten ran inside for warmth.
The white flakes slowing built a small mountain
And it added on and on and on…
The trees got covered in white.
A small boy sitting on the end of the street looking for spare change.
The flakes kept going.
Young men cantered home in three horse-drawn carriages.
Yet none stopped to notice the winter wonderland around them.

Ruby Goldstein de Salazar, Grade 5
Montessori Family School

Blue

Blue is the color of a glistening sapphire in a jewelry store.
Blue is the feeling of rustling wind blowing in your face.
Blue is the sound of birds gently chirping in the twilight.
Blue is the color of snowflakes melting in the sun.
Blue is the taste of scrumptious blueberry ice cream on a blazing summer day.
Blue is the smell of blueberry in the springtime.
Blue is the color of an ocean in a sunset.
Blue is the feeling of warming up after being in the wintry weather.
Blue is the taste of a snowflake souring on my tongue.
Blue is the smell of fresh air on a camping trip.
Blue is the feeling of rising from your bed ready for another day.
Blue is the color of a morning sky.
Blue is the sound of a snowflake gently gliding into a pile of slush.

David Sanguinetti, Grade 4
Heather Elementary School

The World of Yellow

I know yellow.

Yellow smells like the aroma of yellow leaves,
a nutritious banana having its skin shed,
and a sweet scent pineapple when there's a sharp knife digging into its tasty body.

Yellow feels like the smooth and flat surface of a laminated paper,
a yellow, headless teddy bear,
and my old, dirty, worn-out raincoat.

Yellow looks like a swarm of stripped bees attacking an intruder,
the sun as it glides across the sky,
and a wicked bolt of electricity dropped from the sky.

Yellow sounds like crackling lightning striking a tree,
a bee buzzing happily as it drinks nectar from a flower,
and a pencil scratching ideas onto a blank paper.

Yellow tastes like a banana satisfying a growling stomach,
a lemon-flavored ice cream cone,
and a cream soda flavored lollipop that I'll enjoy when my parents aren't looking.

I really know yellow.

Raymond Wang, Grade 4
Dingeman Elementary School

The Nightmare That Was

I am Fever
My only companion is Death
I give no leeway
Whoever I meet is doomed
I devastate lives, ruin families, desolate towns
You cannot run from me
You cannot hide from me
My messenger is so small
Yet carries my duties afar
My height of power
Is in the peak of summer
When no cold showers press me down
To end my reign of death
Few survive my lasting wrath
But once I touch them
Bloodshot yellow eyes will haunt them
Till their days are over
I am a culprit of fatality
Elusive to all around me
I Am Fever

Anna Yager, Grade 6
St Andrew's Episcopal School

I Fell into a Picture Album

I saw me as a baby being baptized.
I skipped a few pages and there was my first communion.
I even saw a few fun birthday parties
And happy family Christmas celebrations.
I was in all the pictures
Growing bigger as the pages passed.
Last — there were pictures
Of my parents' marriage.
It was an exciting book to fall into.
I may do it again tomorrow.

Peter Vu, Grade 5
St Barbara School

A Bear Is

A bear is a type of raging madness
A bear's legs are built of steel
A bear's teeth are made out of the sharpest razors

Jacob Poos, Grade 5
Charles Armstrong School

Computer Virus

Oh User, thou art so vulnerable,
The fatal error you made,
To not download an upgrade
Your firewall, a blockade, a feeble attempt indeed.

Oh User, your hard drive will never withstand
The massive onslaught of my corruption
All files and programs will meet destruction
All your work ending in annihilation…

Aaron Marks, Grade 5
The Mirman School

Best Buds

My best friend Kelly moved in fourth grade
My best bud now is Ilene to say
She is on my softball team
She invites me to play
She encourages me to do my best
She makes me happy on a bad day
She knows exactly what to do and say

Abby Conrad, Grade 5
Jackson Elementary School

Poetry

Poetry is the beach in the moonlight,
pale, yet beautiful,
speaking the unspoken.

Poetry is love.
It will never be diminished.
Poetry can be expressed in many ways.

Poetry is a glowing candle in a dark lit room.
It is the truth in many wavering lies.
Poetry will always find a way.

Lilianne Ephraim, Grade 6
Bernice Ayer Middle School

If I Were…I Would…

If I were a tiger,
I would growl and show my sharp teeth at opponents.
If I were a groundhog,
I would dig up gardens.
If I were a cheetah,
I would chase my delicious prey.
If I were a snake,
I would slither my way through the green grass.

Renee Van, Grade 4
Elder Creek Elementary School

Waiting for You

The dog sits waiting on my front lawn,
Thinking you left her, 'till you're gone

Days pass by, waiting for you
I don't know what to say, or what to do

She waits and waits 'till you come by
Every day, I hear her cry

She sleeps in the gutter with a bone and a ball
She waits until she hears her owner make a call

If you just come, she'll be ok
Please come back tomorrow or today!

Jenna Dahl, Grade 5
Wagon Wheel Elementary School

I Remember

I remember the fear, the everlasting worry that my life could be taken away from me at any given moment.
I remember the wretched stench of the dead bodies being carelessly piled into the mass graves.
I remember watching the tall Nazis herding Jews into cattle cars, not knowing their destination,
and feeling glad that I was not yet one of them.
I remember the loud sound of the Nazis' big, black boots upon the hard ground and the fear it brought to any Jew who could hear.
I remember the sadness, the pure sorrow that cut through my heart like a knife at every moment of the day.
I remember the exuberant joy that I felt when it was all over; finally done with, a part of history.
I worry that once I die, no one would know my past, the whole Holocaust forgotten.
Six million Jews dead, gone forever.
Who am I?
One out of so many chosen, spared from a cruel death?
I remember.
I remember, and I shall never forget.

Elana Muroff, Grade 6
Lindero Canyon Middle School

The Spray of Colors

There I sit on an autumn day in a pile of brightly colored fallen leaves. I look around me and wonder, as the bright colors spray against my skin, do we realize how wonderful the bright, luring colors are? Or do we just treat colors as if they're pieces of trash on our front lawn? God made the rainbow to spray the colors against our world to make it bright, fun, and even colorful. Life would be bland if we lived in a world with only black and white. That's why we humans need color to show our feelings. Without color life would be like getting new Blendi Pens and then finding out they only come in the colors black and white. It would be disappointing and un-lively. That's why I spruce up MY life with colors.

Eden Rae Sedgwick, Grade 5
St Raphael School

I Am From

I am from a home where the Wurlitzer piano gets played, where there's a hallway full of family photos, and a huge pot of flowers.

I am from a yard where a walnut tree sits with lots of beautiful flowers; a bird bath with an angel sits right in front of it, where four dogs are barking and playing, and where three cats are meowing, and sleeping.

I am from a neighborhood where there are orchards everywhere you look! There are also squirrels and birds everywhere in the orchards. Where kids are playing in their yards for most of the time, and where flowers are blooming.

I am from a dinner table where we mostly have steak, fruit, green beans, and salad. Where on Thanksgiving at Sittee's house there is always a turkey, stuffing, mashed potatoes, pie and ice cream!

I am from a family where everyone loves everyone for who they are.

Julianne Ray, Grade 5
Notre Dame School

Half Bear, Half Cat

I have a strange animal; half bear, half cat.
It's as big as a cat and he's black and orange.
He's like some other animals; he purrs and loves to swim.
It's unlike other animals because his favorite food is mac and cheese.
My animal has 2 bearlike eyes, 2 catlike ears, 4 catlike legs, and 4 paws with 3 claws each.
The unusual thing is, my animal hates cat food and fish even though cats and bears love them.
My animal is quiet and tame but also very playful.
When it's happy it says "purr, grr, merr."
When it's sad it goes "sigh, cry, whine."
When people see it they respond with "Wow! Oh! Cool!"
My animal may be different but it is as lovable as a cat and as independent as a bear!

Jordyn Hauk, Grade 6
Big Springs Elementary School

Losing Someone You Love

Memories flashing back like lightning,
Going back to the year of 1969,
During the period of the Cultural Revolution,
Are never pleasant or forgetful.

Those years were tragic, especially of my grandma's death.
Remembering that when I was told that she was shot,
Brings misery and sorrow like a never-ending journey.
My heart was broken as if it were glass.

Hearing it all struck me with horror and pain,
As sadness crawled in and tormented me.
I had always wondered what she was like,
But I never got the chance to meet her.

Thinking of that, I'll never know how it feels,
To have such a grandma like her.
I won't be able to experience having one,
Like most ordinary people do.

Never in my life have I ever known such sorrow.
Is that the way life is supposed to be?
Time passes so quickly and people vanish too.
Now I know the true meaning of sympathy.

Cynthia Weng, Grade 6
Parkmont Elementary School

In California I've Learned

In California I've learned that the redwood trees grow tall,
That the sea shines bright as rain falls down,
The sun shines bright on the valley grass,
The snow covers every inch in a blanket of white,
And the rushing rivers make the gold glow,
As the sun shines down to make one's heart flow.

Morgan Bray, Grade 6
Grant Elementary School

The Beach

I was excited to go to the beach
It was my first time setting foot on sand
Then we ate chicken for fifteen bucks each
And we sat down to watch a real live band

After we went down to a big, cool shack
There were souvenirs and purple t-shirts
We bought a Dorito bag for our snack
And we got fudge popsicles for dessert

Finally we were going to swim now
While in the water I saw a big squid
And I saw it swim fast and I said, "wow"
It turned and it was the last thing it did

It was fun to be somewhere outgoing
But sadly we must be out and going

Beatriz Mopera, Grade 5
El Monte Elementary School

Monkeys

Monkeys in the trees
Swing vine to vine, back and forth
Eating bananas

Audrey Perry, Grade 4
Mayfield Jr School of the Holy Child Jesus

Fever 1793

I am the one who causes your misery
You cannot escape me for I am everywhere
I am elusive
The more you try to defeat me the more danger you are in
No one knows when I attack and they will never find out
I am a tornado destroying everything in my path
I kill the innocent
The dying are now helpless
I watch as people cry, moan, and vomit when they wake up
Animals and plants cry with pain as they die
The only way to get rid of me is to wait till frost
I spread as quickly as wild fires
Many vacate to faraway lands while others stay and suffer
I scour the streets searching for my victims
Many will stay in their houses forever just to be safe
But they are wrong
I'll come get you no matter where you are
Do not infuriate me
Because I am Fever
and I will devastate you

Hannah Kim, Grade 6
St. Andrew's Episcopal School

My Messy Room

Down my hallway, the 3rd door to the right,
It really is a terrible, awful sight,
One solitary patch of my blue carpet,
Leads off to two straight paths,
My side and her side in need of a bath.

My hamster wreaks havoc in my room in the night,
He makes my room messy, I swear I am right.
And then he goes to give my family a fright,
He puts all his bedding all over the floor,
Mixed with my clothes, shoes, and hats, galore.

Then he drags out my clothes from the closet,
And then will carefully, quickly deposit,
My toothbrush and bathrobe and hairbrush on the floor,
Carefully undoing all of my chores.
Wait, don't open that door!

Oh, all I did was put some clothes here,
My hamster makes my room feared,
In the morning, he looks at me
Those eyes as innocent as they could be,
And all the work is dumped on *me*.

Lilli Lawrence, Grade 6
Dorris-Eaton School

Red Roses
On a bush
In a vase
About the petals
From the bouquet
Regarding love
Concerning beauty
With thorns
To his girlfriend
Beside her bed
Under her pillow
Vida Sadeghi, Grade 6
St Anne School

The Ocean of Poems
The Ocean of Poems
dreams of love and happiness.
The Ocean of Poems
makes me feel
like a queen of the world.
The Ocean of Poems
nourishes my heart and soul
and mind.
The Ocean of Poems
is like a basket of hope
filled with glorious days.
The Ocean of Poems
lets me swim in it
until my heart is content.
The Ocean of Poems
is the heart of the world.
The Ocean of poems
is like a waterfall of happiness and joy.
The Ocean of Poems
will always be in my heart.
Malaika Nall, Grade 4
The Mirman School

Please the Bees!!
They are yellow, they are black,
that form stripes on their back.
Making honey is what bees do;
they pollinate flowers unlike you.

If you look you will see
there are three types of honey bees:
Queen, male, and working bees
all in a hive on a tree.

If you don't watch out,
a sting will make you shout.
But if you mind your beeswax,
the hive will relax.
Mariam Kadous, Grade 6
Islamic School of San Diego

Baseball
Baseball
heroes or zeros?
role models?
integrity or cheaters?
character
Home run Hall of Fame
America's National Pastime
ruined?
Why?
Mario Ojeda, Grade 5
Caryn Elementary School

The Fall
Do you like the fall?
The leaves, colors and all.
No one knows when
it leaves you
it's gone when
there is no breeze
but the cold winter snow
that's when you will truly know.
Next year it will come again
grapes will grow,
leaves will fall
that's when it begins
fall is very lovely
fall comes, beautiful.
Irmina Quinn, Grade 4
Coyote Valley Elementary School

Winter
Winter is cold,
Like its white snow,
It will be fun,
To play in the snow.

When snow melts,
What does it become?
Does it turn into water,
No it does not,
It becomes spring.
Elizabeth Rodriguez, Grade 5
St Pancratius Elementary School

Light and Dark
Light
Warm, happy
Flying, dancing, feasting
Animals, oceans, food
Crawling, creeping
Cold, serious
Dark
Alexander Considine, Grade 6
Francis Parker School

Springtime Fever
The reason why I am making this rhyme,
To tell you about springtime.
Flowers bloom every day,
Children are ready to play.
Eggs begin to hatch,
Vegetables grow in the patch.
Flower petals fall on the ground,
Birds chirp pretty sounds.
Vivid colors are everywhere,
In the ground and even in midair.

Spring is a nice season,
And this is my reason.
Because spring is next to summer,
But I think spring is funnier.

Spring is here,
Spring is everywhere.
I am so eager,
Of springtime fever!
Stephanie Salvador, Grade 5
St Linus School

School
When I go to school
Not everything is cool,
Most things are hard
So I can't wait for recess in the yard.

I like to play all kinds of games
Almost with all my friends,
And when it's time for the lunch
All together drink Hawaiian Punch.

Don't think that all we do is play
We also learn during the day,
And from all the subjects I take
Language arts is a piece of cake.

I did this work really nice
I am sure I will get a prize,
Because I make an effort to get
All the credits I deserve.
Adriana Olivares, Grade 6
St John's Parish Day School

A Boy from Spain
There once was a boy from Spain,
He loved to play in the rain,
One day he slipped,
Fell on his hip,
And now he needs a cane.
Blake Burton, Grade 6
St Anne School

Death of My Beloved Friend

I do not know what really happened
Just thinking about it makes me really sapped
I wish I never saw that horrible tale
Because he made my path so bright
It had to be that tragic day
When we both strolled down Shimmer Bay

My inseparable auburn dog and I strolled wondering what to do
Along came a gang team who shot Bang! Bang!
It was coming toward us but my dog shielded me with his love
He fell with a great thump and the gang scurried away
The shot was quick and easy
The thought of it makes me queasy

I looked and to my dismay
My friend, comrade, and family member perished away
I stayed with him day and night
However, I knew he would never awake for my delight
I never knew how death felt
Until my only pal just passed away

Juliana Nghiem, Grade 6
Big Springs Elementary School

Radiant Fog

Fog over harbors,
Hanging like a misty veil,
It is radiant.

Emily Huntsman, Grade 4
Mayfield Jr School of the Holy Child Jesus

Forgive Me of My Sins O'Lord

Forgive me of my sins, O' Lord,
I have abandoned You, my God,
and I have gone another way.

I have betrayed you saying that You were not true.
I have done calumny,
by saying You are wrong.

I have doubted You; though, You never doubt me.
I have been like a bad seed,
and You, like the farmer, still nurture me.

I have stopped praying to You,
wandering off like a lost sheep.
yet, You come for me like a shepherd.

By walking a sorrowful path, I have displeased You.
I have teased and provoked others,
and by doing that I am teasing and provoking You.

Forgive me of my sins, O' Lord,
I gave up on You,
but You will never give up on me.

Joshua Graves, Grade 6
St Cecilia School

If I Were in Charge of the World*

If I were in charge of the world
I'd cancel moldy cheese
Old age
Sharks, and sickness.

If I were in charge of the world
There'd be dogs that don't bite
A billion horses, and
Better horses and lessons.

If I were in charge of the world
There wouldn't be nervousness
You wouldn't have sadness
You wouldn't have spills
You wouldn't have injuries
You wouldn't have tetanus shots.

If I were in charge of the world
There'd be more chocolate
Every horse would never throw you off its back.
And someone who is quiet and very shy
Would still be allowed to be
In charge of the world.

Michelle Espinoza, Grade 6
St Raphael School
Patterned after "If I Were in Charge of the World"
by Judith Viorst

Animal Friends

I have a few roses I see,
So I give them to my love monkey.

Guinea pigs scurry around,
Climbing up and climbing down.

Whimsy dragons are so sweet,
With glittering scales and small, clawed feet.

Pandas climb through the bamboo,
Because they want to be with you!

Huskies run through the soft, white snow.
Just say "Mush" and they will go.

Lots of horses come into view,
Very gracefully they do.

Deer are quick and deer can prance.
It seems they always love to dance.

Animal friends are so much fun.
I like to play with every one.

Kelin Graul, Grade 4
Camino Grove Elementary School

Sundae Delight

My basketball is orange sherbet.
My smile, a sliced banana.
My skin is rich heavy cream.

My curly hair is chocolate drizzle.
My cheeks, cherry red.
My eyes are brown like peanuts.

So step inside and have a bite,
I am an Ice Cream Sundae Delight.

Jordan Gregory, Grade 5
Kentwood Elementary School

My Friends

Water is blue
Ice cream is strawberry
I have a video game
I play with Larry

Brandon Lewis, Grade 4
Clayton B Wire Elementary School

Grandma

Grandma
She was my idol
Low in sodium
So she had a seizer
In a coma for five weeks
She saw my mom
But didn't remember her
We cried for her
She got well
She kept going
I love her
I miss her a lot

Ilene Velasquez, Grade 6
Aliso Elementary School

I'm Concerned About the World

I am concerned about the war
The war that Bush ignored
All the soldiers come home sore
From that monster they call war
And that pollution
That thing with no solution
All that garbage in the water
It's almost as bad as slaughter
The economy is so bad
It's making everyone sad
Everyone will soon be glad
Because Obama is so fab
Obama is cool
He's no fool
Never fear
Obama's here

Liam Hurley, Grade 4
Sonoma Charter School

Through the Eyes of a Foster Child

They come to us both day and night.
Their clothes are torn and faces forlorn.
Each child's expression full of fright and always afraid of the night.
Not knowing what we might do and only knowing of abuse.
A hit, a slap, a hard word spoken, what did I do to make this happen?
Do I dare to think of what this place will bring?
When the sadness is so overwhelming.

Hesitantly eyes are open, to see a new day but they wish they had never awoken.
Grisly memories flood their minds, as it takes them back to another time.
Where pain and fear was very near that the only cure was to escape from there.
A peaceful place in my mind, it's hard to find but I know it's time.
I need to run and play again.
I hope to find this home a friend.

Anxiously, the telephone rings determining what nightmare brings.
No food, no blankets, no kiss goodnight.
They've seal my future; I'm wrapped up tight.
How can I say goodbye to them, they were my only friends.
If I leave I'll never know, what it's like to have a home.
My fate's been sealed for this I know, I'll cease to exist, they'll never know.

Kailen Bell, Grade 6
Big Springs Elementary School

The Life of a Tree

I wonder what it would be like to live the life of a tree.
Nowhere to go and nowhere to be.
It must be easy doing nothing all day.
But the sad part is you wouldn't be allowed to play.
If I were a tree I would be very sad.
Just standing there all day wouldn't make me very glad.
But on the bright side you would be friends with the birds.
The only down side to that is some birds might be absurd.
You also might be able to talk to the sky.
If I could talk to the sky I would say hi.
But the saddest part about being a tree is the woodcutter's saws.
Their blades are so sharp they look like jaws.
So next time you see a tree, have some sympathy.

Christian Brown, Grade 5
Mayfield Jr School of the Holy Child Jesus

My Name

I am right behind you ready to infest
You with my foul disease
You cannot see me but I can see you every
Step you take I am there
I take the lives of you and the people that surround you
I will not forsake I will persevere I will not stop until everything is gone
I make you writhe in pain
You cannot squash me I am too smart
You will need all the stamina you can get to out run
Me
I am FEVER

Jianna Salinas, Grade 6
St Andrew's Episcopal School

High Merit Poems – Grades 4, 5 and 6

Easter Time
They usually shine
Eyes closed 'cuz they're blind
Some are dead because of Lent
White, yellow
Their mood is mellow
They bloom in the spring
Or just not at all
They're as white as a cloud
Touch the leaf and you'll hear a crunching sound
Though some may look tired
And some not at all
Daisies that bloom
Bloom out to the world
Waiting a little bit longer
But they're ready to shout
Ready to praise Lord on high
Eyes almost wide open
For it's almost Easter time
The time that they shine

Klarissa Herrera, Grade 6
St Vincent Elementary School

Sparky City
They call my city boisterous,
unique,
with an individual flavor packed inside its
traffic-jammed avenues.
The sky promises a healthy environment
so it's able to dwell
without smelling the stench
of pollution.
The innocent citizens know
the burden of the earth
and do their best as an individual
to help hold up this blue-green sphere

Nada Alami, Grade 5
Dingeman Elementary School

Green
Go green!
Keep it clean!
Don't always use your washing machine.
Recycle please!
Recycle please!
Do not at all times chop down trees.
Use solar power!
Use solar power!
To save energy every hour.
When the sun is bright, don't use the lights.
Animals are disappearing,
Oh, so fast,
So keep it clean like it was in the past!

Zoe Davin, Grade 4
Alta Heights Elementary School

Harp Seal
I wait for a friend to come home,
It's a very long wait.
I nearly fall asleep
When the door opens.
Since she came home,
I've been jumping up and down,
Being very, very joyful.
When she leaves gain,
I had tasks to do,
Things to ask, and freedom.
When she came home, she was angry,
So I comforted her, and she gradually felt better.
She finished her homework, ate dinner,
Brushed her teeth, flossed and went to bed cuddling with me.
After a long night's sleep my friend leaves me,
Disappearing to someplace called school.
I wait for a friend to come home,
It's a very long wait.

Elaine Hsieh, Grade 5
Daves Avenue Elementary School

Puppy
A silly little puppy
Playing in the grass
On a late afternoon in the summer
In a meadow near a pond
To keep itself entertained

Annabel Genton, Grade 4
Mayfield Jr School of the Holy Child Jesus

If I Were in Charge of the World*
If I were in charge of the world
I'd cancel vitamin pills,
All kinds of shots,
Lots of homework,
And bullies.
If I were in charge of the world,
You wouldn't get scared at night,
Horses would be a little bit shorter,
And fun would be a little more funner.
If I were in charge of the world
I'd make healthier grandmas,
Zippier pets,
No alarm clocks,
Cake would be a fruit,
And less math homework.
If I were in charge of the world
You could choose your own dinner.
I'd make lighter nights and no scary TV shows.
I'd cancel zucchini.
And if you weren't the smartest,
You still could be in charge of the world.

Allison Malone, Grade 6
St Raphael School
*Patterned after "If I Were in Charge of the World"
by Judith Viorst

At the Beach
Down at the beach
kids playing,
waves crashing,
sky clearing,
lots of fun,
hat on my head,
all the fun you can have
at the beach.
Steven Hubbell, Grade 5
Theodore Roosevelt Elementary School

Jesus
Jesus
Faith-filled, loving
Praying, teaching, reading
If you're sad, pray to Jesus
The Magnificent
Darby Carrillo, Grade 4
St Joseph Parish School

Sushi
Sushi, sushi,
It's a dead fish.
Sushi, sushi,
It's a delicious
And interesting dish.

Sushi, sushi,
It's full of crab!
Sushi, sushi,
It is never bad.

Sushi, sushi,
You need some wasabi.
Sushi, sushi,
It's so good for me!
Sean Porteous, Grade 5
Merryhill Country School

Chocolate Cupcake
Batter poured into paper cups.
Warm and moist from the oven.
Can't wait until they cool.
I take one and frost it.
I lick the cream from my fingers.
The cream is melting, running down.
I need the sprinkles hurry up.
At last it's done.
My chocolate cupcake.
I peel away the paper cup.
I take one bite, I cannot stop.
It's gone before I'm satisfied.
Kristina Manankichian, Grade 5
Andasol Avenue Elementary School

Misty Light
As I wonder
I see
The sea is glimmering
right at me
The tides
go in
the waves shout.
The whales,
dolphins and turtles
swift through
the sea.
These sapphire eyes
of a silver seal
stare at me.
The dolphins
swirl among the horizon.
In the foggy night
I see the sea
twirl and twist.
I realize it's the sea
dancing.
Katie Murnane, Grade 5
Bethany Lutheran School

The Rain on the Playground
Little drops falling from the sky
make ripples on the basketball court
splatter on the blue sea of benches
like an artist splattered paint.
The wetness makes the basketball court
turn from light to dark brown.
The rain sparkles on the grass
twinkling like stars at night.
Isabel Wiesenthal, Grade 4
Carlthorp School

Basketball with My Dad
His shot is sweet —
Mine, too
Before I had this shot
I was weak
Every night after homework
He worked with me
Practicing and practicing
The ball still didn't obey me
One day
I did it!
"Nice shot" Dad said
"Your stroke is better than mine"
Everybody he knows
Hears his pride
About his boy
Kyle Lord, Grade 5
Clover Avenue Elementary School

Street
As the hours pass
and the lonely day ends,
I keep looking for a way
to make this broken heart mend

The streets are not easy
full of gangsters and thugs
Idiots die every day
because of drugs

Trying not to join it
but gangsters don't care
If you lose your life
the ones that care about you,
will think it wasn't fair

But now you become
the most wanted by the cops.
Your chance of being in the free world
begins to stop.
Geovani Ardon, Grade 6
Cimarron Education Center

What Is a Book?
What is a book?
A challenge
A fright
An adventure beyond this world
A homework assignment
A novel or mystery
A friend of knowledge
An obstacle of words
A once upon a time beginning
A realistic vision
A resource found in a library
That's a book!
Paloma Palop, Grade 6
Aliso Elementary School

Love
Love is cherished
Love is happiness
Love is eternal
Love is unforgettable
Love is meant for you and me
Wilson Tang, Grade 6
Ramona Elementary School

Rockstar
Standing in line now
Patient waiting for concert
Ready to rock out
TJ Herrera, Grade 6
St Anne School

If I Were Part of Nature

If I were part of nature, I'd have trees filled with marvelous flowers, berry bushes, clean cut grass, and fresh soil. I'd have animals roaming, living in the habitats I provide for them.

If I were a tree, I'd have the loveliest leaves that would change color with the season and sway with the wind. I'd live in a forest with the finest of bark and have birds chirping in my branches.

If I were a flower, I'd grow in a field or in a pot. I'd have bees and butterflies visit me every day taking nectar back to their homes. I could even possibly grow in a tree or bush. I'd have a stem taller than others and petals with a marvelous texture.

If I were a bush, I'd have more branches than leaves filled with juicy berries and red roses. I'd be filled with balls from a child playing fetch with a dog. I might even have prickles protecting my berries.

If I were soil, I'd be thick and rich, nourish the plants, and be soaked with water. I'd have tiny rocks and worms deep within me.

If I were the weather, I'd be the windiest wind, flowing over the ocean, as the rain, I'd pour down into puddles and drip drop off of houses, as the sun I'd shine down on the bathers of the beach, or the flowers of a field.

If I were a season, I'd be the most sunny spring, as fall I'd be the leaves gracefully falling from their trees, in the winter, I'd be the vanilla ice cream colored snow, and in summer I'd be the waves of the beach, the echo of children's play.

If I were one of nature's animals, I'd be the bird in a tree chirping its heart out, as a squirrel, I'd roam frantically through leafy bushes looking for nuts. As an animal with sharp teeth, I'd rip my prey limb by limb.

If I were part of nature, I'd be the cherry scent flowers, hard bark trees, and I'd be a home to all living organisms.

Mykaela Barnes, Grade 5
Aviara Oaks Elementary School

Spring White Lily

The spring Lily feels like velvet and a little bit of rubber on its back,
That's what I feel on my hand.
I see a white waffle cone with a yellow spoon with white sprinkles that fell on the spoon.
Memory of the fresh smell of air freshener.
The touch of velvet makes it feel like the fur of a bunny.
The smell reminds me of those good sugary sugar cookies, the ones that make you happy.
The Spring Lily's many facets are all in my interest.

Katie Dale, Grade 4
Daves Avenue Elementary School

A Winter Wonderland

Outside, the ground is covered with white, icy, wet snow,
just like the pine trees.
The pine trees, more natural and fresher than ever,
are being used as a home for the creatures of the forest.

The birds and squirrels, bundled up with their newly born babies,
open their eyes to a cold, white evening.
Far away, are houses,
with smoke coming out of every single one of them,
and they see us, sitting in front of the television
bundled up in blankets.

We could be enjoying the snow outside,
we could be having snowball fights,
we could be making snow angels and snowmen,
or sliding down a hill in a sleigh
"laughing all the way."

But this spectacular time of year won't wait for us to take advantage of the time it has left
because when spring hits, the snow disappears
along with any chances we have to enjoy this winter wonderland.
But the good part is that spring is near,
and the snow will be back next year.

Monica Morales, Grade 6
St John's Parish Day School

Happy Breakfast Time
Pancakes and waffles
They are super-duper good
They make me feel great
Sam Johnson, Grade 6
St Anne School

Raindrops
Drip, drop, drip, drop
I fall along your windowpanes
Falling hard my body breaks apart
I gently slither down
I plunge again to the ground
Now the wind forces me away
The wind quits pushing
The sun peeks out
I slowly fade and disappear
I am now in the sky
Waiting to drop down again
Gina Kim, Grade 5
Daves Avenue Elementary School

My Life, My Black Cat
You are not bad luck
Whenever I pass you
You are strong when I am weak;
You protect me when I am alone
You are a good luck charm,
A warm blanket different from all others
I am stronger, confident
When you're around
You cheer me up when I'm down
Without you
A piece of my heart is missing
Without you
The ebony soul of our home is gone
Sara Thomas, Grade 6
St Timothy School

Mysterious Storm
As I am sleeping in this lonely place,
The dreadful sky awakens me.
BOOM!
Like a lion clawing on a drum,
Nothing would scare me!
BOOM…BOOM…
There was a silence…
Just as I began to fall asleep,
Another loud, BOOM! tiptoed upon me!
As if it was a big bang on a door…
And no one answered.
But as I peeked out the window,
All I could see were stars
Shining on me!
All of this remains just another mystery!
Erin Gust, Grade 6
John Muir Elementary School

Aqua Green
Aqua green looks like the deep ocean filled with enormous schools of fish.
Aqua green smells like a sweet floral fragrance.
Aqua green sounds like waves smashing against boulders near the ocean.
Aqua green feels like sand that feels as smooth as silk gushing between your fingers.
Aqua green tastes like a freezing, cold bowl of ice cream.
Aqua green looks like wavy kelp but dyed a bit blue.
Aqua green sounds like the ocean and seagulls beckoning to their siblings.
Aqua green smells like the scent after a slight rainfall.
Aqua green smells like sweet, satisfying cotton candy from a carnival.
Aqua green feels like frigid water streaming down your throat after a hot summer day.
Aqua green looks like the color of the atmosphere at the making of night.
Aqua green sounds like people plunging in a pool.
Aqua green smells like mint leaves being crushed on a sturdy rock.
Aqua green tastes like snowflakes landing and melting on your hot tongue.
Aqua green feels like a ball of yarn being tossed on the surface of the water.
Aqua green looks like a line of jellyfish at the deep waters of the sea.
And aqua green is the color that is cold and soothing.
Dina Zheng, Grade 4
Heather Elementary School

Green
Green is the feeling of walking barefoot in a meadow of grass.
Green is the rush of wind blowing in a beautiful forest.
Green is the sound of a hillside when all is quiet.
Green is the taste of a watermelon ice pop on a scorching summer's day.
Green is the sound of a pretty dragonfly hard at work.
Green is the taste of a chilled salad at the end of the day.
Green is the feeling of nature.
Green is the sound of resting in a bed of flowers.
Green is the color of cucumbers being put into an outstanding sandwich.
Green is happy and alive.
Savannah Vold, Grade 4
Heather Elementary School

The Storm
Rain falls gently,
Making a soft dripping sound.
A light wind blows,
And the trees' leaves rustle gently.
A bright white light illuminates the darkness,
Followed by a soft but powerful rumble sounding like distant drums.
The rain falls harder,
imitating a bucket with water streaming.
The winds blow stronger,
And leaves fly around trees.
Now the rain pounds on the roof,
And sharply whips against the windows.
The wind rips leaves and twigs violently from trees.
A blinding flash fills the sky,
Paired to a deafening explosion.
The rain stops pounding,
The howling winds die down,
And once again all is calm.
Kevin Rodin, Grade 6
Francis Parker School

Friends

Friends, friends they're always there for you
Friends that are old and friends that are new
You can play with them
They're as good as a gem
But some things they cannot help you with
That is not a myth
But when you need them they are always there
And that's what shows they really care

Alexandria Reeves, Grade 4
St Pancratius Elementary School

The Reading of the Letters

Please don't call Kelson. Please not me.
"Aronson!"
Thank you.
"Bad news, lad," the captain says.
He reads, "Dear Seaman Aronson,
Unfortunately for you, I have found a
better boyfriend…" Someone laughs.
Then the whole deck falls into a sea of laughter.

Next letter.
Please don't call Kelson. Please not me.
"Phillips!"
Thank you.
"Bad news," the captain says…

Final letter. And, no, it's not Kelson.
It's Stokes.
"What's your first name?" the captain asks.
"Andrew," Mate Stokes replies.
"Are you sure it's not Snuggle-bum?"
Lots of laughter. No one can stop.

"A-vast!" the captain yells.
Well, that certainly stops us.

Hannah Kelson, Grade 5
Carlthorp School

Dr. King

Dr. Martin Luther King Jr. is never the number zero,
But he is really a true hero.

He was the leader of the Civil Rights,
He tried to make everything right.

He is the man that made black and white get along,
and nothing can be wrong.

And the fearness of the people ran
because Dr. King is a true man.

He is the man that works like a team,
He is the man that said "I have a dream."

Alejandro Pineda, Grade 5
Finley Elementary School

Ice

White and glistening, frosting the ground.
Snow has fallen here, as fluffy as a pillow.
Trees bare of leaves with their winter coat.
The coat of snow that wraps the land in a freezing embrace.
Giving the mountains tops of gleaming white.
Leaving drifts of beauty, like scattered gems.
The icicles, teeth of the snow, bared at the world.
Challenging all who see them to disturb the world of cold.
It is a fantasy world with unchecked splendor,
Yet beneath the outer beauty it is cold, unfeeling, brutal.
So in the snow and realm of ice I must not linger,
For, however much I wish to stay, it is a price I will not pay.
For in the realm there is much danger.
And so sadly I must leave,
The land of ice.

James Colwell, Grade 5
Montessori Family School

Seasons

Spring is here, winter has gone.
No snow, only sun and rain all day long.
The seasons change,
Though it may seem strange.
Some seasons I would like to exchange.
Fall is a beautiful season indeed,
Seeing fall colors is something I need.

Like winter and summer,
Oh, what a bummer,
Too hot, too cold, for the bold.
Fall and spring are gold, at least I've bee told.
I believe summer's too hot and winter's too cold.
The seasons change often,
In spring the clouds will soften.

In summer the sun glows
Yet in winter all that shows
Is bare branches and tree trunks,
Big logs and chunks of wood.
Sometimes I feel so misunderstood.
Seasons here, seasons done,
Springtime has just begun.

Misty Hilbourne, Grade 5
Merryhill Country School

At the Dance Studio

Have you ever been to the dance studio?
Stretched on the cold floor,
Felt the vibrations from the radio,
Heard the boom from every step you take?
When I'm at the dance studio,
I feel free.

Kendall Mills, Grade 5
Ladd Lane Elementary School

Samantha
S urrounded by happiness
A lways clumsy
M ostly funny
A bsolutely likes video games
N ever cheats
T houghtful
H as a kind heart
A very good friend
Samantha Flores, Grade 5
Theodore Roosevelt Elementary School

I Love You
I love you more than you love me
I love you deeper than the sea
I love you more than pie
I love you higher than the sky
I love you more than games
I love you more than planes
I love you more than a beyond a wish
I love you more than a beyond a kiss.
Phoenix Hermo, Grade 4
Upper Lake Elementary School

Mother Earth
I am an eagle.
Gliding high above the sky in 48 states.
I have the best view anyone can have.
I coast through the green forest.
I skim the lake with my talons.
I romp with other eagles in the sky.
I love being an eagle.
Please save Mother Earth.
Daniel Hoppen, Grade 4
Ocean Air School

Love
Love is a dream
that one day
will come true,
it all depends on you.
You must open to those,
and one day
your true dream
will come true.
Kelsey Medellin, Grade 6
St Charles Catholic School

Dreams Come True
Caring is sharing
Believing is seeing,
Faith is always with us,
We people make dreams come true.
Leslie Mercado, Grade 6
Blessed Sacrament School

Angels Above…
I wonder why people cry,
at the fact that someone died.
I wonder if they will all fly,
high above in our sky.
I wonder if they will soon show,
to all their loved ones below.
All the love there is to know.
Jose Meza, Grade 6
Lockeford Elementary School

Sunlight
The sunlight is bright,
The sun is hot,
Like a volcano that has just erupted,
Beautiful when it reflects on the water
It shines through it,
All the fish see it,
Do you?
Karina Lopez, Grade 6
Blessed Sacrament School

Blue
Blue is very calm
You can hold it in your palm
Blue is the color of the ocean
It has a very nice motion
Blue is the color of the sky
It is very high
Blue shows that it is proud
Blue is very loud
Hannah Tischler, Grade 5
Eastwood Elementary School

Christmas
Christmas lights are
Flashing bright like
Many shining stars
Paper litters the floor
Like leaves in the fall

Mom holds the camera
Dad is drinking coffee
Lily is eating a fried egg
A gray bobtail kitten
Darts out of the room
Andrew Katsumi Sloan, Grade 5
Clover Avenue Elementary School

Rain
The rain patters down
Coming from the dark night sky
Making a loud noise
Kate Bonde, Grade 6
St Anne School

Shoelace Monster
The monster creeps
onto the empty shoes.
It plans to eat
the knotted laces
in their sleep.
With teeth like
lightning blots
he snaps at them
then gulps them down.
The laces are gone.
It all ends
with a satisfied monster
and torn-up shoelaces.
Layla Moghavem, Grade 4
Carlthorp School

Dolphins
Dolphins…
Dolphins are nice.
They all have gleaming skin,
Gliding through the aqua blue…
Dolphins.

They care,
They love and please,
Care for their young in nurseries.
I love dolphins, and I hope that
You do.
Monique Patino, Grade 4
J L Academy

As if I Never
The ground so cold
as if I never walked

The air so still
as if I never took a breath

The earth so lifeless
as if I never lived

When the moon turns red
and the sun, silver

When the universe twists
and space time bends

The only one God
as if I, we, and everyone
never existed

The world today depends on us
Grace Frome, Grade 4
St Joseph's School of the Sacred Heart

It Passes on Quickly

The girl was dreaming.
She is ready to go.
She kept on dreaming 'till she got to the pow wow.
She dreamed when she had a baby brother.
A baby came. He was cute.
She met her friends, Little Pinenut Festival,
Black Beauty, Rosa, and KL.
But she will grow up. Bring one day.
Her mother tried to wake her up, but she passed on
With a baby brother in her hands.
Her mom cried when the mother passed on.
The son heard coyotes yelling at the moon.
And he fell asleep and passed on.
It goes fast.

Mauricea Two Eagle, Grade 4
Alpine County Elementary Community Day School

World Adventures

There is a world upon your feet,
Treasures of knowledge and more,
From jungles to deserts there will be many to explore,
Adventures await as traveling goes,
Astonishing surprises will meet you along the way,
As you learn from the world
With an adventurous smile on your face.
The stars shimmer brightly in the sky,
The sun warms your heart through the day.
Adventure will begin, but will never end,
It will always be with you as a friend.

Azriel Krista Mostajo Almera, Grade 4
Juarez Elementary School

What It Means to Be Alive

Ask a teddy bear what it means to be alive,
And it would tell you,
Hugged and stuffed by its owner.

Ask a cheetah what it means to be alive,
And it would tell you,
Running free in the savanna with the breeze against its face.

Ask a flower what it means to be alive,
And it would tell you,
Getting watered and taken cared of.

Ask a bird what it means to be alive,
And it would tell you,
Soaring high in the sky feeling the wind on its wings.

Ask me what it means to be alive,
And I will tell you,
Reading all I want.

Caroline Hang, Grade 6
Ramona Elementary School

If I Were

If I were a puppy,
I would be snugly in my own little bed.
If I were a cat,
I would scratch the walls if I were mad at my owner.
If I were a rose,
I would turn around in circles and stare at the sun.
If I were a rabbit,
I would jump around the forest.

Lidia Lupsa, Grade 4
Elder Creek Elementary School

War

One man's greed can lead him very far
leading him to killing men, women, and children
all because of war

War is many things from pride to envy
from friendship to betrayal
When firecrackers sound many people moan in pain
some of them surrender
it feels so in vain
all of this for one man's greed

He does not cry or does not share the pain
One man's greed cares of three things only
his money, his power and his greed

Ulyses Sanchez, Grade 6
Cimarron Education Center

Christmas Dinner

Christmas dinner smells like…
Fresh squeezed cranberry juice,
Chicken cooking with special sauce,
And of course gravy with mashed potatoes.

Christmas dinner sounds like…
Forks and knives clattering on plates,
Mouths crunching with warm, delicious food,
Talking, laughing while having a good time,

Christmas dinner tastes like…
Warm, delicious food especially,
Gravy with mashed potatoes,
Or icy cold fresh squeezed cranberry juice.

Christmas dinner looks like…
Mouths closed while chewing,
Some mouths open while laughing,
Others telling the jokes.

Christmas dinner feels like…
Warmth from the fire,
Happiness in the room,
Love circling around.

Colette Eberle, Grade 4
Daves Avenue Elementary School

Ode to My Sisters

They're as great as one can be. Going to the pool and getting on scary rides with me is the best. Being able to say I'm an aunt at age 11 is so different.

Their hugs, cries, laughs, daughters and love I get to share with 3 wonderful human beings. I share my feelings and secrets and with that they become my accomplices.

They are short and tall, their hair would flow in the wind if only they wouldn't use so much hairspray. Fashion they know a lot about, music too.

They are perfect in every way and even though we don't get along every minute, I still love them. Veronica, Aracely and Esmeralda.

Abigail Benitez, Grade 6
James B Davidson Middle School

Death of a Loved One

I make my uncle a bracelet of blue and brown
It's incredibly sad to see him frown
I see my family's faces walk in sturdy, scrambling paces
I just sit there and beseech for him to be ok
As I tear it became very vague
It's hard to see him die at an early age
I want to be jaunty but I can't

It did not work out the way I planned because my uncle got cremated with ashes not sand
I also felt depleted to watch my relative get deleted from my family's eyes
I thought I saw lies in the darkest blue skies of my life
He crawled through the attic to clean webs and spiders
Which was very dramatic?

As he started to have an asthma attack,
There is no way to bring him back
The paramedics and fire trucks came to see if this was a game but it wasn't
He started to seize but because he couldn't take it anymore we begged him please
He wouldn't listen to us because it felt like getting run over by a bus
My uncle is now in heaven but just to let you know his lucky number was seventy seven

Kelsey Hiroko Wickman, Grade 6
Big Springs Elementary School

A Pool of Aqua

I know aqua.
Aqua smells like the clean, fresh pool filled with chlorine, the disgusting odor of Ms. Morioka's Expo marker,
and the minty smell of aqua scissors.

Aqua feels like the cold water trickling down my throat, the rough pieces of artwork done by Vincent Van Gough,
and the smooth feeling of an aquamarine gemstone.

Aqua looks like my snug jacket warming me up, the square paper cube that Janie made,
and the helpful thesaurus on the desk.

Aqua sounds like the pure water in the lake making peaceful waves, my colored pencil rubbing against my blank paper,
and the drip of water dropping on the wet ground at a water park.

Aqua tastes like sweet, Orbit mint gum, the taste of Tic-Tac mints,
and the clear taste of refreshing water.

I really know aqua.

Emily Hou, Grade 4
Dingeman Elementary School

I Am Proud to Call You

I will never let go of my childhood
To your sweet words that you say
May I have the pleasure to say days without you it's a nightmare
That I will be somewhere else with you
I am like glue stuck to you that way I will never let go
Nowhere is better than somewhere if I don't have you
Who knew I would be so attached with you
You're the people that took care of me
Even to this day on
I'm proud to call you my mother and father
I know you will never let go but when that day comes
I will know as my life
You're my life my mother and my father
I take a pinkie promise I will always and I mean always
Have you in my heart you Mother and Father
And also my sisters and brothers

Jenneffer De Santiago, Grade 5
Canoga Park Elementary School

Sunbeam

I wish I were a warm sunbeam,
Sparkling and straight,
Shining through the window,
Brightening someone's day for a slender second,
Heating up the earth for some fun in the sun.

Ryan Ross, Grade 5
Lake Forest Elementary School

Whatif*

Whatif there was an infinite amount of food.
Whatif you could never be in a bad mood.
Whatif you in your life could never die.
Whatif there was an infinite amount of apple pie.
Whatif happiness never went away.
Whatif you could buy toys and never have to pay.
Whatif everything would be just fine.
Whatif your whole entire house was made of pine.
Whatif there was no such thing as a fight.
Whatif I told you everything would be all right.

Micah Lesch, Grade 6
Grant Elementary School
*Patterned after "Whatif" by Shel Silverstein

Heart of the Jungle

The landscape is lush and oh so green
Filled with things I've never seen
From the great leopard to the beautiful doe
I can tell which ones friend and which ones foe
Although this place is still a mystery I've been here before
Its filled with trees and flowers galore
Suddenly I see a liger
A combination of a lion and tiger
It's strong but slow
I start to run ready set GO!

Carlos Buchanan, Grade 5
Eastwood Elementary School

The Big Save

I saw a girl run down the field,
I was about to take action,
But our best goalie charged and I started to yield,
That girl took a shot which made quite an attraction.
The ball bounced off the girls and they both collided.
The ball rolled toward the net!
I wasn't quite sure but then I decided,
I can get there I bet!
That's when I charged from the far end.
When I came to the ball and I kicked with all my might!
I couldn't tell if it went out or hit my friend,
Until my team cheered at the incredible sight.
We tied thanks to me and my dad called me Ace.
At the end of the weekend my team won first place!

Rebecca Souza, Grade 5
St Louis De Montfort School

Desert Lily

Shines in the sun like thousands of stars.
Looks like bells hanging down,
It can be a bug's umbrella,
It can be a fairy's house,
Feels like a soft smooth blanket,
Smells like the fresh spring wind,
It reminds me of white chocolate,
On the inside it looks like a yellow sparkling dust,
The leaves look like they're hugging the flower.
The sparkling raindrop looks like a diamond in the sun,
The Desert Lily has a multiple of possibilities.

Yuri Hazama, Grade 4
Daves Avenue Elementary School

I Am

I am amazing
I wonder where I go when I die
I hear spirits playing
I see a sparkle in the sky
I want to see the whole world
I am amazing
I pretend to be superman
I feel cared for
I touch the wind blowing softly
I worry about global warming
I cry when my mom goes to work
    because she works for 10 hours and 30 minutes
I am amazing
I understand why people die when they're old
I say Santa is real because the North Pole is
I dream that I will get a job
I try not to get scared when I'm by myself
I hope global warming is not going to happen
I am amazing

Marvin Nelson, Grade 4
La Presa Elementary School

My Mother

My mommy…
You're my hero
So overprotective
But then just so caring
You act so silly like a little girl

You are so wonderful
So lovely and caring
You're a shiny star like a bright night sky
Always shining the most
Than the other stars

Not at all frightening
So independent
You're always there when I need you
Always in a rush
Because you are a true worker

Oh…mom
So overprotective
And still so caring
I love you so much
You are so lovable
And huggable

Sarah Rodriguez, Grade 6
Century Community Charter School

Mother's Day

Happy
Mother's Day!
I want to send you
A waterfall of laughter
To cheer you up
When you're feeling down
Here's a surfboard
To carry you away
From the shore
Filled with blue grains of sand,
You deserve
A bright bucket of sunshine
To caress your spirit
When you are tangled on the inside,

With love
Josh

Josh Hampshire, Grade 4
Dingeman Elementary School

Clouds

The cloud
white, misty, cold
moves silent and slowly
amazing to see from above
The cloud

Jonathan Castaneda, Grade 5
Joseph M Simas Elementary School

Save the Water

Save the brook, babbling like a child
Save the rainfall, pattering on my roof as I sleep
Save the lakes, a source of recreation to all living things
Save the ocean from the monstrous trash, harming all inhabitants
Save the rivers, home to hardworking beavers
Save the freshwater, our shrinking source of life

Jona Plevin, Grade 6
Francis Parker School

An Orange Delight

An orange is like feeling an old man's back,
The bumpy feeling numbs your fingers as they slither across the peel,
The smell refreshes your mind as you breathe in the fresh, zesty and citrus filled air,
The smell makes you feel sleepy and sugary,
The oranges fresh off the tree remind me of a planet far away from earth,
The round orangeness reminds me of the sun,
An orange looks round like the Earth, bumpy like the rocks and orange like the sun.
The taste is like a sugary, sweet and sour taste that no one can resist.
I love oranges.

Elizabeth Monsef, Grade 4
Daves Avenue Elementary School

Crog

Have you ever heard of a crog?
Well now you have!
It is a toad shaped, sage green, four pawed and single tailed beast.
It is six inches wide and eighteen inches tall.
When it is happy, it shouts reow!
But when it is mad, it cries riss!
When it dives into a pond, it makes a humongous splash!
When it sprints, the Earth goes thump, thump, thump!
Part of its diet is flies and mice. Eww!
All it hears are screams and shrieks
From people who are scared.
So what is a crog?
A cross between a cat and a frog!

Amber Sucich, Grade 6
Big Springs Elementary School

Fever 1793

I am unmerciful
I am the what causes people grief and pain
I cause the summer to be dreaded
I am a lightning bolt
speeding through towns
dispatching people instantaneously
People forsake even their own family to keep me from reaching them
The doctors are so inept to my cruel powers
The sicks' blood is boiling
Their eyes are as yellow as the yolk of an egg
Thousands of inhabitants have died so far but I will never end at that
So bring out your dead…
I am Fever

Shannon Vyvijal, Grade 6
St. Andrew's Episcopal School

Nature

N eedles falling from a pine tree
A ir sweet with the scent of flowers
T rees changing colors in the fall
U ncut grass in the meadows
R ain dropping from the sky
E arth orbiting the sun

Holden Groff, Grade 5
Mayfield Jr School of the Holy Child Jesus

Hyenas

Hyenas, scary as light gets darker
Hyenas purr like a pack of growling lions
   Jumping as happy cheetahs
Running in the hot desert,
   As darkness falls
   On their backs
A family of hyenas smile as they see
   Bodies of sleeping dogs
The black eye of a hyena sees,
   And then growls at the enemy
The hyena hides when an enemy appears
   Behind the Rocky Mountains.

Michelle Acuna, Grade 6
St Alphonsus School

Inside This…

Orange is probably nothing,
just little pieces of oranges and a
sweet citrus smell
But are you looking close enough
because you might not know that inside
every orange is a lorange.
What's this you might ask well a
Lorange is a small little troll
that lives in an orange.
Lorange's live in wondrous towns in
the orange always watching out for
those pesky Snoranges, they love
to play and slide down those seeds
So next time think twice when you look
at an orange, never underestimate what's inside,
for next time you just might find a Lorange.

Rosie Melendez, Grade 6
St Vincent Elementary School

Purple

Happy is like purple
And is also like a purple octopus looking for shelter
It spins in my mind
It reminds me of Yosemite's graceful waterfalls
It makes me feel excited like a bird learning how to fly
It makes me want to jump for joy

Benjamin Kraus, Grade 6
St Anne School

Fever

I am Fever
I know where to find you
If I can catch you I will kill you
I billow in like the wind, but am extremely devastating
I will compress the population of the largest cities
Your death will be like a match getting eaten up by fire
I will not let anyone by me without them knowing I am there
I am powerful and persistent and kill all who cross my path
I will besiege whatever is precious to you
Your friends
Your family
Your life
I am Fever

Evie Kinkade, Grade 6
St Andrew's Episcopal School

Ocean

Burning sand under my bare feet
Crabs pinching me till I'm weak
Shells washing up on the shore
I love the ocean
When the sunset fades away
It's dark but there's sounds of the waves
Under water sea animals come to life
The sound of life surrounding me
Awakened creatures having their nighttime fun
I love the ocean
As the sun rises gently
Nighttime creatures
The birds start to sing
I love the ocean
I hope it never leaves

Kelli Holmes, Grade 4
Stone Ranch Elementary School

If I Were…

If I were a cherry tree,
I would give juicy, sweet, and ginormous cherries.
If I were a koala bear,
I would be cute and cuddly.
If I were a rabbit,
I would play jump rope all day long.
If I were a star,
I would be the shiniest star in outer space.

Linh Nguyen, Grade 6
Elder Creek Elementary School

Humble

The boy had faith in God.
Hard work is what the boy did.
He was working with lots of strength.
Being respectful is what he was doing.
He would never lie and was honest all the time.
He wanted everyone to be treated equally all the time.

Vidya Jayaraman, Grade 4
Canyon View Elementary School

My Monkey Friend

I know a girl monkey
She is very funky

Her name is Hannah
She loves bananas

When she gets mad
She calls for her dad

Her dad's name is Fred
He always plays dead

She is my best friend
Until the very end
Patricia Curran, Grade 6
Charles Armstrong School

Globs*

Colorful globs of destiny
Melt in solitude.
They sit waiting
To be loved again.

Colors take rests
When melancholy strikes.
In the smiling rainbow of happiness
They awaken from their rest.
Brandon Brown, Grade 4
The Mirman School
*Inspired by "The Lagoon," 1944
by Henri Matisse

Rain

When I hear the rain,
it washes away my pain.
Later on that day,
I know it's not to stay.
Then I go to sleep,
and dream of lots of sheep.
Then the next day came,
and I heard the rain.
My pain was washed away,
during that rainy day.
The pain's back so now I have to stall,
until the next rainfall.
Troy Oberheim, Grade 6
Chapman Elementary School

Beautiful Butterflies

Beautiful butterflies
Orange, white pretty in every sight
Fun! Fun! Flying in the sun
Cambria Ballinger, Grade 5
Coastline Christian Academy

My Mommy!

My mommy is an awesome cook.
She makes astonishing food
She is smart
But not rude
I love her food
I also love her helpfulness
She shows kindness to you
And is important to me
She is very busy
And she loves me
She has brown hair, brown eyes
Just like me
She is impatient and protective
She looks young to me
She is sweet just like me
But sometimes also demanding
I love her
And she loves me
She likes everything clean
She is nice, caring, and not mean.
Sarah Fuentes, Grade 6
Century Community Charter School

Automobiles

A wesome Lamborghinis
U nhealthy gas polluting Earth
T rucks, SUVs, and cars
O ver the limit engines
M ostly all over the world
O n time for work
B usinesses for selling them
I ntelligent people who made it
L iving life on the road
E ternal exhilaration
S afety is required
Gavin Jaime, Grade 6
Aliso Elementary School

Lightning

Lightning
Cracks bright jagged
Shines in the dark night sky
Strikes across the lawn in anger
Lightning
Machele James, Grade 5
Joseph M Simas Elementary School

Star

S parkling at night
T onight and tomorrow
A shooting star in the air
R acing in the sky for everyone to see
Marissa Barbosa, Grade 5
Joseph M Simas Elementary School

Love

Love is a strong warm feeling
Love is like friendship but stronger
Love happens to everyone
don't be embarrassed about love
People are afraid to show or share love
Love makes you feel happy
Love love
I can't seem to understand
Why people are afraid to share love
Love
it is hard to find
I've found it deep inside me
Love
Asianay Weems, Grade 5
Clayton B Wire Elementary School

Light/Dark

The sun is bright
So let me shine

I gave some flowers light
So let them rise
Til' they die.

Do you know me?
I am light between your eyes
But I am not darkness.

Sunlight is my path
Where you go
Is your light.

I am darkness
Nobody can see me
Except the hollows
Of the full moon.

The full moon
In darkness
I don't attack light,
Light attacks me.
Danica Paras, Grade 5
Oak Street Elementary School

Blank Page

I find myself upon a blank page,
looking for something to write about.
The clock I watch as it ticks on by,
counting while making me nervous.
I turn on some music for inspiration.
The words that I listen to are no help.
Think Melissa, think!
Melissa Kroe, Grade 6
Bernice Ayer Middle School

Faith

Faith is what you believe,
Faith is what pushes us through those tough times,
Faith is believing,
Faith can bring us together,
It is something that cannot be broken,
To me faith is not a fantasy,
It is reality.

Andrew Mueller, Grade 6
Bernice Ayer Middle School

Love

Love is like pink
And is also like kindness
It spreads through my heart
It reminds me of the time my family was cheering
For me at my volleyball game
It makes me feel happy and cheerful
It makes me want to share this feeling

Kayla Demari, Grade 6
St Anne School

A Night Road

Walking against an invisible hand,
Pushing you back,
You smell the slight stench of sulfur in the wind,
But you still push on,
As hard as you can,
Until you find,
Civilization.

Evan J. Guerra, Grade 6
John Muir Elementary School

Sitting Beneath the Trees

I am sitting beneath the trees
Looking at the small buzzing bees
I hear the birds chirping and the lawn mowing
I am away from all my troubles
All the commotion in the house

I am thinking about my future
Will I ever have a spouse?
I am thinking about my mom's past
And how she was oh so fast
Right in front of me is a path
And I remember how I did so badly in math
But I am away from all my troubles
All the commotion in the house

I see red roses
And the outside shower
Oh how it shoots out with power
Then I remember I have practice
But I am away from all my troubles
All the commotion in the house

Sarah Johnson, Grade 5
Mayfield Jr School of the Holy Child Jesus

Mystical Wave

The waves gleaming in the water rushing here and there,
gliding through the water like wind in the air.
They crash upon the shore,
sliding across the sand.
They fly,
They glide,
They slide.
Their movement so peaceful; water on water.

Jesse Parajeckas, Grade 6
Bernice Ayer Middle School

Nature's Fury

Natural disasters are destroying the world
They are destroying us
And destroying animals
Everyone has to be cautious

Tornados twist n' turn with a loud howl
Destroying anything in their path
Hurricanes drench our land
And many people face its wrath

Quakes blast and ripple through the ground
Shaking every bit of life away
Volcanoes erupt with a mighty roar
Ruining our day

Hail falls from the sky
Shattering people's lives
With nature destroying us
We all struggle to survive
Its fury

Jesus Zambrano, Grade 6
Cimarron Education Center

Dogs

Dogs are so messy.
The slobber!
The globber!
The food that turns into poo, eww!
The holes in your mom's new flower bed
Oh what a mess.
Sometimes they're a "pest,"
But there's one good thing,
They can eat your broccoli and other veggies too
You've got to love that!
They cuddle with you all night and they let
You dream you're flying a kite.
So you have your ups and downs with your dog,
But you love them no matter what!
"Katherine your dog is out!"
Oops! "Spot…SPOT!"

Katherine Walker, Grade 4
Oak Grove Elementary School

The Sled Run
The hike
The hike back up the hill
Walking through crusty snow
The first turn, slowly
The second turn, faster
The third turn, high on the bank
Too high and a flip
You keep going
And before you know it the ride is over
The hike
The hike back up the hill
Joshua Temple, Grade 4
Montessori Family School

Mummy
Mummy
Old, creepy
Resting, laying, sleeping
Looking for afterlife
Dead
Katie Santos, Grade 6
Big Springs Elementary School

Music
You can
listen to it.

You can
dance to it.

You can
sing to it.

It's MUSIC!
Maria Garcia, Grade 6
Corpus Christi School

I Am From…
I am from…
A lovely old home
That has been passed down
Where rackety furniture lays
Where I dive off the diving board
I am from…
A worn down school
Where my uncles went
Where I made friends
Where I fall and bleed
I am from…
A street
Where I learned to ride a bike
Where I play in the snow banks
Where I jump over the cracks
Where I will always love
Annie Miziolek, Grade 4
Stone Ranch Elementary School

Football
Pads sitting there getting old
The biggest protection so I've been told
Then swiped down and put on right at the crack of dawn
Going out bright and early getting all muddy and dirty
When the whistle blows the starting kicker sends a blow
Soon caught by the returner
Who shot off so fast he looked like a burner
Then he was met with a hit so big he had to sit
The first play was under way the fans standing and that's where they stay
It was mid-way through the half and the quarter back dropped back
Then chucked it down the line only to be met with a bad sign
Interception by the other team a bad thing it might seem
Then it started the other way
But that's where it would stay 4 straight downs no gain
They punted it extremely far away
Then the ball was taken down the iron grid
Getting yards like taking candy away from a kid
Now only a few seconds left in the game
Fans hoping the score won't stay the same
Then the ball was thrown with a little shimmer
Touchdown a game winner
David Traganza, Grade 6
Francis Parker School

I Am From
I am from a house,
　　Where Lego creations are scattered everywhere.
　　Where the old piano sits next to the wall.
　　Where a lazy cat lugs itself around quietly.
I am from a yard,
　　Where flat balls trip any inattentive person.
　　Where broken light sabers lie from battles long ago.
　　Where an energetic dog barks at any stranger not willing to give him a tummy rub.
I am from a neighborhood,
　　Where Mr. Krause's beat up Jeep sits in front of his families house.
　　Where quail run freely in the bright emerald grass.
　　Where trees line the street casting shade over all.
Dominic Milani, Grade 5
Notre Dame School

The Ocean
I hold some of the most amazing creatures
Dolphins jump, fish swim, and sharks lurk
I sometimes think of how much joy I bring people
I dream that no one will fear my salty blue waves
I worry that rivers, lakes, and streams will take my popularity
I fear that people will drown because of my uncontrollable power
I hope that fishers will stop taking my precious animals
People swim in my luscious waters
They enjoy splashing me with their wet hands
Everyone thinks of me highly
They wish they could see all of my waters
But I go on and on and on
Hannah Leadem, Grade 6
James B Davidson Middle School

I Am

I am a softball player and trying out for track
I wonder if I will make it for track
I want to live with my dad
I see my baby sister every day
I am a softball player and trying out for track

I pretend I'm a queen
I feel my pencil in my hand
I touch the paper
I worry about my dad
I am a softball player and trying out for track

I understand math
I believe in God
I dream about going home when I'm at school
I hope to make it for track
I am a softball player and trying out for track

Brookelyn Lujan, Grade 5
Sundale Elementary School

When Will the World End?

When will the world end?
Will it end tomorrow?
Will it end in sorrow?
Will it come back some day?
Every day I wonder, will it decay?
Will it disappear into a sea?
Or will it return as a green tree?
Will someone ever give me a sign?
Will the world end with the snap of a chime?
Will someone give me a clue?
If they do please make it true.
When will the world end?
Will it end in a flame?
Or will it end in shame?

Hila Revah, Grade 6
Horace Mann School

Freedom

Colder than ice
Clear as glass
I stand silently
Watching the ferocious river path
The roar of a lion
The speed of a cheetah
I close my eyes listening to the ferocious river's cries
As I turn my back to leave
I take one glance at this wild beast
Though it seems its anger greater than any creature
This beast is free
Free for the whole world to see
Free as it swims to the big open sea

Suwayda Ali, Grade 6
Islamic School of San Diego

Undefeated

We enter the field,
and warm up for our game,
the outcome of everything
depends on this situation —
we are undefeated.
The pride in ourselves,
gives us a smile,
for we are the only team without a loss in a while —
we are undefeated.
The whistle blows for the start of the game,
the fans cheer like a roaring flame.
We score a goal with no surprise —
we are undefeated.
The opponent charges with focused expressions,
and hardened anger hid in their depression.
They long to win, they long to beat us —
we are undefeated.
I watch with weary eyes,
the opponents' anger in disguise.
They score two goals and the game has ended —
we aren't undefeated.

Joseph Porges, Grade 6
Cimarron Education Center

Nature Is a Jungle

Nature is a jungle
you never know what is coming your way
you could search forever
and never find that one true place

All around you are trees and bushes
fish jumping and frogs croaking
birds singing and ducks quacking
It is a beauteous sight

You will always wonder what's around the corner
watch out it might be a cougar
creatures will be lurking all around you
through the trees

If you look closer to examine what they could be
you find some of them harmless as harmless as could be
By the end of the week
you're really happy you went on this trip
Before you leave the jungle remember that

Nature is a jungle

Sandra Gamboa, Grade 6
Cimarron Education Center

Fog

Look at the thick fog
Hanging over the harbor
When will it fall back

Christopher Tan, Grade 4
Mayfield Jr School of the Holy Child Jesus

Free Throws
Dribble three times
Spin it,
Dribble two times
Throw it to my left hand,
Dribble once
Spin it two times
Two seconds later,
Swish.
That's my shot,
Dad passes it back to me,
"Same routine," Dad said,
I just nodded
And shot.
Missed,
But Dad says, "Nice shot"
"Bend your knees."
Kan Altice, Grade 5
Clover Avenue Elementary School

How About a Race?
"How about a race?"
said a mate on our boat.
"Down the marina to the last buoy!"
"Yeah!" we all cheer.
Ready! Set! Go!
We all start paddling as
hard as we can.
Heave! Ho! Heave! Ho!

Our boat pulls away!
The first buoy is behind us.
Heave! Ho! Heave! Ho!
The second buoy we pass.
The other boat lags far behind.
Heave! Ho! Heave! Ho!
Here comes the last buoy.
Faster! Faster!
We pass the last buoy.
We win! We win!
The other boat lags far behind.
Zachary Wieder, Grade 5
Carlthorp School

Time
Time is a mystery,
Time is mine,
Time never ever stops,
Time is fine,
Time can change night to day,
Time is cool,
Time can be a nightmare,
But time rules!
Jonathan Rojas, Grade 5
St Pancratius Elementary School

Black
Black is the night
When there isn't a star
And you can't tell by looking
Where you are.
Black is a pail,
Of pavement tar.
Black is jet.
And things
You'd like to forget.
Black is a smokestack.
Black is a cat,
A leopard, a raven,
A high silk hat.
The sound of black is
Boom! Boom! Boom!
Echoing in
An empty room.
Catalina Jackson, Grade 5
PLACE @ Prescott

Changes
Everything is changing,
Everyone is changing,
Trying to keep up
Is the hardest thing to do.
But everyone must move on,
Think about the present,
Not the past.
It may be hard to walk on this journey,
But just remember everyone is with you,
Trying to go on,
Trying to go ahead,
Trying to keep going,
Trying to catch up,
Trying to help,
Trying to save…
Trying to CHANGE.
Sophia Ynami, Grade 6
Corpus Christi School

Tears
Feel a tear roll down your face
Hear your friend run with a worried face
Feel your tear wash away
Hear your friend say "are you okay?"
Ashley Contreras, Grade 4
Montessori Family School

Purple Rose
Flowers grow quite tall,
For they say they're quite lovely,
There are no others.
Mycala Costa, Grade 5
Gustine Elementary School

Target
As if it were yesterday
We walk into the store
It seems like a city of its own
The floor is spotless and squeaky clean
The shelves are full
The toys are toppled
Going to the toy section
The place is huge
With trillions of toys
So hard to choose
Except for one
It was easy for me
No choice at all
Except for the fact
That we have to leave
Andrew Joseph Selvo, Grade 5
Clover Avenue Elementary School

Snow
On the peaceful hill
Sparkling snowflakes fall gently
In the lovely sun.
Angel Campos, Grade 5
Santa Fe Springs Christian School

Highlighter
Stuffed inside a pencil pouch
Just waiting to be used
I hope they don't push too hard
For then I'll be flat
Losing my cap would be
Horrible
I'd get dried up and thrown away
I really wouldn't like that
As long as they use me
I'll be okay
That way I can bring
Joy and brightness to
Those dull, colorless letters
And when my day is done
I settle back into my pouch
With the hopes of being used and
The fears of being thrown away
Katie Clark, Grade 6
James B Davidson Middle School

Chasing
Oh my gosh
look at that
see that dog chasing that cat
the cat found a rat
now they're chasing back to back
Emily Grimes, Grade 4
Marian Bergeson Elementary School

High Merit Poems – Grades 4, 5 and 6

My Likes and Dislikes

I like soccer
But I don't like when I lose.
I like it to rain
But I don't like it when I fall in puddles.
I like school
But I don't like it when I get too much homework.
I like swimming
But I don't like it when the water is cold.

Isabel Spaeth, Grade 4
Elder Creek Elementary School

If

If I were a color, I would be blue
Because blue is the color of the bright summer sky
And the beautiful ocean sea water.
If I were a planet, I'd be Earth
Because Earth is a wonderful place
Where trees and animals are about.
If I were an animal, I'd be the cheetah
Who runs so swiftly and gracefully to catch its prey.
If I were a TV, I would be a 65" Sony flat screen
In a rich person's bedroom.
If I were a band, I'd be AC/DC
And play awesome hard metal rock songs.
If I were a sport, I would be baseball.
Then I could see endless games with a juicy hotdog, soda
And some delicious cotton candy.
If I were a movie, I'd be *The Sandlot*
Because it's a funny, classic baseball movie
About good friends and a kid who becomes a major leaguer
If I were a famous person, I'd be me
Because I'm going to grow up and play pitcher
For the amazing San Diego Padres.

Will Locken, Grade 5
Aviara Oaks Elementary School

Ocean

I know…
the feeling of sea mist whipping my face,
the freedom as I dive deep down,
My hair flowing behind me,
the excitement as I explore underwater coral reefs.

I know…
the sheer terror when I see a guitar shark,
the feel of excitement while looking through murky waters
the overwhelming happiness when I see
angel fish darting around me.

I know…
the desperate need for air,
the sensation when the cold air whips my face,
and beautiful turquoise blue color of the sea
I know the ocean!

Samantha Pryor, Grade 6
Francis Parker School

Excited

Excited is not calm
Excited is a puppy waiting for its owner to come home
Excited is waiting in line to go on a rollercoaster
Excited is going to the airport to catch a flight
Excited sounds like me opening a Christmas present
Excited sounds like screams at a birthday party
Another word for excited is thrilling
One thing about excited is that it's a moment worth waiting for

Amanda Fritz, Grade 6
Big Springs Elementary School

Amazing Grace

Thank You gracious Lord,
My rock and my salvation.
You are the light,
My faith is everlasting.

Thank you gracious Lord,
You sent Your only Son,
To save us all from Satan's power,
So we could share in Your eternal glory.

Thank You gracious Lord,
I glorify Your saving grace.
Your awesome power is like solid gold.
I cherish Your mighty assisting power.

Thank you gracious Lord,
Your kindness is vital.
I will forever be Your servant.
Your mercy is the candle in the darkness.

Thank you gracious Lord,
You have saved me from myself
And my sinful ways.
I confess to You, O' loving and forgiving Lord.

Daniel McNamara, Grade 6
St Cecilia School

Inside This

The words I speak are the words it writes.
It's like the letters it leaves are all of my thoughts.
My thoughts are all coming out.
My test answers just fly out.
It leaves marks on my paper.
It is so smooth.
You cannot feel it on the paper.
It is so magical,
It feels like a dream.
It is all inside a plastic tube.
I can't help to say,
It is all in my pen.

Jose Montes, Grade 6
St Vincent Elementary School

The Forest

Green is the color of the forest,
Surrounded by its choirs.
Made by its beautiful sound,
The sound of animals from all around.
The smell of trees surround me,
If you could only smell and see.
The beauty, the sound, the smell,
Oh, but much has fell.
When people cut them down,
All to the ground,
A thing that makes me sad,
And makes me feel bad.
When people cut the trees,
All the animals flee.
When their homes are cut,
Something they couldn't have fought,
When the trees are cut,
I go nuts.
I wish they would stop,
To something they gave small thought,
When people cut the trees.

Abril Huaman, Grade 6
John Muir Elementary School

Kendall Mills

Kendall,
Weird, silly, crazy, kind,
Relative of her little sister,
Lover of dancing,
Who feels happy and proud,
Who gives love to me,
Who fears spiders and snakes,
Who would like to see the Eiffel Tower,
Who lives in a big blue house,
Mills.

Samantha Corrales, Grade 5
Ladd Lane Elementary School

Agitated

When I'm agitated
I feel annoyed.
I could explode
If it doesn't stop.
It grinds my teeth
It irritates my brain.
I yell and scream
Until it lets up!!!

Noah Scott, Grade 5
Kentwood Elementary School

Summer Days

On a summer day
A lot of big waves crashing
Kids on their surf boards

Keaton Moody, Grade 6
St Anne School

Bodacious Oreo

I smell the sweet, heavenly chocolate and stare at the snowy white frosting.
I take the top off and eat the sugary, circular heaven in front of me.
I feel the soft, sticky frosting move around my mouth.
As I hear the quiet "munch munch" of hard chocolate in my mouth
My spirits feel happier than ever.

Benjamin Don, Grade 5
Morasha School

A Family Is...

To be a part of a family like mine
Is eternal
Where love is shown
And where you own the fun and love
We talk
We titter
We lament
We're always entertained
Whatever we do
We stick together
No matter if we aren't clever
We were put on this Earth for a reason
To have fun in all the seasons
No matter if we go through ills
We will achieve
Don't be shy with your family
And thank every second you have because it's going to pass by very fast
It doesn't matter what happens to me and to you
We'll always make it through
I LOVE YOU FOREVER!
FAMILY FOREVER!

Estefania Corona, Grade 6
St John's Parish Day School

Nature

Sun shines and the day is in full bloom.
The children run like the wind into the trees.
The teacher yells be careful, danger might loom.
A squirrel scampers towards the lunch of a child.

The teacher yells as she's never done before.
The students laugh like hyenas, when in the blink of an eye
The small animal jumps and escapes with a leap.
The teacher makes a fire heating the lazy children.

Now it's time to go back to the place where they can rest.
They sadly, painfully cry that they don't want to go.
The teacher says they'll come back tomorrow for the sun is setting.
The children sigh but say okay, and they start to go.

Finally, it's time for us to part.
Thank you for listening.
Now I will let you go.

Mahdi Nafisi, Grade 6
Dorris-Eaton School

Grades Happen

A's, B's, C's, D's, and F's.
When you get some of these grades
you feel melancholy, despondent,
a rush of anger.
But when you get the others
you feel happy, a rush.
When you find out
you're about to get your report card
your stomach feels queasy
like you're on a fast roller coaster
going down the tracks really fast that's how it feels.

Deja McZeal, Grade 6
St Timothy School

Books

Books are not bad, and are not perfect.
Books can make you feel sad.
They can be funny.
They can be scary.
Books teach you, but books are not perfect.

You need to read a lot of books to be perfect enough.
Books don't teach you everything that you need to know.
That's why books are not perfect.

When books are in just the right place,
They can make this not so perfect world easier to face,
More of us can go in the right direction if you read books.
But you can't be perfect just like books.

Hinano Takahashi, Grade 5
Solana Pacific School

Playing Ball

They call me Alexis and I like to play
When I play ball I play all day
So just hear the words I say
I'll be active in the bay

Playing basketball every day
Hoping everything will be all right
Like sometimes we pick a fight
I know my cousins are cool and tight

I know I lose, it's just a game
But sometimes my cousins say I'm lame
But that's okay because of what I have to say
They are not good at playing a game

But if I lose I have to change my name
That is okay because my name's the same
They started throwing rocks at me but they have no aim
But I'm going to be famous by the end of the day

Alexis Espinoza, Grade 5
El Monte Elementary School

The Treasure

The young boy found a shell of his own,
But who really owned it was not known.

The next day he grabbed his treasure,
And the crab inside pinched him for good measure.

Claire Rowland, Grade 6
James B Davidson Middle School

Life

Life is full of choices some good some bad
some even make people sad

Life is full of fairy tales and happily ever afters
They make this world full of laughter

Making your own decisions some might not be right
But you always make sure to hold on tight

Life is a gift that you get one chance to make true
So make it good and always be you

Kayla Christensen, Grade 4
Palo Verde Elementary School

Rain!

Please rain go away
Let me play in the sun today.
I stay inside as it rains.
I read books and play boring board games.
I see your home, the gray clouds, floating about.
Make the blue sky and white clouds come out.
Or do I have to pout?

Please rain go away
Let me play in the sun today.
How many time do I have to say pretty please?
Replace rain with the sun and a cool breeze.

Please rain go away
Let me play in the sun today.
I look out the window,
The rain has gone away.
I run outside with my kite.
Thank you for letting me play!
You're welcome to come out on a different day!

Angela Murphy, Grade 5
Merryhill Country School

Sadness

We are sad for countless reasons
because our emotions collide.
Sometimes, if your family dies
your emotions will never go by.
Emotions are part of day to day life,
without them your love can never survive.

Sevon Destiny Abdalian, Grade 5
Granada Elementary School

The Things That Make Yellow
I know Yellow

Yellow smells like the sour and juicy ball of a refreshing lemon, the smell of the new sprouted, blooming daisy, the faint smell of the light, but colorful leaves.

Yellow, the tough and rough surface of the dancing pencils on children's desks, the slick touch of the slippery and melted butter, the sticky stroke of a very well frozen, yellow popsicle.

Yellow, the blazing, golden and crisped of the bright way this color shines with these other magical paint, the lonely dot of the camping light piercing the night.

Yellow is the sound of the loud clap of booming lightning, the pop of the yellow confetti, cheep, cheep the sound of a new born chick hatching from its circular yellow egg.

Yellow tastes like the warm, buttery, and small pieces of the popcorn popping with its wonderful scent drifting into the air, the soft foamy and spongy marshmallow coming out of the bag, the taste of the squishy, but still healthy fruit, the banana.

I really know Yellow.

Belle Phommavong, Grade 4
Dingeman Elementary School

If I Were…

If I were a horse,
I'd be a free mustang,
I'd rear up on my back legs and fend off anyone who dares to come near.

If I were a mythical creature,
I'd be an emerald and peridot fiery dragon,
I'd scare off knights and explore through the skies always soaring.

If I were a mountain,
I'd be Mount Everest,
I'd stand tall over the world watching mercilessly as people try to climb me.

If I were a bird,
I'd be a sharp-eyed eagle,
I'd swoop down upon my prey and hear the squeak of it in satisfaction.

If I were anything in the world,
I'd be me.
I'd be my plain self, always knowing I'm more special than a mustang, dragon, mountain, or an eagle.

Kristin Chow, Grade 5
Aviara Oaks Elementary School

Spring Rejoices

I am thankful God made spring,
He gave us this season for new life, flowers, animals, and birds to sing.
He gave us the blue sky, the greens on Earth, and clear water.
All the living beings rejoice in His name with their children and mothers.
God has made this season to let Earth show its brilliant colors.
We show thanks by taking care of His creations with love and honor.
Spring means renewal and new birth.
This season reminds me when everything was happy and joyful when God made the Earth.

Angelica G. Medina, Grade 5
St Linus School

High Merit Poems – Grades 4, 5 and 6

The Candy Shop

Welcome to the candy shop
Where you can find chocolate and lollipops.
You can come here every day
And find some candies made your way.

Eat Milky Ways, Snickers, a jawbreaker treat
Anything you buy here, you know it's sweet.
The special is Ferrero Roche
Ancient chocolate is still here today.

M&Ms, licorice, Hershey's kisses
Root beer barrels, dark chocolate blisses.
The candies go fast, 10 bags by the hour
Some of them are sweet and sour.

Colorful gum balls, I hope you'll like
They have strawberry cakes, in the shape of a bike,
When you come to the shop, you'll never be sad
You come here hungry, and come home glad!

Judy Blancaflor, Grade 4
St Pancratius Elementary School

Laura

Laura,
Funny, nice, smart,
Relative of the Chatham family,
Lover of gorillas,
Who feels funny all the time,
Who gives laughter,
Who fears sumo wrestlers,
Who would like to see herself in a movie,
Who lives in a really big house,
Chatham

Gabby Verdugo, Grade 5
Ladd Lane Elementary School

Fever

I am fever
I kill slowly but surely
You will wither if I touch you
I am not just a minor setback
I slake the young, and the old, the strong, and the weak
You think you are safe from me, but you are not
I devastate towns, cities, countries
I am like a nightmare, but you cannot wake up
You're heart pounds faster and faster
Trying to escape
But escape is impossible
When your enemy is so elusive
Death is imminent
For death does not discriminate
Everywhere you go, everywhere you run
Death will follow
For I am fever

Brandon Luk, Grade 6
St Andrew's Episcopal School

Purple

Purple is the color of the plums.
Purple is the color of the flowers.
Purple is the feeling I get when I'm happy.
Purple is the marker's color.
Purple smells like frozen grapes.
Purple tastes like grape flavor Kool-Aid.
Purple sounds like plums in a blender.
Purple looks like grapes falling off the trees.
Purple feels like I'm pulling radishes.
Purple makes me feel happy if I wear purple.
Purple is my favorite color.

Hong Ngo, Grade 5
Clayton B Wire Elementary School

College

What happens when you go to college?
Do you lower your grades or improve your knowledge?
If you misbehave do you get detention?
Does too much homework give you tension?
Do you get to go to birthday parties?
If you are late do you get tardies?
What time do you have to go to bed?
What if your pencil runs out of lead?
Do you have to make your own meals?
Will the college give you scholarship deals?
There are a lot of questions to be asked
But remember, 6 more years until college is our task.

Sofia Orelo, Grade 6
Horace Mann School

Crazy World

The sense of violence spreads through the whirling wind,
Our souls and hearts are filled with sin.
Dark clouds and rain fill the entire sky,
Many families struggle just to get by.
But many things change and so can we,
This isn't the way the world is supposed to be.
But even when the world is filled with sorrow,
Things can get better by tomorrow.

Imelda Cardenas, Grade 6
St Vincent Elementary School

Evening

The sunset among the land
Clouds fluffy and soft like marshmallows
Drift Away

The sunset disappears under a blanket of darkness
A pale moon sails like a ghostly pirate ship

My eyes slowly close
Dreaming of happy things.

Avi Bhullar, Grade 4
Sierra Oaks K-8 School

Grandparents

Some are sweet
Some are cool
A lot are great
But some are cruel
Some give you money
And some call you honey
But you always love them
Even if they're grumpy

Elias Acevedo, Grade 5
Jackson Elementary School

Waterfall

Roaring waters fall
Down a lovely, blue river
With crystal colors

Angelica Irineo, Grade 5
Joseph M Simas Elementary School

Koala

A koala lives in Australia
Big and fuzzy
Gray with big ears
Like big teddy bears
They eat leaves from the eucalyptus tree
May be friendly
Though their predators are not —
As they lurk in the desert
Waiting and waiting
For the right time
To pounce on the koala
But the koala is clever
It doesn't come out
Bye! Bye!
See you again.

Sierra Hernandez, Grade 6
St Alphonsus School

Presents

Oh presents, oh presents
So many to see
Which ones are for me?

Down the chimney
Who do I see?
It's Santa Claus o'gee

He got us toys
My mom a robe, my dad a globe
What did I get?
A hobo!?
A picture frame
A model plane
A naughty list with my name
OH NO!

Clara Roderick, Grade 4
Oak Grove Elementary School

Midnight

I wait until the clock strikes midnight,
I lay on the wet grass.
Then I hear the clock ringing,
I'm happy that it's midnight.
I look up at the stars,
And at the dark color of the night sky.
I wonder at how beautiful the night sky would be in outer space.
I imagine comets, asteroids, and radiant stars.
I see the comet's beautiful tail pass me,
The large asteroids,
And the giant stars twinkling.
But all too soon I leave my imaginative world,
And I find myself staring back at the night sky,
Lying on the wet grass again.

Erinn Liong, Grade 6
John Muir Elementary School

Holiday

Golden shiny menorah exhilaratingly shining in the darkness,
Great immense presents hiding in gift bags,
Good, close friends happily coming to visit,
Bright, colorful fire happily shining in the dark for eight days,
Big shiny star happily glowing at the top of the Christmas tree,
Green dazzling Christmas tree gratefully standing near the fireplace,
Enormous lighted house being stood out compared to other buildings.

Ori Weiss, Grade 6
Highland Oaks Elementary School

Black and White and Ballet and Contemporary and Morning and Night

black
inky, ebony
blinding, churning, enveloping
darkness, dusk, moonlight, cupcakes
resting, shining, seeking
naive, pristine
white

ballet
serene, outward
flowing, cultivating, dancing
delicacy, expression, floor, grounded
twisting, swinging, falling
unrestrained, inward
contemporary

morning
grayness, foggy
sleeping, waking, dawning
embrace, cosmic, muttered, mourning
darkening, obscuring, waiting
silent, stilled
night

Camille Considine, Grade 6
Francis Parker School

Mother Earth

I am a little baby duckling.
Though I do not need to migrate now,
I will have to someday.
My kin are airplanes flying here and there,
but they need to rest in places with food and water.
Some do not make it because of the pollution.
Save my mother,
Save your mother,
Save our Mother Earth!

Connie Huang, Grade 4
Ocean Air School

Save Mother Earth

I am a polar bear.
I walk low and slow with no sound.
I am waiting for a seal to jump out so I can kill it
After my meal I look for another but then
I drop through the ice.
I swim a mile to shore.
I am so tired, so now I sleep.
It is very hard work.
Please save Mother Earth.

Philip Duvinage, Grade 4
Ocean Air School

Hatfield Beach

Walking
Hot sand on the beautiful beach
A scorching summer day
Mom and Dad hugging me
Searching the ground
For fascinating rocks
Stopping, hitting colorful docks
The lake glowing during sunset
Sitting down, watch the enormous ball of fire hide
Feeling the cold air coming
Fish jumping
Fish never seen before
The sun was down when we got in our old car
What a magnificent time!

Kyla Rave, Grade 5
Clover Avenue Elementary School

Sad Chicken

A rooster is sitting in the barn,
All alone.
The small crown of feathers upon his head is drooping,
He is sad,
He is so sad because he has no friends,
He sits all alone with his crown going down,
Will he be dinner for three,
Or a friend for me?

Ian Keys, Grade 4
Daves Avenue Elementary School

Death

Things are turning black around me.
My fingers are turning numb.
I think my time is over.
My mouth is bitter and my lips are wet with blood.
I think I am going to die now.
But my life has just begun.

Noah Zisser, Grade 5
Montessori Center School

Happy Christmas

Vibrant bulbs dazzlingly blinking on houses
to illustrate alluring, extraordinary colors,
Verdant mistletoe suspending off doors
leading to temperate living rooms,
Prominent, chubby Santa Claus
happily delivering implausible presents
to children worldwide,
Boisterous, intrigued elves hastily wrapping
presents in the remarkable industrial unit,
Exultant children unwearyingly waiting
for Santa Claus to inaudibly put gifts
under the Christmas tree,
Sizable choruses melodiously singing
stimulating songs in the influential night,
Blissful Christmas trees delicately
suspending vibrant, meticulous ornaments shining
in the light,
Frosty flurry silently falling
in the night of Christmas.

Nicholas Lew, Grade 5
Highland Oaks Elementary School

Despair

Despair is like blue
And is also like an empty soul
It chews through my heart
It reminds me of the time I had to leave my friends
And everything I knew
It makes me feel empty like an empty shell
It makes me want to weep and wail and cry

Cameron Eldridge, Grade 6
St Anne School

Up to Bat

A river of sweat pours down your face
Covered in a thin layer of dust
Teammates' encouraging words fill your ears
The ball shoots to the eagerly awaiting hitter
Adrenaline rushes to all your veins
As the bat swiftly slices through the air
Just to be abruptly dropped
Dust cloud forms around scampering feet
Trying to reach its destination
SAFE!

Brianna Millar, Grade 5
Juarez Elementary School

Determination

White black and round
People kick it all around
Excitement in the crowd
You have to be proud
Determination is the key

Getting an A
On a wonderful day
My parents will say "Yah"
Determination is the key

Soccer is my game
Losing is a pain
But I will stand up again
And try to win my game
Determination is the key

Running the mile
Will give my parents a smile
Yet all I need is heart
To get smart
Determination is the key

Kevin Pla, Grade 6
Ramona Elementary School

Clouds

Clouds, clouds
Hanging in the blue sky
What do I see, what do I see
I see a white poodle sleeping in the
white puffy cloud,
Being as cute as a clam!
What a wonderful sight I can see!
Clouds, clouds
Hanging in the blue sky!

Elizabeth Grant, Grade 6
Barstow Intermediate School

Looking at the Landscape

Looking at the landscape
out the uncleaned window,
hearing the whisper of the trees.
Then…
a shock, a feeling
like an earthquake
so scary,
to give my goose bumps, goose bumps.
A car wrapped around a tree like a Frito
frightened to death
thinking we're going to die
running out in our pajamas
scared to death.

Abigail Farmer, Grade 5
Clover Avenue Elementary School

Spider

Home Address: web so neat
Hobbies/Sports: likes to eat
Special Skills: makes design
Occupation: get ready to dine
Favorite foods: clumsy flies
Personality: very wise
Size: very small
Hiding place: in the wall
Working hours; dusk till dawn
Favorite movie: Babylon
Colors looks; brown and tan
Heritage; arachnid clan
Free time: surf the web
Best friend: a snail named Hebb
Favorite song: midnight scream
Favorite holiday: Halloween

Aldo Lamberti, Grade 6
Francis Parker School

Monsters/Alien

Monsters
Huge, strong
Chasing, fighting, roaring
Evil, horrible, scary, war
Stealing, smart, defending
Ugly, weird
Alien

Gen Maeshiro, Grade 4
Heather Elementary School

Warm Jackets

Fire is red
Ice is blue
I love warm jackets
This much is true

Jin Ru He, Grade 4
Clayton B Wire Elementary School

Football

Football, football,
It's the best.
Play football only,
It's better than the rest.

Everybody gets tackled down,
But we want a touchdown.
It's better than baseball,
And played with an odd shaped ball.

If you get hurt it's okay,
But if you break your arm,
Ouch you're not okay.

Jeremy Brown, Grade 4
St Pancratius Elementary School

My Best Friend

Her eyes are closed,
Her body is motionless.
Her life is gone,
And so is my best friend.

She always ran and laughed
When she was awake.
That laugh is now gone,
And so is my best friend.

She liked to sleep a lot.
I usually heard her snore.
The sound of her snore is now gone,
And so is my best friend.

The pain inside me never ends.
I long to see her lively,
But her life is long gone.
She was my best friend.

Justine Sarmiento, Grade 6
Parkmont Elementary School

My Summer

I step outside and take a look around.
I feel, I hear, I sense
nature everywhere.
You cannot stop
the constant rustle of the leaves.
The wonderful scent of the pine trees
and sweet wild flowers
is so mesmerizing.
I never want it to end,
but I know that it must.
My sweet summer
fades away once again.
The leaves on the trees
slowly turn to orange and soon fall off.
There is no more rustling
and no sweet scent.
They have all disappeared.
But I do not despair,
for I know my summer will soon return,
and once again
I will be engulfed by its mighty presence.

Lindsay Bruns, Grade 6
John Muir Elementary School

Dolphins

Dolphins like water.
Swimming in the Atlantic.
They are gray and blue.

Baylee Roop, Grade 5
Eastwood Elementary School

High Merit Poems – Grades 4, 5 and 6

My Milo
He is cute and fluffy,
And as big as a bear,
He is my definite baby,
And has a bottomless stomach.

When we play tug of war,
And he leaps in the air,
I laugh with tears streaming from my eyes,
And happiness in my life.

I will always love him,
And never forget him,
He is the best ever,
I love my Milo.

Bronwen Lane, Grade 6
James B Davidson Middle School

Thinking of a Poem
Listening to music
Asking for help from friends
Sitting down on a chair thinking of a poem
Wondering what should I write?
How would I write it?
What should I write about?
Trying to relax
Getting frustrated
Trying to gain control of myself
Thinking
Thinking way too hard
I just have to realize a poem
takes time

Jovan Sunga, Grade 6
Corpus Christi School

The Kids' Anthem
We are the kids, so bold and brave
We scour the world and heroes we save
We run so fast it'll leave you dazed
And we can see through the thickest haze

Our hands so fast they can catch a fish
We talk so much it'll make you wish
That we would be a lot more quieter
But try as you might we'll never be silenter

We are the kids, so bold and brave
We can see in the darkest cave
We are the kids, we'll never disappear
We are nice and kind and we'll never ever jeer

A blow from us will send you flyin'
We are honest, just; we never start lyin'
We are the kids, we rule the earth
Back off aliens; this is our turf

Ryan Jiang, Grade 5
Dorris-Eaton School

Happy Holidays
Fuzzy, frigid snow falling lightly to the frozen ground,
Tall, evergreen Christmas trees
Covering all the unopened Christmas presents,
Unique, shimmery snowflakes
Appearing in all different shapes and sizes,
Appetizing, scrumptious, ginger bread cookies
Lying on a tray, waiting to be devoured,
Plump, roasted turkey being served
To many starving, happy guests,
Decorative Christmas cards being opened
And read by several grateful families,
Sugary-sweet candy canes
Tasting like the most delicious candy
In the whole, wide, world!

Sophia Meyer-Yen, Grade 5
Highland Oaks Elementary School

Turquoise
Calm is like turquoise
and is also like the ocean
it sways through my mind
it reminds me of the time when I was at the beach
it makes me feel comforted or serene
it makes me want to fall asleep

McKenna Monticone, Grade 6
St Anne School

The Four Seasons
Winter, spring, summer, and autumn,
Which one do you await to come?
Autumn starts, and then it dies,
Sorrowfully wiping tears from its eyes.

Winter rises, winter falls,
Wrap up your shoulders in heavy shawls.
Spring suspends on a string,
As two birds fly and sing.

BOOM! Oh no!
Spring's rage has come!
It's lightning and thunder, everyone's gloom,
Truly it is a sign of doom.

Is it here? It's finally summer!
But it will soon be over, what a bummer.
Again, here's Autumn when school starts,
No more games and no more darts.

Plentiful studying will be tough,
Don't we already have enough?
These are the seasons, I know they're great,
Only one more to go in 2008.

Andrew Nguyen, Grade 6
Dorris-Eaton School

Lily of the Valley

So much etiquette,
No wonder it's delicate.
It sways in the wind like a bell
Ringing out so well.
It makes me sail
Into a fairy tale.
So soft and cozy,
It makes my cheeks grow rosy.
Beautiful, soft, delicate, white,
Looking at it is a delight!

Anahita Yamouti, Grade 4
Daves Avenue Elementary School

Two Paths

In my head
I have two different futures
one path is that
I can see myself
standing on a stage
the lights beating on me
the drums giving the tempo
the guitar doing base
and me standing there singing.

Path two
I see myself
working with animals
people coming
in with sick animals
looking for a reason
on why they are sick.

These paths are
what I think my future is
I am only a kid
a kid can dream
about their future.

Claire Johnson, Grade 6
Bethany Lutheran School

Determination

What is determination?
A river
That never stops flowing
A rock
That never moves
A tree that sometimes will be blown
By heavy winds, and struck
By lightning in storms
But will never move
A source
That keeps you motivated
To reach certain goals
That's motivation

Matthew Amato, Grade 6
Aliso Elementary School

Feelings

Feelings are like big fish in a small tank:
they dream of being free
in the depths of the blue ocean.

Feelings are like a parrot in a cage:
it tweets and jumps,
imagining one day to be free
and explore the wide outdoors —
O it will come someday, to sit on a tree in the middle of May.

Feelings
are like a person reading a book:
when you open the page
you want to explore, imagine, be within and upon the crisp pages.

Feelings just want, wish, imagine to be FREE!

Rylee Rodriguez, Grade 6
St Timothy School

Chocolate Chip Cookie

Cookies are light brown with **C** hocolate chips that are black.
They are nice fres **H** ly baked.
Cookies taste go **O** d mushed up with ice cream.
They are extremely crun **C** hy if over cooked.
Whatever you d **O** , don't let dad find them.
A **L** ways buy more dough to eat.
They always m **A** ke me joyful.
They are spoiled if **T** hey are burnt.
Double the magnificenc **E** with double chocolate chips.

I don't suggest dark **C** hocolate chips.
Who doesn't like t **H** em?
I enjoy them.
They are scrum **P** tious with chunky chocolate chips.

Some have **C** reamy chocolate chips.
I love eating s **O** ft, gooey ones.
Cookies are t **O** tally outstanding. (Don't you think?)
Don't be shy! Ta **K** e them all for yourself.
I w **I** ll choose fresh, homemade ones.
They are d **E** licious!

Hunter Cutting, Grade 4
Daves Avenue Elementary School

Home

the aroma of mothers spaghetti calling me from my room
the fireplace lit with hot chocolate waiting for me on a cold day
the scent of lavender breeze candles every night
the warm bathtub ready for me to soak in every night
on christmas a bundle full of beautiful wrapped presents under the tree
a place called home
home sweet home

Madison Villa, Grade 6
Aliso Elementary School

The Sly Fox

Home Address: The Den
Working hours: From five a.m. to ten
Hobbies: stealing hens from the coop
Special skills: tying my tail in a big loop
Occupation: being sly all the way around the clock
Favorite food: chickens fresh from the flock
Color choice: he prefers the blackness of the night
Age: many moons older than a fortnight
Next of kin: the spy, the thief, and the assassin
Appetite: a great big stomachful of chicken
Cause of death: shot by the farmer's shotgun

Allison Emge, Grade 6
Francis Parker School

Judo

Judo,
The sport
Hear it
The sound of people falling
Feel the force as you push your partner
Take him on your back and…
Bam!
Stick him to the ground as he wiggles himself out
"Mateh"
The match is finished
You have won
Judo,
The sport
Hear it.

Emma Laik, Grade 5
Duveneck Elementary School

Courage

Butterflies in your stomach
Create much discomfort.
Face this uneasiness,
And you have courage.

The time is here — the major test.
You look to the side and see a friend peek.
"What to do, what to do," one will ponder.
Doing the right thing is no little matter.

"Three minutes t'ill show time," the director yells.
Muscles become tense due to the fear.
The crowd looks up, only to find a pleasant surprise.
"Yes, I have done it," one wonders as she is praised.

Courage — a trait only a few possess,
Although many are capable of owning it.
All it takes is a little dedication
And much willpower.

Neha Nagesh, Grade 6
Parkmont Elementary School

Eyes Are Eyes

Piercing as the sharpest bullets,
Frightening as the worst war ever fought,
Catch you as fast as lightning,
Soft as the finest velvet,
Warm as a cup of cocoa,
Affectionate as the most loving parent,
Blue as the brightest sky,
Green as the most polished emeralds,
Parents' eyes are friendly,
While a Navy instructor's are cold,
Warm, cold, scary, beautiful, mean, or nice,
No matter what eyes are eyes.

Kaumron Eidgahy, Grade 4
Stone Ranch Elementary School

The Queen

Oh valiant
Queen Elizabeth
Build a blockade
To keep them away.

Omnipotent powers
Will keep you strong
For this short time.

Valiantly fighting
Martial plans soon won't save you.

The religion of your people will be in your hands,
The Spanish people want to take that away.
But remember always,
It is your duty to protect England.

Your stable hands will begin to shake
On the last battle,
Only God can save you now.

Gwen Snyder, Grade 5
The Mirman School

Green Emerald Palace

Green is the birth stone of May
Green emeralds shine with my name on it
It glitters with spark knowing it's my favorite color
The emerald spreads its green lights into
the green forest leading me to my emerald palace
With a room filled with emeralds to look at
They shimmer with delight as I come in

Gabriella Amon, Grade 4
Stone Ranch Elementary School

Cherry Blossoms

Cherry blossoms fall
Falling like pinkish snowflakes
Littering the ground

Luke McKenna, Grade 4
Mayfield Jr School of the Holy Child Jesus

Fire! Fire! Fire!
The fire is dancing the moon walk
He is very angry

He dances all over the forest
He burns all the trees
He has no mercy
The fire fighters try to extinguish the fire
But he gets even angrier
Raging higher

The people try to flee
But all of a sudden
A flash of lightning strikes
Followed by lots of rain
The fire becomes
Weaker, weaker, weaker
Because of God's mercy
Payaam Elmi, Grade 6
Islamic School of San Diego

Edible World
The trees are broccoli
The mud is brownies
The rocks are marshmallows
The house is a gingerbread house
The people are gingerbread men
but if I eat it all there will be no world.
Karo Torosyan, Grade 5
Andasol Avenue Elementary School

Mom
My mom likes to eat oranges
And is also courageous
She is also lucky
And that makes everything funny
She is joyful
But still playful
Somehow respectful
My mom is brave
And brilliant
She is creative
And active
By playing with me
My mom is funny
Because she is clumsy
She is an animal lover
So I have to love her
And that's me
I can be caring
Just like my mother
And that is why
I love her
Bernard Rodriguez, Grade 6
Century Community Charter School

The Rattler
While watching TV
Near my baby sister's crib,
I heard a rattlesnake hissing
Something was missing.
As I slowly crept forward
Ready to protect,
She had her rattle
Ready for battle.
When she saw me
She gave me a smile,
I was happy to see
It was not a reptile.
Evan Halloran, Grade 5
St Barbara School

Hate Is…
Hate is a deep feeling.
Hate is a bad bug.
Hate is sadness and anger
Hate is broken glass.
Abigail Wise, Grade 5
Jackson Elementary School

Silver
The silver spot turned
It turned into something
From the silver spot
To a silver child

A silver spot turned
It got bigger and bigger
From a silver spot
To a silver city

A silver spot turned
It got bigger and bigger
The silver is now
The silver is now the silver world
Nicole Aguilera, Grade 4
Stone Ranch Elementary School

Basketball
B all
A ll Stars
S hoot
K eep your support
E ffort
T eam
B ounce
A ll players
L ose or win
L ove of the game
Jason Garcia, Grade 4
St Pancratius Elementary School

Mom
Mom, who gives good advice
Who never lies
And keeps promises
Is helpful and caring
When I do something dumb and daring
She is overprotective
And has yellow-brown hair
Is righteous and fair
She is short and huggable
Safer than most
But better than turkey roast
Sweeter than Granny Smith
that was grown from the tree of kindness
But one cannot say
She does not help me
Nay, Nay,
This is the end of what I have to say
Good Day!
Manuel Ceballos, Grade 6
Century Community Charter School

The Wolf
The wolf he howls
and softly growls
but quietly hunts his prey
he's a soft color of grey

He likes to run
while the pups have fun
and he sleeps and sleeps
when the day is done

When he scratches his back
and he's silent until the attack
Slip Slap Slack!
Slip Slap Slack!

If you see a wolf
don't shake with fear
just remember
death is not near
Whitney N. Fay, Grade 4
Sonoma Charter School

Opposites
Coal
Fiery, black
Burning, scorching, roosting
Coal mine, underground, jewelry, stone
Sparkling, shining, glittering
Expensive, pretty
Diamond
Misha Hindery-Nelson, Grade 6
Charles Armstrong School

Candy's So Addicting
I think I'm addicted to candy!
Candy's just so good,
I need to have one more bite
But I'm just so full.

I think I'm addicted to candy!
Don't ask me why?
My mother says I eat too much
But she is really lying
Candy is so heart breaking
I think you should try it sometime.
Candy could be the best thing in your entire life!

Macy White, Grade 4
Oak Grove Elementary School

My Ancient Family
My family oh my ancient family,
I can't just let you go,
I have feelings in my heart,
You can't just pass away,
I watch them as they disappear,
There's nothing I can do,
But they would always sail through my heart,
And bring back memories of the past,
I release the water drops in my eyes,
But I have to let them go,
As I see their bodies disappear,
To a new life in their soul.

Zhibing Liu, Grade 4
Stone Ranch Elementary School

Rain
Tip, tip, tip
The rain gently splatters on the window,
Inside it is dark,
The drumming of the drops drifts towards my ears.
As I look through the blurred window,
Among the tall trees,
I see nothing besides rain striking the icy ground,
Above as the clouds brew a harsh storm, the rain falls.
Near the ocean, between the sky,
The rain comes and goes as a shy fly,
Different from a clear blue sky,
Tip, tip, tip

Ishani Synghal, Grade 6
Seven Hills School

Leon's Pooch
L ovingly takes care of his
E nergetic but small dog who is always getting
O n his nerves. He doesn't know why, but she
N ever stops barking at people.
  "Woof! Woof!"
  "Will you please shut up, Lila?"

Leon Martin, Grade 5
Ecole Bilingue de Berkeley

Waiting
The warm sand submerges our feet
Waiting with the breeze in our faces
Hand in hand
For our friends to come
For our afternoon to begin

I feel something on my cheek —
A kiss
For a long time we sit silently
"When are they coming?"
She had a distant look and whispered, "I don't know"
Feelings of anxiousness and sorrow were overpowering

Every second,
Every time the lifeguard ran by
More anxiety
Finally…
They arrived.

Claire Smith, Grade 5
Clover Avenue Elementary School

Ten Things About Spring
I love spring,
Here are some of my favorite things.
The Easter holiday,
The following month is May.
Outside it's sunny,
To have this much fun it should cost money.
March Madness is in full swing,
If you win your bracket you will be king.
Baseball season is about to start,
Perfect time to do some art.
April showers,
Bring May flowers.
This time of the year I go to Palm Springs,
Oh there are so many things.
I can't get enough of the spring weather,
It's as light as a feather.
A time to relax, a time to kick back,
A time to play on my Mac.

Michael Lira, Grade 5
Mayfield Jr School of the Holy Child Jesus

Friendship
Friends like you there's very few,
You're honest and helping, and always true,
No matter what kinds of fights we've been through,
I will always be there for you.
Just like the light in my heart,
You're always there to help me start,
Even though we may twist and bend,
The friendship we have will never end.

Rhea Sanghani, Grade 6
Heritage Oak Private School

Clear Crystals
Crystals clear as water,
Flowing through the air, gracefully
As girls and boys play and play,
The crystals go everywhere
Like small invisible thieves,
They come and go all around!
Merceden Khazaieli, Grade 4
Sierra Oaks K-8 School

Should I
What should I do?
Should I walk?
Should I talk?
Should I run?
Or should I dress up as a nun?
Should I have a race?
Should I wash my face?
Should I learn to dive?
Or should I burn a beehive?
Should I sleep?
Should I read?
Should I go to the mall?
Or should I play handball?
I think I'll just be me!
Gaby Rasson, Grade 6
Horace Mann School

Beauty
Water reflects sun
Palm trees swaying back and forth
Orange skies above
Avery Castro, Grade 4
Ladd Lane Elementary School

Peace
Peace,
What used to be
Something that everyone
Loved to see.
It was war that started this.
Now
No one can stop this
But the power of
Almighty
God.
Mohamed Buul, Grade 6
Islamic School of San Diego

Guinea Pigs
Guinea pigs
Soft, cuddly
Eating, running, hiding
Small eyes with a big body
Animals
Justin Jones, Grade 4
Daves Avenue Elementary School

If I Was…
IF I was an ice cream sundae
I'd tempt people with my ruby red cherries, and my rainbow sprinkles
I'd be devoured and loved
IF I were a lion
I'd play hide and seek, I'd hide, seek my prey and jump out and eat them
I'd be beautiful, and graceful
IF I was "Thriving Ivory"
I'd sing a smash hit
I'd be famous
IF I was a bubble
I'd float gracefully in the water
I'd be popped
IF I was a Ford F150
I'd be grey with an awesome inside
I'd be fast and furious
IF I was a jellyfish
I'd mind my own business
I'd sting anything in my path
IF I was the Atlantic Ocean
I'd glisten in the sunlight
I'd glow in the dark
Matthew Blake, Grade 5
Aviara Oaks Elementary School

My Life
I am from beautiful colors all around, from music filling the room,
from sweet smelling aromas, from unique furniture, and bright lights,
I am from home — peaceful, tidy, happy, unique, home with smiling faces.

I am from smiling faces, from laughter and talking,
from mouthwatering smells, from reading, from cats meowing and dogs barking.
I am from home, happy and fun.

I am from Stockton, California, from freedom, and beautiful beaches,
from courageous police officers, and strong firefighters.

I am from Mexico and Italy, from farmers to Master Chief of the Navy,
from happiness and pride, and thankfulness.
I am from music, from sports, from optimism and fun, from happiness and clear,
from strong, big and safe, from family.
I want to be very successful.
Isabelle Rodriguez, Grade 6
John Muir Elementary School

Happy Halloween
Frightening costumes roaming the dark, dark streets,
Scary haunted house with a skeleton watching little kids collect candy,
White ghost terrifying the kids that cross its territory,
Startling mummy hanging from a lamppost,
Scary pumpkins startling kids with their intimidating faces,
Groups of kids collecting scrumptious candy to enjoy,
People hiding behind trees waiting to scare little kids.
Tyler Rivera, Grade 5
Highland Oaks Elementary School

Rainbow

I wish I were a beautiful rainbow,
Shining and colorful,
Arching through the misty sky,
Painting over the heavens with all my colors,
Reflecting on the ground until my colors fade away.

Jallyn De la Torre, Grade 5
Lake Forest Elementary School

Gillette Stadium

100 yards long and 53 yards wide.
Green, cool grass.
Fans roaring, "Go team!"
Big and strong players.
QB screaming, "Hike!"
Coaches wailing, "Pick up the ball!"
Vendors announcing, "Get your cotton candy here!"

Nachos melting in your mouth.
Players tasting blood after a big hit.
Beer splattering on the seats.
The smell of buttery popcorn.
Someone cheering, "Touchdown Patriots!"
Gatorade soaking the coach on the sideline.
A big win for New England.

Danny Lavery, Grade 5
Solana Pacific School

A Day at the Beach

Waves crashing
Children playing
Along the sandy shore

Waves are running
To the playing children
As if it was a game of tag
Bringing foamy bubbles,
They hit the shore
And scare the kids away

They crash towering sand castles
And make the children cry
But when they hit again
They tickle the children and wipe away their tears
Instead of tears, smiles now spread across their bright faces

So when it's time to leave the beach
They cry in disappointment
Then the ice cream truck comes
Their sadness fades away
But inside their little hearts
They're waiting for their next
Day at the beach.

Zaineb Boulil, Grade 6
Islamic School of San Diego

Insect City

The morning dew comes and leaves the grass wet
The bees speed by in their snazzy jets
    The towering blades of grass are just like skyscrapers
And the insect colony is enjoying their morning papers
The fantastic ladybugs buzz
And the young green caterpillars just leave around fuzz
The grasshoppers get to places in a hurry
Whereas the butterflies flitter around in a flurry
When it comes time for lunch
The butterflies and bees drink the flowery punch
    The crickets and Grasshoppers could eat grass all day
While the ladybugs eat aphids HOORAY!
As it gets dark the critters scurry home
And the wandering night creatures go out to roam
The moon comes out and the grass shines white
While the crickets chirp their lullabies through the night
Again the morning sun arises
Another day in the insect colony may bring more surprises.

Riley Kim, Grade 6
James B Davidson Middle School

My Special Place

My special place is my front yard.
Whenever I get the chance, I go
And visit my special place.
Quite often, I lay down, I look at
The flapping wings of the birds, and
Soft, fluffy clouds like giant pillows
Begging me to fall asleep on them.
When I look down, I see the green grass
And tiny insects and bugs, crawling about.
When all is quiet, I can hear the wind,
Blowing through the leaves, creating a rustling sound,
And the bird, chirping to one another, calling to each other.
I can smell the soft, fragrant smells of the flowers,
As well as the lemons, waiting for me to pick them.
I can feel the grass, so smooth, and the flowers,
So soft and delicate and sweet.
In my special place, I feel calm, relaxed, and happy.

Selina Chang, Grade 6
Joaquin Miller Middle School

Your Heart

The thing that holds you together
It makes you feel as light as a feather
It is a battery that keeps you running with infinite power
A safe that holds your love
A very delicate thing
Where your feelings get stored
There is a key
That you have to give to the right person
A key that holds all your secrets and all your loved ones
It is your heart
A precious thing to keep

Danielle Lizarraga, Grade 6
St Vincent Elementary School

I'm a Know-It-All

I know yellow,

Yellow smells like the scorching fire roaring in the fireplace, the savory lemon growing from the beautiful plant
and the grotesque smell of the soft gauze wrapped around my cast,

Yellow looks like the delicious popcorn that I eat every Monday night, the bright lights that come from the overhead light
in my room, the slip of paper that I bring home every Tuesday,

Yellow sounds like the noodles steaming in the pot, the crunch of salty potato chips in my mouth,
the sound of the yellow autumn leaves crunching as I step,

Yellow tastes like the ripe bananas waiting in a bowl, my vitamins that I eat every night
and juicy mangos that I hate so much,

Yellow feels like my foot slamming into the painful, yellow hardwood floor, the smooth plastic Easter eggs that I put
in my basket while searching for more and the hot sun against my nearly sunburned face,

I really know yellow.

Stephen Kasmir, Grade 4
Dingeman Elementary School

The Good Fight

Charge! Yelled the captain, both armies ran together in a clash very large,
Both armies fighting slicing and dicing,
The rifles roared, and men fell to the ground, nothing others could do as they found,
The enemy was losing the hero was winning as the enemy's blood ran thin and slightly oozing,
The fight was won with good men dead, but still alive and wounded the captain said
"We're going home, all of us."

Alex Ziemba, Grade 5
St Louis De Montfort School

The Months of the Year

January is the first month of the year. With God, there's nothing to fear.
February is when we show our love, coming from our Father up above.
March is the month that can be very windy. It is also the birthday of my mom, Sindy.
April is the month for storms and showers. These are examples of God's mighty powers.
May is a month when it is fun to play. When you are busy, remember to pray.
June is the month when school is done. Jump in the pool and have some fun.
July is the month for celebration, for the freedom of our nation.
August is hot, there is no doubt. It's a month to play and shout.
September is the time when we crack the books. We do our homework while Mama cooks.
October is when we change the clocks. Around the house, we'll take a walk.
November is when thanks we say, to almighty God whom we pray.
December has trees, stars and lights. In baby Jesus the people delight.

David Richards, Grade 6
Heritage Christian School

The Mirror

In the mirror I see myself confident, strong, and brave.
Outside the mirror I am shy.
I am confident, strong, and brave because I see myself playing, and dancing, and having fun.
I am shy outside the mirror because I have no friends and I am always stuck in my room studying.
But, the mirror is my only friend so I guess that is why I am confident when I am in the mirror.

Daniela Romero, Grade 4
Garden Grove Elementary School

I Am

I am 12 and a boy
I wonder if I would go to space.
I want to be happy all the time.
I see my family every night and day.
I am 12 and a boy.
I pretend like a soccer player.
I feel people's feelings.
I touch what I see.
I worry when something is wrong
I am 12 and a boy.
I understand when it's no.
I believe we can be better.
I dream of being a pro soccer player goalie.
I try to not get in trouble.
I hope you like the poem because
I am 12 and a boy named Hector Enriquez.

Hector Enriquez, Grade 5
Sundale Elementary School

What If

What if the world was a better place?

What would it be like?
What if there was no violence, guns, or weapons.

What if we never died?
What if there were no schools or homes?
How would we know?
"What if" is the question we all ask.

Jake Casaus, Grade 5
Theodore Roosevelt Elementary School

Spring

What is spring?

The season of growth
the season of birth
the stop to cold
the beginning of fun
a break from school
the time of beauty
the migration of butterflies
when basketball ends and baseball begins
the celebrating of Easter
That is Spring!

DJ Moore, Grade 6
Aliso Elementary School

Sunshine

I wish I was a radiant sunshine,
Glowing and glistening,
Rising from the east and setting to the west,
Covering the planet in a warm and welcoming blanket,
Fading away at sunset until I'm gone...

Adison McGill, Grade 5
Lake Forest Elementary School

Nature Zoo

Nature is so pretty and colorful too
That's why I call it my nature zoo
All nature is unique
There are so many kinds
Let's see what flowers come to mind
Pink flowers
Purple flowers
Yellow flowers too
Here are some more in our nature zoo
Red leaves
Green trees
There's much more
Let's see what else I've got in store
Rose buds
Lavender
Bamboo trees
Oh, we've even got some bees
Nature is magical
Who knew that there are so many types in our nature zoo!

Perry Hotchkis, Grade 5
Mayfield Jr School of the Holy Child Jesus

The Beach

I lie on the sand of the beach
I look at the moon its white as bleach
The breeze is cool and it blows through my hair
The seagulls fly through the air
The ocean is at my feet
And there in the air a fleet of seagulls
The dolphins jump in the sun's light
The sun is so bright
I go swim with the dolphins

Kyle Galvez, Grade 4
Coeur d'Alene Avenue Elementary School

I Am

I am lovable
I wonder what I will look like when I grow up
I hear the sound of a shark coming
I see a vision
I want to be a better climber
I am lovable
I pretend I am a werewolf
I touch a hand
I worry when my parents yell at me
I cry when I lose my friend
I am lovable
I understand why people love each other
I dream to be a werewolf
I try not to higher my temper
I hope to have a great future
I am lovable

Travis Graham, Grade 4
La Presa Elementary School

Love
Mom goose baby geese
Follow mom goose in green grass
Love is everywhere
Lorena Ornelas, Grade 5
Ladd Lane Elementary School

Amanda
My books are for reading
My heart is beating
I have nowhere to go
I also have a foe
My mother is here
My father is near
So many rhymes and riddles
I sang the fiddle diddle
Amanda Rita Al-Habre, Grade 5
Andasol Avenue Elementary School

Mountains
Mountains are beautiful
Mountains are high
Mountains can be big
Mountains can be small
Some mountains are brown
Some mountains are round
Mountains are cool
Just like you.
Haley Sheets, Grade 4
Upper Lake Elementary School

Flight
Sailing through the sky
A rush of wind
Through my thick soft feathers
Over my white hollow bones
The heat of the drafts
Pushing my bright blue body
Over the clouds
Gliding onto a branch
What a flight!
Kevin Potts, Grade 4
Daves Avenue Elementary School

Love Is…
Love is…
patient like your mother and father
kind like your brother and sister
like two friends stick together
through tough times
created by two but
enjoyed by many
stays in your heart forever
Ravi Sandhu, Grade 5
Santa Fe Springs Christian School

Space
Space
It's in outer space
Making no sound at all,

Blending into its surroundings
Floating listlessly into the void.
Mason Chiao, Grade 6
John Muir Elementary School

Umbrellas
Umbrellas are big,
Umbrellas are small,
Umbrellas are colorful,
They're like big flowers,
They pop up in the rain,
But, not in the snow.
Elliot Moser, Grade 4
Ladd Lane Elementary School

Who Am I?
I swing from branch to branch
I don't eat very much
I have big ears
Kevin Flahavan, Grade 6
Charles Armstrong School

The Eagle
This bird,
Predatory,
Soars high in the deep sky,
Sharp talons reaching toward its prey.
It kills!
Andrew Kim, Grade 4
J L Academy

The Winds of Poems
The winds of poems
flutter all over.
The winds of poems
go into the morning mist
and then go into
people's pools of joy.
The winds of poems
go and come
here and there.
The winds of poems
float like winds
of songs.
The winds of poems
dazzle the superb earth
and then get absorbed
into the universe.
Brandon Broukhim, Grade 4
The Mirman School

My Perfect Mummy
Here when I am sick
She cheers me up
I can trust her with secrets
Is kind to others
Sharing
Is sweet as cherry pie
Is caring
Is loving
Can get upset
Talks a lot
Can be playful
Hugs my bear
Is hopeful
Loves sports
Loves red
Is friendly to others
Mummy can be joyful
Can be afraid
I am glad to have a mummy like her
Maria Villapando, Grade 6
Century Community Charter School

Black
BLACK, burnt trees,
Like anger and pain,
Alone in an open field.

BLACK, night sky,
Like an optimistic, hopeful future,
That goes on forever.

BLACK, volcanic ashes
Like a disturbing past,
That won't leave your head.
Sean McGovern, Grade 6
James B Davidson Middle School

Sweets
There are many kinds of sweets,
There are kisses and hugs,
There are M&Ms and Skittles,
There is licorice and gummy worms.

There are Hershey Bars and Milky Ways,
There are Starbursts and Nerds,
There is cake and cookies,
There are donuts and Dots.

There are Snickers and lollipops,
There are Crunches and Kit Kats,
There are many many more but,
I really wish to eat some candy!
Rachel Croft, Grade 4
St Pancratius Elementary School

High Merit Poems – Grades 4, 5 and 6

Happy Feelings
Video games make me happy
When my mom lets me skate at the skate park I am very excited
Jokes that my cousins make up are funny
Computer makes me very happy
Friends are everything
They help me with everything like problems and school work
Kristian Alarcon, Grade 5
Kentwood Elementary School

Gorillas
Running through the jungle
Babies born in the LA zoo
Also living in Australia
Pounds powerfully on the ground with long arms
Scary Silverbacks frighten people
Gorillas beat their chest when angry
Fascinated people observe them.
Manuel Villarreal, Grade 6
St Alphonsus School

Timothy Scott
Timothy
Active, kind, friendly
Sibling of Blair and Chelise
Lover of soccer and football
Who feels everyone should be treated equally
Who needs kind family and friends
Who gives respect to each and everyone
Who fears getting in a car accident
Who would like to see Kobe Bryant in person
Scott
Timothy Scott III, Grade 5
Kentwood Elementary School

Maxy
Seeing Maxy come to me when I'm home
Maxy would sing to the sweet girls he likes
He takes a shower and gets me the comb
But sometimes he would try to get the mic.

Out back is his favorite place at home
When hungry he could chew his bed apart
He likes the backyard 'cause there is no mouse
But he would bark at a slow moving cart

When he likes to jump he does so quite high
I could touch his warm fur when I pet him
When I look at him he has two brown eyes
In the morning, he can't find the dog gym

Maxy would always be wild at the park
And that is when he would begin to bark
Abigail Nicely, Grade 5
El Monte Elementary School

The Sunset
How you can find a quiet sunset,
But the moon must rise, it is for the best.
You can find the orange skies,
All of a sudden saying, "Good-bye."
Over the mountains it goes,
When will it set? I do not know.
The bright sky is slowly fading away,
For the gloomy night is coming its way.
I shall not worry of the dying sight,
Because the stars will come this very night.
The orange swirl slowly dies,
But it will all come back, at the sunrise.
Anthony Nguyen, Grade 6
John Muir Elementary School

The Mountain
a mountain is a part of nature that lies
beneath the morning clouds,
it looks like a peach blossom flowing in a stream.
Marco Flores, Grade 6
Blessed Sacrament School

Dream of a Shadow
I am shadow,
Sulking in the darkness unnoticed,
A speck in the millions of things around me,
I am nothing,
But maybe with one small hope,
And one small wish,
Please someone notice me.
Olivia Henry, Grade 6
Grant Elementary School

The Puppy Did It*
A dog barked, "You won't have time."
A puppy sighed, "I haven't tried."
"You aren't going to have time."
The puppy barked as he took his first try,
A moment later, the time was up,
But he had accomplished his homework.
The work that couldn't be done was done.

Some dog snapped, "You can't do that."
The puppy exclaimed, "I haven't tried."
"It's a waste of time, you won't do that."
With a wag of his tail he set off to work,
A minute later the puppy pranced proudly around.
What couldn't be done was done.

There are tons of things to be done,
Most of them will not be done.
With just a wag of your tail you can do the thing.
What cannot be done, will be done.
Nicolas Williams, Grade 5
Solana Pacific School
*Inspired by Edgar A. Guest

Flip Flops
Funny noises that you make
Love my feet will always stay
Interesting colors, neon through gray
Perfect fit can't get away

Follows me everywhere
Loves to walk
On the beach
Please stay on purple flip flops
Faith Hayden, Grade 5
Joseph M Simas Elementary School

Sports
I like to play ball
Baseball, basketball, football
My favorite games
Dillon Kohler, Grade 6
St Anne School

Untitled
At midnight
you could hear
little fish whispering,
while foolish wolves
try to catch them.
You could hear
the wolves splash
as they try to catch a fish,
just like when you skip a stone
in the water.
Isai Bustos, Grade 5
Henry Haight Elementary School

Love Is…
Love is…
gentle as a baby's hand
growing stronger like a child
sticks with you like super glue
peaceful as a floating feather
not jealous of anything
never gets an F (fails)
Chloe Winter, Grade 5
Santa Fe Springs Christian School

Out in Nature
Scouting through the woods,
Wondering where you are,
Looking around, and seeing nothing,
But nature's wonderful goods,
The sun is setting now,
You're hungry and so you weep,
You cry, and cry,
Very sadly, and lonely,
Until you cry yourself to sleep.
Amanda Guarino, Grade 5
St Pancratius Elementary School

If I Were in Charge…
If I were in charge of my home
I would live in a mansion that had a room where you can have ANY pet
I would play video games, watch movies, and fly my personal jet

If I were in charge of my school
I would have no tests or homework
School would be on Wednesday and Thursday from 10:00-11:00

If I were in charge of the world
I would make summer two weeks longer
I would make a shelter for the sick and poor
I would keep everyone happy
Charlie Badger, Grade 5
Duveneck Elementary School

Merry Christmas
Exultant, patient families waiting for Santa Claus,
Opaque, comatose snowman being made in the dawn of the morning,
Chilly, mysterious nighttime examining people giving presents in houses,
Emerald evergreen tree waiting in the midnight breeze,
Dusty, old ornaments being cleaned for the holiday,
Appetizing food being prepared for a wonderful, enticing, family feast,
Snowy, deafening carolers on the hard, pavement street singing in melodious voices,
Merry, innocent children throwing inflexible, blistering snowballs,
Old, gloomy fireplace waiting for a benevolent person to light it,
Green, skinny elves packing surprising presents for the long, exhilarating night,
Crimson, rusty chimney feeling the brand new year approaching.
Royal Gong, Grade 5
Highland Oaks Elementary School

My Messy Room
Stepping through the haunted door, I wonder what it holds in store.
Grimy pasty paint peeling slowly off the morbid walls,
I try not to glance in the direction of where it falls.
Insects creep all over the dirty room,
Turning into the likeness of a pharaoh's tomb.
Paperback books strewn in every direction,
To them I feel so immediate connection.
A carpet is encrusted with filthy socks,
As hard as I try I cannot find my toy box.
A tsunami of blanket is falling off the bed.
In their midst I spy a crust of decaying bread.
In the corner are a pile of belts tied in knots,
Even they are bursting of repulsive olive spots.
My fractured mirror is layered with dirt,
Around it I must always stay alert.
Small white flakes fall from the ceiling,
But unlike snowflakes, they give me a dreadful feeling.
When my sister comes in she goes to her bed,
Wishing, hoping she won't bump her head.
Like a dumpster my room is in disarray.
I hope like this it will always stay.
Marianna Del Matto, Grade 6
Dorris-Eaton School

High Merit Poems – Grades 4, 5 and 6

Two-Hour Night Watch

The cold never stopped.
It was an evil cold, a nippy cold,
a torturous prick at the eyes or toes.
Four layers were only a summer sheet
helpless in this cold.
They say, "Forty degrees."
They say, "Wear layers."
They say, "I told you so," at the end.
But none of that, not a single word of that
could prepare me for the cold
that tugged on the halyards,
pulled on the main block,
and yanked *me* leeward
like I'd been shoved from behind.
No, nothing helped me
on my two-hour night watch
when the cold, that frosty cold, kept on.

Nicholas Steele, Grade 5
Carlthorp School

Bittersweet

Oh S'more, so sweet yet so vulnerable
Robust flames devour your every crumb,
While my staunch logs make me indestructible
But for you, you soon will succumb

You now lay wrapped in the comfort
Of feeble chocolate and graham,
But you are not safe, as after the fire
Comes the devouring man.

Jadon Yariv, Grade 5
The Mirman School

The Church Walls

The night is wet, and cold, and dreary
it snows, and the wind is never weary;
the leaves still cling to the crumbling wall;
but at every gust the dead leaves fall,
and the night is dark and dreary.

Troy Mestetsky, Grade 4
Montessori Family School

Cats

Cats are fluffy
Cats are nice
Bonus point: they eat mice.

Cats are cuddly
Cats are cool
It really stinks ya can't take 'em to school!

Cats are clean
Cats are neat
They are really hard to beat!

Maggie Luque, Grade 4
Sonoma Charter School

Oceans

The salty air tickles my nose
While the grainy sand is underneath my toes

As I crash through the waves my heart beats so fast
I come up for air, the ocean so vast

A couple of times the waves got me
Thank goodness I got free

The ocean is diverse so broad and wide
It makes me feel all good inside

It's home to many creatures both big and small
But the jetty is my favorite of all

At the end of the day, as the sun says goodbye
It leaves a beautiful glow that encumbers the sky

Noel Kildiszew, Grade 6
La Costa Heights Elementary School

Shoes

Shoes are great
I have a shoe colored plate
There are many types of colors
let me tell you others
purple, blue, black
there are some in the store called Mack
tie them up
zip them up
gold, bold colors
special made rubbers
slip and slide
on either side
I like shoes, I like them lots
there's also polka dots
they are really cool
you know there are also some for the pool

Carolina Oviedo, Grade 6
St Charles Catholic School

I Am

I am a tiger cub, playful and young,
but sometimes I am a tiger dad, fierce and strong.
I am a turtle, slow as molasses,
but sometimes I am a cheetah, quick and silent.
I am a cat, sly and quiet,
but sometimes I am a howler monkey, loud and annoying.
I am a baseball player, athletic and quick thinking,
but sometimes I am a manatee, huge and slow thinking.
I am a surfer, balanced and in control,
but sometimes I am a bull rider, wild and out of control.
I Am Kenny

Kenny Abbott, Grade 5
Wagon Wheel Elementary School

Lunar Dance

The moon dances in the sky
leaving starry
imprints.
Her mysterious step
has garnered the name
aurora
in the north.
Her work
surrenders
glistening
droplets
of
liquid
crystal.
As the dawn breaks,
her dance
is at
an end.

Diego Sanchez, Grade 5
Bethany Lutheran School

Little Joey

I used to be a little joey
until a fox ate me
I used to have a family
until a fox ate me
I used to be small and soft
until a fox ate me
I was loved and I loved them
until a fox ate me
I was little and cute
until a fox ate me
I loved my life so much
until a fox ate me
Now I'm in a fox's belly

Kejhana Maydelle Taylor, Grade 4
Upper Lake Elementary School

Dysrockxia

I have a cool band called Dysrockxia
We're cool because we all have dyslexia

We play all sorts of songs
All afternoon long

I play the guitar and vocals
We like play for all the locals

Spencer Sutter, Grade 6
Charles Armstrong School

Deadly Forest

The deadly forest
Where trees are old and leaves fall
With snow over the top

Mikaela Williams, Grade 6
St Anne School

The Abuse

When I walk down the street
All I see are complete strangers
Sometimes I may see horrific or sweet
But I never knew it was going to end in danger

These complete strangers may be criminals
Or they can be innocent
But you can never assume until something hits you like an animal
Five years old when this terrifying event occurred

A man looks at me in a suspicious way
I close my eyes and pretend he's not there
I turn around and we're face-to-face
I scream for my mother

There's no use she's gone
The man grabs, pushes, hits, and pulls me
I shout, "Let Go!" but the man wasn't done
A woman saw the actions and decided to help

At the end of this nightmare the woman was my hero
My mother noticed I'm gone and starts to run toward me
She thanks the woman with all her heart and takes me home
I'll always remember that horrible man that abused me.

Leslie Chinchilla, Grade 6
Cimarron Education Center

Ode to Creation

To imagine seeing stars in the night sky,
to see an ocean of wonders in front of your eyes.
Can you imagine a world shaped by our dreams?
We can all succeed just as it seems.

A will for power is consumed by our desire,
because we live in a world of war.
Lost by the era of love and peace,
for our friendship and compassion will increase.

For we live in a world carved by imagination,
our love for life which spreads across the nation.
Hate and war infects our mother Earth,
which is shown by our journey beginning at birth.

We lived in a place that changed since forever,
but nothing disappeared, for we stand together.
From the past, we learned.
Our life, we earned.

Now we have discovered a purpose to live.
We have learned to not take, but give.
God gave us life, so let's live it long,
for we have 2 paths ahead, so take the one that's right, not wrong.

Matthew Quintanilla, Grade 6
St Dominic Elementary School

Trust and Friendship

Trust is the engine of friendship.
She wears travel clothes and running shoes, ready to follow you with a backpack of helping hands.
Trust is always there, ready to catch you if you fall.
She floats down a stone path, never resting.
Trust travels with Friendship; they never separate.
Friendship wears a flowing pink and blue gown, gracefully gliding alongside Trust.
She makes sure you are never lonely; you always have somebody to lean on.
Friendship, forgiving and comforting, walks next to Trust in a meadow of daisies and wildflowers,
taking each step as if she is walking on tightrope.
They are tied together with unbreakable rope, illuminating the path to a brighter future.

Zoe Brown, Grade 5
Wagon Wheel Elementary School

If I Were A...

If I were a hamster
I'd burrow deep, deep down in my soft, tender shavings
I'd munch and chew on salty sunflower seeds all day till there was no more left
I'd nuzzle in my luscious green plastic igloo and sprint on my noisy wheel, all day long

If I were a tiger
I'd be the king of the colorful damp jungle
I'd stalk my prey with my sharp, jet-black eyes and I'd show my pearly-white, five-inch canines

If I were a horse
I'd be an American Saddlebred with a hot rude attitude
I'd be the center of attention in the show ring and I'd be the high stepping action with the first place, blue ribbon in position

If I were a dragon
I'd guard a cave full of the finest glistening gold and treasure in all the world
I'd breathe my red hot flaming fire on anyone who trespassed in my cave and I'd flap my wings with enormous power

If I were a viper
I'd slither and slide my way around the ground, looking for a juicy victim
I'd hiss and show my venomous, sharp chompers
I'd hide in my quiet, cool hollow which would be deep under the dark ground and
I'd speedy-quick catch my prey wandering around the hot surface

Madison R. Nelson, Grade 5
Aviara Oaks Elementary School

I Dreamt

I dreamt of baskets filled with hope for all
I dreamt of meadows with joy and happiness
I dreamt of flowers blooming with golden glory
I dreamt of scarlet trees with buckets of laughter
I dreamt of my worries and problems fading away by the minute
I dreamt of children playing and laughing and having so much fun
I dreamt of birds singing about the crimson ponds of hearts
I dreamt of sitting on the beach watching the beautiful sunset
I dreamt of you and me resting watching the shimmering moon glistening on a ruby night
I dreamt of citrus roses and plum sunflowers encircling me
I dreamt of living in a violet castle on a jagged mountain
I dreamt of soaring up to the navy blue clouds
I dreamt of watching glimmering shining stars dancing around me

Malaika Nall, Grade 4
The Mirman School

My Mom

My mom makes astonishing food
She wishes to give to the poor
But she can only afford for us all
She is my hero
However, my mom is too over protective
I never get to see her,
But only on the weekends
She works all night
Which can take her energy
I know she is a hard worker
To other people she is helpful
And very generous
My mom hates animals,
But is still loving
Always busy
Never impatient to kids
My mom is gentle
And very kind
And forever
She will be sweet as a strawberry

Jocelyn Contreras, Grade 6
Century Community Charter School

If It Weren't for Immigrants

If it weren't for immigrants
I wouldn't be here
For America's a place for
People far and near

I love America so
It's just the right place for me
But if immigrants hadn't come
Beauty wouldn't be here to see

Just today I saw a man
Sitting on the street
Looking for a job to find
And buy something to eat

Just think of all the culture here
Shamefully going to waste
Think of how much history can be made
And on who it can be based

Faith Randall, Grade 5
El Monte Elementary School

Blizzard

I wish I were a severe blizzard,
Bitter and brisk,
Covering the houses with a coat of white,
Providing snow for the kids to play with,
Melting away when the sun comes up.

Adela Barriga, Grade 5
Lake Forest Elementary School

Orange

Orange, the early morning
sunrise shining at me and
my friends like the bright sun

Orange, fresh rays of warmth
and joy flowing my way
just as a cold, river
stream flows downstream

Orange, the light that
makes one feel loved
and happy like a newborn
puppy warm and excited

Orange, bright and shining
like neon orange shoe laces
tied on my feet

Orange

Taylor Ping, Grade 6
James B Davidson Middle School

Summer Fun

S uper
U ltimate
M agical
M erry
E ntertaining
R elief

Amber Anderson, Grade 5
Coastline Christian Academy

Crashing Ashore

Waves crashing ashore
Children building sandcastles
Dolphins singing beautifully nearby
Surfers shredding curling waves
It's time to leave, how dull
But wait, the waves will crash ashore.

Samir Sandhu, Grade 5
Merryhill Country School

Food and Clothes with Toothpaste

My shirt is green as green pepper.
My pockets are as blue as blue gum.
My knacks are as black as black beans.
My socks are vanilla ice-cream.
I have gray and white toothpaste shoes
With bumpy noodles laces.
I wish to eat everything.
But then I will have no clothes
Or nothing to brush my teeth with.

Carlos Salazar, Grade 5
Kentwood Elementary School

My Dad

My dad was great
My dad was strong
My dad was fun
My dad was big
My dad was funny
I want him back
I really do
I hope he hears this
I want him to
I really do
He will be happy
He was fun
He throws me in my pool
He is fun in the pool
I really miss him
I want him back
I am glad he is
Somewhere special
I really am

Max Dearth, Grade 5
Theodore Roosevelt Elementary School

Mommy

Oh mommy you are my lucky star
Isabel you have taken me far
How crazy can you be
Filling my heart with glee
You are very wise
With you high I will rise
You are so independent
Yet so attentive
You're bold
And you shine like gold
I love you
You are awesome
For you don't leave me lonesome
You are my sport
Even though you are short
Always in a mood
That's why you are my mom
I Love You Mommy

Alondra Becerra, Grade 6
Century Community Charter School

Lady Bugs

Lady bugs!
Lady bugs fly so high,
They fly so high, to reach the sky.
It's not fair for lady bugs to share
So they shouldn't care what they share
Lady bugs lady bugs fly around
They fly around to go downtown.

Tiara Brown-Sloan, Grade 4
PLACE @ Prescott

My Grandfather

I never got to meet my grandfather
I was told he was wonderful
I was told he would of taught me many things
He would have taught me about sports
He would have taught me many more things too

I never got to meet my grandfather
I wish I would be able to
But before I was born he passed
And then I was born
And I have only heard stories about him

Jonathan Partamian, Grade 4
Mayfield Jr School of the Holy Child Jesus

Messy Room

Sticky spiders creeping and crawling all over the wall,
The overwhelming smell makes you want to fall.

A snake of clothes slithering all over the dirty floor,
Many of armies of ants roaming all over some door.

The closet dragon roaring with it's mouthful of clothes,
When entering the room the fierce bed lion knows.

Cupboards shooting at you with dirty, disgusting socks,
While looking you see an old, ripped cracker box.

Old pizza is hanging from the huge, sticky ceiling,
This gives the room a very uncomfortable feeling.

Looking on the dark floor you see a ripped book,
As well as a newspaper hanging from a sharp hook.

Underwear monsters lurking here and there,
Their presence makes one beware.

Burnt, old bread from an unusual store,
This makes you run away in horror.

Adeel Pervez, Grade 6
Dorris-Eaton School

Clean Up

Why do people treat janitors horrible?
Do they pick up food on the floor because they're mad?
Would you like to clean up trash?
Would you want to be bad at a job and crash?
Don't you think they deserve some respect?
You wouldn't want to clean up people's speck?
What if they had technology to know who throws the trash?
Maybe you will stop the float?
Don't you feel bad?
Do they grab your attention in trash?

Jordan Petito, Grade 6
Horace Mann Middle School

Winter Angel

Flying in the east
The red bird and the white snow
Blessed cardinal

Christopher Dinkel, Grade 4
Mayfield Jr School of the Holy Child Jesus

Friendship Was Falling

I am hanging onto the edge of the cliff
Waiting for a hand to come and catch me
But as I lose my grip more and more
I see the world is empty

There is nobody around me
No birds flying in the air
No fish swimming in the lakes
And that's when I feel despair

I am starting to lose hope
And cannot hold on much longer
But just then I see a face lean over
It says take my hand and do not be afraid
For I am the one who has caused this to fade

I grab the friendly person's hand
And realize that I had someone to believe in
From that day we have been friends
And have never even reached that cliff again

Brianna Rutherford, Grade 6
Santa Rosa Technology Magnet School

My Mommy

My mom is a funny fellow
And one of her favorite colors is yellow
She's happy every day her birthday is in May
She talks a lot
And likes to shop
My mom is loud
She's very proud
When I get good grades
My mom chants Hooray
Almost every day

My mom is very helpful
She really isn't doubtful
She helps me with my homework
When I do not understand
My mom is overprotective
When I act suspicious
She acts like a detective

My mom is lovable
She is also very huggable
Therefore she is special to me
My mom is a funny fellow

Eva Lopez, Grade 6
Century Community Charter School

Sports
Football
Sweaty, hard
Running, tackling, passing
Touchdown, Super Bowl, fun, friends
Kicking, passing, defending
Goalie, head butt
Soccer

Jerry Charette, Grade 5
St Louis De Montfort School

Warm Spring Day
Leaves falling through air
Thrown wildly by the warm breeze
Gracefully float down

Charlotte Trefethen, Grade 6
St Anne School

A Peach Tree in Spring Day
Flowers blooming,
On a peach tree,
Spring day has come,
New life has begun
Teaching me
One peach is gone,
All is gone,
Then, comes a new generation,
It's born again.
Once you fail
Try again, and it
will be possible!

Taherah Abbas, Grade 5
New Horizon School

Ode to My Eraser
O, thou great eraser,
You who were in that store
So rubbery and pink
Your shape being so exquisite
I just had to buy you —
If I didn't my heart would sink.
O, how thee hast fixed my errors,
Hither on my page. Without you
My paper would be a terrible mess.
If thee shall sit there upon my page
I shall admire thee
Until all is well made.
Whoever uses thee shall succeed.
And how hast thee made my errors
Vanish?
How hence do I deserve to be treated
With such kindness?
Thou art my hero
For thee make my mistakes
Disappear into the darkness.

Natasha Sachs, Grade 5
La Jolla Country Day School

I Wish
I wish I were Selena Gomez in India next to the blue Indian Ocean.
I wish I were Vanessa Hudgens under a brown tree at Elder Creek School.
I wish I could meet Miley Cyrus in my orange room in San Francisco.
I wish I could meet David Henry in Canada in the black theater.
And I wish I could meet Mrs. DeSplinter in my cousin's blue pool.

Cindy Campos, Grade 4
Elder Creek Elementary School

Flat
Flat is not a skyscraper
Flat is a bug on the windshield
Flat is when your tire pops
Flat is the head of a nail after hammering it into wood
Flat sounds like a pancake frying on the griddle
Flat sounds like the machine reading a person is dead in the hospital
Another word for Flat is smooth
One thing about Flat is I don't like listening to it sing

Dayne Johnson, Grade 6
Big Springs Elementary School

If I Were…
If I were an electric guitar
I'd be a shiny white Fender Telecaster
I'd be helping Joe Strummer play a face melting guitar solo
and I'd be getting to be the world famous Clash every day of my life
If I were an amplifier
I'd be a 78" specially made glassy looking black Marshall
I'd be amplifying Peter Townshed's heart stopping rock
and I'd be breaking the world record with Jimmy Hendricks
for the loudest guitar solo ever
If I were a band
I'd be the world famous band The Who
I'd be in England for the first stop of our world tour
and I'd be writing a future No. 1 hit on UK's rock charts
If I were a song
I'd be *Sweet Child of Mine*
I'd be blowing out people's ears while Slash hit all of the high notes in his guitar solo
and I'd be at the top of the world rock charts
If I were rock n roll
I'd be helping construct the next generation of bands
I'd be sending requests to the Rock n Roll Hall of Fame every minute
and I'd be helping keep rock alive for all the generations to come

Andrew Clexton, Grade 5
Aviara Oaks Elementary School

Mother Earth
I am a gray whale.
I flutter on a pair of sleek water wings.
My speedy body swims through the water in search of food.
I hungrily search as the fish are disappearing into the claws of fishermen.
One of the fisherman's claws threw a thin fish out.
Please save Mother Earth.

Connie Chen, Grade 4
Ocean Air School

Basketballs

Basketballs are cool and brown,
you can bounce them up and down.
You can shoot them in the hoop,
you can also do an alley oop.
You can play the game horse,
although it could be very coarse.
You can bounce it down the hall,
and that's what you can do with a basketball.

Carley Forester, Grade 5
George Washington Charter Elementary School

Planet Iraq

Bombs around,
Fighting to get out,
"Help us" people are screaming
Bullets at a hundred miles an hour
Running, begging to stop
People are wondering, Americans,
Why are they here?
Now they get it,
Spare us our lives,
Iraq needs it.
People on streets, like a crowd not applauding,
But wondering,
People running and scream in terror,
AMERICA, they wanted us,
They've got us!

R.J. O'Malley, Grade 4
Stone Ranch Elementary School

I Am From

I am from a home,
Where three girls take over while
One boy fights to the top.

I am from a yard,
Where a tree holds a tree house
Nice and strong.

I am from a neighborhood,
Where my friend lives down the
Street and someone is always on a bike.

I am from a family,
Where Aunt CK and little cousin Ryan come over often.

I am from a mother,
Who speaks Spanish at dinner
When she is happy.

I am from a hill,
Where I like to relax and get
Away from the excitement
Of where I AM FROM.

Emma Johnson, Grade 5
Notre Dame School

Taking a Test

I'm taking a test,
But I didn't study.
I looked at the clock,
Oh no, 10 minutes to go.
Well, I guess I can ask my buddy for the best answer.

Tick, tick, tick

My heart is beating fast,
It's all I can hear.
Oh no, my teacher is near to take the rest of the test.
He picked up my test.

I blinked and opened my eyes tick, tick, tick

Oh, wow it was just a dream,
Or was it really reality.

Lorraine Felix, Grade 5
St Pancratius Elementary School

I Am From

I am from a home where a fish swims
back and forth and pictures hang on the wall.

I am from a yard that has a swing set laying on the lawn
peaches scattered in the back yard and cactus grows.

I am from a neighborhood where kids play on the street
and a big tree is blooming flowers.

I am from a home where my relatives like Aunt Lucy,
Uncle Omar, Grandpa Arnulfo, my cousins Bree, Melissa,
Caty and Wendy all talk to each other.

I am from a home where my dad says
"Big Kahuna Will Take Care of Every Thing!"

I am from a home where my mom makes tamales when
My grandma comes over and special food for special occasion.

I am from a home that memories are kept in a family album.

Yvonne Arevalo, Grade 5
Notre Dame School

Light Blue Sea

Her eyes were blue sea sculptors
Diving into the water
As quiet as can be
A breath could be taken
The moonlight was shining
Beautiful as can be
Dark waves splashing down, down she goes

Claire Pelote, Grade 4
Sierra Oaks K-8 School

I Am From

I am from a home,

Where an aquarium sits with fish swimming in it. Where Aztec sculptures bring tradition to our family. Where baby photos of my brother and I hang on the walls. And where an grandfather clock chimes every day.

I am from a backyard,

Where two porches lay built by my dad. Where an old swing set sits there with the wind blowing its way. Where a pear tree gives fruit every spring. And where peacocks fly and turtles crawl in their cages.

I am from a neighborhood,

Where palm trees blow in the wind. Where a bunch of kids play together sports. Where birds fly around us. Where basketball hoops lay their while kids make shots. And where Mexican people fill the neighborhood.

I am from a family,

Where my brother's name is Angel but I call him "LiL Devil." Where my mom, Pilar and my dad, Juan Jose are married. Where my uncle, Jorge, is graduating. Where my cousins, Edward, Hugo, and Jose live one house away from me. And where my grandma Socorro and my grandpa Secundino take me to the ranch.

Juan Jose Valencia, Grade 5
Notre Dame School

Inauguration 2009

Cheerful, people screaming loudly in the cold
Shouting "Obama, Obama, Obama, Obama!"
All the people in the Obama Administration walking out on stage,
but people still chant "Obama, Obama!"
Soon enough people on the loudspeaker announce, "Barack Obama."
It's like the entire crowd pauses, there is no more chanting;
It is like a person sleeping soundlessly on a bed at night.
All of a sudden, people scream and yell wildly as Barack Obama walks onto the platform.
Then there is the oath; he gives the people of America an uplifting speech.
While that goes on people are silent, tears of joy streaming down their faces.
When he finishes, people know that change has come to America,
Now everyone is excited, to have a new beginning and clean up our big mess.

Rachel van Gelder, Grade 5
Duveneck Elementary School

The Beach

When we go to the beach we carry our surfboards out of the car and walk down to the beach.
My mom is pulling my sister in the wagon with all our food.
We pull our bags and towels on our boogy-boards and surfboards down to the beach.
We help our dad pick the spot.
We lay out our towels and our beach umbrella.
Then my mom lathers us up with suntan lotion or sunscreen and then we run out on the grainy sand to the ocean to surf.
I can smell the salty sea.
It smells like a sweet sea rose.
We run into the waves.
Whoo! The water is icy cold.
Oh well, I will get used to it.
Then we are riding the waves, and before we know it the sun is about to set and cast its sunny glow.
It is time to go home.

Rachel Blackburn, Grade 5
St Louis De Montfort School

Snow in San Francisco

I wish it would snow in San Francisco —
Little kids making snow angels,
Boys and girls having snowball fights.
And to look out your window,
To enter a world of white, fluffy snow —
What a joy it would be
To run outside and make snowmen,
To laugh and run around with your friends!
Snow gives a chance to spend time together,
To really get to know each other.
There would be laughter and joy all around.
That feeling of pure happiness —
It's all I really want.
And that is the true reason
I wish it would snow in San Francisco.

Samantha Geronimo, Grade 6
Corpus Christi School

My Fear

Every day my parents
Make my breakfast,
My lunch,
My dinner,
Help me with my homework,
Give me things,
I want and need.
But if one day,
I wake up
And my parents just disappear,
What would I do?
How would life be without them?
I cannot imagine living
Without my parents.
They are my supporters…I depend on them.
I love them, I thank them
For what my parents have done for me.
Nothing could ever replace my parents.
My only fear in this world
Is to lose the ones I love.

Justin Kabiling, Grade 6
Corpus Christi School

Me

Chris
Smart, crazy, naive
Son of Steven Harvey
Lover of video games
Who feels I need more sleep in the morning
Who wants more sleep
Who gives nothing
Who would like to see Europe
Harvey

Christian Harvey, Grade 5
Kentwood Elementary School

O'Neill Park

O'Neill Park has beautiful sights,
And you can travel to its heights.

Wild life is easy to find,
This place creates good thoughts in your mind.

Snakes slither, hawks soar,
This place is right outside your door.

The bright yellow mustard plant tastes spicy and hot,
From missionaries it was brought.

Be careful of the nasty oak,
This poison stuff does not joke.

O'Neill Park is part of the great outdoors,
Like a high flying bird it makes spirits soar.

Aaron Canter, Grade 6
Morasha School

Yellow

Yellow, vibrant and strong,
Like the afternoon sun
As it sinks behind mountains.

Yellow, hyper, but calm,
Like a child on his first day of school,
Waiting for the bus that matches his mood.

Yellow, joyous and intelligent,
Like Albert Einstein
As he finds the solution to his first math problem.

Yellow, glittery and glowing,
Like the rippling waves
Under the setting sun.

Yellow, bright and alive,
Like the long, glorious days
On the shimmering sands of summertime.

Xania Eileen Bytof, Grade 6
James B Davidson Middle School

Obama's Inauguration

Barack Obama's inauguration
Made a turning point for this nation
From the Emancipation Proclamation
To Martin Luther King's determination
To end all racial discrimination

Which sadly led to his assassination
And now we come back to the inauguration
Of Barack Obama and his destination to change this nation
And I hope you enjoyed this presentation.

Sanjay S. Singh, Grade 6
Francis Parker School

Black Cat

Fur black as coal
With shining green eyes clear as crystals
Staring deep in you

Its voice clear as a bell
Purring in the deep alley
Calling for you

It's like a human
It has emotions
It has personalities
It has friends

It does not prey on animals
But can deliver some bad luck

When it lands from a high building
It looks as if a dark angel landed
So graceful and so elegant

It's the black cat who silently
Creeps in the night as a stray
Wandering in the darkest place
Of the alley.

Cathy Tran, Grade 5
St Barbara School

Snow-White Clouds

Inside a cloud
You rest gently on a
Soft bed of mini clouds.
In the lush white world
You relax.
Floating, tumbling, drifting
In what seems like a cotton ball.
On foggy days you feel
As if you will fall through the
Thin wisps of the cloud!

Cameron Kao, Grade 6
Carlthorp School

Scary, Scary Night

Scary, scary night.
The sky is black
The moon is red.
I hear monsters under my bed.
I hear the screech, I hear the scratch.
I feel its breath blow up my back!
The nightmares are on the walls.
The nightmares are walking the halls.
I scream!
My voice screeches.
Hoping! Hoping, someone will hear.
But all I hear is…silence.

Samuel Blake, Grade 6
Barstow Intermediate School

Winter

Winter blows in like the tornado of a helicopter
with ice appearing and rain coming to the ground like bullets
as if the ground is a giant magnet on a warlike day
that shows it is time for the winter battle
soldiers retreat from the incoming flashes and booms
they run to find cover from the loud barrage
they enter a shelter bringing the booming in with them
then drink hot chocolate from cannon-shaped mugs to warm their hopes
later, they go back out to help fight the winter war

Thomas Jodry, Grade 5
San Gabriel Elementary School

The Yellow Sun

Yellow is a very special color,
The sun is the color yellow and it is very important.
I see the sun every day when I go outside, but sometimes, the dark
clouds block the sun's bright yellow light.
It is high up in the blue sky shining down on us.
Every day it comes up in the day, and every night it comes down.
So the moon comes up to take its place.

Adam Vang, Grade 6
John Muir Elementary School

Bosco

My dog makes me happy because he is always there for me
Sometimes he makes me mad because he ruins my stuff
But I love him no matter what
When I am scared he always knows and he is ready to protect me
Bosco is a dog who likes you rich or poor
That's why I love him so much

Adrianna Borgatello, Grade 5
St Raphael School

Ocean

Listen, hear that, here comes a wave.
Boom, swish, boom, splash, burrr, cold.
Ahh here comes a shark, it's coming our way swim away swim away.
Swimming in the water crunch, crunch the fish is his lunch,
He's getting closer I screamed, Ouch!!!

Isabella Boatman, Grade 5
Sundale Elementary School

Violin

Strings vibrating, emanating sounds of love and sorrow, all in one.
The bow strokes the strings gently, accenting every note.
The sounds bounce around in its wooden heart before
Breaking out and filling the awaiting air.
Every feature of the instrument is perfect, slightly curving
But never too much.
When set down it still shines brightly, its wooden surface
Glowing with the sounds of music ringing in the air.
Delicate yet so strong it is like no other and refuses to be beaten.

Megan Roudebush, Grade 6
Francis Parker School

Imagination

Dreams are a creation where in your mind
there is an image.
Image is imagination.
Imagination is thinking of thoughts and things
that we may come across.
This will filter into dreams.
This is a whole process of the dream.
Imagination creates the dreams we have.
Many ways of dreaming,
is simply letting
our minds create an image and that image
becomes a dream.

Elijah Valdovinos, Grade 6
Cimarron Education Center

Save the Dolphins

Dolphins, so beautiful and swift,
They have such a wonderful gift.
Gentle and kind and silky and wet,
Swimming so fast, as fast as a jet.

This is when the dreaded nets,
Get caught around them as horrible threats.
Struggling to get out, and running out of breath.
Then it's time for their innocent death.

Now all these creatures get harmed,
So now it's your turn to be alarmed.
Help save the dolphins today,
Tell the others, and lead the way!

Alexis Funaki, Grade 6
Ada W Harris Elementary School

Red Rose

Characteristics: Never being able to share
Special Skills: Being beautiful everywhere
Home Address: Calm and peaceful garden
Favorite Hobby: Swaying in the open
Appetite: Just a tiny bite
Favorite Color: Blue as the midnight
Favorite Animal: Baby Ladybugs
Favorite book: Diary of a Mad Rose by Mildred McPug

Sophie Minteer, Grade 6
Francis Parker School

Power

There was a boy who was humble just like his friends.
He had power and greatness.
They all had different skin colors but were treated equally.
All of them cared for each other.
He also had courage.
His friends also had color and they never gave up.
They'll fight and fight and reach their goal and
they will always be at the top.

Ryan Marmion, Grade 4
Canyon View Elementary School

Leaves and Pea Soup

A long, dingy tree
Hibernating like a bear.
See the veins swarm up,
To the tip of the distorted branches.

The tree and I are alike,
We grow
Each and every day.
Behind the tree
Is grass that looks like a field of pea soup,
But the strands of grass
Are as piercing as a knife.
Although the day is young and the sun is beaming,
It is still as cold as a winter's day.
It's so cold I can feel the chill crawling
Up my spine.

You can hear the whistling of the wind,
As it passes by.
The day is fading away…
As the moon slowly awakes,
And the stars
Appear.

Dakota Tan, Grade 6
Bethany Lutheran School

Orange

The orange,
It looks like the earth,
The peel is the land we live on,
The zest is the hot lava mantel.
The sweet juicy goodness is like the hard non-breakable core.
Tastes like the candy we eat at a sleepover,
It seems that I never get enough!
One slice looks like a seesaw.
Those honeycombs sting my lips.
It has 6 chunky pieces.
It sticks to your mouth like a piece of tape.
It gives you a charge,
It is bumpy like the moon,
Juicy like the pomegranate.

Makayla Krumbholz, Grade 4
Daves Avenue Elementary School

My Edible Clothes

My shirt is cheddar cheese
My hat is blueberries
My pants are black eyed peas
My shoes are vanilla ice cream
My socks are strawberry's with string bean shoes
they had spaghetti laces, but I ate them
I wish I could eat my clothes.

Connor Jongewaard, Grade 5
Kentwood Elementary School

Gold Bee
Gold bee in oak
Buzzing around in huge tree
Gold bee flying by
Sarah LaCasa, Grade 4
Ladd Lane Elementary School

At Midnight
At midnight a diamond sizzles
a dark narrow puddle and a million
hurricanes twist around
and melt on a hill
Jafet Oidor, Grade 5
Henry Haight Elementary School

I Used to Be
I used to be a beautiful horse
until my owner forgot to feed me
I used to be brown
until my owner forgot to feed me
I used to be happy
until my owner forgot to feed me
I used to be fat
until my owner forgot to feed me
I used to be pretty
until my owner forgot to feed me
I used to be wonderful
now I'm just a white old horse.
Dakota Fugate, Grade 4
Upper Lake Elementary School

Snowball
I wish I were a chilly snowball,
White and frosty,
Global as the Earth itself,
Soaring like a wingspread eagle,
And finally landing softly on the
Cold, winter ground.
Zeina Elhanbaly, Grade 5
Lake Forest Elementary School

Comfort
Snow falls all around
Floating down to the ground
Tromping through the snow
Thinking of the soft crackle of the fire
Reading about hobbits, outside the Shire
Laughter and gift-giving
This comfort I'm living
Friends and family
Greeting with glee
Feelings of home
That I'm not alone
Theresa Westphal, Grade 5
Montessori Family School

Under the Lights
Atop a stage
Among fellow actors
Until the audience claps
Behind the curtain
In the theater
Near the props
Under the lights
Between shows
With a microphone
Becoming a star
Grace Villa, Grade 6
St Anne School

Fierce Tornado
I wish I were a fierce tornado,
Spinning and swirling,
Spiraling like a breathless drill,
Rotating like a rapid top,
And finally dying down.
Elijah Nelson, Grade 5
Lake Forest Elementary School

Snake
The poisonous snake
Harnesses the bear
As it climbed the high tree
After the snake
Sneaking up to a rat
The predator slithered fast.
Mario Flores, Grade 6
St Alphonsus School

Hawk
The Hawk that flies high,
It may be hungry for food.
Hawks are wonderful.
Their feathers are beautiful.
I love to watch Hawks fly high!
Bailie Smith, Grade 5
Gustine Elementary School

John
John,
Funny, nice, silly,
Relative of Samantha Sanchez,
Lover of church,
Who feels happy,
Who gives hugs,
Who fears sharks,
Who would like to see dolphins,
Who lives in Salinas,
Serrato.
Jade Sanchez, Grade 4
Ladd Lane Elementary School

The Mountain Peak
The mountain peak very tall
pretty and orange in the fall
the water reflects off the sun
as it sets.

The mornings are fun
especially with the sun.
I love the morning dew
as the May flower petals flew.
Emily Dunn, Grade 4
Upper Lake Elementary School

Scout
What's a Scout?
a trustworthy young boy
a loyal helper/friend
friendly, courteous, and kind
considerate of the outdoors
obedient, cheerful and brave
adventurous outdoorsmen
a hard worker, a camper
a determined individual
prepared for anything
That's a scout!
Ian Halter, Grade 6
Aliso Elementary School

The Death Fall
I slipped down a canyon yesterday
My bones are split, there is nothing left
I'm laid out in a hospital

I don't think I am gonna survive
All I have is my head and flesh
They already have my coffin built

These are my final words forever:
I hate unicycles and birds!
Johnny Jansen, Grade 5
Merryhill Country School

On the Horizon
Flower sits so tall
With shiny green stem, green leaves
Smells so good, so rich
Justin Brown, Grade 5
Joseph M Simas Elementary School

A True Love
One for everyone
Fills their heart with emotion
Forever as one
Nina Charlene Ann Harris, Grade 5
Clayton B Wire Elementary School

The Mirror

In the mirror I see me as a baby,
Wondering as much as I can.
In the mirror I see the beautiful sky of endless dreams,
Will we ever get that far?
Come with me and we will see!

Eqleema Kakar, Grade 4
Garden Grove Elementary School

My Mom Is Special

My mom is generous
She is nice and sweet like ice cream
She also likes to eat ice cream
She likes to be neat and friendly
She takes care of me and my family
She also gives me good advice
She makes my lunch for school
She sometimes understands me
She reminds me of the stuff I need
She cooks really great
She takes me to McDonalds
She is sometimes funny
She lets me sleep at 10:00 p.m.
She wakes me up at 6:00 a.m.
She gives me money on Tuesday for pizza
She buys me clothes and video games
She also buys me candy
She buys me the supplies for school
She gave me the money to pay for "The Egypt Game"
She helps me on my homework when I am stuck

Jose Roque, Grade 6
Century Community Charter School

The Alligator

There's a gator in the river,
Looking around,
Carefully waiting,
And not making a sound.

Soon a zebra comes,
To get a quick drink,
But the gator grabs it,
And it begins to sink.

The gator tries to bite,
But the zebra fights back.
And then for the gator,
Everything goes black.

The gator's knocked out,
And the zebra runs away,
And still the gator thought,
The zebra had to pay…

Alec Sahakian, Grade 5
Mayfield Jr School of the Holy Child Jesus

Weather

Dangerous hail striking farm animals,
Gigantic typhoon making land disappear,
Big storm destroying villages,
Chilly blizzard shivering people,
Humongous thunderstorm killing people,
Hard wind blowing trash everywhere,
Dark cloud scaring children.

Yumeji Takehiro, Grade 6
Highland Oaks Elementary School

Ocean

Choppy waves crashing on giant cliffs and white sandy beaches
Home of sea animals clinging, hiding, and swimming
Ships sail using oars, wind, or a motor
Made of salt water that covers most of the Earth

Matthew Benson, Grade 4
Daves Avenue Elementary School

My Silent Friend

It's following me no matter where I look
It's staring at me behind every cranny and nook
Casting a shadow upon my back
Hanging over me
Lighting my way
Showing me ahead
Always by my side
The moon
The magnificent moon
Up there with his pride and joy
Like a friend who's always there
Twinkling and smiling down before me

Sarah Suad, Grade 6
Islamic School of San Diego

Tension

In the living room, smaller than a mouse,
I lay in a corner like a discarded doll in a girl's room,
Mom and Dad are yelling at each other like crazed hyenas,
It's a throat squeezing moment.

The air with thundering booms, is thick and tight
I can't say anything
Even if I dare.
Mouth dry, scared face
And a sinking heart
I lay with my eyes open;
My mouth shut,
Watching the penetrating glare
Of a thousand laser beams cutting through time,

It's over,
I can breathe,
I can talk
And mom and dad say, "Sorry."

Nicholas McCauley, Grade 6
Vista Verde Middle School

The Solar System
The sun is in the middle.
The planets going around.
Neptune and Uranus
are the farthest from the sun.
Jupiter and Saturn
are above the Asteroid Belt.
And all the outer planets
are gas giants in space.
The inner planets are
under the Asteroid Belt
like Earth, Mars,
Venus, and Mercury
all these planets are in our
Solar System in space.

Anastasia Pupo, Grade 5
St Pancratius Elementary School

Space
I wonder what's beyond the sky,
up in the air way, way up high.
I wonder where the planets are,
far out there beyond the stars.
I wonder if there's life up there,
like down on Earth and everywhere.

Brandon Ollar, Grade 6
Lockeford Elementary School

Raindrop
I wish I were a beautiful raindrop,
Delicate and stunning,
Bursting from a cloud like tears,
Sparkling like a crystal gem,
Splashing gently on the Earth below.

Hannah Dahlstrom, Grade 5
Lake Forest Elementary School

Spring Time
Colorful, green and quiet
the grass blows peacefully

You are lying in a big meadow
where the sun is shining bright

You can hear the bees buzzing
hummingbirds singing,
and crows chatting among their flock

Trucks are passing by
as butterflies fly
up into the beautiful, vast sky

You fall asleep dreaming about
the wonder of spring time,
and hope that it never comes to an end.

Olivia Bowen, Grade 4
Charles Armstrong School

The Beach
Down at the beach, with the sweet sea breeze,
A bunch of beach bums in bikinis and T's.
Surfers surfing, boogie boarders boogie boarding,
Hawaiian music ringing in my ears. How great is the beach,
Just sitting here, a coconut in my hand, and my toes in the sand.

Kelly Blankenship, Grade 6
John Muir Elementary School

Love
One day, this one single day…
For twenty-four hours you are exposed to cupid's arrows.
Just calmly walking down the street,
Unaware of your carelessness, you have now become his target.
Just one single strike can make you fall
Head over heels for anyone
Eyes locked on your crush, heart beating fast,
Losing breath, face turning blush-pink.
Are these signs of everlasting love?
Is this truly known as desire running through your veins?
One answer can change your life,
And one answer might overcome your soul.
Yes, the answer is yes!
You are now a victim of love.
Can you ever escape this trap?
And will your crush ever feel the same?
That, you must find out for yourself.
Swallow your pride, and gather your courage.
Things may become bleak, they may become pointless.
But if you don't try, you alone will be the one disappointed…
Listen to your heart, and Happy Valentine's Day!

Sarah Abughrib, Grade 6
Corpus Christi School

Arguing Between Families
Fights spring out of arguments about silly things
House held chores lead to arguments
Do this. Do that. Right now. Not now.
On the contrary there's something else needed to be done
Some arguments no one wins
Some dislike arguing so much they deliberately give in

When I heard one argument going about I would always scurry out
Mom always wanted to scrub one of our mouths out with soap
Arguments can lead to impulsive name calling
Arguments lead to shouting and hurt feelings
Tempers flare
Anger rises

Avoid the one topic
Discuss things calmly, don't over react
Break the argument early then come back to it
Mentally prepare for the argument
Families should not have to abandon each other
Family love should be stronger than any argument

Sean Rea, Grade 6
Big Springs Elementary School

Autumn

The last fading sunshine rays,
Reflect the end of summer days
The leaves of the trees are amber and gold weave,
The logs are cinnamon sticks brewing in tea,
Thanksgiving is here,
Let's all give a cheer.

It's time to be thankful for all that we have,
To celebrate this time of year and never be sad,
Pass around the pumpkin pie,
Look, my grandpa is wearing a bow tie.
The turkey tastes delicious,
And it is very nutritious.

There is a whirlwind of leaves outside,
The wind blows them as children laugh and hide.
The twister of autumn leaves swirls around my head,
Whoosh, Whoosh, Whoosh, the end of autumn is sad.
It's hard to leave this stunning time,
But winter is here, and I'm ending my rhyme.

Anna Satterfield, Grade 6
Dorris-Eaton School

Even So…

Even so, I am thankful for cleaning my room
because if I didn't I would have a messy room.

Even so, I am thankful for my sister playing the clarinet
because then I wouldn't learn clarinet music.

Even so, I am thankful for my cats biting me
because it teaches me to be nice to them.

Even so, I am thankful for cleaning my fish's water
because then she won't get sick.

Even so, I am thankful for doing my chores
because it teaches me responsibility.

Maya Paulo, Grade 4
Heather Elementary School

Happiness

Happiness is seeing stars in the sky.
It is watching ladybugs crawl,
Or hearing birds sing.
It is watching butterflies during the day,
And fireflies at night.
Happiness is watching the sunrise,
And the sunset on a sandy beach.
Happiness is the feeling you have
From people who love you.
Happiness is all of these and much more.
It's what makes you
Happy!

Becka Chase, Grade 5
Stone Ranch Elementary School

Heaven

I start to nestle in my bed,
there is nothing that I dread.
It feels like heaven.

Counting sheep two by two,
sleep invades and dreams pursue.
Can this be heaven?

Whiteness surrounds me,
happiness has found me.
This must be heaven.

Clouds in the air,
the wind rustling through my hair,
and heaven; almost there.

The swirling mist, rocking me back and forth
will never leave, never mourn, always there,
while guiding me north.

I see a light ahead
and it captivates me,
so forward I sped.

It's now getting clear,
and I know there's nothing to fear.
I wake up, I saw you there, I knew I was here.

Frances Abalos, Grade 6
Cope Middle School

Feelings

It is hard to talk
For when I do I feel like crying
Tears fight my eyes, trying to make me cry
Fear and anger lay inside of me
As if happiness never comes
It feels like a curse
One that will never go away
All I ask is to get happiness

Renz Olivar Caceres, Grade 5
El Monte Elementary School

Midnight

There is a black cat on my fence
When he comes around, my mom gets tense
I tell her not to worry,
'Cause it's just a cat who's furry.

I named him Midnight, for that seemed good.
My mom would name him Demon, if she could.
When he comes over he says, "Meow, meow!"
We like him very much now.

Sarah Juhl-Harris, Grade 5
Packinghouse Christian Academy

Green, Green, Green!
Fresh, ambrosial limes waiting patiently to be picked in the pulchritudinous meadow,
Recycling signs hanging for a considerable time to help the environment,
Lanky palm trees being blown in front of the resplendent sunset at the windy beach,
Four-leaf clovers standing motionlessly, finding a person to give good luck to,
Incandescent emeralds being polished in the new-opened museum,
Nutritious broccoli being eaten by healthy children at the restaurant,
Crafty leprechauns deviously giving people fake gold on St. Patrick's Day,
Scrumptious green tea being poured cautiously at the Japanese restaurant,
Aquamarine sea water rushing against the sandy shore.

Olivia Xu, Grade 5
Highland Oaks Elementary School

Love to My Mom
My mommy is a fashionable lady
She runs to the mall because she is the opposite of lazy
My mommy is very protective her love is very effective
She is as cute as a button her touch is as soft as cotton
My mommy is a first grade teacher she is often compared to great leaders
She is my pillow at night and intolerant to fights
My mommy thinks she must diet but I don't think she should try it
She is always there for me even when she sees a bad attitude deep inside of me
My mommy is the perfect listener even though she has a fist on her
She tries to be positive by being very talkative
I love it when she kisses me I feel a little tingle inside of me
My mom can find the greatest inside of me I hope she always stays with me
I love her with all of my heart looking at her is like looking at my favorite piece of art

Lorren Walker, Grade 6
Century Community Charter School

Courage
Courage is a male lion, roaring fiercely, and impatiently pacing his territory to protect his pride. It shows up when he defends his home and family. Courage displays its strength when an elephant lifts a tree trunk out of the path, so others can get through. Courage has a large brain. Its intelligence is evident by astronauts that learned to fly to the moon and back! It is also extremely quick like Jesse Owens running like a flash to earn a gold medal. Courage is colorful like bold brushstrokes on a canvas painting. But most of all courage is war heroes who sacrifice themselves for others!

Michael Abbott, Grade 5
Wagon Wheel Elementary School

I Am From…
I am from a house, where a chinchilla named Chilli lazily lounges, where laughter lines the walls, and loud music bursts through the windows.

I am from a family, where practical jokes are not a strange thing, and where mistakes are accepted like Mom's chocolate chip cookies.

I am from a neighborhood where a peacock named Oscar proudly struts the gravelly streets lined with ancient trees, where my brother plays sports with me, and hurtles footballs at my legs.

I am from a town, where happiness flies around like a rosy winged bluebird, where people whiz around on skateboards, smiling to each other as they ride by.
I would not trade the world for this.

Caroline Sajben, Grade 5
Notre Dame School

Index

Aaron, David 53
Abalos, Frances 219
Abbas, Dhouha 100
Abbas, Taherah 210
Abbott, Kenny 205
Abbott, Michael 220
Abdalian, Sevon Destiny 187
Abed, Kate .73
Abughrib, Sarah 218
Aburajab, Rayyan 96
Acevedo, Elias 190
Acosta, Ariana 53
Acosta, Giana 132
Acuna, Michelle 179
Adair, Kelsey 44
Adams, Katreena 41
Adams, Mason 54
Addamo, Skyler 90
Addas, Elizabeth 120
Adigopula, Tanuja 108
Agaba, Ibraaheem 39
Agarwal, Sharanya 57
Aguilera, Nicole 196
Ahmed, Fariza 43
Ahmed, Roshan 75
Akella, Prathima 101
Al-Habre, Amanda Rita 202
Alamango Shapiro, Grayson 51
Alamango Shapiro, Leila 107
Alami, Nada 169
Alarcon, Kristian 203
Alba, Jaiden 30
Alejandre, Oriana 112
Alexander, Mary 136
Alfaro, Savannah 24
Ali, Suwayda 183
Allen, Emily 38
Alley, Austin 82
Almaraz, Milla 158
Almera, Azriel Krista Mostajo 175
Altice, Kan 184
Alvarez Jr., Fernando 49
Amato, Matthew 194
Amer, Trevor 90
Amid, Saba 72
Amid, Saba 151
Amon, Gabriella 195
Anderson, Abby 102
Anderson, Amber 208
Anderson, Taylor 154
Andrews, Xavia 107
Angulo, Luis Angel 24
Antabli, Sarah 155
Aponte, Keelan 34
Applebury, Jonathan 126
Ardon, Geovani 170
Arevalo, Yvonne 211
Arguelles, Janelle 130
Arias, Crystal 62
Arias, Matthew 102
Asenas, Danielle 29
Asif, Aisha 148
Astamendi, Cole 24
Attaway, Lawrence 142
Attia, Zinab 113
Attwood, Tommy 79
Avery, Eden 91
Avila, Alex 117
Awad, Ramzy 149
Aznar, Brianna 32
Babbitt, Katie 65
Badger, Charlie 204
Badilla, Andrei 117
Baer, Zoe 23
Bagheri, Kian 72
Bahn, Jennifer 104
Bakkila, Baylee 139
Ballinger, Cambria 180
Banda, April 37
Barbosa, Marissa 180
Barcellos, Anna 121
Barcelona, Samuel 101
Barnes, Emma 103
Barnes, Mykaela 171
Barrera, Evelyn 45
Barrera, Noel 148
Barriga, Adela 208
Barsky-Ex, Elijah 55
Barta, David 70
Bartlett, James 122
Batson, Caroline 156
Bea, Matthew 83
Becerra, Alondra 208
Becerra, Anthony 45
Becker, Sydney 49
Bell, Kailen 168
Bell, Sarah 144
Benitez, Abigail 176
Benjamin, Carson 119
Bennett, Charlie 23
Bennett, Sofia 119
Benson, Matthew 217
Benson, Quade 65
Benson, Taylor 60
Bentley, Spencer 130
Berardi, Lindsay 91
Berglass, Ellie 62
Bergman, Ryan 144
Berja, Joshua 153
Bernard, Elijah 162
Berson, Emma 67
Bertrand, Claire 148
Bess, Nikita 144
Bettis, Nellesha 77
Beverly, Justin 154
Bhullar, Avi 189
Bianchi, Bryce 126
Bibriesca, Yvonne 155
Bidar, Sajia 135
Biley, Nicole 156
Bishop, Shea 159
Bistagne, Alex 156
Black, Khyra 28
Blackburn, Rachel 212
Blackwood, Nicole 47
Blair, Olivia 110
Blair, Sophie 136
Blake, Matthew 58
Blake, Matthew 198
Blake, Samuel 214
Blalock, Lilah 140
Blancaflor, Judy 189
Blankenship, Kelly 218
Bloom, James 54
Blough, Jessica 24
Blount-Singletary, Devaughn 81
Boatman, Isabella 214
Bockholt, Ryan 124
Bonde, Kate 174
Bonilla, Zaira 76
Borgatello, Adrianna 214
Boulil, Zaineb 199
Bowen, Olivia 218
Bowen, Trevor 70
Boyd, Eryn 38
Boyer, Natalie 96
Bragg, Adriana 110
Brandt, Jenna 96
Branstetter, Jalissa 147
Bray, Madeleine 64
Bray, Morgan 165
Britt, Taylor 158
Brock, Julia 99

Broukhim, Brandon 202
Brown, Brandon 180
Brown, Christian 168
Brown, Jeremy 192
Brown, Justin 23
Brown, Justin 216
Brown, Tiara 61
Brown, Zoe 207
Brown-Sloan, Tiara 208
Brownell, Rachel 98
Brunkal, Melissa 90
Bruns, Lindsay 192
Buchanan, Carlos 177
Bui, Helen 50
Bullard, Charlie 45
Burns, Harrison 139
Burton, Blake 166
Buss, Katie 49
Buss, Tiffany 88
Bustos, Isai 204
Butler, Madison 133
Buul, Mohamed 198
Bytof, Xania Eileen 213
Cabezas, Kieran 98
Caceres, Renz Olivar 219
Cai, Samuel 28
Calderon, Caleb 57
Caldwell, Thomas 72
Calk, Brandon 139
Camacho, Taylor Rose 63
Camargo, Angelo 83
Campion, Andrew 147
Campos, Angel 184
Campos, Cindy 210
Campos, Kristie 62
Caniglia, Matt 12
Cano, Ivanna 85
Cano, Stephanie 76
Canter, Aaron 213
Cantor, Jordan 133
Cantos, Chelsea 26
Cao, Anh 89
Caprini, Brandon 109
Capulong, Roland Theo 48
Carbone, Sydney 120
Cardenas, Imelda 189
Cardozo, Augustin 162
Carey, Mac 97
Cariello, Marissa 121
Carothers-Liske, Chloe 13
Carrillo, Christian 119
Carrillo, Darby 170
Carvalho, Ana Marie 113
Casaus, Jake 201
Castaneda, Angelica 34
Castaneda, Jonathan 178
Castillejo, Veronica 60

Castillo, Brianna 109
Castro, Avery 198
Castro, Talisa 98
Ceballos, Manuel 196
Ceresola, Danyelle 84
Cervantes, Stephanie 90
Chaarawi, Adam 94
Chamberlin, Layla 103
Chan, Anna 35
Chan, Anna 87
Chance, Shannon 113
Chang, Caroline 69
Chang, Jasper 122
Chang, Selina 199
Chapton, Jenna 52
Charette, Jerry 210
Chase, Becka 219
Chatlani, Nima Usha 40
Chavarria, Edward 96
Chavez, Sergio 58
Chen, Connie 210
Chen, Ellie 105
Chen, Emily 137
Chen, Jamie 131
Chen, Jason 152
Chen, Tiffany 159
Cheng, Kimberly 103
Cherekdjian, Christina 133
Chew, Sam 72
Chiao, Mason 202
Chick, Annabel 72
Chiem, Emily 29
Chinchilla, Leslie 206
Ching, Annie 110
Chiong, Christopher 76
Chiotti, Giovanna (Gigi) 75
Chism, Darren 158
Cho, Nathan 24
Cho, Ruth 95
Choi, Hankyul 132
Choi, Jonathan 60
Choudhary, Sakshi 33
Chow, Kristin 188
Chow-Ise, Ian 62
Choye, Camryn 112
Christensen, Gracie 144
Christensen, Kayla 187
Christopher, Cami 51
Chu, Carolina 155
Chun, Isabelle 26
Ciup, Joshua Krishna 85
Claiborne, Bruce 93
Clancy, Megan 31
Clark, Katie 184
Clark, Madison 82
Clexton, Andrew 210
Clinkinbeard, Sonia 57

Cloyd, Haley 71
Cobarrubia, Sophie 14
Cobian, Ashly 113
Coffey, Sarah 92
Colston, Shane 126
Colwell, James 173
Combes, Chloë H. 60
Cong, Iris 59
Conrad, Abby 163
Conrad, Nico 36
Considine, Alexander 166
Considine, Camille 190
Constant, Sheridan 119
Constantin, Charlotte 88
Contreras, Ashley 184
Contreras, Jocelyn 208
Contreras, Mariah 61
Cook, Jade 66
Cooney, Delaney 44
Cornwall, Maggie 100
Corona, Estefania 186
Corrales, Samantha 186
Correa, Alexander 37
Cortes, Gabriella 144
Corwin, Katherine 153
Costa, Mycala 184
Costa, Pascal Sy 74
Covarrubias, Leo 79
Crane, Courtney 126
Creasy, Alexandria 132
Crockett, Matthew 69
Croft, Rachel 202
Cronk, Alyse 138
Crowell, Holly 137
Cruz, James 86
Cruz, Paulo 78
Curran, Patricia 180
Cutting, Hunter 194
D'Souza, Alexander 24
Dahl, Jenna 163
Dahlstrom, Hannah 218
Dale, Frebrenie 74
Dale, Katie 171
Daniel, Shanice 43
Daou, Kayla 97
Dardis, Alec 58
Daughtry, Amber 157
David, Aili 38
Davin, Zoe 169
Davis, Jonah 64
Davis, Kyle 84
Davis, Reese 85
Day, Kayla 72
De Camara, Cady 52
De La Espriella, Sean 55
De la Torre, Jallyn 199
De Santiago, Jenneffer 177

Index

Deahl, Briana 137
Dean, Damani 137
Dearth, Max 208
DeGuere, Milena 154
Deiranieh, Asmaa 154
Del Matto, Marianna 204
Dela Cruz, Corinne Elyse 120
Delgadillo, Kennedy 106
Delgado, Vanesa 137
Delos Santos, James 160
Demari, Kayla 181
Desai, Mihir 150
Dhuey, Katherine 105
Dieteman, Izzabella 53
Dimarucut, Richard 76
Dinkel, Christopher 209
Djahanchahi, Olivia 25
Dodge, Dylan 161
Dodson, Emma 154
Domergue, Fiona 147
Don, Benjamin 186
Doney, Faith 25
Doppalapudi, Vishnu 131
Doss, Skylar 55
Dovan, Kimmy 94
Dow, Sabrina 50
Downing, Danielle 69
DoyLoo, Ryan 62
Drazovich, Logan 72
Drew, Macy 158
Duarte, Danny 76
DuBeau, Joe 49
Dumiak, Rachel 159
Dunn, Emily 216
Dunnet, Sara 22
Duran, Joey 36
Durnin, Bailey 39
Duval, Christina 145
Duvinage, Philip 191
Eaton, Andrew 161
Eberle, Colette 175
Echevarria, Alyssa 40
Edgin, Jordan 152
Eherenfeldt, Hannah 43
Eidgahy, Kaumron 195
Eldridge, Cameron 191
Elhanbaly, Zeina 216
Elmi, Payaam 196
Emge, Allison 195
England, Sydney 159
Enmark, Madeline 40
Enos, Kelsey M. 89
Enriquez, Hector 201
Ephraim, Lilianne 163
Erlendson, Emily 138
Escalona, Vytas 112
Escobar, Natalia 45
Escobar-Lopez, Jezelle 158
Espinoza, Alexis 187
Espinoza, Michelle 167
Esquivel, Frances 30
Estrada Linares, Katherine 86
Etessami, Giselle 114
Euyoque, Sarah 100
Fang, Lisa 114
Farin, Kian 142
Farmer, Abigail 192
Fast, Jake .52
Fathollahi, Niloo 87
Fay, Whitney N. 196
Feitzinger, Lauren 159
Felix, Lorraine 211
Fermenic, Alexus 138
Fernandez, Isabella 114
Ferral, Sarah 63
Ferrer, Drew 25
Fidler, Olivia 102
Finlay, Nicole 134
Fish, Libby 95
Fisher, Greg 77
Flahavan, Kevin 202
Flores, Jasmin 86
Flores, Marco 203
Flores, Mario 216
Flores, Samantha 174
Flores, Yovanni 100
Foellmer, Lena 98
Folsé, Anthony 59
Fong, Kristina 107
Fonseca, Suseth 130
Fontaine, Beverly 102
Fontes, Mykaila 31
Foody, Shannon 106
Ford, Michael 134
Forester, Carley 211
Fortin, Will 46
Fortner, Sophie 161
Foster, Eric 96
Foster, Sabrina 34
Fox, Hannah 54
Franco, Alyssa 66
Frastaci, Brian 125
Freels, Alexandra 100
Freeman, Alexander 43
Freeman, Miranda 31
Fritz, Amanda 185
Frome, Grace 174
Froomer, Maddie 72
Frutkoff, Amaya H. 141
Fuentes, Sarah 180
Fugate, Dakota 216
Funaki, Alexis 215
Gabski, Jillian 25
Gallagher, Daniel 90
Gallardo, Alexa 28
Gallardo, Katrina 145
Gallastegui, Alexander 139
Galvan, Itaide 26
Galvez, Kyle 201
Gamberale, Mia 88
Gamboa, Sandra 183
Gao, Emily 51
Garcia, Aaliyah 90
Garcia, Erika 28
Garcia, Jason 196
Garcia, Madeline 59
Garcia, Maria 182
Garcia, Maricarmen 158
Garcia, Rebekah 25
Gardner, Nina 42
Gardner, Sarah 69
Garrity, Bridget 83
Garza, Unica 147
Gates, Lillian 92
Gauthier, Soline 66
Gaylord, Hank 99
Genton, Annabel 169
George, Rebecca 93
Geronimo, Samantha 213
Gharineh, Donya 90
Ghassemi, Ryan 116
Giambastiani, Seth 106
Giddings, Haley 116
Gilman Dye, Sydney 32
Gimena, Anabell 89
Gionet-Gonzales, Julia 106
Givens, Vanessa 62
Goe, Morgan 120
Golanka, Spencer 82
Goldberg, Brianna 51
Goldman, Jodi 128
Goldsmith, Caroline 129
Goldsmith-Morgan, Zeque 148
Goldstein de Salazar, Ruby 162
Gomez, Aaron 120
Gomez, Alysa 86
Gomez, Anastasia 132
Gomez, Carley 24
Gomez, Erika 57
Gomez, Evelyn 86
Gong, Royal 204
Gonzales, Ariana 44
Gonzalez, Adolfo 93
Gonzalez, Mario 100
Gonzalez, Paulina 28
Goodwin, Adam 89
Gordon, Isabella 15
Gordon, Nicholas 121
Gosart, Thomas 130
Graham, Travis 201
Grant, Elizabeth 192

Name	Page
Graul, Kelin	167
Graves, Joshua	167
Greenberg, Natalie	141
Grego, Angelina	111
Gregory, Jordan	168
Grimaldi, Vincent	113
Grimes, Emily	184
Groff, Holden	179
Groll, Jacob	85
Guarino, Amanda	204
Guerra, Evan J.	181
Guerrero, Angel	148
Guerrero, Isaiah	98
Guerrero, Jacob	146
Guerrero, Rosie	122
Gujral, Heena	62
Gussman, Katherine	154
Gust, Erin	172
Guthrie, Katie	41
Gutierrez, Jazmin S.	69
Gutierrez, Lucero	54
Habib, Caroline	123
Hacker, Hannah	134
Hahn, Siena	149
Halas, Justine	137
Hall, Shaun	66
Haller, Lauren	33
Halloran, Evan	196
Halsell, Joseph	66
Halter, Ian	216
Hammel, Grace	153
Hampshire, Josh	178
Hanaoka, Maya	104
Hang, Caroline	175
Hansen, Morgan	110
Hanson, Ian	126
Harari, Caroline	84
Harelson, Claire	94
Hargrove, T.J.	135
Harris, Jack	136
Harris, Nina Charlene Ann	216
Hartzheim, Alyssa	135
Harvey, Christian	213
Hassane, Salma	46
Hasty, June	99
Hatch, James	97
Hauk, Jordyn	164
Hayden, Faith	204
Hazama, Yuri	177
He, Jin Ru	192
Hebri, Samantha	91
Heinen, Alexandra	82
Hellwig, Sasha	156
Hemphill, Candice	45
Henriksen, Cole	85
Henry, Olivia	203
Heriman, Robert	155
Hermo, Phoenix	174
Hernaez, Reggie	67
Hernandez, Angel	124
Hernandez, Cristian	160
Hernandez, Cynthia	151
Hernandez, Eddie	49
Hernandez, Jennifer	150
Hernandez, Kirsten	76
Hernandez, Melani	46
Hernandez, Sierra	190
Herrera, Klarissa	169
Herrera, TJ	170
Herrero, Ashley	118
Herrero, Cody	90
Hilbourne, Misty	173
Hindery-Nelson, Misha	196
Hinds, Kaycie	162
Hiromoto, Kaylen	136
Hobson, Katie	54
Holman, Alexis	82
Holmes, Kelli	179
Holmquist, Justin	146
Holve, Grant	80
Hoorfar, Emily	118
Hope, Camille	66
Hoppen, Daniel	174
Hopper, Cassidy	145
Hotchkis, Perry	201
Hou, Emily	176
Houghton, Lucy	47
Houshanian, Negin	71
Hovey, Zak	22
Howard, Kenneth	71
Howard, Tyler	92
Hsieh, Elaine	169
Hu, Amy	130
Huaman, Abril	186
Huang, Connie	191
Huang, Mira	155
Hubbard, Madison	70
Hubbell, Steven	170
Huezo, Joshua	96
Huitron, Stephany	149
Huizar, Madison	118
Hulse, Madison	132
Hunt-Silva, Jasmine	37
Huntley, Miranda	154
Huntsman, Emily	167
Hurley, Liam	168
Huston, Garett	91
Hwang, Janet	45
Ibarra, Daisy	134
Idan, Gony	127
Im, Edward	16
Infante, Alexie	119
Irineo, Angelica	190
Islas-Chavez, Jasmin	57
Iverson, Jamie	76
Jackson, Catalina	184
Jackson, Elizabeth	86
Jackson, Jocelyn	24
Jacobo, Karina	138
Jacobson, Halli	59
Jaffe, Erica	17
Jagger-Wells, Tess	29
Jaime, Gavin	180
Jain, Vishal	151
Jama, Ayan	91
James, Machele	180
Janett, Natalie	123
Jansen, Johnny	216
Javelosa, Airelle	79
Jayaraman, Vidya	179
Jensen, Erika	89
Jiang, Ryan	193
Jimenez, Josue	70
Jimenez Mendoza, Nayeli Anahi	84
Jodry, Thomas	214
Johnson, Avalon	122
Johnson, Claire	194
Johnson, Dayne	210
Johnson, Emma	30
Johnson, Emma	211
Johnson, Sam	172
Johnson, Sarah	181
Jones, Jess	123
Jones, Justin	198
Jones, Mia	65
Jones, Rionna	109
Jongewaard, Connor	215
Joseph, Matthew	117
Joslin, Kevin Michael	142
Juhl-Harris, Sarah	219
Jurich, Michael	113
Kabiling, Justin	213
Kadous, Mariam	166
Kakar, Eqleema	217
Kamerman, Brittany	161
Kaminskis, Griffin	87
Kao, Cameron	214
Kappes, Julia	61
Karlous, Rebecca	114
Kashani, Saam	25
Kasmir, Stephen	200
Kelkar, Saumitra	112
Kelley, Donovan J.	84
Kelly, Joshua	106
Kelly, Mikey	99
Kelly, Tatianna	132
Kelson, Hannah	173
Kendrick, Thomas	160
Kent, Alyssa	158
Kerievsky, Sasha	112
Kershner, Isaac C.	106

Index

Kessler, Nick 35
Keys, Ian 191
Khan, Suduf 36
Khazaieli, Merceden 198
Khoe, Ethan 67
Khullar, Kristy 141
Kildiszew, Noel 205
Kim, Andrew 202
Kim, Christina 135
Kim, Eric .122
Kim, Gina 172
Kim, Hannah 165
Kim, Janie .68
Kim, Riley 199
Kim, Young-Kyung 54
King, Asia .57
Kinkade, Evie 179
Kinlow, Carlin 153
Kirk, Hanna 31
Kirste, Sarah 67
Klein, Danielle 103
Klein, Emily 90
Klembith, Skylar 129
Knapp, Corryn 82
Knerr, Adam 23
Knight, Jared 115
Knowles, Johnny 71
Kohler, Dillon 204
Kolb, Katelyn 108
Koler, Ethan 24
Kong, Taylor 97
Kong, Vivian 108
Krasnodemsky, Ilona 79
Kraus, Anne 109
Kraus, Benjamin 179
Krishnakumar, Rohan 126
Krisik, Matthew 106
Kroe, Melissa 180
Kroemer, Ryan 52
Krumbholz, Makayla 215
Krutonog, Sam 35
Kugel, MacKenzie 149
Kuhn, Jason 144
Kuhn, Joey .64
LaCasa, Sarah 216
Laik, Emma 195
Lam, Christine 96
Lamberti, Aldo 192
Lambrecht, Sophia 27
LaMere, Miranda 76
Lamphear, Cassidy 145
Lane, Bronwen 193
Langenbahn, Michael 141
Lara, Leticia 148
Larson, Jessica 134
Lasken, Halie 54
Lavery, Danny 199
Lawrence, Lilli 165
Lay, Jonathon 29
Le, Jade 50
Le, Krystal 132
Leadem, Hannah 182
Leal, Carlos 136
Lee, Andrew 119
Lee, Jake .125
Lee, Jessica 36
Lee, Nathan 159
LeMasters, Maddie 44
Lemons, Riley 76
Lemos, Joey 103
Lesch, Micah 177
Lester, Ariana 50
Leventis, Alex 151
Levy, Jason 59
Levy, Jen .109
Lew, Nicholas 191
Lewis, Benjamin 70
Lewis, Brandon 168
Lewis, Staycee 136
Li, Andrew 133
Liang, Matthew 42
Lin, David 118
Lin, Maya .85
Lindley, Savannah 141
Liong, Erinn 190
Lira, Michael 197
Lisitsa, Freddy 22
Liu, Joanna 86
Liu, Tony 83
Liu, Zhibing 197
Lizarraga, Danielle 199
Lo, Jennifer 40
Loaiza, Alexis 65
Locken, Will 185
Logan, Alaena 129
Lona, Andrew 58
Long, Madelynne 128
Long, Sutter 146
Loo, Yi-Ling 41
Lopez, Eva 209
Lopez, Karina 174
Lord, Kyle 170
Lovett, Zoe 111
Lowance, Christian 40
Lowe, Robbie 96
Lujan, Brookelyn 183
Luk, Brandon 189
Lunday, Thomas 57
Luong, Jade 114
Lupsa, Lidia 175
Luque, Maggie 205
Lynch, Brandon 132
Lynch, Carly 127
Lyton, Errin 85
MacAskill, Ashley 34
Macatangay, Alexandra 46
Macatangay, Andrea 138
Machetta, Sarah 61
Machuga, Julia 37
Maciel, Carlos 74
MacVean, Margaret 63
Madan, Marissa 98
Madha, Asiya 91
Maeshiro, Gen 192
Maestas, Dominique 136
Magaling, Jemm 77
Magallanes, Isabel 54
Magana, Leopoldo 65
Magaña, Natalie 155
Mageno, Marilyn 40
Mahoney, Aryana 105
Malcolm, Guy 145
Malone, Allison 169
Maly, Gwen 23
Manankichian, Kristina 170
Maniti, Joanna 67
Mann, Jordan 26
Manter, Hunter 138
Marcus-Willers, Aaron 47
Marin, Heriberto 131
Mariolis, Emilia 110
Marks, Aaron 163
Marmion, Ryan 215
Marsh, Jacob 100
Martin, Annalee 28
Martin, Leon 197
Martinez, Braianna 73
Martinez, Marlene 66
Martinez, Natalie 18
Martinez, Skyler 64
Martinez, Yves 35
Marx, Noah F. 33
Maryamian, Mayan 64
Mascarenhas, Kristen 153
Matais, Grant 140
Mataraarachchi, Nirosh 28
Mayet, Rabeeya 146
McCann, Michelle 152
McCarthy, Tara F. 41
McCaul, Kiana 154
McCauley, Nicholas 217
McCaw, Andrew 133
McClellan, Sonora 122
McClure, Catherine 94
McColl, Alexandra 115
McCowan, Taylor 47
McCoy, Allie 109
McCullough, Kaiya 149
McDonald, Melissa 123
McDowell, Carrington 127
McGill, Adison 201

Name	Page	Name	Page	Name	Page
McGovern, Sean	202	Morin, Kyono Chantal	143	Nowikow, Josh	77
McIntyre, Morgan	66	Morse, Kate	64	Nunberg, Rachael	110
McKee, Michelle	42	Moser, Elliot	202	Nussbaum, Claire	63
McKenna, Luke	195	Moses, Tucker	40	O'Malley, R.J.	211
McNamara, Daniel	185	Mosley, Mitchell Lou	112	O'Neill, Emily	106
McZeal, Deja	187	Motz, Mattie	108	O'Sullivan, Matt	76
Meave, Naomi	78	Mould, Tyler	54	Obasi, Effy	27
Meda, Elizabeth	29	Mueller, Andrew	181	Oberheim, Troy	180
Medellin, Kelsey	174	Muenzenberger, Savannah	68	Oberman, Katie	116
Medina, Angelica G.	188	Mugnai, Krista	154	Ochoa, Xochitl	134
Mejia, Juan Carlos	126	Muirhead, Ryan	158	Oidor, Jafet	216
Melendez, Rosie	179	Mujic, Francesca	99	Ojeda, Mario	166
Melgar, Dalton	158	Mulbarger, Freddy	80	Olascoaga, Zabela	62
Mello, Mary-Catherine	46	Munkres, Christopher	121	Olivares, Adriana	166
Melton, Nicholas	108	Muratalla, Zoe	117	Ollar, Brandon	218
Mendoza, Jannelle	76	Murillo, Kassandra	120	Oney, Jeff	75
Mendoza, Joseph	122	Murnane, Katie	170	Oppenheimer, Ron	150
Mercado, Ashley	73	Muroff, Elana	164	Orellana, Lilly	101
Mercado, Leslie	174	Murphy, Angela	187	Orelo, Sofia	189
Mestetsky, Troy	205	Murray, Dwight	95	Orloff, Alexis	49
Methot, Nils	134	Nadel, Jesse	131	Ornelas, Lorena	202
Meyer, Nickolas	42	Nafisi, Mahdi	81	Orr, Sam	136
Meyer-Yen, Sophia	193	Nafisi, Mahdi	186	Ortiz, Lorenzo	42
Meza, Jose	174	Nagesh, Neha	195	Oson, Kira	23
Mikus, Zach	44	Nakamura, Megumi	40	Osorio, Kimberly	96
Milani, Dominic	182	Nall, Kamilah	121	Oswald, Maddie	111
Miles, Ariana	49	Nall, Malaika	166	Ottilie, Madeline	52
Miles, Helene	49	Nall, Malaika	207	Oviedo, Carolina	205
Millar, Brianna	191	Nam, Courtney	141	Pagarkar, Dania	34
Mills, Kendall	173	Napoli, Amanda Allessa	115	Palakodeti, Samhita	38
Min, Rachel	31	Naqui, Shazia	129	Pallett, Samantha	157
Min, Seyeong	150	Narag, Andrew	110	Palomino, Bryan	37
Minteer, Sophie	215	Nelson, Elijah	216	Palop, Paloma	170
Miranda, Lance	153	Nelson, Erik	24	Pan, Ariel	122
Misshula, Sophie	71	Nelson, Grant	157	Pan, Ryan	58
Miu, Megan	129	Nelson, Madison R.	207	Panferov, Gene	112
Miziolek, Annie	182	Nelson, Marvin	177	Parajeckas, Jesse	181
Moghavem, Layla	174	Nelson, Olivia	87	Paras, Danica	180
Mohamed, Abdirahman	60	Nelson, Ryan	132	Paredes, Esteban	144
Mohan, Sanjay	145	Nevarez, Luke	134	Pariseau, Gabriela	154
Molina, Nicholas	22	Newman, Mark	124	Park, Flora	63
Monsef, Elizabeth	178	Newton, Hailey	101	Park, June	77
Montanez, Pia	37	Nghiem, Juliana	167	Park, Sarah	121
Montes, Jose	185	Ngo, Hong	189	Parkes, Faye	119
Monticone, McKenna	193	Nguyen, Andrew	193	Parnala, Genny Lhyne	124
Moody, Keaton	186	Nguyen, Anthony	203	Parra, Alejandra	35
Mooney, Remi	63	Nguyen, Belle	143	Parris, Erica	131
Moore, DJ	201	Nguyen, Derek	100	Partamian, Jonathan	209
Mopera, Beatriz	165	Nguyen, Linh	179	Partha, Mira	129
Morales, Gabriella	33	Nguyen, Matthew	82	Paschal, Gabbi	115
Morales, Giselle	145	Nguyen, Vanessa	150	Paschal, Harrison	114
Morales, Monica	171	Ni, Yu-Shien	136	Patino, Monique	174
Morallos, Alisaundre	19	Nicely, Abigail	203	Pattinson, Gabriela	143
Moreira, Aylene	108	Nicholson, Colin	62	Paulo, Maya	219
Moreno, Isaiah	72	Nievera, Roni	93	Pearson, Ellie	133
Morey, Thomas	88	Nolet, Tiffany	115	Pelosi, Sophia	20
Morgan, Alec	95	Nour, Abdurashid	144	Pelote, Claire	211

Index

Peña, Karla 48
Perez, Brian 115
Perez, Maximilian 118
Perry, Amber 141
Perry, Audrey 165
Perry, Madeline 113
Perry, Samuel 70
Pervez, Adeel 209
Perzabal, Marcos 156
Peterson, Alexandra 51
Petito, Jordan 209
Petrovskaya, Nelli 106
Pham, Catherine 52
Pham, Judy 64
Pham, Justin T. 65
Phelps, Megan 99
Phommavong, Belle 188
Pineda, Alejandro 173
Ping, Taylor 208
Pinto, Andrew 147
Pizaña, Morgan 110
Pizarras, Raphael 127
Pla, Kevin 192
Plant, David 27
Plett, Taylor 72
Plevin, Jona 178
Polizogopoulos, Peter 122
Poos, Jacob 163
Porges, Joseph 183
Porteous, Sean 170
Poston, Alissa 106
Potts, Kevin 202
Prior, Sean 74
Pryor, Samantha 185
Psaila, Miranda 114
Pupo, Anastasia 218
Qi, Matthew 125
Quesenberry, Quinn 26
Quinn, Irmina 166
Quintanilla, Matthew 206
Quinteros, Briana 24
Quinto, Lyric 131
Raasch, Jon Michael 146
Raber, Adam 80
Radovic, Dylan 36
Raff, Alexandra 109
Raff, Olivia 83
Rahmanian, Brandon 101
Rajsombath, Christin 81
Ralda, Kevin 61
Rall, Bailey 46
Ramirez, Alanie 39
Ramirez, Carlos 73
Ramos, Jesus 152
Ramos, Micah 45
Randall, Faith 208
Raptis, Sofia 53
Rasson, Gaby 198
Raulet, Gabriel 69
Rave, Kyla 191
Rawjee, Natalia 160
Ray, Julianne 164
Rayala, Michael 25
Razvi, Zareb 97
Rea, Sean .218
Redd, Nia .125
Reedy, Ali .39
Reeves, Alexandria 173
Refaat, Aly 50
Rego, Austin 96
Reinhardt, Tess 155
Renteria, Geraldine 126
Revah, Hila 183
Revelle, Ajna 84
Reyes, Anthony 104
Reyes, Isabeau 88
Reyes, Miguel 100
Reyes, Rachel 46
Ribeiro, Gabrielle 28
Ricci, Caroline D. 153
Richards, David 200
Richardson, Hannah 103
Richardson, Laney 84
Ridley, Asia 29
Rieckhof, Devon 28
Riis, Erik .126
Rivera, Amanda 130
Rivera, Anthony 24
Rivera, Bella 34
Rivera, David 36
Rivera, Taylor 90
Rivera, Tyler 198
Rizvi, Sabine 98
Roberts, Emily 95
Roderick, Clara 190
Rodgers, Thomas 66
Rodin, Kevin 172
Rodriguez, Bernard 196
Rodriguez, Elizabeth 166
Rodriguez, Guadalupe 58
Rodriguez, Isabelle 198
Rodriguez, Kyndal 62
Rodriguez, Marisa 78
Rodriguez, Rylee 194
Rodriguez, Sarah 178
Rojas, Jonathan 184
Rojas, Leida 106
Rokhman, Jennifer 135
Roll, Jacob 40
Romero, Daniela 200
Romero, Eduardo 83
Roop, Baylee 192
Roque, Jose 217
Rose, Catherine 34
Rosenblatt, Dillon 38
Ross, Jon .140
Ross, Ryan 177
Rossi, Abel 158
Roudebush, Megan 214
Rowland, Claire 187
Rowley, Amanda 74
Ruhstaller, Florian 127
Ruiz, Angelina 127
Ruiz, Wendy 65
Russ, Brendan 86
Russell, Justin 111
Rutherford, Brianna 209
Saad, Matthew 102
Sachs, Natasha 210
Sadeghi, Sara 111
Sadeghi, Vida 166
Saephan, Ariel 42
Sahakian, Alec 217
Sajben, Caroline 220
Salazar, Carlos 208
Salem, Mariel 73
Salinas, Jianna 168
Salino, Lilian 70
Salmeron, Jahiro 55
Salvador, Stephanie 166
Sanchez, Analyssa 65
Sanchez, Diego 206
Sanchez, Ilene 77
Sanchez, Jade 216
Sanchez, Natalie 96
Sanchez, Ulyses 175
Sandhu, Ravi 202
Sandhu, Samir 208
Sandoval, Blanca 101
Sanghani, Rhea 197
Sanguinetti, David 162
Santiago, Michael 68
Santos, Katie 182
Sanvictores, Gabriel 89
Sarmiento, Justine 192
Sarshar, Shauna 74
Sasser, Allegra 67
Satterfield, Anna 219
Savdharia, Asir 146
Savoie, Reese 81
Savoor, Rohan 160
Sawaya, Ysabella 111
Schall, Alana 117
Schiller, Andrew 120
Schoen, Patric 79
Schoolsky, Noah Lev 104
Schroder, Theo 55
Schuyler, Jay 46
Schwartz, Sydney 149
Scott, Brian 146
Scott, Noah 186

Scott III, Timothy 203	Souther, Maddie 42	Tesfamicael, Sewit 50
Scotti-Goetz, Francesca 39	Souza, Rebecca 177	Thao, Che 36
Seda, Gabriela 23	Spaeth, Isabel 185	Thao, Kong 60
Sedgwick, Eden Rae 164	Spagnola, Kylee 154	Thao, Selina 152
Sek, Sarah .82	Specchierla, Dante 94	Thomas, Genny 33
Selvo, Andrew Joseph 184	Spralja, Sophia 54	Thomas, Maddie 100
Serna, Kayley 43	Springs, Bethany 37	Thomas, Sara 172
Serrano, Claudia 34	Sraberg, Adam 59	Thomason, Taylor 61
Sette, Pietro 124	Stanley, Joseph 48	Thompson, Charlie 40
Sevor, Domenick 110	Steele, Nicholas 205	Thompson, Corrina 158
Sevor, Kira 34	Steffon, Bethany 122	Thompson, Jackie 66
Sexton, Alexandra 76	Stephens, Shelsey 154	Thompson, Jenna 43
Shali, Shatu 79	Stephenson, Sara 23	Thompson, Paige 40
Sharma, Arjun 139	Stevens, Erol 151	Tisch, Connor 142
Shawkey, Garret Lee 116	Stevens, Kelsey 114	Tischler, Hannah 174
Sheets, Haley 202	Stevens, Megan 53	Toker, Tal 117
Shelton, Trejon 105	Stinson, Natea 160	Topete, Idalis 72
Sheps, Monique 24	Storvold, Camryn 156	Torosyan, Karo 196
Sherden, Steven 93	Stratton, Tai 73	Torres, Isabel 105
Sherpa, Mingma 143	Strausbaugh, Ryan 148	Torres, Sebastian 22
Shetty, Nishita 147	Stubbs, Steven Hughes 78	Toulouse, Ryan Alexander 55
Shoemaker, Kelsey 87	Stuhaan, Ariana 93	Tovar, Ana 53
Shore, Trenton 81	Suad, Sarah 217	Tovar, Ariana 105
Sibony, Ilana 48	Sucich, Amber 178	Traganza, David 182
Siemens, Benjamin 128	Sullam, Mariella 54	Tran, Cathy 214
Sievers, Zak 157	Sullivan, Brooke 95	Tran, David 46
Silva, Alexandra 100	Suman, Samantha 94	Tran, Emily 84
Silva, Fredric 126	Sunga, Jovan 193	Trando, Cameron 97
Simenc, Joseph 142	Sutherlan, Cara 125	Trefethen, Charlotte 210
Simmons, Isaiah 81	Sutter, Spencer 206	Tretheway, Cole 51
Simon, Stephanie 72	Swall, Kelsey 148	Tropp, Justin 157
Sims, Ashley 50	Sweeney, Michael 159	Tsai, Samantha 58
Singh, Sanjay S. 213	Synghal, Ishani 197	Tsay, Katherine 144
Singh, Sapna 149	Tadena, Stephen B. 81	Tse, Davis 107
Sirott, Eric 45	Takahashi, Hinano 187	Tsu, Eric .108
Sledge, Dylan 134	Takehiro, Yumeji 217	Tuavao, Sepi 138
Sloan, Andrew Katsumi 174	Talgo, Julia 82	Tuazon, Rafael 125
Sloop, Nico 103	Tan, Christopher 183	Two Crows, Aja 51
Slosberg, Noah 114	Tan, Dakota 215	Two Eagle, Mauricea 175
Smallson, Brooke 66	Tanega, Rachelle 35	Udall, Devan 21
Smart, Carlin 118	Tang, Wilson 170	Ung, Kaitlyn 48
Smith, Asia 87	Tangney, Niamh 82	Uribe, Damian 31
Smith, Bailie 216	Tarzjani, Shawdi 81	Vahid, Jaydlin 91
Smith, Cameron 160	Taswell, Koby 70	Valadez, Maria 148
Smith, Casey 50	Tatman, Alex 136	Valdez, Maria 22
Smith, Claire 197	Taylor, Allison 52	Valdovinos, Elijah 215
Smith, Demi 162	Taylor, Evelyn 54	Valencia, Juan Jose 212
Smith, Hiram 110	Taylor, Joshua 144	Valenciano, Samantha 161
Smith, Josh 85	Taylor, Kejhana Maydelle 206	Valinoti, Austin D. 72
Snider, Joannie 108	Taylor, Nash 148	Vallejo, Thomas 34
Snider, Madeline 82	Taylor, Theresa 30	Valverde, Nick 58
Snyder, Gwen 195	Teagarden, Jenna 124	Van, Renee 163
Snyder, Weston 114	Teincuff, Josh 30	Van Dyke, Aubrey 62
Solar-Sanchez, Pablo 151	Temby, Michelle 124	van Gelder, Rachel 212
Soliman, Salma 35	Temple, Joshua 182	van Keulen, Carolina 78
Solorio III, Ruben 53	Templin, Amanda 157	Vang, Adam 214
Song, Anna 143	Tervet, Maddy 88	Vang, Erik 50

Index

Vang, Holly 39
Vargas, Nicolas 27
Vargas Jr., Oscar 107
Vasquez, Coletta 161
Vazquez, Nathalie 80
Velasquez, Ilene 168
Velazquez, Sofia 53
Velez, Chris 93
Veloff, Logan 50
Venezia, Bridgette 77
Verdugo, Gabby 189
Verhoeven, Kora 46
Verma, Megan 56
Vescio, Karina 28
Villa, Grace 216
Villa, Madison 194
Villamil, Montana 143
Villapando, Maria 202
Villarreal, Manuel 203
Viray, Noah 47
Vo, David 150
Vogel, Cassandra 59
Vold, Savannah 172
Vollkommer, Emma 153
Vu, Peter 163
Vu, Quinn 142
Vu, Richard 50
Vuceta, Christian 78
Vyvijal, Shannon 178
Wagner, Amanda 161
Waldenberger, Thomas 40
Walker, Katherine 181
Walker, Lorren 220
Wallace, Stephanie Peyton 105
Walters, Savanna 144
Walthall, Sydney 154
Wang, Raymond 162
Wang, William 90
Ward, Ryan 132
Warraich, Gurjeet 41
Warren, Ashlyn 46
Washington, Theran 101
Waters-O'Mohundro, Spencer 41
Watkins, Katie 83
Weems, Asianay 180
Weinstein, Sam 84
Weiss, Ori 190
Wellington, Justin 100
Welter, Nick 34
Weng, Cynthia 165
Westphal, Theresa 216
Wexler, Debra 56
White, Jordan 95
White, Kyara 71
White, Macy 197
Whittington, Sarah 32
Wickman, Kelsey Hiroko 176

Wieder, Zachary 184
Wiesenthal, Isabel 170
Wiggins, Dalton T. 139
Wiggins, Nathan 102
Williams, Beatrice 99
Williams, Bryan 26
Williams, Dustin Michael 33
Williams, Ethan 122
Williams, Jayson 55
Williams, Mikaela 206
Williams, Nicolas 203
Wilmot, Andrew 63
Wilson, Anna 85
Wilson, Celeste 92
Wilson, Lauryn 27
Wilson, Sydney 120
Winglewich, Sam 66
Winter, Chloe 204
Wise, Abigail 196
Wittbrodt, Jaclyn 156
Wixon, Samantha 48
Wolf, Jessica 111
Womack, Lucy 31
Wong-Appel, Alexandra 56
Wordelman, Madelyn 36
Wright, Adam 107
Wright, Bree 161
Wright, Luke 79
Xu, Olivia 220
Yabuki, Anthony 64
Yager, Anna 163
Yamouti, Anahita 194
Yang, Chang 106
Yang, Ger 46
Yang, John 68
Yang, KaBao 28
Yang, Salena 64
Yang, Sophia 86
Yanovsky, Dylan Samuel 78
Yap, Katrina 28
Yariv, Jadon 205
Yavercovski, Chris 121
Yavorkovsky, Eva 150
Yi, Hannah 148
Ynami, Sophia 184
Young, William 135
Youssef, Nebil 38
Yuan, Amanda 90
Yuen, Joshua 60
Zakhour, Chloe 86
Zalmai, Aaron 27
Zambrano, Jesus 181
Zamil, Arif 143
Zavala, Jacob 100
Zelaya, Henry 110
Zemtseff, Sara 138
Zhen, Andrew 132

Zheng, Dina 172
Zheng, Michelle 78
Zhong, Andrew 126
Zhu, Lauren 30
Ziemba, Alex 200
Zisser, Noah 191
Zurek, Sofi 160
Zweerink, Sarah 47

Author Autograph Page

Author Autograph Page